Up in the Rocky Mountains

Up
in the
Rocky
Mountains

WRITING THE SWEDISH IMMIGRANT EXPERIENCE

Jennifer Eastman Attebery

University of Minnesota Press

MINNEAPOLIS • LONDON

An earlier version of chapter 1 was published as "Swedish America in the Rocky Mountain West, 1880–1917: Folkloric Perspectives on the Immigrant Letter," *Scandinavian Studies* 77 (2005): 53–84. Parts of chapters 1, 2, 4, and 7 appeared in "Peasant Letters Revisited," *Swedish-American Historical Quarterly* 56, nos. 2–3 (2005): 126–40. An earlier version of chapter 5 was published as "Swedish Immigrants and the Myth of the West," *Swedish-American Historical Quarterly* 60, no. 3 (2004): 179–93. Parts of chapters 4 and 5 appeared in "A Lonely Guy in Rocky Bar, Idaho: Imagining Swedish America from the Mines," *Swedish-American Historical Quarterly* 54, no. 3 (2003): 164–84; and "Lonely Guys on the Fringe of Swedish America," *Swedish-American Historical Quarterly* 53, no. 3 (2002): 163–78. Parts of chapter 3 appeared in "Being Swedish-American in the Intermountain West: The Experiences of Immigrants to Idaho and Utah," *Swedish-American Historical Quarterly* 49, no. 3 (1998): 234–44; and "Transplantations of Swedish America in Idaho: The Role of the Churches," *Swedish-American Historical Quarterly* 46, no. 2 (1995): 122–40.

Published by the University of Minnesota Press
111 Third Avenue South, Suite 290
Minneapolis, MN 55401-2520
http://www.upress.umn.edu

Library of Congress Cataloging-in-Publication Data

Attebery, Jennifer Eastman, 1951–
    Up in the Rocky Mountains : writing the Swedish immigrant experience /
Jennifer Eastman Attebery.
        p.   cm.
    Includes bibliographical references and index.
    ISBN-13 978-0-8166-4767-5 (hc : alk. paper) — ISBN-13 978-0-8166-4768-2 (pb : alk. paper)
    ISBN-10 0-8166-4767-4 (hc : alk. paper) — ISBN-10 0-8166-4768-2 (pb : alk. paper)
    1. Swedish Americans—West (U.S.)—Correspondence. 2. Swedish Americans—Rocky Mountains Region—Correspondence. 3. Immigrants—West (U.S.)—Correspondence. 4. Immigrants—Rocky Mountains Region—Correspondence. 5. Letter writing—West (U.S.) —History. 6. Letter writing—Rocky Mountains Region—History. 7. American letters—West (U.S.). 8. American letters—Rocky Mountains Region. 9. West (U.S.) — Social life and customs. 10. Rocky Mountains Region—Social life and customs. I. Title.
    F596.3.S23A88 2007
    978'.004397—dc22
                                                                                    2007007489

Printed in the United States of America on acid-free paper

The University of Minnesota is an equal-opportunity educator and employer.

14 13 12 11 10 09 08 07   10 9 8 7 6 5 4 3 2 1

For Barbara and Louie Attebery

Contents

Acknowledgments

*M*Y THINKING ABOUT IMMIGRANT LETTERS began in 1998 while serving as a Fulbright Scholar at Gothenburg University in Sweden. For the research and writing of this book I am grateful for support from Idaho State University's Humanities and Social Science Research Committee, Faculty Research Committee, and College of Arts and Sciences Sabbatical Fund. Work at the Swedish Emigrant Institute, Växjö, Sweden, was supported in part with funding from the institute's annual fellowships. Travel to archives in the Rocky Mountain West was funded by the Idaho Humanities Council through its research fellowship program.

I am grateful for assistance from archivists and research staff at the Swedish Emigrant Institute, Idaho State Historical Society, Idaho State University Intermountain West Collection, Utah State University Special Collections, Brigham Young University Special Collections, Montana State Historical Society, Colorado Historical Society, and the Swenson Swedish Immigration Research Center at Augustana College, Rock Island, Illinois. The Swedish Emigrant Institute has kindly granted permission for reproduction of the letters used in this study, including the twenty translations in the appendix.

Several scholars read and commented on parts of the book as I developed the manuscript. I am deeply grateful for their astute comments. I owe thanks many times over to Philip J. Anderson, Brian Attebery, Louie Attebery, Ulf Jonas Björk, Dag Blanck, Maria Erling, Barbro Klein, Orm Øverland, and Larry E. Scott. In addition to translating the letters in the appendix and offering superb guidance on my translations within the book, Christina Johansson provided comments on the contents and argument of the project. Without her patient and thorough efforts, this book would never have progressed to publication. Any lingering infelicities or errors in translations or contents are entirely my responsibility.

A Note on Translations

CHRISTINA JOHANSSON, head of archives at the Swenson Swedish Immigration Research Center, Augustana College, Rock Island, Illinois, was essential to the translations that appear in the text and appendix of this book. Not only is she a native speaker of Swedish, but she is also well versed in nineteenth-century Swedish manuscripts, with all of their foibles in handwriting, spelling, and idiom.

Translations in the appendix are Johansson's work. For translations in the text of the book, I produced a first draft of the English translations and Johansson corrected my draft with much line-by-line consultation. In the notes for translations, readers will find the original Swedish language. As with the translations, I produced the draft of the notes and Johansson closely checked these Swedish passages against photocopies of the original manuscripts. These notes follow the manuscripts as closely as is feasible, including spellings, punctuation, and sentence length. For example, when Elin Pehrson writes to her cousin Maria in a letter dated May 13, 1896, "för flickor är det bra här om di är starka och orka arbeta," we retained her nonstandard spellings of *de* and *orkar* so that Swedish readers interested in dialect and literacy levels can read for those concerns. In very few cases we introduced punctuation and added diacritical marks where a correspondent's writing was so incorrect as to be unreadable. The note for such passages mentions these changes.

For further comments on translation, especially regarding Johansson's full translations of twenty letters for the appendix, see the introductory comments to the appendix.

Expanding Swedish America Westward

❧

I FIRST BECAME INTERESTED in Swedish immigration to the West
through hearing stories of my husband Brian's grandfather Mounie
(originally Magni) Olson, a successful farmer near Payette, Idaho, who
had left Sweden in 1897 at age twenty to join his older sister Emma. He
left behind his parents, a sister, Marie, and a brother, Carl-Emil Ohlsson,
on the family's rocky Småland farm. By the time I heard of the family's
Swedish connections, Mounie and Carl-Emil were both deceased, but
Carl-Emil's daughters were still in touch with the family in America.
During a trip to visit my husband's cousins in Sweden, I became more
intrigued when I saw direct evidence of Swedish immigration as we traveled to the family farm, Eknes; to Skatelöv, the church to which Mounie
and his family had walked seven miles every Sunday; and to the Swedish
Emigrant Institute in nearby Växjö.

A regular part of many trips to Sweden by Swedish Americans is a visit
to the Swedish Emigrant Institute, where one learns about emigration's
"push" and "pull" factors. There, on display in the exhibits area, we were
startled to see a newspaper clipping bidding Swedes in the Midwest to
"Come to the Snake River Valley" (*Kom till Snake River dalen*) of Idaho.
The institute also has an archival section where, among the numerous
collections showcasing the emigration to the Midwest, I discovered a significant number of donations related to Western settlement. A review of
the geographical index revealed numerous collections for Colorado, and
a few from Wyoming, Montana, New Mexico, and Idaho, including an
extended collection of letters, a scrapbook, and a reminiscence of a miner,
Leonard Nilsson, who lived in Rocky Bar, Idaho, during the 1880s.

Mounie Olson's experience living in Payette had been fairly isolated,
with only a handful of other Swedes in the Payette area. Like him, most

*This photograph from 1910 records a Fourth of July picnic at New Sweden, Idaho,
with a Midsommar pole in place. Photograph courtesy of David A. Sealander;
preserved and gifted to Sealander by Anna Margaret Nygaard Cobb.*

had married non–Swedish speakers. We were told by the Swedish cousins that Mounie eventually lost his native language to such an extent that
his letters became difficult to understand. I had assumed that his experience might have been representative, that there were no significant enclaves of Swedish settlement in the inland West, that all those western
Swedes were in Seattle or perhaps California. But the Swedish Emigrant
Institute's collection revealed to me what indeed should be obvious to
those involved in history of the American West, that European immigrants,
though not always clustered in homogeneous ethnic communities, were a
major component of American expansion into the West.

The historian Frederick Luebke has made a case for more study of
these Western immigrants, noting that "European immigrants are the forgotten people of the American West," because they do not fit comfortably
into the frameworks used by labor, Western, and immigration historians.[1]
Luebke calculates the percentages of first- and second-generation Euro-
Americans in the 1900 census, in which figure high percentages of Irish,

Swedish, German, and Norwegian immigrants. The Swedish composition of the Western immigrant population has been examined by Dag
Blanck, who calculates that by 1920 one-fifth of Swedish immigrants were
living in the West.[2]

My first trip to the Swedish Emigrant Institute inspired me to investi-
gate whether enclaves of Swedish settlement existed in Idaho. Rocky Bar
was not a Swedish settlement; in the 1880s, when Leonard Nilsson worked
as a miner there, there was only one Swedish family in the area. Nilsson
falls into a category I later identified as "lonely guys": isolated and itinerant workers whose paths can be traced through their letters written home.
Some of these men returned to Sweden; many simply disappeared, blended
into Western culture. But a few pockets of contiguous Swedish settlement
did emerge from my search: Troy and nearby Nora in the Idaho panhandle,
which were centers for Swedish farm families living along creek drainages
on the eastern fringe of the Palouse region; Swedes in the logging towns
of the Idaho panhandle, where towns like Orofino had "Swedetowns"; the
agricultural communities of New Sweden and Riverview in southeastern
Idaho near Idaho Falls, where small Swedish Mission and Baptist congregations established farms along a privately developed irrigation system;
and clusters of Swedes living alongside Danish, English, Swiss, and other
ethnic groups in Mormon villages like St. Charles, located in the southeastern corner of the state.

The patterns of Swedish settlement in Idaho reflect those we can identify throughout the Rocky Mountain area, each with a unique kind of
contact with the non-Swedish world. Many men came to the West as laborers, some finding a community of fellow countrymen among the labor
pool and in the unions. A few, however, were ethnically isolated and found
their chief contact with Swedish America through newspapers. There were
also single Swedish women who ventured West for work, mostly to urban
settings where domestics were needed and where small Swedish congregations and secular organizations provided networks of ethnic support.
The religious groups that migrated westward tended to move as families
and to create contiguous agricultural settlements, with the exception of
the agricultural villages of the Mormons, in which Swedes interacted with
immigrants of many northern and western European origins, who were
all making the adjustment to being Mormon and being American while
retaining selected parts of their European heritage. Urban neighborhoods

Mounie Olson working his farm with his son Glen at Payette, Idaho.
Photograph courtesy of Barbara Attebery.

also emerged in the region's larger cities, such as Denver, where they were often focused around Lutheran churches.

Indeed, I found the presence of Swedish immigrants in the emerging Western region of the late nineteenth and early twentieth centuries was significant enough to warrant further study. In 1988 I had the opportunity to begin a study of Idaho Swedes when Brian and I moved for six months to Uppsala, where he served as a Fulbright scholar. In a brief inquiry printed in the Idaho State Historical Society's newsletter before our departure, I invited Idahoans of Swedish heritage to contact me. I was rewarded with a telephone call from Philip Swenson of Riverview. Our phone conversation led to many pleasant visits with Philip and his wife Edith after my return from Sweden and launched my study of the farms in New Sweden and Riverview, which was funded by the Idaho State Historic Preservation Office. In Uppsala I met scholars engaged in the study of Swedish emigration at MESK (a center for multiethnic studies); there, Harald Runblom and Dag Blanck were interested in my attempt to push our understanding of the Swedish immigrant experience westward. During my return to Sweden with my own Fulbright scholarship in 1998, along with shorter trips supported by the Swedish Emigrant Institute and Idaho State University in 1997 and 2002, I was finally able to spend time in the archival collections that had originally intrigued me.

*Mounie and
Blanche Olson.
Photograph
courtesy of
Barbara Attebery.*

My findings at the Swedish Emigrant Institute included fifty-four collections of letters sent from the Rocky Mountain states of Idaho, Montana,
Utah, Wyoming, Colorado, and New Mexico. These collections include
texts by seventy-four writers, who produced 331 letters during their time
in the Rocky Mountain region. It became immediately apparent that I was
dealing with fascinating material. Each collection read like an epistolary
autobiography, though often cut short and lacking a narrative conclusion
that neatly answers all the reader's concerns. These autobiographical and
psychological merits of immigrant letter collections have recently been explored by David A. Gerber in his 2006 book, *Authors of Their Lives.*

What intrigued me about the letters was somewhat different from
Gerber's concerns. Trained as a folklorist, I recognized the letters' formulaic language as a kind of folk expression, possessing the aesthetic qualities

we more ordinarily encounter in traditional oral prose forms such as folk-tale, legend, and personal experience narrative. Certainly we can read these letters as historians or literary scholars, I thought, but we can also pull the ideas of folklorists into our reading. Throughout *Up in the Rocky Mountains*, that is exactly what I have done. I have turned first to the ideas of folklorists for aid in interpreting the letters. Doing so yields new insights both into the immigrants' cultural affiliations and into their expressive abilities in using a traditional form, the vernacular personal letter. While we could reach some, though certainly not all, of the same insights through the avenues of sociolinguistics and rhetorical analysis (for example, by using Bakhtin), I leave it to others to make such comparisons.

What draws me to the letters is their informality; they are as close as we can get to the vernacular level of culture that most interests me as a folklorist. But to say that the immigrant letters are simple, informal texts is not to say that they readily reveal their meanings. How to interpret the immigrant letter is an ongoing point of discussion among historians and literary scholars, who are finding that reading the letters as texts as well as documents yields new understanding of the letters and their writers. This exciting new work is summarized in chapter 1, and in chapters 1 and 2, I add a folkloristic method for reading letters.

My main goal in studying the letters, then, is to acknowledge their expressive power as a folk form. But a folkloristic study of vernacular letters serves other purposes as well, pushing our understanding of Swedish America westward. Swedish immigration, in and of itself, is a gratifying subject for its imaginative links to the past, and for Swedish Americans, it is a link to their people. Swedish immigration to the West is a subject with connections that are far-reaching and multiple, resonating through some of the most important issues in Western and immigration history and in ethnic studies.

Swedish immigrants were among many peoples converging on the West during the nineteenth century. Patricia Nelson Limerick calls the American West "one of the great meeting zones of the planet."[3] In the West, Swedes joined others who could claim the label "white," establishing their potential power over the people of color who migrated to or who were already present in the region, primarily Hispanics, Chinese and other Asians, and American Indians. Swedish immigrants to the West could claim to be "Westerners," "Swedish," or "Americans," or they could place their religious beliefs at the fore and claim primarily to be "Mormons," "Friends," or "Baptists." Thus, immigrants' stories are part of much larger issues of identity. How is it that those entering the region during the nineteenth century came to view themselves as Westerners? What did they keep of their Swedish or Swedish American cultural baggage; what did they jettison? What became part of a blended identity? These are queries about the traditional culture of the past, yet for nineteenth-century immigrants we cannot use the direct interviewing techniques of folkloric or anthropological fieldwork.

In a 1992 essay, Limerick espouses the need for "cultural study of verbal activity" in the West, "a study that can encompass Indians, Hispanics, Asians, blacks, and Euroamericans of all backgrounds."[4] She points, for example, to the many languages that have been and are spoken in the West, represented by non-English-language newspapers, as an area ripe for comparative study. Yet, as a scholar using English-language sources, Limerick demonstrates the limited way in which Western history has availed itself of these materials by emphasizing Anglo-American examples for this "verbal activity": she cites Anglo-American newspapers, the English-language and common-law-based American legal system, and Henry Nash Smith's reading, in *Virgin Land*, of dime novels and the myths and symbols they employ.

This is not to fault Limerick's or Smith's significant work in our understanding of the cultural history of the West, work that has influenced my own studies. Rather, I hope to point out the difficulty of any multilanguage comparative study. As we immerse ourselves in the products of any one language group's verbal activities, the task becomes overwhelming. Among the Swedes of the Rocky Mountain states, a central verbal activity was the writing of personal letters. Other verbal activities ranged from playbills for stage productions to minutes of Lutheran congregations, from newspaper advertisements to socialist literature, from documents relinquishing inheritances in Sweden to grocery accounts listing Christmas food purchases. And we should not forget that the Swedish literates of the West were bilingual: they were English speakers and readers as well. An array of Swedish and English texts allows us insight into the lives of Rocky Mountain Swedes.

Such texts are used in chapter 3 to provide context for personal letters. What socioeconomic niches did the Swedish immigrants fit into? What was their social and physical environment? Did letter writers represent a literate minority among the immigrants, or a majority that used writing to reforge connections broken by their having left Sweden? "Verbal activity" in manuscripts and printed sources, demographic sources, and local-history materials helps us characterize the Swedish population and track its literacy levels and its distribution throughout the Rockies. In the appendix, I provide thumbnail biographical sketches of each letter writer. The appendix also includes twenty fully translated letters—the work of Christina Johansson, head of archives at the Swenson Swedish Immigration Center at Augustana College.

We can read the immigration letters for many kinds of meaning, including implicit and explicit identity claims, and evidence of identity formation. The traces of identity expressed throughout the immigrants' letters take up the bulk of this volume. In chapters 4 through 7 I examine, in turn, occupational, ethnic/national, regional, and religious identities that could be claimed by the Swedes, and in chapter 8 I examine how mixing and blending could occur. Through their expressive use of commonplace phrasing, metaphors, and stories, the immigrants laid claim to religious belief, to the West, to gender, to ethnicity, and to nationality, but few of these identity claims were singular. Instead, the immigrants mixed and sometimes blended their identities in what we recognize today with unhyphenated labels like "Mormon," or with what Mounie Olson would have recognized himself to have become, a "Westerner."

ONE

Vernacular Writing

LETTER WRITING AS A FOLK PRACTICE

I sit down right away to write to you because there are so many
thoughts and feelings that come to me when I receive a letter, but
that I can't hold onto for very long; therefore I prefer to write
them down immediately if I can; in any case I will do my best.

Clara Jeppsson, 1912, LaJara, Colorado

*I*N THEIR PERSONAL LETTERS, writers like Clara Jeppsson wrote, as
she describes above, as well as they could, but often with the urge
to say as much as possible under hurried circumstances.[1] There is no
wonder, then, that Jeppsson relied on what we can call *vernacular writing*.
By using the modifier *vernacular* I do not mean the medieval emergence
of vernacular-language literature such as Chaucer's *Canterbury Tales*,
or the use of dialect by a writer like Samuel Clemens in *Adventures of
Huckleberry Finn*. Vernacular writing is produced in informal situations
like Jeppsson's—everyday and routine—and uses language that is similarly everyday, pragmatic, and, most importantly, traditional.

The letters written by Swedish immigrants were produced in just
these circumstances and using just such language. The term *vernacular*
begs further definition. However, I would like to set aside definitions
until later in this chapter in order to first turn to a few of the letters
themselves, then to the kinds of study that letters have thus far received
from scholars in various fields, and finally to some ideas from one field in
particular, folklore, that will aid us in reading the letters.

Of all the materials available from the Swedish immigration to
North America, personal letters perhaps provide the greatest quantity of

material from ordinary people. H. Arnold Barton, in his *Letters from the Promised Land*, estimates that "millions" of letters were sent from America to Sweden, of which "only a few thousand have survived"—still a massive amount of material.[2] My own search for letters sent from the Rocky Mountain region turned up fifty-four letter collections, housed at the Swedish Emigrant Institute in Växjö and representing all parts of the region and sent to all parts of Sweden. These collections include 331 letters written by seventy-four individuals. As Barton notes, these materials are invaluable historical documents in which "the Swedish immigrants tell their own story." For Barton, their quality is limited by their very everydayness, their tendency toward clichés, platitudes, and hearsay. "Most immigrant letters," he concludes, "have in fact little of interest to relate" from a historian's point of view.[3]

To avoid boring his readers with these qualities, Barton did not select letters for *Letters from the Promised Land* on the basis of representation alone. He also chose them based on interest and readability. With the major exception of Orm Øverland and Steinar Skærheim's four-volume *Fra Amerika til Norge*, this is also true of the other major collections of Scandinavian materials: Danish American letters selected by Frederick Hale for *Danes in North America*, and Norwegian American letters selected by Theodore Blegen for *Land of Their Choice*, by Frederick Hale for *Their Own Saga*, and by Solveig Zempel for *In Their Own Words*. Zempel writes that she selected "to remain faithful to the original writer while at the same time holding the interest of the present-day reader."[4] Similarly to Barton, Zempel values the personal letter for its ability to give social history a personal voice, even though she expects that many readers will find them "mundane, repetitious, and formulaic" in comparison to literary texts.[5]

The repetitiousness of personal letters can perhaps become dull as one sits in an archive reading letter after letter, sensing that one can predict the topic that the writer will take up next and the sorts of phrasing that she or he will use. So, too, can we become frustrated with the limitations of letters as documents, telling us only a fraction of what we want to know. The documentary limitations of letters are exemplified dramatically in a case explored by Virginia Walcott Beauchamp. Beauchamp juxtaposes a letter manuscript with a sharply contradictory diary entry written on the same day in 1867 by a wealthy Baltimorean, Madge Preston. In her

Clara Jeppsson explains to her sister that she has moved from Denver. Image courtesy of the Swedish Emigrant Institute.

letter, Preston represents herself as a contented mother and wife, but the diary entry reveals that Preston wrote in the midst of profound domestic strife.[6] Few archival collections provide this kind of comparative evidence, but readers do sense omissions, often without knowing whether they are important.

We can choose at random from letters written from the Rocky Mountains for an example of these literary and documentary limitations. In the Clara Jeppsson collection, a letter written to her sister Sigrid on October 13, 1911, from Carmel Ranch, Colorado, begins with news about Clara's move to Carmel Ranch from Denver to join her husband at a farm: "As you can see, I have now left Denver. . . . We are together again on a farm but the difference is that this time I have my own house."[7] Clara goes on to report on their living conditions and pay: "it [the house] isn't large; it has only 2 rooms; occasionally I can do some hours' work for the boss, but there isn't much profit in it. Johan earns 50 dollars per month and then we have free housing."[8] Clara worries about the slow economy, explaining that she and her husband have made their move not for profit so much as to be together. Earlier in her correspondence, she explained to her sister that she and Johan have had to find work apart: she doing housekeeping in Denver, and he on a farm outside the city.

In her October 13 letter, Clara next offers a description of her trip to the new place, to explain why she did not write immediately on arrival. During the trip it "rained as though heaven was open and all the roads were full of water."[9] She had been forced to stay at a hotel even though her destination was only a day's journey from Denver. Returning to her worries about finances, Clara notes the especially good economic position of her husband's uncle, who claims to possess $100,000, "but he lives poorer than an old man in a poorhouse in Sweden. He is unmarried and he does all of his housework himself as well as his farm work."[10] The old man's penny-pinching ways are the subject of local gossip, according to Clara, who may have been embittered because she hoped that the uncle would employ her as a housekeeper. The final two pages of Clara's letter are increasingly conventional; she turns to news of common acquaintances and to well-wishing those at home in Sweden.

Clara's October 13 letter illustrates both the usefulness and the limitations of personal letters as documents. We do indeed obtain interesting information as we read, for example, about Clara's separation from her husband, the limited work for women in her new location, and the difficulties of travel in 1911 Colorado. Even more interesting to social historians is Clara's concern about the economy and its effects on her family's ability to negotiate a good wage, and about the undesirability of being too parsimonious, as represented in her criticism of the uncle. But we always want to know more than Clara tells us.

For example, we want to know more about the writer's emotional state, which is often left out of immigrant letters.[11] What was the nature of Clara's relationship with her husband? Was the strained relationship between Clara and the uncle based only on economics? We also want to know more details about everyday life. Was Clara's two-room house a tar paper shack or a frame house with insulation? Did she write by lamp or by electric light? Was the "work for the boss" solely housework or did it include some outdoor labor? What kind of vehicle did she take from Denver that was so affected by a sudden rainstorm?

Very few correspondents are as revealing or as detailed as we in the future audience would like them to be. In part, this was for good reason. Their audience of close contemporaries did not need or want much of this information, being much more concerned with the simple contact provided by personal letters and the news that everyone across the Atlantic was in good health and faring well. The simple need for contact is most apparent in the letters' many repeated themes and formulaic phrases. It is not just that unnecessary information is elided, but also that the information imparted is underscored with repetition.

The thematic recurrences in Clara's October 13 letter are not so obvious to someone who has not read her letters written in May through August of the same year, and those letters that followed in 1912. The repetitions would have been obvious to Sigrid, however, who read them in letter after letter. Clara was typical of many workers, female and male. She was preoccupied with work conditions and comparisons between the American and Swedish economies, returning to these themes in much the same words. Before October 13, Clara repeats herself in telling Sigrid that "Johan has stayed on the farm, so I think I may also go there; more can be saved if we live in the country."[12] Before and after her move to the countryside, Clara returns to the theme of saving money, an arduous task for her and her husband: "I only want to earn money so that I can come home."[13] A line in Clara's letter from September 29, 1911, suggests another reason that economics so dominates her writing. Commenting on the prospects of another young immigrant couple, she writes, "the love might cool soon when the money is gone and they have to work until their backs ache."[14] Money, then, had an intimate connection with social relationships. Accompanying social relationships were responsibilities and reciprocity. When her sister reported to her that a family had given her a present, Clara comments that "perhaps they have come to realize how much money you scraped together for them."[15]

The themes chosen by Clara are as typical as the verbal formulas she uses to express them, including repetitious phrasing and the overall organization of her letters. If we bring literary expectations to the letters, we experience these features as well-worn clichés and conventional presentation. At key points in her October 13 letter she uses commonplace phrasing to accomplish the shift from section to section. She opens with "as you can see" to explain her move from Denver, she signals her shift to news of mutual acquaintances with "I have gotten a letter from," and she uses "you must greet mother and everyone for us" to signal the closing section of her letter.[16]

In terms of organization, each of Jeppsson's letters works from individual to community, from America to Sweden. Clara begins by noting her receipt of Sigrid's last letter, continues by describing her current situation, and then expands her view to the surrounding community and other Swedes in America with whom she is in contact via letters. In some of her letters, Clara expands her view further to a more abstract, national perspective on American events or issues; for example, her hope that the upcoming 1912 presidential election will yield a better economic climate (all four candidates—Eugene Debs, Theodore Roosevelt, Woodrow Wilson, and the incumbent, William Howard Taft—could lay some claim to addressing workers' concerns). From the American scene, Clara turns to the scene in Sweden, to those left behind in Sweden, and finally to her wishes for their health and well-being. Similar themes, phrasing, and overall organization can be found not only in Clara's other letters, but in letters written by other immigrants at the time as well.

In Barton's and Zempel's descriptions of immigrant letters, and in my own description of Clara Jeppsson's letters, two terms for repetitiousness are used: *cliché* and *formula*. *Cliché* expresses a literary expectation that writers will enliven their texts with fresh phrasing even if the ideas are not completely new. The term *formula* is less judgmental, allied as it is with the study of oral language use, in which formulaic composition can be admired and enjoyed by a live audience. Probably the best-known oral formulas are the epithets of Homer: "swift-footed Achilleus," "godlike Priam," or "Hektor of the glancing helm."[17] Humbler oral forms such as the joke and the personal anecdote also rely upon formulas to set up and play with audience expectations; for example, "knock knock" or "that reminds me of the time." In these vernacular contexts, repetition is not trite, but a virtue.

We should consider, then, the approaches that can be used in analyzing the personal letter as a text. While it is not an oral form, it exhibits some of the tendencies of oral genres: the repetition of phrases and themes and the adherence to patterned organization. This is the "paratactic impulse," according to John Miles Foley, "a primary trope in oral tradition."[18] Foley broadly uses the term *parataxis* to mean any kind of repetition, from smaller units such as formula to larger units such as the repetition of themes and story segments.

Could it not be that the categories used by folklorists, who study oral texts, would open up new insights? By subtitling this chapter "Letter Writing as a Folk Practice," I have tipped off the reader regarding my own view. I find the ideas of oral studies useful because the social context in which the letters existed was in some ways similar to oral culture; in fact, it was an extension of the oral culture left behind in Sweden. Filling a void left by the lack of personal conversation with Swedish family and friends, the letters were written by people who had previously relied on orality for everyday interactions. In this intermediate position between oral and written forms, the letters frequently partake of what Walter Ong calls "residually oral composition."[19] They are similar to works written by "bilingual" poets—writers fully competent in oral composition who write what Foley calls "written oral poems."[20]

I am not the only scholar to see the similarities between folklore and immigrant letter writing. Adopting William I. Thomas and Florian Znaniecki's term *peasant letters*, Linda Dégh wrote in 1978 that the letters written by and to immigrants "invite the folklorist to an important field of folk literacy . . . *written* folklore related to territorial mobility and migration."[21] The "traditional [organizational] formula of peasant letters," according to Dégh, is three-part. Letters begin with an opening "informing that the writer is in good health, wishing the same for the addressee," followed by a middle section in which Dégh finds an "elaboration of the main objectives of writing," and ending with a closing section in which there is a "repetition of [the] well-wishing formula and blessing to addressee and family."[22] This organizational scheme certainly describes the immigrant letters that I have read, but it is very general. We could particularly stand to refine our understanding of the middle section, a task I undertake in chapter 2.

Another folklorist who has noticed the immigrant letter is Robert B. Klymasz. Rather than analyzing its form, Klymasz discusses the social function of the letter for Ukrainian immigrants to Canada: "In common with other immigrant groups on this continent, [they] found that the letter alone could replace the casual, everyday verbal contacts once enjoyed with friends, relatives and loved ones back in the Old Country."[23] Klymasz finds that Ukrainian folk texts such as ballads recognized the importance of letters with frequent references to their drafting and receipt. Much more recently Wolfgang Mieder examined letters from one famous writer, Wolfgang Amadeus Mozart, for their use of proverbial phrases. Mieder found that Mozart used, for example, the opening formula "praise and thanks be to God," which is similar to opening phrases found in Dégh's peasant letters. Mieder characterizes Mozart's earthy, often scatological prose as "written orality."[24]

Dégh cites a few predecessors in her study of peasant letters, especially Thomas and Znaniecki's work with Polish letters, *The Polish Peasant in Europe and America*; and "Das Kann Ich Nicht Vergessen," Georg R. Schroubek's work with German letters, which he calls *Volksprosa*. However, what Dégh and these others began in examining the form of the letter has not been followed up by folklorists in any extended way. In a 1989 article about Norwegian letters, "Personal Letters as Research Sources," Knut Djupedal proposed that letters could be examined as folklore-like texts using performance theory. Heda Jason also recognized the potential for folkloric study of personal letters as a genre of "private manuscript creativity" in "Literature, Letters, Verbal Texts," a 1992 article systematizing the many genres of folklore.[25] And in "The Traditional Craft of Christmas Form Letters," Diane Tye recently analyzed Christmas form letters as a kind of folklore.[26] However, these efforts have been too sporadic and dispersed to create a general acceptance of the personal letter as a folkloric genre. For more intensive work with personal letters we must turn instead to the work of American studies and literary scholar Orm Øverland and of social historian David A. Gerber.

Øverland proposed in 1996 that we need to be able to read immigrant letters as texts because they represent "one of the earliest substantial bodies of a written folk literature," requiring a separate "textual theory" that can enhance both our understanding of immigrant history and our appreciation of the letters as writing.[27] He deals with the immigrant letter as a traditional genre with particular characteristics, including clichés and conventional themes, and a characteristic social context that includes public availability, limited literacy, and marginal writing circumstances. True to Øverland's combined American studies and literary perspectives, his work with letters achieves a dual focus on content and form. He is as interested in what we can learn about Norwegian immigrants through their letters as he is in how the letters can be read, and he sees the two processes as informing each other. For Øverland, the important content is the series of themes found in the Norwegian immigrant letters, including health, religion, and racial identity.[28]

While not really folkloristic, Øverland's approach is more ethnographic and contextual than that of purely literary scholars and linguists, who have tended to focus on letters written by well-known individuals or to analyze communicative form per se. For literary scholars and linguists, the letter is a quasi-literary text with a number of social communicative functions. Its generic development is seen as intertwined with that of the epistolary novel. As texts, letters have special qualities; their writers are able to signify dualities such as "bridge or barrier . . . presence and absence."[29] Letter writers can play with tense and person to indicate their uncertain position: Is the letter writer *I* or *you*, is it then or now, as a Swedish recipient reads a letter written weeks earlier in the Rockies? These are important qualities of both letters and epistolary novels, as illustrated in *Epistolary Practices*, William Merrill Decker's work with the letters of American literati like Emerson and Dickinson, and by *Epistolarity*, Janet Gurkin Altman's work. However, while these qualities are present in the immigrant letter, immigrant writers do not necessarily manipulate them toward an artistic purpose. As explored in chapter 2, their vernacular epistolary aesthetic is instead based in oral forms, having a close relationship to conversation, custom, and storytelling.

Through their concern with discourse communities and everyday language use, linguists offer insights that approach the contextual concerns of Øverland. David Barton and Nigel Hall argue in their introduction to *Letter Writing as Social Practice* that letter writing is important as a textual form that is all-pervasive and that has social functions that differ from culture to culture. In her essay "Letters," Patrizia Viola combines these issues of form and function in defining the letter as tending to be more or less self-referential, to be patterned in organization and use of codes, to be personal, to use markers of orality, and to include implicit meanings.

Historians have approached letters with similar insights. Charlotte Erickson takes a social-historical point of view in *Invisible Immigrants*, her 1972 study of English and Scottish letter writing from nineteenth-century America. Like Barton, Hale, Blegen, and Zempel, she reads across letter collections in order to generalize about the immigrant experience. Religious historians Maria Elizabeth Erling and Jay P. Dolan also read across collections of immigrant letters to, as Dolan puts it, "understand the religion of the people" through reading for repeated religious themes, an approach very similar to that of folklorists.[30]

What sets Gerber's work apart is his use of ideas from discourse analysis in a two-part process: he analyzes letters as texts that use particular modes of discourse, and then draws social-historical conclusions. Gerber analyzes letters of nineteenth-century English-language immigrants, seeing "letters as *texts* with their own specific conventions and codes."[31] He also builds on the work of David Fitzpatrick, whose *Oceans of Consolation*, a study of Irish Australian immigrant letters, has provided a new model for anthologizing letter texts with as much contextual information as possible.

Gerber focuses on familial and other close relationships. When an emigrant left home, when an immigrant arrived in a new place and culture, there was a profound impact on such relationships, which, according to Gerber, may already have been shaky.[32] Gerber suggests that "many of these immigrants seem to have come out of family backgrounds that were tense, troubled, or tentative. . . . Indeed, such personal problems in the human relationships of families . . . may be the major undiscovered dimension of immigration history."[33]

Gerber categorizes the discourse of the immigrant letter as regulative, expressive, and descriptive. Through these modes of writing, immigrants shaped new relationships with their family and friends across the Atlantic at the same time they were reshaping their sense of selfhood in their new surroundings. Gerber includes in his analysis the most repetitious parts of the letters, especially those referring to letter writing itself and those operating as seemingly merely phatic greetings: the "Hello. How are you?" segments that tend to fall at the beginning and at the end, where, for example, immigrants apologize for not having written or for the quality of their writing, worry over the unreliability of the mail service, consider how private or public their letters should be, and express the joy of receiving letters.[34] Like Øverland's comparative analysis, Gerber's work makes the repetitiousness of the letters meaningful.

Put simply, if immigrant letters are repetitious, there is good reason, and scholars should pay attention to the repetitions as much as to the occasional, fortuitous documentation of events and social customs. Repetitions are the key to elements in the letters that were important to the writers. Gerber's analysis of these repetitions opens up for us an understanding of how the letter was used to renegotiate personal relationships within very small groups such as the family. Using ideas from folklore, we can shift the focus somewhat to larger cultural groups. Folklorists are interested in people's participation in a variety of folk groups that share cultural values, as expressed through folkloric genres. A folklorist would see the letter as a genre in which not just personal relationships but the relationships to larger cultural communities were renegotiated as the immigrant attempted to position himself or herself in American surroundings.

Sandra Dolby Stahl's analysis of the personal experience narrative as a folkloric form provides us with a model for these multiple relationships. For each of her personal storytellers, Stahl draws a pie chart with eight divisions.[35] Each "slice" of the chart represents a folk group with which an individual may interact, based on family relationships, ethnicity, religion, place or region, age, gender, occupation, or other social networks. For any one individual, the slices of pie may be more or less important, but most of us would have at least some interactions and identity claims based on each slice. For example, one of Stahl's storytellers expresses the importance of male identity in his story about staying in an unheated garage through an Indiana winter and encountering a rat there. This emphasis is more than just a matter of personal identity; it becomes a basis for establishing common ground with the audience, through emphasis and through hailing the audience with insider knowledge embodied in brief references, for which Stahl uses the literary term *allusions*.[36]

For an immigrant, the pie chart becomes very complex. If we take Clara Jeppsson as an example, we can see her participation in relationships with family members in both Sweden and America and on both her and her husband's sides of the family. She mentions attending a Swedish church in Denver, without identifying it as Lutheran, Methodist, Baptist, or another specific denomination. She expresses fondness for Denver but not for the rural West, where she is forced to live if she wants to be with her husband. She interacts with her sisters on the basis of common age and gender. Thus, loving relationships and the possibility of having children take the foreground in many of her letters. As a paid housekeeper, she is a member of an occupational group, concerned about wages and working conditions. Finally, she is Swedish; she mentions her interactions with other Swedes in America, identifying Swedish subgroups from Värmland and Dalarna, as well as Americans, Mexicans, and Mormons as cultural groups with which she is in contact.

Jeppsson's letters can be read for the ways she perceived relationships with all of these groups. This is a particularly important and interesting consideration for Swedes in the Rocky Mountain West, who were sundered from Sweden, whose interaction with the Swedish Midwest was filtered through popular media, and who came into contact with Americans of varying backgrounds (including American Indians), with a variety of other immigrant groups, with various religious groups (especially Mormons), and with some whose primary identification was with the West itself.

When we turn to the immigrant letter with the perspective of a folklorist, particular qualities take on importance. Elliott Oring points out that folklorists tend to focus on "the communal . . . the common . . . the informal . . . the marginal . . . the personal . . . the traditional . . . the aesthetic . . . and the ideological."[37] Immigrant letters like those of Clara Jeppsson exhibit these qualities. Clara follows a format shared with many other writers. She uses that format in common, or everyday, settings, and she does not seek to formalize her letters through publication, though in them we can perceive an attempt to shape her experiences according to a folk aesthetic. She writes from the margins of both Denver society and Midwestern Swedish society—marginal in Denver by virtue of class and ethnicity, and marginal to the Midwestern Swedes by virtue of region and gender. Her letters express, at least implicitly, the cultural values she shared with others in the same situation. (I prefer the term *cultural values* to *ideology*, limiting ideology to the elite/popular realms of culture.) Finally, Clara's letters are both personal and traditional. While expressing personal concerns, she also uses a conventional format, themes, and formulas that can be identified in the letters of others.

Those conventions may have borne the distant imprint of letter-writing manuals, which existed in Sweden and America during this period. However, that imprint was probably slight. Nineteenth-century Swedish letter manuals presented models for those with middle-class pretensions to write letters for particular social occasions; for example, a plea for a privilege or an introductory greeting sent by a bride to a soon-to-be sister-in-law. In her study of these models, Stina Hansson finds that there was rarely a close correspondence between actual letters and the models presented in the manuals. Rather, the general influences of the manuals may have included the idea of a tripartite form, with some of the language used for opening and closing sections, and the idea of style and content for love letters. The last influence came with the publication of love-letter manuals that were read for pleasure, as though they were epistolary novels.[38]

In America, manuals were businesslike, presenting brief model letters demonstrating how a correspondent could write for specific occasions, such as for a social invitation, an acceptance or rejection of a marriage proposal, or an introductory letter recommending the bearer to a potential employer. The *Fullständig Svensk-Engelsk Bref- och Formulärbok* (Complete Swedish-English letter- and formbook) was clearly intended for a businessman who also needed to be able to manage his social life. Under one cover, it included model letters and letter-writing advice, guides to American money and measures, balance sheets, and interest and price tables. The letter manual's general advice was to keep introductions and closings brief, and to present in the main body of the letter a well-ordered series of thoughts.[39] The letter-writing section of *Allt-Omfattande Svensk-Amerikansk Uppslagsbok* (Comprehensive Swedish American reference book) advised writers to follow its models for business letters, but for personal letters, not to allow the manual's formulas to stifle the natural feeling that can be a letter's greatest delight.[40] *Allt-Omfattande Svensk-Amerikansk Uppslagsbok* devotes as much space to advice on letter-writing tools and posture as to the form and rhetoric of the letter itself.

As we shall see in the chapters that follow, very few of the model letters found in manuals were applicable to the situation of nineteenth-century immigrants in the American West. Even if general characteristics recommended in the manuals, such as the tripartite form, did influence the immigrant letters, they were never slavishly reiterated. Once put into use, they became an informal means of expression, reshaped by reuse and reinforced by the sharing of letters among recipients.

It is important to note that my use of *vernacular* here does not mean bad, mediocre, inartistic, lowbrow, lower-class, or unself-conscious. *Vernacular* derives from the Latin *vernaculus*, meaning indigenous, native, or domestic. In literary studies, *vernacular* identifies the language of everyday discourse, as opposed to language used formally in institutions such as a university, a definition so closely related to societal status that its object is constantly shifting. In nineteenth-century academics, for example, English literature was admitted into the curriculum alongside Greek and Latin, leaving American English as a vernacular. In the late twentieth century, the new admissions were women's, multicultural, and multilingual literature.[41]

Within folklore studies, though, the term *vernacular* is linked to the culture concept. Folklorists have been drawn to the term *vernacular* as perhaps clearer than *folk* to describe the parts of a culture that are informally learned in small groups that interact with each other face-to-face on a nearly daily basis. The distinction is clearer if we consider what for the folklorist is *not* vernacular: Vernacular culture is *not* the formal culture of larger groups whose interaction is usually mediated through broadcast, publishing, or other means that require institutional support. When a folklorist labels a genre as vernacular, it is not intended as a comment on quality so much as an indicator of how a genre is learned and used within a particular culture.

To interpret an immigrant letter as vernacular is to emphasize its use within the informal context of a shared culture and to partition it off from other sorts of letter writing. Personal letters written to family or close friends tend to fall into this category. Letters written to newspapers generally do not. "America letters" written to be shared throughout a whole village in Sweden are on the margins between vernacular and broadcast. In fact, Blegen uses the metaphor of broadcast to describe such letters, calling them a nineteenth-century "voice of America."[42] Many other kinds of letters—business letters, letters of application, reference letters, and other sorts of official epistles—are clearly not vernacular. The kind of personal letter writing we can label as vernacular uses informal, everyday language without concern for formal grammatical correctness. It fits generic expectations that are maintained informally through practice rather than set forth in letter-writing manuals (although, as I have noted above, letter-writing manuals may have had some impact on the form). It has a small audience, usually a family audience, rather than an audience of hundreds or thousands. The writer's intent is not to be an "author," nor to be authoritative. When the letters are published, it is in a venue well outside the writer's society and era, as in Barton's academic anthology, *Letters from the Promised Land.*

I have cited repetition as a chief characteristic shared by immigrant letters and oral texts. This characteristic has, in fact, been the focus of a major effort to understand the nature of oral narrative, especially the epic and the ballad. Milman Parry first framed an understanding of oral formula as the basic building block for oral composition of epic poems. His work with his student Albert Lord led to *The Singer of Tales*, in which Lord extended the idea to repetition of story units, which he called themes, and to the genre itself, which he called the song. Parry and Lord's work in turn influenced Walter Ong's *Orality and Literacy* and John Miles Foley's *Immanent Art*.

Foley's work is the fullest exposition to date of how oral texts convey meaning to their listeners. He sees meaning-making in the epic as chiefly a system of metonymic reference that is very similar to Stahl's allusions: repeated formulas and story units are references to a larger traditional system, in which inhere the values of a culture's worldview. Thus, formulas are able to tap into meanings present in the larger culture but never fully developed in the epic itself, meanings that are simply assumed by the reciter and the listener and to which outsiders have limited access. In Serbo-Croatian epic, for example, references to a "white dwelling" might seem just that, but Foley points out that the implicit, traditional meaning of "white dwelling" is a home base for the characters and the narrative action. A listener from the culture would know that "white dwelling" indicates "the still core around which the often unpredictable and unruly events of the story evolve."[43] Foley calls this kind of meaning-making *immanent*.

Another way of putting it is that members of a culture group communicate in a kind of shorthand that is well understood by insiders and poorly understood by outsiders. The insider's reaction to the formula is not "How boring. I've heard that before," but rather a reaction of pleasurable recognition, "I know what that means; it brings to mind other stories that I know. I've been hailed as an insider." According to Foley, who intentionally uses a term referring to oral rather than written language, the repetition of "white dwelling" or variations on that formula "brings to its surroundings a deeper traditional resonance" for an insider audience.[44]

Perhaps this pleasurable recognition is not so apparent to those of us who did not grow up with extended oral forms like the epic. But the epic is not the only oral genre based on repeated units; it is merely the longest and most complex, and therefore the most celebrated. In British ballad, Barre Toelken has discovered a system of metaphorical reference in which the formulas are multivalent—able to refer to several meanings at once.[45] Even the audience for very loose forms such as the joke or the personal experience story enjoys hearing allusions that compress whole stories into catchphrases or kernel stories.[46] Such catchphrases might be shared by a very small group. For example, in my family, "Don't step there" refers to a story used by my husband and children to tease me about my obtuseness in a near miss with a rattlesnake. "Why does it rattle when I step here?" I had asked them, repeatedly stepping on a rock on the path down to the Snake River at Pittsburg Landing. Within my small family group, the catchphrase is enough to evoke the full story and to accomplish the teasing. Gradually, the catchphrase "Don't step there" has become a general, humorous cautionary phrase.

Formulas also can be used to indicate genre and its attendant expectations. Hearing "What do you get when you cross a Unitarian Universalist with a Jehovah's Witness?"[47] immediately alerts a listener that the speaker is telling a joke likely to comment on the character of two groups at once by making a pun or a witty comparison. This example illustrates how a folkloric form can play on insider knowledge to tap into an implicit group code while using explicit labels as well. Full understanding requires access both to explicit public statements about a group and to implicit, coded insider knowledge. The entire cycle of jokes shared among Unitarian Universalists would include many that are simply puzzling to an outsider, requiring too much explanation to be understood quickly enough for genuine laughter.

A final characteristic of folklore as a field of study is its empiricism, accompanied by an understanding of a text or kind of text as the focal object of study. Typically, folklorists do fieldwork or archival research, collecting together as many examples of traditional texts as is possible and examining the resulting mass of material for shared characteristics and patterns. Further analysis is informed by a variety of theoretical approaches, but this empirical basis underlies most folkloric work. For example, my study of log construction in Idaho began with amassing a field record of hundreds of buildings, which constituted the "texts" I intended to analyze. *Text* is related to the Latin word for *weaving*, and so is often used by folklorists in this extended sense, applied to artifacts and customary practices as well as verbal materials. This gathering of data was followed by looking for patterns in construction techniques and their combination. Further analysis pulled in the idea of cultural and historical contexts of mid-nineteenth-century Euro-American settlement in Idaho, and the semiotic ideas of icon, index, and symbol.[48]

Folklore's empirical impulses suggest that we should begin with a close look at the letters as texts; its emphasis on meaning-making through a cultural shorthand suggests that in doing so we should look for the letters' building blocks. In letters, we can begin reading to look for shorter formulas, longer subgeneric units, and an overarching structure. However, these units are likely to exist with linguistic features that are peculiar to letter writing. Certainly they would be different from epic, since the letter is both prosaic and written. Because of its recursiveness, writing does not have to be as saturated with formulas as oral epic, and because the letter is a prose form, it allows for flexibility in such considerations as diction, rhythm, and sentence and paragraph length.

Following Dégh's lead, we can begin with the opening and closing formulas. While many scholars omit openings and closings in their editions of immigrant letters,[49] Dégh, Fitzpatrick, and Gerber note the patterning of greetings and closings as significant parts of the letters, worthy of analysis. The formulaic opening and closing is a characteristic of the personal letter generally, noted in letters outside the immigration context by Beauchamp, for example, in her analysis of Preston's letters.[50] In the Swedish letters from the West, these form important components too.

Clara Jeppsson's greetings are brief but still patterned. While some correspondents use the initial greeting as an opportunity for elaboration on their feelings for the recipient, Clara limits her initial greetings to "Dear [recipient]." Following this opener, she typically writes, "Thanks for your letter which I received today [or on a specific time or day]," or a variation on that expression.[51] Twice she instead notes the receipt of a letter from a mutual relative or friend, and then launches into the news of that letter. Twice she opens instead with "As you can see, I have now"[52] to explain a move or other circumstantial change. And in one letter, she skips a greeting sentence, launching into an informative statement: "I got a letter from Axel last week."[53] Most correspondents spend more time establishing contact with their readers through elaborate introductory phrasing. Clara's practice, while using two typical strategies, does not use the most common ones, which we will consider in some detail in chapter 2.

Closing patterns also are present in Clara's letters. She uses a paragraph-long closing beginning with an expression commenting on the writing process itself: "I will now close," "Write soon," or "I have no more to write this time." The closing section typically moves on to extend greetings to specific relatives and friends, and then ends with a general and formulaic greeting such as "Dear regards."[54]

Openings and closings are flexible forms, but Jeppsson treats the body of her letters even more flexibly than the openings and closings. We can describe the middle sections of her letters both through their structure and their content. I have already noted the general outline of Clara's October 13 letter, which is typical of her approach. In structure, the bodies of her letters tend to move from the personal to the communal. Often Jeppsson notes having received a letter from her sister in Sweden, which triggers reflections on the situation of the family, separated by the immigration of some of the siblings. A sister, Ida, was in California, and a brother, Axel, in Canada. Axel, who apparently had left behind a wife and children, was of particular concern to the three sisters. From these opening concerns, Jeppsson moves to a description of her and her husband's current situations, to a description of the Swedish American community in Denver and other Colorado towns, and to a description more generally of the American economic and social milieu. Finally, Jeppsson shifts to concerns about the communities left behind in Sweden, the second-tier community of extended family and friends. Toward the ends of her letters she expresses the strong desire to return to Sweden to be reunited with friends and family there. These comments are usually bracketed with comments about the American and Swedish economies and about her sending money home to her sister. The overall trajectory of the letters is a movement outward from self to communities near and far. Thus, Jeppsson's letters imaginatively bridge the Atlantic.

Immigrant letters also focus on particular content. One might dismiss this statement by saying that of course the immigrant letter would revolve around issues of everyday life such as climate, work, familial relationships, money, and travel. As Øverland points out, at least some of the similarities in content have to be traced to similarities in the immigrant experience.[55] Indeed, these subjects dominate Clara's letters. However, we should note that a great deal is either not mentioned or mentioned only briefly. For example, the everyday consumption of food is rarely the subject of comment, even though foodways would have been a point of difference in Western American culture and even though Clara would have prepared much of her own food. Learning English also receives short shrift, even though it posed a problem for many immigrants. Music was important to many Swedish Americans, but it is rarely mentioned in letters. Clara mentions English only once, commenting on her desire to learn the language better. She mentions music only once, when she reports being able to hear music coming from a nearby park. Clara writes during spring 1912 that she is pregnant; however, she tells her sister about her condition in a roundabout way, following a passage in which she expresses her strong desire to travel home to Sweden: "But it is not only for that reason I wish to travel home. I might as well tell you that we are expecting an heir."[56]

Swedish workingwomen like Clara Jeppsson were typically hired in domestic service. This photograph from the 1890s depicts a maid cooking in a Denver kitchen. Courtesy of the Denver Public Library, Western History Collection, call number X-18395.

Clearly, letter writers had a choice of subject and selected and emphasized certain topics over the full range of everyday experience. Additionally,
they treated those topics in characteristic ways. In some cases, the characteristic treatment of a subject was idiosyncratic, a pattern exhibited by just
one writer and revealing a concern specific to his or her situation. Clara,
for example, was concerned about the separation of couples. She usually
brings up the subject in the context of migration, during which a separated
husband and wife could drift apart or even become divorced; this topic is
the subject of a clipping that Clara sends to Sigrid. Clara also is concerned
about Sigrid's separation from a young man in Sweden, with her brother
Axel's separation from his wife and children, and with her own separation
from her husband, Johan. Clara's circumstances influenced her treatment
of male-female relationships.

In some cases, the characteristic treatment of a subject is patterned
throughout several collections, indicating that the way of thinking about
the subject extended throughout the migrant culture; in other words, it
was part of a vernacular epistolary tradition. Clara's treatment of money
and relationships is a good example. Like the letters themselves, money (in
the form of checks that could be redeemed for Swedish crowns), enclosed
in the letters or otherwise transacted, was used to establish and maintain
connections. If money was not enclosed or sent, then its absence became
the focus of content in the letters themselves. Long explanations of the
lack of money (and attendant lack of work) substituted for the American
dollars that could not be sent. Money is written about characteristically as
something to be saved or sent, not spent. Just as the exchange of money
by relatives becomes a means of expressing reciprocal relationships, the
mention of money takes on an importance in the letters as a distillation,
a metaphor for these relationships that I will explore further in chapter 5.

Approaching letters as a folklorist requires identifying a body of texts
from a place and time, analyzing their parts, and looking for the patterns they embody. A single collection like the letters of Clara Jeppsson,
however engaging, is inadequate to define the genre, which has to be approached by describing the genre as it is ordinarily practiced—the subject
of our next chapter. The question is really an empirical one: What do we
encounter as we read across the whole corpus of Swedish letters from the
Rocky Mountain West?

TWO

"Thanks for the Letter"

THE SHAPE OF THE GENRE

Many, inexpressibly many warm and heartfelt thanks for the dear
letter I received the 3rd of April. I could not have been happier,
when I once more—without expecting—got to receive a letter
from you, full of news and more important occurrences, that have
taken place in my home village.

John A. Leonard, 1884, Lake Valley, New Mexico

MOST OF US RECOGNIZE the shape of an informal letter, and use
that form throughout our lives in letters from summer camp, love
letters, and thank-you notes, and, now that Internet use is so common,
in their e-mail equivalents. Recognition and use of the letter form is not
instinctive or unconscious, though. The letter genre is learned through
observation of letters we receive or have read to us and through trial efforts of our own. Our use of the form is both imitative and original. In the
passage above, John A. Leonard opens a letter to his brother-in-law following a typical format, by thanking his correspondent for a recent letter.
But Leonard also elaborates on the usual formula, *tack för brevet* (thanks
for the letter) by expressing how very welcome it is to receive a letter and
by explaining the kind of news that is especially interesting to him.[1]

M. M. Bakhtin places personal letters like Leonard's in the category
of simple speech genres. These are forms, spoken or written, that take
shape in everyday interactions such as conversation. Along with the letter, Bakhtin lists "short rejoinders of daily dialogue" and "everyday narra-
tion."[2] Each of these genres has a recognizable style that both binds writers or speakers to the form and allows them some flexibility in its use.[3] In

folklore studies, Barre Toelken has referred to this same principle as the "spectrum of dynamism." The spectrum of dynamism is the pull between change and resistance to change, between variation and formula, in any one performance of a folkloric text, making the text both recognizable and creative.[4]

Writing letters is not a magical process. Writers of letters do not just sit down and allow words to flow onto the paper as though the words are springing from a well hidden in the psyche. They write to produce a text that satisfies their and their recipient's idea of a letter. Leonard wrote knowing that his brother-in-law would expect thanks for his recent letter. But many letter writers also strain at the boundaries of the genre, as they write letters that play with the form, or, as we shall see, as they on occasion violate it. Leonard works to make his thanks even more expressive than the typical formula by expanding it with modifiers and specific detail. In this chapter, as we explore the shape of the immigrant letter, we will be examining the genre's spectrum of dynamism, looking both for what is stable and for what allows for expressiveness.

Letters are tangible texts, recognizable even before read on the basis of their size, shape, and packaging. Leonard describes this moment of recognition. He received an envelope, sealed and addressed, and knew that he had received a letter, or something akin to a letter. Our recognition of the letter as artifact sets up our expectations for the kind of writing we will find inside. We expect first to see a salutation. We then have expectations of the letter's contents (for Leonard, news of his home village), and we expect a proper closing in which we receive greetings and well-wishing from those who know us. If our expectations are violated, the violation registers with us. If a letter misses a salutation, for example, we think to ourselves, perhaps huffily, "Well, she just launches right into it." The salutation and closing signature are so basic to the letter form that, coming across a manuscript that has neither, we have to question whether the whole text is present.

The salutation, which serves to mark the beginning of letter texts and to hail the reader, is formulaic. Usually the salutation includes the recipient's name and/or relationship to the writer. It also communicates the writer's degree of personal attachment to the recipient: *kära* (dear) or *älskade* (beloved) or *hjärtligt älskade* (dearly beloved). These greetings and the formulas that follow, such as *jag/vi mår bra* (I/we are doing well) or *jag lever* (I am alive), represent the writer as though he or she has walked into the room. The important fact of the letter writer being alive and healthy would be obvious at first glance during a social visit. In the letter, the tangible text is a metonym for the writer, in whose hands it recently has lain. Lacking face-to-face observation, writers have to explicitly establish critically important information about their health. Hailing establishes literal hale-ness, or whole-ness.

In Clara Jeppsson's letters, we saw an unusually brief use of the formulas for beginning a letter. Because Jeppsson has a great deal to say to her sister, she greets her as briefly as possible and moves quickly on to the meat of her letter—important family matters. The beginnings of Jeppsson's letters are like a meeting with a friend who has hardly any small talk, who walks briskly across the threshold to launch right into a discussion of the point of the meeting. Jeppsson's letters stand at one end of a continuum of formula use: At another end are letters like John M. Swanson's, in which we see a heavy use of repetitious formula in greeting the recipient. Swanson opens a letter to his parents written October 1, 1911, as follows:

> Thank you for your very welcome letters which we have received. It made us very happy to hear that you are fairly healthy and doing well, all things considered. I can also let you know that we are all doing well here so we have much to offer God thanks for, both at home and away, that we have been spared all misfortunes to body and soul.[5]

Swanson moves through acknowledging receipt of a letter, to recapitulating its "ideational core,"[6] to informing his parents about his family's health and spiritual well-being. Only with his fourth sentence, near the end of his first page, does Swanson get to information more particular to his situation in Denver, a comment on the unusually dry weather. The structure of Swanson's opening is symmetrical:

a (your letter received)—*b* (your health and well-being)
b' (our health and well-being)—*a'* (here is our letter)

Swanson uses a typical order for his opening, in which the letter becomes a physical link between correspondents, like a handshake. Its receipt is expected to prompt a corresponding assurance of physical and spiritual well-being. The mirroring of content parallels the reciprocity of letter writing and letter-writing relationships. This $a/b{:}b'/a'$ formula for social contact is so important that many writers feel compelled to represent it even in the absence of reciprocity. Here is how Nels Pearson opens a November 30, 1908, letter to his sister Annie:

> It is such a long time since I heard anything from you so I want to send you a few lines and let you know how I am, so you know that I am alive and well and work, as usual.[7]

In Pearson's opener, a (your letter received) is represented in the negative, *not a* (no letter received), so that Pearson can move on to a' (here is my letter even so). But unlike many correspondents who complain about the lack of correspondence, Pearson manages this statement more gracefully, without explicitly blaming his sister for not having written.

These opening formulas might sound oddly formal in a personal letter were it not for the context in which the letters were exchanged. If we take seriously Robert B. Klymasz's idea of the letter's function as a stand-in for the many oral and face-to-face contacts of the immigrants' lives before emigration, we can define more precisely the kinds of customary practices being replaced. Many of these would have been at least quasi-public: a conversation on encountering a friend along a path, conversations over a family dinner, or exchanges during a dance or a Christmas festivity. The formality we detect in the letters mimics the manners of conversational discourse that one knows may be overheard and that is therefore governed by public expectations such as asking after mutual acquaintances and sending greetings to them.

In these immigrant letters, such expectations would be governed by Swedish custom, which for these working-class immigrants to North America would have included a blend of ensconced rural folk traditions and urban working-class customs bearing some influence from Sweden's emerging middle class.[8] An example is the saying of thanks, which occurs in Swedish conversation at different junctures from those one would expect in American English. Jens Allwood describes the Swedish "duty to

Nels Pearson begins a letter to his sister Annie. Image courtesy of the Swedish Emigrant Institute.

say 'thank you' in situations where such a duty does not exist in any other cultures," including saying *Tack för maten* (thank you for the food) at the end of a meal, *Tack för sällskapet* (thank you for the company) after conversing with someone in a public place, and *Tack för senast* (thanks for the last time).[9]

This last formula, *Tack för senast,* used when first encountering someone who has hosted a party or dinner, most closely parallels the intent of the phrase *tack för brevet* (thanks for the letter). The formula fits a larger pattern of Swedish conversational use of *tack* to establish that one has an equal and reciprocal relationship of mutual gratitude. This is especially appropriate to the relationship required in letter writing, and indeed *tack*

för brevet is the most frequent opening formula in the immigrant letters
from the West.

We see both Swanson and Pearson using this phrase and the formula
jag lever och har hälsan (I am alive and well), or a variation on that phrase,
demonstrating the immigrant's concern about health.[10] Throughout the
chapters that follow we will see the importance of health expressed when
immigrants write about work, nationality and ethnicity, life in the Western region, and their religious life. The topic of health crops up on all
fronts. While we could, of course, simply say that the immigrants were
health-conscious because of the precarious state of physical well-being in
the nineteenth century, that fact does not entirely account for the topic's
all-pervasiveness. The nineteenth century was also an era, in Sweden and
elsewhere, of improvements in public health as a result of cleanliness campaigns. These campaigns could have reinforced the topic's importance in
everyday discourse. According to ethnologists Jonas Frykman and Orvar
Löfgren, "people in the [Swedish] countryside were exposed to a sys-
tematic barrage of propaganda aiming to teach them better morals and
hygiene."[11]

Both Swanson and Pearson link the ubiquitous *jag/vi har hälsan*
formula with a reference to a shared value of importance to them, and
presumably also to their readers. In Swanson's case, the shared value is
religious; in Pearson's, the value of having work. This is a typical opening
strategy that accomplishes the functions of an immigrant letter's initial
section: establishing contact, expressing thanks for the last letter, testifying to the writer's well-being, and citing important shared values. This
most common strategy was not the only strategy, though. Throughout the
sample of letters written from the West, we encounter a few alternatives,
which include pointing out one's new location, expressing the emotions
the writer felt upon receipt of a letter, or providing a religious greeting or
admonishment such as "God's peace" or "Live well." A more secular opener
is that of the kind used by Emma Hallberg, who typically begins her letters to her parents by writing immediately after her salutation, "Be now
and always well is my daily wish."[12] She uses this opener even when writing to her parents about the death of her brother, John M. Swanson, in a
letter in which the formula acts as a delaying device before she writes the
terrible news: "Be now and always well is my daily wish. Also I ask you to

be courageous and read this sorrowful letter; you can probably presume what it contains."[13]

Each letter writer has a distinctive manner for using formulas, placing the imprint of personal style on community practice, but tradition becomes most apparent, perhaps, when we see it violated. Abruptness like Jeppsson's is also found in Bernhard Rydberg's long letters, whose scrawling handwriting gives the appearance of hastiness. Indeed, as he writes about social events in Red Lodge, Montana, and his trips into the surrounding countryside, Rydberg seems to have so much to say to his mother that he often begins abruptly and then interrupts himself with the usual formulas. For instance, he begins a letter dated October 15, 1901, "I sent some photographs yesterday," then interrupts himself to write the obligatory "Thanks for the letter," and then continues, "The photographs are from a place up among the Rocky Mountains."[14]

Another violation of form appears in two unusual letters from women—Karna Anderson and Genny Andersson—both of which are pious letters most closely resembling religious testimony, an oral form inscribed on paper. The writers begin with religious greetings, continue for pages with pious sentiments, and then turn to secular news. In both cases, the writers demonstrate idiosyncrasies that suggest an incomplete literacy, making it even more likely that they were attempting to re-create an oral form on paper. As discussed in chapter 7, these letters function differently from secular letters by creating sacred space for worship within the text itself.

The openers of Leonard Nilsson's letters are unusual in another sense. Nilsson, an avid reader of Esaias Tegnér and the Swedish and Swedish American poets who appeared in Chicago's *Svenska Amerikanaren* (The Swedish American), especially Magnus Elmblad, appears to have been little influenced by biblical reading, church services, or oral discourse. Nilsson's bookishness is revealed in his attempts to restate the typical letter-writing formulas and to make the beginnings of many of his letters formula-free. In his letters to a friend, Johan Westerberg, Nilsson uses his own way to thank Westerberg for writing to him: "For your letter of the 18th June last—which came to me the 20th July—I am thankful to you with my whole heart."[15] In his letters to his fiancée, Lovisa Borg, a similar acknowledgment of a letter received becomes poetic:

Oh, my little angel, if you could see how happy, how delighted I became—when the 30th October last I had the pleasure and joy to, at the Post Office, here in R.B. [Rocky Bar], receive a letter, which I immediately recognized to be from my sweet, faithful, and patiently (with an angel's patience) awaiting *Lova!*[16]

In this example, Nilsson's periodic circumlocutions reveal how very direct the formula *tack för brevet* really is. When Nilsson does not begin his letters with such an acknowledgment of a letter received, he uses two main strategies, both of them similarly writerly. He begins either by expressing his love and appreciation for Lovisa, with compliments to and descriptions of her, or by describing his situation, including his natural surroundings, his writing situation, and his frame of mind. For example, here is the beginning of a letter written to Lovisa in May 1880:

Clear, warm, and radiant shines the sun down on the now green valleys. All of nature is breathing the rejuvenating forces of spring. The trees are clad in summer garb. The rivers ripple swiftly. The birds send their chirping as offerings to nature's lord. Everything is beautiful and lovely. Flora's children are beginning to open their mouths. The Old Man *[Gubben Bore]* appears seriously to have disappeared from this place.[17]

Thus far in our look at the shape of the letter, we have not gone beyond the introductory handshake. Albeit important, this part of the letter usually takes up no more than the first page. The main segment of a letter, in which more particular news of family and friends, locality, economy, and current events are imparted, falls in the middle. While a full treatment of the middle section of the letter is the main subject of the chapters that follow, I here devote some attention to the form and style of the middle segment. This is the point at which Linda Dégh's analysis of the peasant letter becomes vague, and at which letter-writing manuals tend to offer very general advice or to invoke formal rhetorical tropes that were apparently rarely followed. Yet this middle segment of immigrant letters demonstrates a sequencing that has a special logic.

As evidenced by Clara Jeppsson's letters, the overall framework of the middle section is based on the immigrant's personal point of view, moving from self to outer circles of relatives and acquaintances, first in physical locality and then in communities of the imagination. Figuratively, this organization follows the trajectory of the letter itself, which moves from the writer to the recipient. For additional examples of this organizational principle, we can turn to the letters translated in full in the appendix. A simple example is Johan Håkansson's letter to his wife Britta. The middle of Håkansson's letter begins with the statement, "Today I am sending money," along with instructions on how Britta should use the money. Johan comments on his work and the fact that he is idle due to broken machinery. He then pleads for information from home and inquires about the money he has already sent: "I am wondering if the money I sent last has reached you. Write about that when you write."[18]

This general framework is used by some writers with special emphasis on the sending or the receiving ends of the letter exchange. Fritz Lindborg focuses most of his letter from December 1888 on the situation in Helena, Montana, ending with a brief plea for news from home.[19] On the other hand, Oscar Wall focuses his attention on Sweden, saying very little about his situation in America. He begins his middle section with "I have had good luck ever since I came here to this country." He then shifts to information about the presence of an aunt in Seattle. Halfway through his short letter, Wall asks a series of questions about the situation of people he knew in Sweden. The questions dominate his letter, enough that Wall apologizes at the end of his middle section with "You have to excuse me for asking so much, but I like to know a few things about the old country."[20]

In addition to illustrating the general framework of the letter's middle section, these previous three examples also display the dialogic principle of turn-taking that guides many of the Swedish immigrant writers. In conversation, turn-taking is a simple process of sharing a dialogue through alternating chances to speak. In letter writing, the writer has the power of speech without interruption; yet many Swedish writers mimic the turn-taking of conversation by alternating the points of view from which they write. Their incorporation of a simulated turn-taking in their letters assumes a social equality of writer and reader.

The structure used in many introductory sections, $a/b:b'/a'$, is an example of this dialogic structure. We see similar alternations of point of view within middle sections. Håkansson alternates points of view when he writes, "*You* should write as soon as *you* receive this letter so *I* will get to know how things are *at home* this summer. [It] has begun to get cold during the nights so *we* will soon have winter. *I* am wondering if the money *I* sent last has reached *you*."[21]

Dialogic structure is also created by many writers who, when asking questions of their correspondents or when sending them wishes or instructions, follow through with conjectural answers to their own statements. Fritz Lindborg, for example, expresses his hope that Nils's "stay there [in Skåne] . . . may altogether become pleasant." Then he answers this concern with the comment (standing in for the missing response), "Naturally there is no reason to assume the opposite."[22] In Oscar Wall's October 1906 letter, the series of questions is briefly interrupted with such a response: "Have you had any letter from him [father]? I would like to write him."[23]

While letter writers usually use the idea of movement from writer to reader as an overall framework and break into it with brief bits of alternating dialogue-like prose, these principles are sometimes at odds with each other. In Emma Hallberg's September 1902 letter to her mother, for example, the dialogic principle overrides the me-to-you framework. Her letter's middle section can be outlined as follows:

> *Sweden*: the *weather*—*America*: the *weather*
>
> *America*: a wish that her parents could *visit*—*Sweden*: inquiry over *relatives' visits*
>
> *Sweden*: two *relatives* wish to immigrate—*America*: they could find *the relatives* work
>
> *Sweden*: a *relative* has *revisited* home, *behaved* poorly
>
> *Sweden*: inquiries about another *relative's* fiancé; this *relative* is well-*behaved*
>
> *America*: the *children's* schooling
>
> *Sweden*: inquiry whether they have *eggs*—*America*: they have *eggs* and a cow

At the end of her letter, Hallberg, like Wall, apologizes—in her case, for the "rambling"[24] of her letter. Indeed, our first reaction to this chain of subjects, shifting back and forth between Sweden and America, is that she is a rambler. However, in the concerns italicized above, we can detect associational chains; that is, chains of topics that Hallberg perceived as connected to each other.

Hallberg's letter is organized very much like a series of personal experience stories, which, according to folklorist Barbara Allen, "tend to occur in clusters or rounds" that are "linked by similarities in topic or theme."[25] Hallberg's chains of associated topics include the subjects of visits and of having eggs available. But it is important to note that associations exist not just on the topical level. Like a cluster of personal experience stories, in which stories are often related to each other without an explicitly stated link, some of what Hallberg writes is also related thematically. She is concerned not just with whether a particular young woman has visited her parents, but also with how she has treated them:

> We have heard that she begged from you your gold ring last
> time she was home we think that at least she could let you hold
> on to what you have. When you needed it, she did not give you
> much either, now she could help you a bit if she understood it.
> She ought to be ashamed of herself.[26]

Hallberg moves from this judgment to a statement about another young woman, Betty, and her fiancé: "Have you heard what Betty's boy is doing or if he is as great as she brags. Betty is certainly a nice girl so she is worthy a good man."[27] The theme linking the two women is their behavior. Are they nice to others, and therefore worthy? They are the Unkind and Kind girls, as in the folktale,[28] but unlike the folktale's end, the Unkind Girl is here unfairly rewarded.

Some of the letters' thematic links occur regularly throughout the collections as what we can term "idea clusters." In chapter 4, for example, we will see that many writers link the themes of work, regularity of work, compensation for work, the camaraderie of male workers, and the dangers of work. The parts of such an idea cluster—phrases like "I work every day," for example—are like leitmotifs, parts of a culturally shared work ethic. A writer can briefly cite a leitmotif to evoke the entire cluster of concerns circling a worker's life during this era.

Thematic links and idea clusters are similar to formulaic language and the mimicking of turn-taking in that they employ characteristics of orality.

At least three other characteristics from oral genres appear in the middle sections of the letters: writers frequently use metaphorical or metonymic images, often imparted through formulaic language; they frequently use epithets; and they sometimes shift into past tense to relate their or another's experiences as stories.

An example of an image that works metaphorically is that of standing to talk while holding one's hat. This is a literal image, of course, but it also once had iconic significance. It was the posture and etiquette appropriate in Sweden when encountering someone of higher social position. Åke Daun cites this custom as one of the rituals that "recall a past, more hierarchical Swedish society."[29] That society was shifting toward more social mobility and equality during the time of the immigration to North America; hence, standing "hat in hand" became a frequently cited image that metaphorically was related to the idea of social inequality. More analysis of the hat-in-hand image can be found in chapters 4 and 5.

An example of an image that works metonymically is the fumes of smelting, of which we have several examples in chapter 4. Describing the experience of work at a smelter is attempted by workers who suffered from the heat, sulfurous smoke, and physical exertion of such work, but each of these elements was only part of an overall experience that was very difficult to describe in its entirety. Hence, the mention of fumes briefly referred to that experience metonymically. A metonymic image may also bear further significance. For example, when the fumes of smelting are mentioned in the same letter in which a correspondent emphasizes the everlasting snow on the nearby mountains, there is an implied opposition, of pure snow versus a polluting industry, and of salubrity versus unhealthy working conditions.

Metaphors and metonyms are often expressed in formulaic language. For example, the formulas "God's gift" and "gift of God" were understood metonymically by the pious writers who used these phrases. In this case, the formulaic language comes from biblical sources, as will be detailed in chapter 7. The image "God's gift" is somewhat less concrete than standing hat in hand or than the fumes of smelting, but it became concrete for the immigrants when they repeatedly associated it with health. Health is seen as a "gift of God," and for the most literal of believers this would have indicated a causal relationship, good health being God-given.

The influence of orality on vernacular letter writing is especially apparent when the writers use epithets and when they create stories based on their or another's experiences. In chapters 5 and 6, we will encounter the many epithets used for places that were important to the immigrants: Sweden, America, and the West. Usages like "the old country" for Sweden, "a free country" for America, and "the Wild West" for their new region in the United States are common throughout the letters and are expressive of the writers' attitude toward the West and toward their native and new-found countries.

To create narratives, the writers shift away from the ordinary discourse of letters, which is cast in present tense and which is heavy with lists, greetings and other commonplace expressions, and self-referential comments on letter writing itself. In so doing, the writers create characters, however minimally, that move through at least a brief series of actions that are related in past tense. The combination of character and action imparts a core theme or value to the audience. These three features—character, value, and event—are the essentials noted by Sandra Dolby Stahl in her study of the oral personal experience story.[30]

Personal experience stories, which are told in the first person, and the closely related form, the anecdote, both appear in the letters. The anecdote is a third-person form that, according to Dégh, "characterizes a person, a memorable event, or a place through a representative personal episode." Besides its point of view, the anecdote's main difference from the personal experience story is that it is often an underdeveloped, or fragmentary, narrative—as Dégh puts it, possessing a "gossip-like formlessness."[31]

To develop narratives or narrative fragments with these essentials of character, value, and event is probably rarer in letter writing than in face-to-face interaction. But by doing so, the writer re-creates the kind of social interaction missed by the immigrants; "a substitute for direct interpersonal verbal communication," according to Klymasz.[32] As readers coming to the letters a century after their composition, we become most aware of the genre's function within a folk community when we encounter brief references to a story that we do not know but that is so well known to the writer and the recipient that only a catchphrase has to be used.

An example of this kind of brief narrative reference occurs in a letter written by John Hedin to his "Friend and brother" Ole (Olof Larsson). In 1889, Hedin wrote from Helena, Montana, that he often thought of his and Ole's time together in Sweden: "I remember various places where we traveled with our belongings on our backs."[33] "Our belongings on our backs" is a catchphrase for an experience so well known to Hedin and his friend Ole that it can be distilled in a single phrase. Hedin uses the brief narrative reference, characterizing himself and his friend as vagabonds, in order to compare the old times in Sweden with his situation in America, where he testifies to having broader opportunities as a worker. Ole would have been able to understand Hedin's meaning better than we do, because he had access to the specifics of their shared past.

In the immigrant letters, narrative is not unusual, but neither is it a standard letter-writing practice. Hence, when a letter writer breaks into storytelling, the level of importance is immediately heightened for the reader. Some of the subjects that one might expect to evoke a narrative— subjects that mattered to these writers—are in fact not developed to the point of character, value, and event. Those who had children, for example, frequently mention them, with the obvious motivation of keeping relatives in Sweden apprised of the family's well-being and accomplishments. However, none of the many references to children in my sample do more than mention or describe children and their activities. Similarly, the festive Christmas season, mentioned many times throughout my sample, evokes but one narrative (the text of which is provided in chapter 5). Other topics that dominate the letters, such as the immigrant's work or the writing of letters, are shaped as narratives in a few striking instances related in chapters 4 and 5.

Topics that particularly seem to evoke stories include tales of misfortune (including death), adventures, personal relationships, good fortune, and occasionally news that had been emphasized in the press, such as the shooting and death of President Garfield. The topic of Garfield's death was a nineteenth-century media event widely covered in newspapers. The tragedy caught the imagination of Leonard Nilsson in Rocky Bar, Idaho, who wrote of it to two letter recipients, Johan Westerberg and Lovisa Borg. Nilsson wrote to Westerberg soon after the event, emphasizing the particulars of the shooting:

> The President arrived at the train station in the company of
> "Secretary of State["] Blaine. Just as they walked into the waiting
> room—holding each other under the arms—two shots were fired
> from behind and this noble, excellent man, cherished by the whole

nation, fell to the floor. The one bullet only slightly wounded the shoulder, but the other went in through the back on one side, shattered a rib, went through the liver and was embedded in the area of the groin—it is still not removed, not yet successfully.[34]

The description of the second bullet's trajectory is as detailed as the descriptions of spear thrusts in the *Iliad*, and it has a similar effect, as it raises Garfield to the status of hero. The implication is that Garfield becomes a hero by virtue of placing his body directly in harm's way. Earlier in this correspondence with Westerberg, Nilsson praised Garfield as a man of the people, a perhaps not entirely accurate image that had been promoted during Garfield's campaign for president: "The current President has begun as a woodcutter, been a carpenter, and now they say that from the planer's bench to the President's chair is only—one step."[35] Westerberg would have agreed with Nilsson that this apparent ability of a worker to become president was a good thing. In Sweden, they had shared interests in a local workers' association, and Nilsson's letters to Westerberg frequently cite the welfare of the common worker as an issue.

With Westerberg as his audience, Nilsson tells the story of a fellow workingman raised to hero status and tragically cut down in his prime. Nilsson writes to Lovisa Borg a little later, emphasizing the sorrow of the family and of the nation on Garfield's death:

President Garfield died Monday, the 19th of September. Mourned by wife and children, as well as (50) fifty million citizens. This is a nation that mourns a chief chosen by the people. This is a country that mourns a worthy son, who was born into poor circumstances. Who from the ax and the plow as well as the planer's bench, through his own merits—work, diligence, and enterprising spirit with the help of good character—gifts, pulled himself up to the highest achievement in the whole world that you can earn—a leader chosen by the people, for the world's richest and mightiest nation. Also the most enlightened and progressive.

I said he is mourned by wife and children. He is also mourned by an 80-year-old mother. The old woman has borne him in her arms. She has seen him work hard to provide for her and his younger siblings. She has seen him ascend higher and higher until

he finally reached eminence—and she had to see him fall—a
victim to an assassin's bullet. Life is after all a riddle—impossible
to solve.[36]

With Lovisa Borg as his audience, Nilsson focuses on the impact of
Garfield's death on those who grieved for him, especially the family members and, among them, Garfield's elderly mother. A worker ethic still lies
at the core of the passage, but the details of the murder give way to the
idea of grief. The contrast between the two passages reveals the impact of
the reading audience on how letter writers shape their letters.

The passage written to Lovisa also exemplifies the way in which letter writers can embed a variety of orally derived forms in the middle sections of their letters. Lacking a focus on a sequence of events, the passage
is more eulogy than narrative. In good funereal speech-making fashion,
Nilsson develops the passage with parataxis; that is, with repeated phrasing that indicates and emphasizes meaning through parallelism. We see
parataxis in the repeated ideas of a nation in mourning and in the qualities ascribed to Garfield by workingmen like himself: "This is a nation. . . .
This is a country"; "who was born. . . . Who from the ax and plow"; and
"He is mourned by." Through this use of parallel structure, Nilsson is able
to compare the nation and the mother, suggesting a similar relationship
to Garfield, the son. Nilsson ends with another oral form, a proverbial expression, using it as a moral comment on the situation but also suggesting
its general applicability to his and Lovisa's life. Garfield's death is a riddle;
so, too, is Nilsson and Lovisa's separation a difficult riddle to solve. As we
will see in the chapters that follow, many other oral forms can be used by
letter writers: sermons, religious testimony, hymns, and folk songs.

Nilsson's material for both anecdote and eulogy came from his newspaper reading. But the materials for most of the stories and other embedded genres appearing in letters came from personal experience. At the
heart of many stories are the ways in which immigration, American culture, Western experience, and religious experience worked changes in the
immigrants. This is the gist of stories like those of Peter Peterson, who
wrote during the period 1892 to 1902 from Gunnison, Utah, to a friend,
Jonas Danielson, about the successful conversion of his carpentry shop to
steam-driven equipment, about the places in the American Midwest that
Mormon theology identifies with Old Testament characters, and about

the foolishness of a local Swedish inventor who had sold a patent. In turn, Peterson thus touches on occupational, religious, and ethnic status. The story about the local Swedish inventor is typical of Peterson's narrative brevity:

> A few weeks ago there was a Swede close by Salt Lake City who received a patent on a new kind of trap that catches larger and smaller pests, and he sold the patent for 25,000 dollars but I am [not] so foolish that I wanted to sell my patent for $25,000.[37]

Although very brief, this anecdote displays character, local event, and a value judgment. We read of a Swedish inventor characterized by Peterson as "foolish" for selling his patent. Peterson uses the inventor as a foil for his own intended action, to sell his own patent for as much as he can get for it. The value here, the "point" of the story from Peterson's point of view, is to avoid naïveté, to have entrepreneurial savvy in the context of American business.

Personal experience story and anecdote are very flexible and sometimes fragmentary oral genres, but they also employ strategies of more highly structured genres of oral storytelling like the magical tale (*Märchen*), including contrast, repetition, parallel structure, and traditional and popular motifs. Peterson develops his brief anecdote of the Swedish inventor as a kind of cautionary tale against which he can measure his own future actions. He develops this theme through a simple and explicit narrative contrast: the inventor is foolish, but Peterson is not. Ulrika Wolf-Knuts identifies narrative contrast as a technique used commonly not just in oral stories in general, but more specifically in the narratives of emigrants. Her study of Swedish Finns in South Africa reveals explicit and implicit comparisons of nations, eras, generations, environments, and personal situations. She observes that "the concept of emigration is in itself contrastive."[38] Not surprisingly, then, we see contrasts developed throughout the letters in their formulas, images, and storytelling. We have already seen one other example of contrasting images in the previously mentioned everlasting snow on mountains above valleys smudged by smelters.

In a personal experience story that is much more fully developed than Peterson's anecdote, we encounter the effective use of repetition and parallel structure in addition to narrative contrast. Charles Flodin tells of a trip into the mountains of central Idaho in a letter written October 9, 1890. Flodin was an avid storyteller, and this letter in particular is composed of back-to-back anecdotes and personal experience stories. One long travel account dominates the letter. After explaining that he had met a Civil War veteran with whom he had joined forces to seek gold, Flodin describes their provisioning for the trip. He then describes in detail their passage through the mountains:

> So on top of all that [clearing their way through dense forest and travel over ice and snow] after we had advanced up a stream, we found ourselves wedged in among high mountains from which at first sight there seemed to be no way out other than the way we had come. But after two days of searching we finally found a pass, through which we continued our troubled travels until the next hindrance, which represented itself in a big stream that we had to build a bridge over, on which we carried our things over, and our horses swam over. Now everything was as usual again until we had to cross a high mountain chain with high snowdrifts that were solid enough to hold us and our horses up. One time I came close to losing my horse. He fell into a mountain crevice but got away with a few nasty scrapes and wounds.[39]

This is just a part of Flodin's long story of the journey. He and his companion come across a large and impassable river, which diverts them another two days "through forests, swamps, over creeks and streams. We found ourselves at the top of a high mountain chain from which we could discern in the distance the contours of a green valley."[40] The pastoral vision of the far-off valley becomes their immediate goal, as they have reached an elevation where grass for their stock is not easily available. Flodin's story ends with their encountering "two old prospectors"[41] who help them find their bearings in the confusing country. They do locate gold, but the find is not workable, so "there was nothing else for us to do except go back, which we did."[42]

This is a sequential adventure story in which Flodin, cast as the protagonist, has to overcome a series of ever-harder barriers to his journey. He and his companion are saved through the agency of two helpers, old-timers who know the terrain better than they. By spending time to write more fully about this event, Flodin is able to develop character, event, and place—and hence, his thematic point about his experience in the West—well beyond the level of Peterson's anecdote about the inventor. Flodin shows us that traveling through the mountains took courage and perseverance, and he leads us to conclude that perhaps the testing of his perseverance was more important than his failed attempt to seek gold.

Flodin sets up a contrast between the pastoral valley, where his horse may find forage, and the snow-packed crags that earlier nearly swallowed up his horse. He repeats the phrase *höga berg* (high mountains) several times throughout the letter, emphasizing the mountainous setting. As in Nilsson's eulogy, Flodin uses parallel structure. Toelken calls this strategy "connotative structure." When narrative structures are doubled, tripled, or repeated in other multiples, each repetition, according to Toelken, can add "a connotative dimension to the narrative that provides a depth of meaning it did not have before."[43] Flodin's narrative breaks his travels into a series of parallel segments. In each segment, Flodin first describes travel through or over a series of barriers, and he then describes a pause at the top of the mountains, during which he and his companion take in the view and attempt to discern where they are. Each segment is described as more challenging than the last. In the chapters that follow, we will encounter several other examples of connotative structure that repeat sequences of action or thought.

The shape of an immigrant letter is completed by its closing segment, in which the letter writer tends to again use more highly formulaic language. Often this language includes a return to self-referential language that describes the act of letter writing and the particular letter-writing situation. Correspondents often mark the beginning of the end with a rather abrupt-sounding statement like "I have no more to write," as Jeppsson does in a June 1911 letter.[44] Writers follow this statement with greetings to all those at home in Sweden, sometimes a long list that inspires the writer to interpose queries about friends and relatives. This practice was shared by Norwegian immigrant writers, whose closing greetings, according to Theodore Blegen, "often include virtual rosters of entire families and neighborhood circles."[45] It is a customary inclusion that has logic within the immigrant situation, although we also see it in other kinds of personal letters. An elaborate closing of a personal letter outside of the immigration context is exemplified in Madge Preston's letter to her daughter May at a parochial boarding school: "With love and good wishes to Anna and the girls, in the Happiest of New Years to dear [May's teachers], I am as you already know your loving Mama. With all the love imaginable from each member of the family to 'dear May.' "[46]

The setting for a letter to relatives closely resembles the setting for a family visit, in which leave-taking certainly is expected and may become extended with, for example, the saying of thanks several times over. The saying of thanks, which is so important at the beginning of a letter, is usually missing from the closing section, but leave-taking is instead extended and made ceremonial through a redundancy of greetings and well-wishing. Here is the entire closing of Jeppsson's June 1911 letter:

> Signal that the end is beginning/self-reflection on letter-writing: "I have no more to write this time."
>
> Greetings: "except many greetings to you all."
>
> Reference to the correspondence: "Write soon."
>
> Request for specific information: "and say how things are at home in Sweden—whether you have a pretty summer."
>
> Well-wishing: "Hope that you all are healthy and hale."
>
> Complimentary closing: "Dear regards"
>
> Signature: "Clara."[47]

But, as with many letters, that is not the end. After her signature, Jeppsson includes the statement "My address is"[48] and provides her full address. She then adds the line "I do not get to see my old man [*gubbe*] for a whole week. It hurts."[49] This brief testimony of her personal feelings offered outside the bounds of the genre is perhaps the most important content in her letter. She places it as her last words, in a location where her sister will notice it and sympathize with it, rather than burying the line in the newsy middle portion of the letter.

Several correspondents use the space outside the boundaries of letters—the space before the salutation or after the signature—to write something extra. In examples in the appendix, we see Emma Hallberg adding greetings from a third party; Peter J. Johansson giving instructions

Clara Jeppsson adds a final comment to her sister, "Det käns," to explain how diffi-cult it is to be separated from her husband. Image courtesy of the Swedish Emigrant Institute.

regarding money he is sending; Ola Svenson requesting some specific news from home; and John A. Leonard providing miscellaneous informa-tion he had overlooked in the body of his letter. A few correspondents use this space in the way Jeppsson does, to write something that is markedly important. Anni Dickson, who writes to a man she would like to see as a sweetheart, inscribes a poem above her salutation.[50] In the letters of pious writers, this space is put to use for religious formulas, a matter that will be addressed in chapter 7.

Jens Allwood characterizes Swedish leave-taking as abrupt or even ab-sent. He writes, "possibly there is a tendency in Sweden to make a greater use of greetings than farewells." In work settings it is "common" to leave "without saying goodbye" to coworkers.[51] The immigrant letters do reflect a general tendency to have long opening sections and briefer, sometimes abrupt, closing sections. Several examples of brief, abrupt closing sections are found in the fully translated letters in the appendix. "I do not have time to write more this time but many thousand dear regards to you mother," writes Oscar Wall.[52] Olof Larsson writes, "I do not have anything else to say this time but end with many dear regards to you all back home."[53] And Aron W. Johnson simply writes, "Many dear regards to you from me."[54]

Jeppsson's, Wall's, and Larson's reflections on the act of writing are representative of a general tendency for writers to return in their closing sections to self-conscious comments on the letter-writing process. Sometimes this return to self-consciousness is also marked with an apology. Anni Dickson says she has been ironing all day and is too tired to continue writing. Ida Sandberg notes she has to end her letter because her infant son is awakening. Peter J. Johansson breaks off so he can travel to town to fetch a paycheck. In each case, the writer brings the letter to a close with a return to his or her everyday surroundings.

David A. Gerber notes the frequency with which letter writers refer to the difficulties of writing and to the situations in which they write.[55] This self-consciousness frames the genre, marking its opening and closing sections. In the middles of letters, the intrusive writer disappears behind the content, especially in storytelling or in other lengthy embedded genres, such as Nilsson's eulogy. But at the beginning and the end we have the writer clearly before us. The self-consciousness of the letter's frame reminds us that letters are intimate productions. As Gerber says, "letters inscribe the bodies of correspondents ... the letter has been touched by the other writer, whose handwriting is the material mark of a physical presence."[56] Self-conscious reference to the writing of a letter, phrases like "now I must send you a few lines" or "now I must stop," which appear throughout the openings and closings of the immigrant letters, are more than just conventions of expression. They point to the letter's role as a tangible text linking the correspondents physically as well as intellectually and emotionally.

Our analysis of the immigrant letter has revealed a number of common characteristics we can see as providing the stable shape of the genre. Like folk-narrative genres, the letter has beginning, middle, and ending sections that meet writers' and readers' generic expectations. Appropriate content exists for each of these: formulas, metaphors, metonyms, personal experience stories, anecdotes, testimonies, and more. But our analysis has also revealed the writer's use of the genre to express innumerable concerns. A letter can be stretched, as Ola Svenson does, to serve as a sermon to a sister. Or it can be used to create a private space for courtship, as Leonard Nilsson does in his love letters to Lovisa Borg.

All these characteristics of the vernacular letter use the paratactic impulse to create immanent meaning. The paratactic impulse is apparent from brief repeated phrases such as "high mountains," to repeated greetings, to repeated motifs, to connotative structure in the doubling or tripling of sections within narratives. As noted in chapter 1, immanent meaning is meaning created through brief reference to a larger shared tradition that is never fully stated. The idea is very similar to what Stahl calls a "frame of reference" and to what an earlier generation of American studies scholars called a mythology, "a complex of narratives that dramatizes the world vision and historical sense of a people or culture, reducing centuries of experience into a constellation of compelling metaphors," according to Richard Slotkin.[57] The mythic body of metaphor explored by Slotkin is the myth of the West as frontier, to which we will return in chapter 6. Stories like Charles Flodin's refer to that larger context, a mixture of folk tradition and popular mythology, through their characters, setting, and storytelling structure. The myth of the West provided a frame of reference for Flodin's stories.

Swedish immigrants coming into the Rocky Mountain West wrestled with new community affiliations. Some, like Flodin, perceived themselves as Westerners, but other affiliations were available. They could position themselves as workers, Swedes, Americans, Swedish Americans, or members of a particular religious group. These frames of reference will be explored in chapters 4, 5, and 7. But before considering each of these potential identity claims, we need to set the scene for immigration to the West. The following chapter will sketch an overview of Swedish immigration to the Rocky Mountain West, taking a brief look at demographics, settlement history, and ethnic institutions, before turning to the way immigrants wrote about their experiences in the Rockies.

THREE

"Here Are Many Swedes"

NODES AND NETWORKS OF SWEDISH SETTLEMENT
IN THE ROCKIES

❧

To drink and shoot each other are part of everyday life; here you
live a quite wild life; any church or similar establishment cannot
be found in more than 100 miles.

Pet Stred, 1891, Bay Horse, Idaho

[We want you to visit because] you don't believe that we have it
as wonderful as we do. Streetcars go by on the next street over so
that we can go wherever we want in the city for 5 cents.

John M. Swanson, 1891, Denver, Colorado

$\mathcal{T}$HE SWEDISH EXPERIENCE in the West varied as much as the re-
gion itself. Passing through Utah on his way to the Idaho mines,
Leonard Nilsson observed a distinctive religious group, the Mormons.[1]
John A. Leonard encountered American Indians in New Mexico;[2] August
Johansson wrote of seeing African Americans in Denver.[3] Pet Stred noted
the lack of social and religious institutions in Bay Horse, Idaho,[4] and
John M. Swanson told of his enjoyment of Denver's urban amenities.[5]
These immigrants' basis for judging their new surroundings included
comparisons with the eastern United States and with Sweden. Typically,
the Swedes coming into the West had spent some time in the Midwest or
on the East Coast working in communities that had a significant Swedish
presence. They began their adaptation and contributions to American
culture within those Swedish American communities.

Moving to the West took them into a region that was more ethnically and religiously diverse than any other region in the country at that time. The crazy quilt of Western demographics was the result of convergence, as noted by Patricia Nelson Limerick. Asians, Mexicans, Canadians, eastern Americans, and Europeans converged from all directions onto lands already occupied by American Indian groups.[6] This mixed population made the West in the late nineteenth and early twentieth centuries truly a place to reexamine one's ethnic, national, or regional identity.

Swedish immigrants were important in the westering movement. By 1880, after parts of the northern Rockies had experienced mining rushes for a good twenty years, the Norwegian- and Swedish-born population of Colorado was 2,526—1 percent of the state total. The Swedish-born part of that population increased significantly, to 9,659 by 1890, equaling 2 percent of the state's total population. Similarly, the Swedish-born populations of Idaho, Montana, and Wyoming grew to 2 percent to 3 percent of the total state population by 1890.[7] By 1900, Swedes made up 3.4 percent to 5.3 percent of the first- and second-generation immigrant population in the northern Rockies, ranking third in Utah; fourth in Colorado, Wyoming, and Idaho; and fifth in Montana. The only European immigrants from a primarily non-English-speaking country to rank higher were the Germans.[8] Moreover, in his classic study of Swedish settlement in the United States, Helge Nelson found that Swedes were "proportionally somewhat more strongly represented in the mountain regions than in the United States as a whole."[9] We may associate Swedish Americans primarily with the Midwest, but that leaves out the roughly 20 percent of Swedish immigrants who were by 1920 located in the West.[10]

Important in establishing Swedes as a group that could support ethnic institutions was the way the population clustered both locally and within particular sectors of the workforce. The Swedish-born population was as dense as 5 percent to 7 percent of the population in some counties, leading to the creation of a few population centers, some called New Sweden or Swedetown, with enough Swedish residents and resources to foster Swedish American churches, social groups, and newspapers. After 1880, Swedes moved to the West primarily in pursuit of good work, satisfying the labor hunger of the region's expanding industrial base, particularly in mining extraction and processing but also in railroad construction and logging. Thus, Helge Nelson found slightly higher concentrations of first-

and second-generation Swedes in the urban population of the mountain states of 1910 than in the rural.[11]

In Colorado, clusters of Swedes began to form as early as 1880 in Arapahoe, Lake, Clear Creek, and Summit counties; Swedish communities grew up in Denver and Leadville, for example.[12] In Idaho, Shoshone County, a major silver-producing area, was 4 percent Swedish by 1900.[13] Montana's Jefferson County, home to the mining town of Butte, was 7 percent Swedish by 1900, and there were similar concentrations in the mining towns of Anaconda and Helena.[14] In Wyoming, a concentration of Swedes developed in Albany and Carbon counties, where they found work hewing ties for railroad construction.[15]

All these states also experienced some Swedish settlement in agricultural areas. Ryssby, Colorado, on the eastern edge of the Rockies northeast of Boulder, was established in 1869 as a direct transplantation of Swedish settlers from Ryssby, Småland, and became well known for its 1881 Lutheran-church building.[16] In Idaho, transplantations of Swedish immigrants from the Midwest took root in Troy and nearby Nora, in the panhandle, and in the southeast, which was dominated by Mormon immigrants but which also had a Swedish Baptist settlement called Riverview, and a New Sweden settled by Mission friends located between Blackfoot and Idaho Falls.[17] Like Colorado, Wyoming and Montana developed agricultural settlements where the plains meet the mountains. In Wyoming, Swedish cattle ranchers were located in Laramie, and sheep ranchers could be found in Rawlins.[18] Montana's rural Swedes were more evenly distributed, creating no major contiguous Swedish settlements.[19] Utah held clusters of Swedish agricultural settlement in the villages of Sanpete and Sevier counties, south of Salt Lake City, where Swedish Mormon converts lived alongside Danish, Norwegian, British, Swiss, and other European immigrants.[20]

U.S. enumerators reported that most of the Swedish immigrants to the mountain West were laborers.[21] In the 1890 U.S. census, more of the Swedish- and Norwegian-born population in Wyoming, Colorado, Montana, and Utah were designated simply as "unspecified laborers" than by any other occupation. In Idaho, farmer slightly edged out unspecified laborer as the more common occupation. Those male laborers more specifically accounted for were miners, steam-railroad employees, and farmers or farm laborers, except in Utah, where "apprentices" accounted for nearly 10 percent of male workers. Swedes and Norwegians were engaged in skilled crafts; carpentry in particular was a craft in which Scandinavians had a presence disproportionate to their quantitative standing in the general population. In Utah in 1890, for example, Swedish- and Norwegian-born carpenters made up 10 percent of the carpenters working in the state, while the overall Swedish- and Norwegian-born portion of the male population was 5.6 percent.[22] Census statistics for 1900 yield a similar picture of Scandinavian workers, although farming and ranching had by then become more important in Idaho, Utah, and Wyoming.

Among women, those working outside the home were overwhelmingly listed as domestic servants or waitresses. In Colorado, 82 percent of Swedish- and Norwegian-born women in 1890 were working as servants; Utah's figure was 57 percent, and Idaho, Wyoming, and Montana's figure fell between Colorado and Utah's percentages. By 1900, these percentages ranged between 35 percent (Utah) and 61 percent (Colorado). A few Swedish women were laundresses, a few pursued skilled crafts such as millinery, and some were farmers. The only state in which such pursuits registered a significant percentage in the census is Utah, where in 1900, 12 percent of Scandinavian-born women were dressmakers, and 9 percent were farmers, planters, or overseers. These figures may represent a degree of female autonomy achievable in polygamous marriages in which women maintained separate households and farmland.

By 1910, the U.S. Immigration Commission depicted the Swedish immigrant population as largely literate. According to the commission, it was typical for a Swedish immigrant to be able to read and write his or her own language and to speak and read English. Most Swedes were reported as able to write English as well.[23] Recent studies in Sweden have questioned some of the historical data regarding Swedish literacy, but these studies, even while suggesting that literacy in early nineteenth-century Sweden may have been less than previously estimated, agree that by midcentury "93–96 per cent of the children born in [the] 1850's became literate."[24] This high literacy rate enabled those coming to the United States to create and participate in networks that reached outside their immediate communities through print communication in Swedish, as well as allowing immigrants to remain in contact with relatives and friends at home through letters. While letter writing posed a challenge for some writers—examples of which can be found in the chapters that follow—many Swedish immigrants arrived on the shores of North America with a basic literacy level that allowed them to at least make an attempt at letter writing.

Cultural geographer D. W. Meinig identifies two cultural regions in the Rocky Mountains: the Colorado Complex, with Denver as a focal point for a "mining hinterland" farther west, and Mormonland, with Salt Lake City as a focal point for Mormon settlement in the valleys north and south.[25] Denver and Salt Lake City emerged as nodes for a network of Swedes living in the Rockies outside these cities. To gain a sense of life in one of these cities, Denver, we can turn to the letters of Clara Jeppsson.

Writing on May 19, 1911, Jeppsson tells her sister, "judging by what I [have] seen of Denver it is a prettier city than San Francisco."[26] Jeppsson had only recently moved to Denver with her husband Johan. The couple had lived previously in California, where Johan had been a farm laborer. Finding in Denver large parks, neighborhoods with "villa-style"[27] houses surrounded by lawns, attractive streets with room to accommodate both trams and automobiles, and a population of fellow immigrants, Clara and Johan were hopeful they could also find a good living there.[28] When they become geographically separated by the work that is available, Clara evaluates her situation as she considers whether to join Johan: "I have developed a taste for Denver and therefore it is a little hard for me to go back to a farm again."[29]

For a perspective on Swedish-immigrant life in Salt Lake City, we turn to the letters of Peter Peterson, who, like Jeppsson, writes of being drawn to the city. Peterson was a carpenter and farmer in the village of Gunnison, which lies 125 miles south of Salt Lake City. In 1902 he wrote to a Swedish friend that he had purchased a small plot of land in Salt Lake City and is thinking of moving there. Salt Lake City, he says, is so well lit by electricity that it is "brighter than the United States capital city, Washington D.C."[30]

By 1910, the Swedish-born population of Denver County, Colorado, was 2 percent, or 4,500 residents. In 1910 the "Swedish Denver Colony,"[31] its people, businesses, and organizations, were enumerated in a special directory in which it was claimed that 6,500 Swedes lived in Denver, a figure that probably included the second generation. Similarly, Salt Lake County at the time had 3,900 Swedish-born residents, or 3 percent of the

county population.[32] But the character and history of the two communities differed considerably, providing some interesting distinctions between
the circumstances of those living in the Colorado Complex and those living in Mormonland.

Denver served as an important urban center for male laborers drawn to
the region by the mining, timber, and railroad industries. West of Denver,
Colorado counties dominated by mining and ore processing had up to
7 percent Swedish-born population.[33] In his 1985 study of Colorado's
Swedish population, Carl V. Hallberg identifies Leadville, Cripple Creek,
Idaho Springs, and Telluride as mining camps with concentrations of
Swedes, based on his own count of names in the 1900 census.[34] Hallberg
singles out Denver as "the center of Swedish activity in Colorado"[35] as a
consequence of having the highest percentage of Swedish residents in
Colorado.[36]

Clara Jeppsson enjoyed the advantages of a number of Denver's
Swedish institutions. The city was a base for several Swedish American
churches, one of which Jeppsson visited in 1911. As she describes it, the
church was a place to hear a good choir and to meet up with fellow
Swedes: "The people who go to church here are not particularly religious,
they mostly go to meet others."[37] Although there was a secular side to the
Swedish Lutheran, Baptist, Methodist, Covenant, Seventh-Day Adventist,
and Free congregations of Denver, their leaders were, of course, devoted to
spreading faith, not just within Denver but also to communities throughout the Colorado Rockies.[38] The Lutherans, for example, had established
congregations in Longmont by 1887, and in Pueblo by 1891.[39]

The Swedish Free Evangelicals, organized in Denver in 1880, placed an
emphasis on missionary work, using Denver as their base of operations.
By October 1887, the congregation was supporting preachers at the nearby
Argo smelter and Grant smelter, and in West Denver, and was discuss-
ing additional extension work farther west in towns like Leadville. The
church formally organized a Colorado Mission in 1891, eventually resulting in separate congregations in Leadville, Boulder, Aspen, Idaho Springs,
Central City, and Pueblo.[40] In Denver the congregation supported chari-
table work through its sewing auction and its active young people's association.[41] The depth of the group's resources was apparent in their ability
to sustain organizing efforts for the Colorado Mission at the same time
they were mustering support for a second church building in Denver.[42]

According to Jeppsson, Swedish immigrants in Denver were "well-off, if not rich."[43] The population was apparently wealthy enough to include a segment that could enjoy a number of secular amusements and institutions. The one such city amenity mentioned by Jeppsson is music. Jeppsson enjoyed the choir at the church she attended, and she also enjoyed the music that drifted in her window from the city park: "I can lie in my bed and hear the music."[44] Denver's musical groups included the Orpheus Sångförening (Orpheus singing society), organized in 1901.[45] This organization was involved in plays, such as the popular *Anderson, Petterson och Lundström* (Anderson, Petterson, and Lundström), in festive New Year's events, and in concerts.[46] Members of the Orpheus Sångförening joined with the local Vasa Order lodge to form Svenska Dramatiska Sällskapet (the Swedish dramatical society), a group that hoped to establish a Swedish meetinghouse in Denver by 1920. Although there is no evidence of success in that venture, the group did put on a very popular Swedish American play, *Värmländingarne* (The Värmlanders), at the El Jebel Temple in 1917.[47]

Clara Jeppsson's gender and her position as a house servant afforded limited access to some of these events. Even though she appreciated music, she does not mention the Orpheus society by name, nor does she note the existence of Swedish democratic and republican clubs or the involvement of club members in fund-raising balls and promotional events for political candidates, some of whom were Swedish.[48]

Jeppsson also fails to mention local fraternal organizations such as the Foresters of America, Court Valhalla, and Vasa Order,[49] or the city's Midsommar (summer solstice) picnics.[50] Jeppsson did not come to Denver until after the Swedish community's 1903 relief fund for those suffering from crop failures in the northern province of Norrbotten, a natural disaster noted by John M. Swanson, who writes to his parents that he has read in the Swedish American news that "the poor people in Northern Sweden are terribly afflicted with hardship."[51] The Denver Swedes sent money directly to Luleå, in Norrbotten, rather than through the central relief committee located in Stockholm.[52] Denver's Swedish Relief Committee, joining efforts around the United States, mustered nearly $1,000 in relief aid by combining income from a theater performance with individual donations.[53]

Alongside such organizations were the many local merchants who catered to the Swedish population through newspaper advertising and who supported the various organizations' entertainments and charities. Merchandise explicitly labeled as "Swedish" in *Svenska Korrespondenten* (The Swedish correspondent) advertisements of the 1890s were primarily personal items: clothing, shoes, snuff and tobacco, jewelry, bakery and delicatessen goods, groceries, and medicine. One could patronize a *Svea* bar[54] or dine at a *Svenska Gästgifvargården*[55] (literally, the "Swedish Inn," but translated by the ad writers as the "Last Chance Hotel"—perhaps as the last chance to enjoy Swedish food before traveling farther west). Some services and professions catered specifically to the Swedish population, advertising themselves as Swedish barbers, Swedish dentists, and so forth. For example, photographer Chas. E. Emery advertised on August 12, 1897, that his studio had a *Svenskt biträde* (Swedish clerk),[56] and Dr. John E. Nordlund identified himself as a *Svensk Läkare* (Swedish doctor).[57] Two doctors serving the Swedish population, John Lindahl and Charles A. Bundsen, created a Swedish National Sanatorium in Englewood, Colorado, in 1909.[58]

Jeppsson did have access to one of the most important unifiers of the local Swedish population: the newspaper. She mentions newspapers twice in those of her letters to which we have access. As both references come from letters written after she had left Denver to live with her husband in LaJara, Colorado, they attest to the importance of the Swedish press for those living away from the city's ethnic institutions. Jeppsson's references to the press also attest to the way immigrants could use a newspaper to participate in a distant community through what Todd S. Gernes calls "active reading."[59] Jeppsson's active reading included clipping items to send to her sister, accompanied by her own commentary. In an undated fragment from LaJara, Jeppsson writes:

> I will send a newspaper clipping from the Swedish newspaper we have here [probably the Denver paper]. You can see there the various opinions that the immigrants here have about America and Sweden. But you cannot take many [of them] seriously because those who left Sweden 20 or 30 years ago base their opinions on how it was then and cannot comprehend that Sweden has moved forward as well as America.[60]

Jeppsson sent her sister a clipping from the legal question-and-answer section of the Swedish newspaper. She uses the case, in which an immigrant had obtained a divorce because his wife never chose to immigrate, as a parallel for the case of a mutual acquaintance.[61]

To the extent that they had write-in columns for readers, turn-of-the-century newspapers displayed an early form of interactivity.[62] These columns reached outside the city to help create an ethnic network. The Denver *Svenska Korrespondenten* made several efforts to launch a letter-to-the-editor column. It appeared first in 1890 as *Fria Ord* (Free words), was revived in 1892 as *Ordet Fritt* (The free word), and in 1900 as *Insändt* (Submitted) and *Från Våra Vänner* (From our friends). Although none of these formats were long-lived, they did provide a forum for communication of the concerns of Swedish immigrants, a role that folklorist Barbro Klein has identified as persisting into the 1960s in one of the few long-term Swedish American newspapers, Chicago's *Svenska Amerikanaren Tribunen* (The Swedish American tribune).[63]

Sometimes letters written to the editor reflect the same generic characteristics of the personal letters that were written home to relatives and friends. They include self-reflexive passages referring to the act of writing;

for example, *två Denver-flickor* (two Denver girls) begin a letter printed February 5, 1891: "We would like to write."[64] Similarly, A. J. Anderson's letter dated March 26, 1891, begins "I want to send the newspaper a brief greeting"—a similar introduction as what he might write to a friend.[65] These sporadic contributions from *Svenska Korrespondenten* readers range over a variety of subjects. The two Denver women who wrote in 1891 expressed a desire for more social events at which they could meet young men. A. J. Anderson wrote describing the harsh winter weather at Beech Hill, in the Boulder County foothills. He was concerned that many Finns had arrived destitute and were unprepared for the severity of climate. Other immigrants wrote solicitations for charities, descriptions of the weather, comparisons of Sweden and America, and promotions for Swedish businesses or clubs. A prominent writing topic is warnings: against a swindler posing as a debtor, against ruffians traveling the region, against the general wickedness of Western communities. Hallberg sees one major debate emerging in letters to the editor and in the work of regular correspondents: that of Americanization and the degree to which it should be resisted, especially as it affected women's conduct and dress.[66]

The Denver population was perhaps just barely large enough to sustain a Swedish press, which had a shaky beginning in the 1880s. Hallberg identifies seven efforts to publish a Swedish-language newspaper in Denver, beginning with *Colorado-Posten* (The Colorado post) in 1882.[67] A retrospective report in Denver's *Western News* gave credit to "our first vice-consul" for establishing *Colorado-Posten* as a publication that "helped initiate . . . [the Swedish newcomers] into the mysteries of the West."[68] *Denver Veckoblad* (Denver weekly paper), begun in 1888,[69] was the precursor to a Swedish-language newspaper that was able to maintain an extended run. *Svenska Korrespondenten* took the place of *Denver Veckoblad* in 1889. By the turn of the century, when *Svenska Korrespondenten* was taken over by J. R. Newton and renamed *Svensk-Amerikanska Western* (The Swedish American West), its publishers and editors—who included well-known Swedish poet, journalist, and humorist Ninian Wærnér— had already successfully expanded the newspaper's range to the larger northern Rockies region.[70] When declaring its name change on the front page of its March 28, 1901, edition, the newspaper boldly declared that it had 7,000 subscribers and 20,000 readers.[71]

Svenska Korrespondenten created through its correspondence column a regional network in which one could read submissions of regular correspondents from all over the Colorado mining country, including Aspen, Colorado Springs, Cripple Creek, Leadville, Pueblo, Ouray, Telluride, and Victor, and ranging north into Butte, Montana, and Burke (just north of Wallace), Idaho. Some correspondents wrote from their homes; others traveled in order to better describe these outlying communities. Often adopting pen names, these writers combined descriptions of the mountain towns with comments about their Swedish populations and institutions and the issues faced by Swedish immigrants. For example, Anna Stina wrote from Leadville on June 25, 1891, after having just moved to that town:

> There is also a beautiful small church here and it is supposedly situated at the highest elevation on earth. The church is also used by the Norwegians, and I have heard that sadly enough it is the cause of much division and dissension between Swedes and Norwegians in this area. This is bad and does not uphold the Scandinavians' reputation among Americans and people from other nations who have settled here.[72]

The ethnic dispute described by Anna Stina eventually led to the dissolution of both congregations.[73] Anna Stina noted that if Ninian Wærnér chose to print her letter, she would write again after settling in Leadville. She followed through with two more Leadville letters.

These contributions from Anna Stina suggest the way in which newspaper correspondence might become a regular feature. Others who developed into frequent contributors throughout the 1890s included Jack, also from Leadville; Kurre (a nickname for Kurt that can be used in a generic sense to mean a guy or fellow), from Butte; and Cire, from Colorado Springs. The pen name *Jack* falls into one category used by Swedish American correspondents: names that can be seen as typically Anglo-American. *Anna Stina* and *Kurre* represent another category: names seen as typically Swedish. Kurre was also the name of a weekly humor magazine published in Chicago between 1884 and 1887, in which some of Wærnér's work appeared.[74]

Through these many institutions—churches, social groups, music groups, businesses, and newspapers—Denver served as an important node for a network of Swedes in the Rockies. Salt Lake City formed a similarly important node, but for a very different community, one principally composed of those who had converted to Latter-day Saint (LDS) beliefs before traveling to America. The dominance of the LDS church in Utah made it nearly impossible for the few non-Mormon Swedes to support Lutheran or other Swedish churches. Mormon Swedes dominated efforts to organize secular ethnic organizations as well.[75]

Most Swedish converts emigrated as whole families and traveled with fellow converts in what William Mulder characterizes as a "shepherded migration."[76] The emigrants enjoyed the guidance of missionaries and received advice in a church publication produced in Denmark, *Skandinaviens Stjerne* (Scandinavia's star), although for the most destitute the trek across the Great Plains states was in a so-called "handcart company," in which immigrants themselves provided the muscle for pulling their belongings in carts.[77] Salt Lake City was the terminus of this long journey.

a   b

Two Swedish LDS leaders in Utah: (a) Anthon H. Lund and (b) Ole N. Liljenquist. As a member of the Quorum of the Twelve (the group of immediate advisors to the LDS president), Lund was involved in Scandinavian services and events. Liljenquist was an LDS bishop and mayor in the mostly Scandinavian town of Hyrum, but he also traveled throughout Utah to assist recent Scandinavian immigrants. Photographs courtesy of Utah State Historical Society; all rights reserved.

Until 1904, when a Swedish mission was established, the converts were served by a Scandinavian mission based in Copenhagen, resulting in demographic percentages that reversed the usual pattern of Swedish/Norwegian immigrant dominance.[78] More of the Mormon Scandinavians were Danish, and fewer were Swedish. Norway contributed the fewest Mormon converts. Within Sweden, the missionaries had their greatest success in the southern province of Skåne and in Stockholm.[79]

Although it was against official church policy, many of these immigrants settled near each other, forming a concentration of Scandinavian settlement south of Salt Lake City in Sanpete and Sevier counties, where Peter Peterson's village of Gunnison was located. There were also specifically Swedish concentrations in Salt Lake City and in a few villages such as St. Charles, Idaho, and Grantsville, Utah.[80] But these ethnic concentrations always existed in the larger context of Mormon settlement. The LDS church encouraged church affiliation rather than ethnic connection, although it did set up a Scandinavian Meeting that enabled immigrants to hear services in an amalgam of the Scandinavian languages and to participate in secular activities organized around ethnic holidays.[81]

Peter Peterson is typical of the Scandinavian immigrants in that he was both a farmer and a carpenter. His letters are full of reports of the bounty, as he perceived it, reaped from irrigation of the Utah desert, but Peterson also comments in 1886 that he was able to make more money with his carpentry.[82] Like Peterson, roughly half of the Scandinavian immigrants to Utah were farmers, but there was also a large population of skilled craftsmen.[83] As Mulder explains, "nearly everyone, regardless of his former occupation, had to turn to farming at first, [but] the town system made it possible for some to follow familiar trades."[84]

Peterson reports visiting Salt Lake City three times during the summer of 1902. He was impressed by the electric streetcar system that provided cheap travel throughout the city from its northern to its southern extent. Besides appreciating the convenience of the urban transportation system, Peterson gives lavish praise to the city's natural surroundings, especially its water supply: "Salt Lake City is located on the slope of the mountains and it is built as high up on the mountainside as it possibly can be, spring water is used over the whole city, in the houses and to water grass and flower gardens."[85]

It is notable that neither of these valuations is markedly Swedish, unless we see valuing nature as a Swedish cultural trait. Moreover, Peterson does not place an emphasis on Swedish or even Scandinavian communal interaction elsewhere in his letters. This lack of specifically claimed ethnicity was characteristic of the Mormon population, for whom religious identity came first and ethnic identity came second or even third, below claims to being part of America or of the Western region. Kenneth Bjork describes the active discouragement of ethnic ties by the Mormon church. Yet, according to Bjork, "Scandinavian and even distinctly Danish, Swedish, and Norwegian feelings were and still are much alive among converts to Mormonism, though subordinate to church loyalties."[86]

Thus, unlike Jeppsson, Peterson does not explicitly rejoice at having Swedes and other Scandinavians nearby. His ambiguity toward ethnicity is evident when he distances himself from the Scandinavian population by criticizing their work:

> I know many good workers both from Sweden and Norway
> and Denmark, their work is not acceptable until they have been
> here a long time and there are many who cannot give up their
> habits from the old country. I will mention one of the simplest
> things, driving in a nail. To hear whether it is a Scandinavian
> or an American, a Scandinavian if you hear five or six blows, an
> American if you hear no more than one blow.[87]

Swedishness is subsumed here into the panethnic category—Scandinavian—and Scandinavians are compared unfavorably to Americans. Peterson presumably would have placed his own work in the American camp; his letter implies that he was one who was able to leave behind his old Swedish habits.

It is only through the implicit gesture of writing in Swedish to his friend Jonas Danielson that we can see Peterson participating in ethnic culture. Of course, this was a necessity; how else could he communicate with his friend? Language much more explicitly and voluntarily expressed ethnic connections in Salt Lake City's Swedish-language press. Kenneth Bjork interprets the Scandinavian press in Salt Lake City as supporting "a persistent Scandinavianism that . . . was . . . too potent to be wholly contained within the forms and routine functions of the church."[88] Writing in a language other than English was also significant, according to Mulder, because the Mormon church saw English as "the Lord's favored language in which he had spoken his will in [the text of the Book of Mormon, understood by the Mormons to be a translation by Joseph Smith]."[89]

Danish and Norwegian newspapers were the first established: *Utah Posten* (Utah post) in 1873, *Utah Skandinav* (Utah Scandinavian) in 1875, *Bikuben* (The beehive) in 1876, and *Familie Vennen* (The family friend) in 1877. All but the anti-Mormon *Utah Skandinav* were publications by LDS members, although not necessarily with monetary support from the church.[90] Swedish-language publications came a bit later. J. M. Sjödahl, one of the editors of *Svenska Härolden* (The Swedish herald), was a president of the LDS church's Scandinavian Meeting. *Svenska Härolden* was established by the Swedish Publishing Company in 1885, and ceased publication after an 1892 fire. *Utah Korrespondenten* (The Utah correspondent) was edited by Otto Rydman, a printer and writer trained and educated in Sweden. Published from 1890 to 1915, *Utah Korrespondenten* was joined in 1900 by a Swedish *Utah Posten*, which was soon taken over by the LDS church as an official publication for its Swedish members.[91] Also briefly published were the Swedish republican *Fyrbåken* (Lighthouse beacon) and the Lutheran *Salt Lake Bladet* (The Salt Lake paper).[92] Peter Peterson apparently read at least one of these newspapers, as he sent a newspaper, presumably in Swedish, to his friend Jonas Danielson in 1902, without comments on the contents.[93]

Although the three main Swedish newspapers were edited by Mormons and supported LDS beliefs, the official church position in favor of panethnicity over ethnic- and language-specific groups was a point of contention. Rydman's editorials delivered heated criticism of Sjödahl, *Svenska Härolden*, and *Utah Posten* for espousing the church position on Scandinavian rather than Swedish, Danish, or Norwegian church services. His "Swedish Uprising," through which he hoped to establish LDS Swedish-language services and celebrations, was unsuccessful in introducing a Swedish julotta service (Christmas morning service), and it resulted in his excommunication.[94] Ironically, those supporting the church position later established separate Swedish meetings, including a 1907 julotta.[95]

As proponents for preserving Swedish language and culture, Rydman and his newspaper provided an important Salt Lake City–based forum for Swedish Mormons. Like Denver's *Svenska Korrespondenten*, *Utah*

Korrespondenten featured correspondence and letter-to-the-editor columns, but unlike the Denver paper, it emphasized poetry and included a weekly riddle in addition to Rydman's own column, written under his pen name *Tomte* (Brownie).[96] The locations of *Utah Korrespondenten* correspondents suggest the extent of the newspaper's reach. They were located south of Salt Lake City in Sanpete and Sevier counties; farther south in Cedar City, a town situated in Utah's southeastern corner; east of Ogden in the Wasatch forests at Huntsville; and north to Rexburg, Idaho, which lies about 130 miles north of the Utah-Idaho border. The locations of correspondents sending letters to the paper's *Insändt* and *Fria Ord* columns exhibited a similar distribution. Salt Lake City was the center of a smaller, more unified cultural region than was Denver. The region of the Salt Lake City paper coincided with Meinig's Mormonland.

Columns devoted to readers' comments were used more actively in *Utah Korrespondenten* than in the Denver paper, although Rydman appears to have been inconsistent, sometimes using *Insändt* for reports from regular writers. Nels Forsberg, writing simply as "Nels," wrote *Insändt* letters that were really accounts of the LDS Scandinavian Meeting. Forsberg was a stockholder in the newspaper who contributed other kinds of writing as well.[97] Although formally similar to the Denver letters, the topics of letters in *Utah Korrespondenten* varied considerably, ranging into religious and philosophical arenas in a way not evident among the Colorado letter writers. For example, O. T. V—n. wrote in 1893 about the results of his calculations based on Milton's depiction of Satan. After having figured the speed, acceleration, and heat from friction in Satan's fall from Heaven, he concluded his letter with a question: "What kind [of] material was Satan made [of], that he could endure 2,000 times more heat than a diamond without melting?"[98]

Other topics included the importance of Mormons' understanding the Christian trinity; a plea for financial assistance for a fellow Swede whose son in Sweden was in danger of being placed in the poorhouse; advice that men should always lift their hats when meeting female acquaintances; reflections on the status of the Bible as inspirational gospel or as a history of God's relationship with mankind; and the possible articulation of the Scandinavian Meeting with groups arranged by nationality.[99] This last issue was taken up by numerous writers beginning in 1894, and generated exchanges in which letter writers engaged with specific points made by earlier writers. "The undersigned hereby humbly requests that these lines may be printed in your newspaper in connection with Mr. Nilson's writing in the last issue," writes Gus Almquist in an 1894 letter. "I believe that everyone who has submitted something to the newspaper about the unsatisfactory state of affairs with the Scandinavian meetings would and could stand by the same without apology and equivocation."[100] Almquist's tone is typical of these politely emphatic exchanges.

Generally, *Utah Korrespondenten* nurtured a livelier sense of community than did the Denver newspaper. Not only was more at stake, as with issues such as Swedishness versus Scandinavianness, but also the Swedish speakers had more in common as part of a subculture within Mormon Utah and Idaho. A lively use of the press also emerged in areas outside the letter columns: the newspaper featured numerous poems and riddles labeled as *Insändt*. In his examination of *Utah Korrespondenten*, Ernest Olson notes that many of the poems were by local writers, such as Nels Forsberg and Alfred Rydelius, who wrote moralizing verse on conventional subjects using picturesque imagery. Rydman himself was a frequent poetry contributor.[101] The riddle column was even more interactive than the poetry column; readers sent in riddles, and then vied to provide answers. Many of the riddles are versions of traditional lore. For example:

There was a man, but there was no man. He went on a road, but there was no road. He found a thing, but there was nothing. Had he seen it, he would not have picked it up, but because he didn't see it, he picked it up. How can that be explained?[102]

The answer, sent in by Erik I. Mogren of Santaquin (south of Pleasant Grove), is: "The man was a boy. The road was a forest path. The object that he found was a nutshell. He thought it was a whole nut, but had he seen that it was only a shell, he would never have picked it up."[103] Thus, the newspapers served as conduits for Swedish folklore.[104]

Like the Denver papers, Rydman's newspaper served readers by advertising the wares and services of merchants who catered to the Swedish population, by providing announcements for Swedish democratic and republican organizations, and, in the early years of the paper, by providing announcements and reports of the Scandinavian Meeting. The newspaper also promoted the celebration of Midsommar and of Christmas, to which

Tomte devoted columns describing typically Swedish customs. Norden, a Swedish literary club organized by Rydman in 1896, sponsored yearly Midsommar festivities.[105] The Stor [S]kandinavisk Midsommar-Fest (Big Scandinavian midsummer celebration) planned for June 24, 1896, was held in Salt Lake City's Calder's Park, accessible via the streetcar system that Peter Peterson so admired. The 1896 Midsommar featured music and singing, speeches, races, dancing, and prizes, but the Midsommar pole so commonly associated with the celebration is not mentioned in the newspaper's advertisement of the event.[106]

It is interesting to note that the Rydman-endorsed Midsommar was labeled as Scandinavian at a time when his newspaper readers were engaged in a heated discussion of Scandinavianism. Panethnicity also pervaded the other secular entertainments available to Salt Lake City Swedes. Representative is the performance of the Scandinavian Dramatic Committee at the Salt Lake Theater on March 5, 1900, in which a Swedish play, A Midsommar Night in Dalarna, shared the billing with An Adventure at Fodrejsen, labeled as Danish and Norwegian. This performance was to benefit a Scandinavian Jubilee Fund.[107]

The panethnicity that was church policy for the Mormons of Utah was necessity for many of the Swedish immigrants who lived outside of metropolitan centers like Denver and Salt Lake City. In many places, the Swedish population was sparse enough that ethnic institutions were created by the combined efforts of Swedes, Norwegians, and sometimes Danes. Swedes living in Montana were served, for example, by local Scandinavian newspapers, in which Norwegian was the dominant language but which included Swedish-language correspondents' submissions. Extant issues of such newspapers are few, but we can verify that there was a Montana Posten (The Montana post) in Helena during 1890–93. The first issue, dated October 11, 1890, was written entirely in Norwegian and set in Gothic type. By issue 21, the typeface had changed to Roman, and the masthead declared that Posten was "the only paper in Montana published in both the Norwegian and Swedish languages."[108] Page 3 of issue 21 presented Swedish news and Skizzer och berättelser af SIGURD (Sketches and stories by Sigurd), but local and state news was written in Norwegian.

The Butte Montana Skandinav (Montana Scandinavian), published in 1893, merged with Montana Tidende (The Montana times) to become

Montana Tidende og Skandinav (Montana times and Scandinavian), advertised in 1894 as "the only Scandinavian paper in Montana."[109] Unlike *Posten, Tidende* intermingled its Swedish-language features with Norwegian features, rather than segregating Swedish on a separate page.

The only entirely Swedish newspaper extant from nineteenth-century Montana is *Bergs-Väktaren* (The mountain guardian), begun in 1898. Published by the Evangelical Lutherans (Augustana Synod) of Helena, this paper was edited by pastors in Helena and Missoula, who reported on meetings held in outlying communities like Anaconda, East Helena, Marysville, and Livingston.

These mixed-language newspapers reflected a panethnicity that was also present at Montana social functions, in business advertising, and in church organization. While there were social groups and functions devoted to the Swedish population, there were also many that were more broadly Scandinavian. In Helena, a Swedish group, Svea, met regularly every Wednesday at the Merchants National Bank Building, according to an announcement in *Montana Posten*.[110] Svea organized a Midsommar picnic on June 25, 1893, the day declared by the Chicago Exposition as "Swedish Day," a day that would be "celebrated with more than usual magnificence among all of the Swedes in America."[111] The Swedish identifier Svea also appeared in the name of Svea Lodge No. 52 of the Odd Fellows (IOOF) in Butte.[112] The Vasa Order began a district lodge in Montana in 1912 that organized local lodges in Butte, Anaconda, Missoula, and Great Falls.[113]

Much more commonly, social functions were identified as Scandinavian and promoted to a mixed Swedish-Norwegian audience. Föreningen Scandia (The Scandia society) was congratulated by Helena's *Posten* for its May 17 celebration in 1893. Attendees included many Swedes, who must have had mixed sentiments about celebrating Norwegian Constitution Day, the day marking the end of the 1814 hostilities between Norway and Sweden that had brought about a degree of independence for Norway. *Posten* urged Scandinavians to attend picnics held in Helena and Butte. In Butte, "all of the Scandinavians were on their feet and taking part in the celebration."[114]

The celebrations described most markedly as Swedish were held by the Evangelical Lutherans. The missionary efforts of pastors C. E. Frisk, Helena, and A. E. Gustafson, Missoula, reached to communities like East

Helena, six miles east of Helena. There, according to Frisk's report in *Bergs-Väktaren*, smelters were kept going night and day, seven days a week. As Frist saw it, the Swedish men who worked there found the work hard both for the body and the soul, therefore welcoming the religious services he brought to the community. But the Lutherans provided more than religious services. In 1898 the Helena church sponsored its third *Årsfest* (yearly celebration), for which the church was decorated with portraits of the Swedish king and Martin Luther, and with Swedish, American, and other flags. Entertainment included music, declamations, and dialogues, and attendees were served oyster soup and coffee by members of the youth group.[115]

While many Swedish churches were established in Montana, *Scandinavian* was a banner available for smaller religious groups. Perhaps the most multiethnic of Montana towns was Butte. By 1905, Butte had numerous religious groups serving specific ethnicities—Norwegian, Finnish, German, Jewish, Chinese, and Welsh—as well as Catholic services that would have attracted the town's large Irish population. The Swedish congregations included Swedish Baptist, Evangelical Lutheran, and Mission churches, but the Butte Methodists were broadly Scandinavian.[116] Helena's Lutheran and Free Evangelical congregations for Swedish speakers were also "Scandinavian."[117]

Scandinavian was also a designation used in advertising. The Broadway Meat Market (John Beck, proprietor) advertised: "Fresh and salt meat. The only Scandinavian butcher shop in Helena."[118] Similarly, Helena dentist A. C. Sandberg advertised himself as "the only Scandinavian dentist in town," and a Missoula pharmacy advertised that it stocked a "Scandinavian pharmacopoeia" and that it had a "Scandinavian pharmacist."[119]

Not all of Montana's Swedes were happy with panethnicity. The multilingual Midsommar celebration in Butte was not to the taste of the correspondent Åskådare (Spectator), who wrote to *Posten* complaining that the celebration had been a "fiasco" marred by the "Babel" of Norwegian; Swedish dialects from Småland, Skåne, and Dalsland; and "skandinaviska"—by which we can assume the writer meant an impure mixture of Scandinavian languages.[120]

In Idaho and Wyoming, Swedish settlements also were sparse, making it logical for those interested in preserving ethnic heritage to join forces with other Nordic groups, as was done in Montana, or to look to the out-

side world for Swedish connections. We have no evidence of there having been a Swedish-language newspaper in either Idaho or Wyoming, so
the availability of the Denver, Salt Lake City, and Montana publications
would have been important in creating and sustaining networks in those
states. However, those living in the northern Rockies could also subscribe
by mail to Midwestern and West Coast newspapers such as Chicago's
Svenska Amerikanaren (The Swedish American) or Spokane's *Svenska
Nordvästern* (The Swedish northwest), which began to serve the region,
including north Idaho, in 1907.[121]

Newspapers were mentioned by several Idaho letter writers as a means
of staying abreast of Swedish news as well as Swedish American concerns.
Olof Larsson, for example, wrote from Kellogg, Idaho, in a 1905 letter: "I
see in the newspapers that they have had some trouble between Sweden
and Norway."[122] John R. Johnson of Moscow, Idaho, read about Norway's
break from Sweden, and asked his relatives for more information than he
had been able to glean from the newspapers.[123] Leonard Nilsson looked
forward to receiving *Svenska Amerikanaren*, which sometimes arrived in
large batches when mail delivery into Rocky Bar, Idaho, was delayed by
snowstorms.[124] For Nilsson, the newspaper was more than just a source
of news. He clipped poetry, favoring Magnus Elmblad's work, and he assembled his own poetry scrapbook by pasting the clippings onto the pages
of a general mercantile catalog.

Although immigrants like Nilsson and Pet Stred of Bay Horse, Idaho,
lived in isolation from any sort of Swedish institution, some Swedish and
Scandinavian institutions did develop in Idaho and Wyoming in areas
where there were greater concentrations of Swedish settlers. In Idaho,
Swedish Lutheran congregations were established in Moscow by 1884,
and in Troy by 1886, later followed by congregations in Firth (between
Blackfoot and Idaho Falls), in Idaho Falls (1890s), and in Blackfoot and
Boise (1900s). The New Sweden Mission Church was founded in 1895,
and the Riverview Swedish Baptist Church in 1903.[125] Wyoming similarly
developed Swedish social organizations and churches. Hallberg notes
that Cheyenne, Laramie, and Rawlins had North Star Benevolent associations and Vasa lodges, and he identifies Lutheran churches that served
the Swedish population in Cheyenne, Laramie, Hanna, Rock Springs,
and Sheridan. Other Swedish congregations included Mission, Baptist,
and Methodist, all focused in the southeastern part of the state.[126]

In spite of religious, geographical, and occupational distinctions, Denver, Salt Lake City, and outlying Swedish settlements in the northern Rockies did share some characteristics. The kinds of secular events planned throughout the region were similar. These were the sorts of events characteristic of middle-class sponsorship throughout America during the nineteenth century: celebrations taking the form of picnics and programs mixing skits with declamations and music. The Swedish stamp on these events appeared in scheduling at the summer and winter solstices and in using particular symbols, including Swedish foods and Swedish-language songs.

The Swedish population in the Rockies also shared with middle-class Americans a reliance on the press as an important medium for exchanging ideas and fostering a sense of community. But here, the letter writers' reactions to places like Denver and Salt Lake City should give us pause and encourage us to consider divisions within the Swedish population. Jeppsson reveals interest in but limited access to the city's ethnic institutions, and Peterson demonstrates indifference. The comparison underscores the different kinds of evidence we have available. When we are reading newspapers and play programs, we have evidence of what was available to the immigrants. When we turn to ordinary writing such as personal letters, we gain a sense of the immigrants' degree of involvement in those institutions. Throughout the following chapters, our reading of the immigrants' letters as vernacular texts will unfold the many affiliations that were relevant to writers like Jeppsson, Peterson, and their fellow immigrants in the Rocky Mountain West.

FOUR

"I Work Every Day"

BECOMING AMERICAN WORKERS

~~~

I am well and work and grind away a little every day but I have
been sick, not so that I was bedridden, but I was very ill a few
days ago but am now completely healthy again. I have worked
at various jobs this summer. For a while I worked on a road that
was being built. One month I worked for a farmer and now I
work at a smelter where they smelt ore that is taken out of the
mines. That is hard work and takes real Swedish strength to bear
with it. The work is very tough and it is hot like a certain *place*
[meaning Hell; underlined in original]. I do not know how long
I will stay here, when I get tired of it [I] will have to try something else. Those who are young and inexperienced should try
everything.

Pet Stred, 1891, Bay Horse, Idaho

*P*ET STRED'S LETTER to a friend, written August 9, 1891, is typical of
most of the letters from immigrant men in that Stred emphasizes
his work.[1] Stred opens his letter with the usual thanks for a letter received
and acknowledgment of news of his friend's good health. The section
quoted above immediately follows. Reassurance to his friend that he, too,
is healthy prompts Stred to write, "I work . . . every day."

Work is the most universal topic in the letters. All but eight of the
Rocky Mountain correspondents at least mention their or their relatives'
work.[2] As in Stred's letter, work ordinarily takes the first position in the
body of a letter, immediately following the obligatory opening formulas
for greeting and health. The formula for mentioning work often includes

67

more than simply "I work" or "he/she works." Many letter writers qualify their statements, as Stred does, with "every day" or some other modifier that indicates the frequency and regularity of their work. Stred assures his friend that he works "a little every day." Peter F. Erlandson writes in 1880 from Morrison, Colorado, "I have worked steadily."[3] In 1888 Johan Håkansson reports to his wife, "I have worked every day."[4] "I work every day," Charles M. Bloomberg writes in 1910, "and my little woman she has so much to do with washing and cooking."[5] Carl Boline writes in 1915 from Leadville, Colorado, "I work every day, Sunday as well as Monday."[6]

When an important concern takes precedence over the usual formulas, a few writers delay references to work until later in their letters. This was the case when John M. Swanson wrote to his parents and siblings to announce that he had gotten married. Swanson mentions his work only after describing the wedding; expressing hopes that his parents will visit him and his bride, Tilda; promising to send photographs; and describing his new house and furniture. Following all this news, Swanson echoes the kind of passage usually found much earlier in the immigrant letters, using conditional language: "So now I wish that we may keep our health and that I could work, so I hope that everything will go well for us."[7] Swanson's return to the linked subjects of health and work represents the usual formula, just displaced to the letter's end section.

Work was also an important topic in the letters of women who worked at home. Married housewives such as Bengta Olson of Midvale, Utah, and Swanson's sisters, Emma Hallberg and Ida Sandberg of Denver, open their letters with thanks for the last letter received and a report on health. They then turn quickly to family news, especially news of their children. This topic may indeed be seen as their form of reporting on work, even though it does not carry the same economic import as "I work every day." Of course, Hallberg and Sandberg literally worked every day in their homes, but they do not use that formula to describe their own non-wage-earning work. Their account of work is instead similar to the kind of account of work and barter found in women's diaries at the turn of the century.[8] Sandberg, for example, comments on the amount of sewing she has to do to keep her baby clothed: "I have sewn so that the little one has 9 or 10 white dresses as well as slips and coat."[9]

Married women also report on men's work and on the work of their adult children. As in Swanson's nuptial letter, these reports are displaced to later in their letters. "Albert sends special greetings to you both; he works every day as before,"[10] Ida Sandberg writes in the fourth page of her letter. On the second page of a letter, Bengta Olson proudly reports the success of a young daughter: "She now has worked at a place for over two years and she has for the past year earned seven dollars per week."[11] This kind of work was worth noting, perhaps because it was wage earning rather than simply an unreimbursed expectation based on one's gender.

However, displacements toward the ends of letters are the exceptions to the rule, which is to mention work first after the opening of a letter by writing "I work every day." Is this formula, which recurs throughout the letters from 1880 to 1917, a reassurance or a complaint? Either is possible. The formula could reassure the reader not only that one worked but also that work was regular. As Stred notes, "on the whole it is somewhat slow times here in this country at present and very hard to find any work."[12] Comments like this acknowledge that the American economy was in a slump during the 1890s, and particularly during the 1893 depression year. Therefore, to write that one worked every day is not entirely a complaint. Regular work was a boon in an uncertain economic climate, especially for a newcomer who hoped to better his or her situation and to send money home.

The workers who write home "I work every day" came of age in a country that was only slowly industrializing and in which a rural work ethic was important. Åke Daun's study of the "Swedish mentality" notes, not surprisingly, that "life was dominated by work" in preindustrial Sweden, and that "the household was first and foremost a unit of production."[13] Work was, perforce, every day, with long days regulated by the seasons and the available hours of daylight.

Accompanying this regularity of rural work were the holidays, especially Midsommar and Christmas, that punctuated the yearly cycle. Coming at the darkest time of the year, when there were fewer farm chores, the Christmas season was elevated to special importance in peasant life, and it was a standard expectation that workers could have several days available at Christmas for family celebrations and visits to friends.[14] Other nonwork activities, such as visiting markets, going to church, and attending funerals and weddings, provided a leisure component to peasant life. As Daun notes, "'Leisure time' existed, even though the term did not."[15]

In the new industrial era, Swedish workers brought into the workplace their expectations of time off for holidays that had developed to fit agricultural activities, and this became the basis of power struggles between workers and managers.[16] In the American labor movement, this was an era during which the idea of limiting working hours per day and days per week, along with providing regular vacations, was also a point of contention. Even though the idea of an eight-hour day was proposed much earlier in the nineteenth century, in 1880, United States laborers worked on average 10.3 hours per day and six days per week. By 1896, that figure was 9.9 hours per day. Even in 1916, the work week was greater than forty hours: on average, 54.9 hours per week.[17]

It is not surprising to see that the Swedish workers immigrating to the Rocky Mountain region to work in mining, smelting, logging, and railroad construction were disturbed when they had to work every day, including Sundays and at Christmastime, days marked in Sweden not only by time off from work but also by ritual activities such as bathing, donning Sunday clothes, and cleaning and decorating one's home.[18] At the same time the statement "I work every day" reassures the reader that the writer was employed, it can also express a complaint from the point of view of a worker who had grown up expecting time off from work to mark holidays, especially the traditionally more-than-one-day Christmas observance.

Throughout the period 1880 to 1917, Swedish workers expressed that they felt the lack of Christmas. Leonard Nilsson, a mine laborer, writes in 1881, "for me, Christmas has been rather gloomy. I have not noticed that it was Christmas at all. Only saw it in the almanac."[19] Twenty-seven years later, Victor Johnson, another miner, observes, "I *had* some days off but now there is work every day so I don't know if there will be time to be off on Christmas Day."[20]

Workers on both sides of the Atlantic were affected by the industrial era's move to quantify work in hours and wages. This quantification of work is one of the several topics regularly associated with the idea of work in the immigrant letters. As already mentioned, other idea clusters include work and health (and dangers to one's health), and work and companionship among workers. These idea clusters suggest the several ways in which work was both valued and a source of worry.

The detailed accounts men give of their wages and hours are reminiscent of the accounts of housework that Jennifer Sinor finds in women's diaries. While, according to Sinor, a woman keeping a diary might use "imprecise language" to evade emotional subjects, in passages describing work accomplished, the same diary writer could be very precise.[21] The immigrants are similarly exact in their letters when they account for their work. Work is quantified by hours and dollars (or sometimes Swedish crowns *[kronor]*) with a specificity that letter writers grant to few topics.

Whether evaluations of wages are positive or negative, the letter writers are equally specific in their language. Peter F. Erlandson's comment that he "worked steadily" is part of a list of ways in which he considers himself fortunate at the beginning of a new year, 1880. His list includes that he is in good health and that he is earning a good wage, specifying for his audience: "I receive between 7 and 8 crowns per day."[22] Olof Larsson also considers himself fortunate when in 1904 Kellogg, Idaho, he earned "3 to 3.50 per day [hewing timbers for mine tunnels] and yet don't work hard."[23] But two years later, Swan Smith finds his work as a mine laborer in Idaho Springs, Colorado, to be harder, while the wage is only adequate: "you have to work plenty hard but the pay is fairly *good*. When I work for daily wages I generally get (3.50) 3 dollars 50 cents per day, sometimes a little more, but it also costs to live."[24]

Smith's comments bring to mind the image of a ledger with credit and debit columns, and his concern was that the credit column would only slightly balance the debits. A similarly detailed verbal account comes from Peter J. Johansson, whose work with railroad construction crews took him to Montana in 1891. In January that year, he writes from Great Falls to tell his brother that the railroad company has sent him to Fort Buford, where he worked during December, but that work was shut down after Christmas: "We got our daily wage reduced in December to 1 dol. 50 Cent and then [I] paid 50 Cent more for food per week so there was not much profit that month."[25] By July, Johansson was working at Neihart in a railroad construction job that concerned him because the laborers would have to blast through mountainous terrain at high altitude in order to construct the roadbed: "I do not know what we are going to earn here for the job we are doing now, but the last [job] got only 2 dollars in excess of daily wages. I think that we are earning a bit more here because we have [a] 1500 (meter) *yard* mountain in this job, but we have had to purchase rock blaster tools [perhaps percussion caps] for about 5 per dollar."[26]

Again, there is attention to how the credit column will or will not balance the debits.

Work and the careful accounting of wages and hours was also a concern for women, both as workers and as potential employers. As workers, women, like men, sought the best pay they could find. At about the same time that Johansson hoped to be able to get ahead by making more money than he had to pay out for expenses, Charles H. Anderson hoped to tempt his sweetheart Hanna Gustafson to travel from Minnesota to Limon, Colorado. He could not offer her a better working situation, though: "You say that you have a small salary, and I believe it is the same *all over.* Girls here get 2 to 4 do. per week as better cooks, but they have to work hard."[27] Anna Olson finds wages sufficient when she writes in 1889 from Denver to report that she has found work: "I . . . have a really good place; I have the same kind of work that I had in Topeka paying 20 dollars a month."[28] But the good market for Swedish maids was a disadvantage to the Swedish housewife who hoped to employ a maid. When she had a baby, Elin Pehrson employed a maid for two months before it became too expensive. "It is too expensive for us to have a maid," she writes. "She [maids in general] now has 25 doll. per month, so it is good here for girls if they are strong and have the strength to work."[29]

Clearly, one of the reasons that immigrants discussed their wages and work hours was to advise those who might be thinking of emigrating to America, or, as with Anderson's letter to Gustafson, to advise those already in America who might be thinking of moving to the West. This prompted some specificity in the letters. Sometimes the advice includes an accounting of the cost of passage as well as a detailed account of hours and wages. John Renström, in a letter to a friend whose son had America fever, provides precise information about the cost of passage to America, along with a strategy for timing the passage:

> My idea is then he should stay home over the winter because it
> is pretty cold at sea that time of the year and another thing it is
> easier to get work in the spring for someone who has to do outside
> work until he learns some English and then if he would like to go
> in and work in the mine then you can get work at any time.[30]

Other kinds of advice are somewhat more general. Clara Jeppsson worries about a brother-in-law who wants to come to America, explaining that the economy in both countries is suffering during the early 1910s, but she describes the economy with only a vague descriptor, "bad times": "It is better for him to stay in Sweden since there are such bad times here."[31] Regarding work conditions, she is somewhat more specific: "This place is so full of male workers so there are many who have been here for many years who are without jobs. . . . I am wondering if he [yet another potential emigrant] has perhaps thought about going down into the mines or out in the forest, which is not exactly the worst work there is, and working on Sundays and every day year-round."[32]

Thus, work was closely associated with quantifiable concerns such as money and time, but less easily quantifiable qualities were also of concern. One such quality is good health. The position of the topic of work in the letters, after opening comments about one's health, expresses an implicit connection between work and health, but many of the writers also state the connection explicitly. Stred and Swanson, quoted earlier, both make a connection between their health and the ability to continue working. The hard physical labor of mining, smelting, logging, and railroad construction made it imperative that one be fit. But also these were very dangerous sorts of work, and workers were well aware of the threats to their health. The connection was circular: To be able to work, one had to remain healthy, but working itself could threaten one's health. To express these dangers, writers move beyond simple formulas, such as "I work every day," to use imagery, proverbial language, and storytelling.

Acknowledging to his fiancée, Lovisa Borg, that mining is bad for his health, Leonard Nilsson deflects her worry by joking using a proverbial expression:

> Darling! You want me to quit mine work. You are right; it is harmful to your health. So I think about giving it up soon. But there is nothing else here in this place. . . . Here I have "gone at rocks" [*huggit i sten*], and that in the words' full meaning, speaking literally.[33]

The Swedish expression *huggit i sten* is in a literal sense appropriate to describe his work, but its figurative meaning, "to be mistaken," is also appropriate for his situation. What he desires most is to own his own business or farm, and mine labor is only an indirect route to that goal, figuratively a mistake along his life's path.

To Lovisa, he admits that mine work might harm his health and that it makes him "somewhat tired after going at rocks' the whole day."[34] To his friend Johan Westerberg, Nilsson is willing to admit more in a passage that also makes light of his work through rhyme and rhythm, providing a more colorful description of his work and how it makes him feel:

> The pay is good, 3.50 per day. Yes—you drill and you blast, you grind and you hurry, you hack and you pick, you curse and you beg, you chug down water, getting drunk,—All for the almighty buck.[35]

To Westerberg, Nilsson also admits that he knew "the ore in this mine contains arsenic, which does not exactly prolong life."[36] Arsenic is present naturally in the kind of crushed rock produced at stamp mills like those in Rocky Bar, Idaho, and can be breathed in with airborne particles.

Nilsson's description of his work goes well beyond the simple quotation of wages and hours and the formulaic "I work every day." Others write somewhat less emphatically of the dangers of work, but their reports help us understand that, as much as regular work with good wages was appreciated, Swedish workers knew their work made them vulnerable. The pursuits most readily available to Swedish workers involved using heavy equipment and being exposed to pollutants in an era long before there was any consistent guarantee, from industry or from government, of workers' compensation and standard regulation of safety and environmental concerns. It is common to read of injuries that affected a worker's abilities yet left him hoping to be able to return to work. August Peterson writes in 1900 from Gem, Idaho, that he had been in the hospital for twelve days: "I got one finger injured on the right hand. I can just now hold a pen to write but I cannot work yet so that has cost me (yes that it has)."[37] In his next sentence, Peterson mentions that a friend is also recovering from surgery.

In some of the letters, we see descriptions of injury and illness cast as positively as possible, as if to say "This is a bad event, but it could have been worse." This serious, resignedly pragmatic tone reflects qualities that Daun identifies as components of Swedishness,[38] but it additionally reflects a muted optimism. When Emma Hallberg's husband Olof was injured in his railway work, his brother-in-law, John M. Swanson, reports the incident to his parents in a letter dated July 28, 1906. Immediately after his formulaic opening statement that everyone in the extended family living in Denver has good health and is doing well, Swanson writes his report as a brief story:

> But you perhaps have heard that Hallberg has injured his hand. He pinched off the thumb on his left hand. It happened on the train at the station where he works. He was going to couple the railway cars together and got his thumb between so it pinched it off. It is four weeks this evening since it happened. So he had to go to the hospital right away and he had to stay there for two weeks, then he came home. It is not really well yet but he thinks that in a couple of weeks he can work again. He had the hospital stay and doctor's care free and he thinks that he should get a little workers' compensation. So it is good that he didn't lose the whole hand.[39]

This occasion warranted, in Swanson's mind, the fuller treatment of storytelling. Swanson marks his narrative's beginning with a clue that something important has happened—"you perhaps have heard"—and then shifts to past tense to relate the series of events that led to Hallberg's loss of a digit, the loss of which will make his work difficult. Swanson emphasizes the severity of the injury through the repetition of the story's strong, central image, "*klämde af tummen* [pinched off the thumb] . . . *klämde af den* [pinched it off]," and through detailing the swiftness, duration, and expense of Hallberg's medical care. Swanson marks the end of his story with a sentence commenting on the incident, as if delivering a moral that things could have been worse.

Pollution was as strong a concern as injury. The dangers and discomforts of smelting are represented frequently in the letters of smelter workers through the senses of sight, smell, and touch, including the feeling of the heat and the physical effort of stirring and shifting molten ore, the smell of fumes and the sight of the furnaces' fire. None of this work was pleasant; indeed, it was potentially quite injurious to the workers' health. In 1891 at Bay Horse, Idaho, Pet Stred would have been working in a lead-silver smelter fueled with locally produced charcoal.[40] Lead-silver smelting would have exposed him to arsenic, sulfur dioxide, and other sulfurous fumes. It is not surprising that he considered moving on to a different kind of work.

EASTERN SECTION OF RICHEST HILL ON EARTH, BUTTE, MONT.

A view of Butte, Montana, in the 1890s depicts the town's residences abutting the industrial landscape. Image courtesy of the Denver Public Library, Western History Collection, call number X-62607.

August Peterson made just such a decision when he left Butte, Montana, a town where a multiethnic population of workers was employed at numerous copper smelters. At the Butte smelters, in addition to more standard smelting processes in furnaces that released fumes through tall stacks, ore was roasted outdoors. According to Donald MacMillan, this outdoor roasting process produced a slowly smoldering mass that at ground level "continuously release[ed] clouds of toxic smoke and fumes composed of undiluted oxides of sulphur and arsenic, particulates, and a host of fluorides," which left the city and its surroundings completely denuded of greenery.[41] August Peterson wrote to his nephew, "I worked in Butte City only one month, and then I thought it was best to quit before my health was gone. Fritiof quit some days before me because the heat and gas were too dangerous."[42]

A more graphic description of a smelter is offered by August Johansson in a letter to his younger brother. Johansson had moved to Denver in 1891, hoping to find work. While he waited for an opportunity to open up for him, he visited the smelter where his host, Andrew, worked: "I have been and watched them at the smelter [and] know how it goes there, and Androw's work is like standing and stirring in [the middle of] a baking oven, the ore is red as fire which they have to stir and turn so it is terribly hot."[43] John M. Swanson writes that in his work at the Argo smelter near Denver he had "to stand and rake [the ore] at a hot smelter furnace and smell the sulfurous smoke."[44] Even though Johansson had experienced this environment, this was work he hoped to get.

In 1894, Swanson writes that he is glad to be back at work after a summer of having been laid off from the Argo smelter, but also that "it is so hard to work at the smelter, there is no wonder that some people quit if they can, but it is hard to get anything else."[45] After one month back at work, Swanson reports he had been away from work so long that it was very taxing to start up again: "It was almost as though I had never worked. I got so sore in my hands and in my whole body so I [was] almost ashamed of myself."[46]

Johansson and Swanson had been drawn to the Denver area by the three smelters established in 1879 and soon after: Argo, Grant, and Globe. Swanson's employer, Argo, was the first, opened by the Boston and Colorado Smelting Company just north of Denver along the Colorado Central Railroad. Originally modeling its lead-silver processing after smelters in Swansea, Wales, the company initially favored hiring experienced smelter workers from Wales, but during the 1880s the company shifted its hiring policy to favor employment of Scandinavians, especially Swedes. By 1892, a drastic reduction in silver prices precipitated much lower production at Argo, putting even long-time workers like Swanson temporarily out of work.[47] Among such periodic lulls, Swanson continued at Argo until the company's dissolution in 1909. That year, he sent his parents a photograph of himself to "see if you recognize me again."[48] He had been away from Sweden for twenty-one years, and felt that his work had changed him: "After hard work at a smelter, even a machine of iron and steel would fold, and so also do I."[49] Using the common Industrial Revolution image of man as machine, Swanson is able to impart not only that he felt physically worn out but also that he had been used like a machine by Boston and Colorado Smelting.[50]

The physical duress of smelting work was paralleled by the dangers of mining, which could have tragic consequences. August Peterson died in 1902 from gas in the mine where he was working in Victor, Colorado.

Workers Ino George and Charles Johnson pose beside a furnace chimney and hopper inside the Argo Smelting Works near Denver, 1892. Image courtesy of the Denver Public Library, Western History Collection, C. H. Hanington, photographer, call number X-61405.

According to historian Elizabeth Jameson, in the late 1890s the Victor newspaper "reported nearly a thousand accidents in under four years," and workers' unions repeatedly pointed to mine timbering that was insufficient, causing cave-ins.[51] Peterson's death prompted his friend, P. N. Johnson, to write to Peterson's nephew Hjalmar in the old country. This was another occasion when a dramatic occurrence warranted telling a story:

> I want to inform you so far as I can about Gust Peterson's death. He worked in a little mine that is called "Mackey." He went to work there at 8 in the morning. He and a buddy went into the bucket and [they] were lowered about 200 feet when they gave the stop signal and they stopped. In a few seconds they rang 3 times, which means [an emergency] on the bucket. The engineer waited 4–5 minutes for another signal; when he didn't receive any, he thought of the bad air that often was there and tried to hoist the bucket but found it was stuck down there. Then the foreman and

3 more *men* went down the ladders but found they could not get any closer than 30 feet because of the gas. Then they had to blow compressed air in for a while before they could get to them. When they got there Peterson lay in the bucket dead and his buddy lay 10 feet below him dead. Presumably his buddy had stood up in the bucket when he rang the bell and then become overpowered by the gas and fell and took the bucket with him and so it got caught in some timbering and could not be hoisted. It took about 2 hours from the time they went down to [when] they got them up. I was at the inquest and heard there how it was. Gust was like himself in death. You could see he hadn't had any pain. He had not been in Victor long but had often come to visit me and we were always good friends; he was here the same evening that he received a photograph from you. [Johnson continues with a discussion of the funeral costs, which were mostly covered by the miners' union.][52]

Like Swanson's, Johnson's storytelling is effective in many ways. He marks the beginning of his story with an opening statement of purpose, and closes with a memorial statement from his own point of view. The body of the story is a compelling narrative in which Johnson first sets the scene with the two miners going into the mine, and then recounts the consecutive perceptions and actions of those trying to rescue the men. Reading this narrative, Hjalmar must have felt as we do, imagining the wait for another signal from the mine, the attempt to hoist the mine bucket, the concern that it was stuck—all the time hoping for a different ending, even though the result was already known to him. He probably also appreciated Johnson's memorial statement as a way of valuing Peterson's life.

Johnson emphasizes that Peterson died with a *kamrat* (buddy).[53] This idea of the camaraderie of male workers is another important idea cluster in the letters. That Peterson valued his fellow workers is clear from his earlier letter from Gem, Idaho, in which he writes, "We traveled here and found work immediately, met up with Walfrid Chals *and* Gust Ehrneberg. Gust is foreman so we have been doing well."[54] Before his time in Idaho, Peterson expressed the loneliness of being entirely among strangers while he was serving in the military at Fort Leavenworth, Kansas.[55]

John A. Leonard emphasizes being among other Swedish workers when he moved west to Leadville, Colorado, in 1881: "I am presently in the company of I. B. J. Magnusson from Granhult and other acquaintances." Referring again at the end of this letter to Magnusson's being in town, Leonard assures his correspondent, "We live well and enjoy ourselves."[56]

The importance of working among fellow Swedes is corroborated in a reminiscence of work at Telluride, Colorado, originally written in the early 1910s. In *Hellhole on Earth*, Waldemar Holmberg mentions at several junctures the presence of Swedish buddies as traveling companions and as contacts for finding lodging and work. Describing a situation when two Italian workers with whom he could not communicate refused to work with him, Holmberg emphasizes that a fellow Swede rescued him by inviting him into his work group.[57]

The salutation used by many workers when they write to male friends is a simple but eloquent indicator of the importance and closeness of the bond among Swedish men. Many write *broder* (brother) to address men who are not relatives but are close friends. Leonard Nilsson's friend Johan Westerberg, to whom Nilsson clearly was not related, is to Nilsson "Friend and brother Johan!"[58] Fritz Lindborg addresses a letter "Honored brother Nils!" yet signs it "your true friend."[59] This was not exclusively a working-class practice. There were groups—religious, fraternal, and union—that formalized the idea of brotherhood during this era. In vernacular letters, we encounter a more general and informal sense of brotherhood among Swedish men that appears to have been adapted by working-class men to their particular blend of shared relationships: ethnic, occupational, and socioeconomic.[60]

To have regular work, to earn good money, to have health, and to work among buddies was "to be doing well"—another formula that frequently appears in the portions of letters dealing with work. A letter from Johan Håkansson provides an excellent example to illustrate this point:

> I am healthy and doing well up to the moment of writing this. I work at a smelter in Leadville. I and Johan from Jedhult so we are doing nicely here. We work together every day, we work at a *furnace [fanis]*. It is hot but it goes well when you get used to it. I have worked there 2 months every day so I have earned a little money for you which you need.[61]

Håkansson felt he was "doing well" and "doing nicely" even though his work at Leadville would have been very similar to that described by Stred and the other writers who worked at smelters: hot, noisy, reeking with sulfur, and physically draining. In addition, Håkansson was living a lonely life, separated from his wife Britta and their children. A freeholder, according to the Swedish emigration register, Håkansson had left Sweden for America in 1886 in order to work and send money home to his family.[62] What made all of this bearable to Håkansson was the combination of regular work, good health, good pay, and, most important, a fellow worker who was Swedish. That was what it meant to be "doing well" as a worker.

Among themselves, these workers were "brothers," a greeting that represented their fraternity and their equality within the working class. The workers' understanding of class status emerges in the frequently cited image of a worker having to remove his hat in the presence of a supervisor or a gentleman. In Sweden, this was expected etiquette. In America, the workers' letters celebrate the fact that one did not have to stand hat in hand when talking with the boss. The hat-in-hand image was embedded in the larger idea of America having a society in which classes were fuzzily defined and class mobility was possible, a myth current among native Americans and decidedly embraced by Swedish Americans and other immigrants.[63]

John A. Leonard uses the hat-in-hand image amid his explanation of the ways in which America was a better place than Sweden for workers. Leonard had moved west in 1881, after a year of work on an Illinois farm. His sister had asked about his situation. From Silver Camp, New Mexico, where he is employed as a mine worker, Leonard replies that he finds "it is much better to be a worker here in this country than in the old." He feels this is the case "partly because the workers are esteemed and respected . . . you don't have to use titles of rank and respect, stand up, or doff your hat when you meet influential men [*storgubbar*] and want to talk with them."[64] Leonard had apparently found a good work situation, or perhaps simply had a very positive outlook. He also tells his sister that workingmen can count on receiving the wages they deserve for the work they do, and that they can choose their days off from work—the latter situation very different from that reported by other workers.

Victor Johnson also uses the hat-in-hand image when he reflects on being back in America after a trip to Sweden to visit relatives in 1908. Returning to America, Johnson writes that he feels free again; the trip reinforced his strong sense of difference in the ways the two countries treat the working class: "You can walk around freely and be yourself and you do not have to stand with your hat in your hand in front of wooden characters with badges in their caps or a big fat belly or anything like that."[65] Here, rather than using *storgubbe* (literally, "great old man") to indicate the Swedish men of high status to whom those of the lower class had to defer, Johnson provides humorous descriptions of such men. From Johnson's viewpoint in America, it would be ridiculous to have to stand hat in hand for a man so stiff he appears to be made of wood, a man whose significance comes only from the badge attached to his cap, or a man whose fat belly indicates how well fed he is.

The hat-in-hand image and Johnson's manipulation of it suggest the new way Swedish immigrant workers were looking at socioeconomic class as they adapted to American working conditions. "I work and drudge," Pet Stred writes, characterizing through his use of verbs his work as an activity. This is an unremarkable usage in English, but it is meaningful in the Swedish context. Stred and the other workers cited thus far came from Swedish parishes where the local priests had listed them in catechetical registers (*husförhörslängder*) with titles through which "they tried to characterise the family socially."[66] Formal titles existed for nobility or for church and other authorities, but titles assigned to workingmen were ordinarily based on a combination of occupation and land ownership, when applicable.

Thus, for a Swedish worker of this era, social position was officially linked to the kind of work he did. The few immigrant letter writers who can be traced to the catechetical registers were either nonlanded farmers (*åbo, torpare*) or their sons, or they were laborers in occupations requiring some skill and training—*gjutare* (foundry worker), *mjölnare* (miller), *snickare* (carpenter), *smed* (blacksmith), *urmakare* (watchmaker)—and also, with the exception of watch making, requiring physical strength.[67] In the title-conscious society of nineteenth-century Sweden, this standard assignation essentialized one's identity as bound up with class and occupation. It was not that Leonard Nilsson's father "farmed." Rather, his father was *Torparen* Niklas Nilsson (the crofter Niklas Nilsson).[68] Similarly, John M. Swanson's father didn't "farm." He was *Brukare* Sven Jonsson (the farmer Sven Jonsson).[69] The existence of these and the many other titles for farmers of various sorts indicated levels of socioeconomic status.

Nilsson's own changing status in Sweden was reflected in his title before he left in 1877, and after his return in 1884. He left simply as a *son*, and as a son of a non-land-owning *torpare*, his prospects for an improved position were very limited. As mentioned earlier in this chapter, Nilsson's ambition was to be what would have been called in Swedish an *owner* (*ägare*; spelled *egare* in Nilsson's day), an owner of either a farm or a small business. On his return to Sweden, he was able to achieve that ambition. By 1889, he and Lovisa, whom he married soon after his return, lived in their own home in Söderköping, and Leonard had become both *Gårds egare* and *Bryggaren* Nils Leonard Nilsson (the house owner and brewer) in the records kept by the parish priest.[70]

In letters from the Rockies, we see the workers referring to themselves by occupation only occasionally, and not ordinarily in the major labor pursuits of mining, smelting, railroad construction, and logging. Answering a friend's inquiry about what he does nowadays, John Renström of Spring Gulch, Colorado, replies: "You ask what I do nowadays, and I will here let you know. As you perhaps have heard already I am a manager of a tavern [*källarmästare*]. 'Saloon keeper' in English."[71] Claiming a work title in this way is unusual in the letter collections I have examined; more commonly, a correspondent might write, "I *work as* a saloonkeeper."

In Sweden, the importance of titles and their use in formal conversation ("Does the Captain wish coffee?") was sustained into the mid-twentieth century.[72] In America, the link between work and social position could be severed upon immigration. Rather than being a *torpare*, one might say he did farm work, or, as Stred puts it, "worked for a farmer." Rather than being a miner or a logger, one could say, "I work in a mine" or "I work in the forest." Not only did this usage turn one's occupation into a verb, it also recognized the way in which what one did for wages could rapidly change with the season or the available opportunities. Stred's letter makes this abundantly clear. Within a few months' time, he had done farm work, road construction, and smelting.

Applying titles from the Old World could become awkwardly incorrect. In Renström's example, this worked in his favor. To be a manager of a tavern in Sweden was not exactly the same kind of work as being a saloonkeeper in Spring Gulch, Colorado, in 1892. Indeed, in Sweden it was a more respectable position that could include authority over maids and other tavern workers. On the other hand, to be a farmer in western America usually meant that one was self-employed and either a landowner or working toward that status through homesteading. The many terms for farmers in Swedish represented a much broader range of class distinctions.

By far, most of the immigrants in the Rockies were members of the working class—that is, they were in positions with industrial companies for which they were paid by the hour and they answered to supervisors. But a few were not, or, like Leonard Nilsson, aspired to rise above working-class status. A few immigrants owned their own businesses: Bernhard Rydberg, a jeweler in Red Lodge, Montana; P. J. Johnson, a liquor distributor in Rawlins, Wyoming; and Victor A. Hallquist in Denver and Peter Peterson in Gunnison, Utah, who were self-employed carpenters (Peterson also farmed). Ole Pedersen, John Peterson, and John E. Jernberg had their own farms, and Aron W. Johnson had a sheep ranch.

These men who owned their own businesses write differently about their work and their leisure time. We do not hear from them that they "work every day." Their descriptions of work are either very slight or are made from an owner and manager's point of view. For example, they write of the purchase of new equipment. Also, they express the emergent middle-class values of their era by showing an interest in a variety of secular, leisure-time pursuits that were marked neither as holiday nor ceremony. Some of them were readers, and demonstrate in their letters that they were engaged with the news and literature that was available to them through both Swedish- and English-language newspapers.

Bernhard Rydberg is an interesting case in point. Rydberg mentions his jewelry store, but only in very general terms. Had he not written his letters on his professional stationery, which featured *tomtar* balancing on rolling rings and watch cases, we would not detect from the contents of his letters that he was a jeweler when he mentions, for example, that he opened *butiken* (the store) after a night out at a dance sponsored by the Elks fraternal organization.[73] Instead, Rydberg's letters dwell on his avocations, which were all secular: his unsuccessful run for the office of public administrator under three parties—Democratic, Labor, and People's parties; his participation in the Elks Lodge and his desire to join the Masons; his writing, under the pen name Benedictus, of an English-language newspaper column for the Red Lodge *Carbon County Democrat*; his participation in the Montana militia; and his trips into the beautiful forested mountains around Red Lodge with a close friend, David Smethurst, who was a British immigrant. Single until he returned to Sweden to marry,

Rydberg busied himself with these various activities, many of which bore the imprint of middle-class civic-mindedness and an attraction to the Western region and to American institutions and media.[74]

Like Rydberg, Peter Peterson of Gunnison, Utah, had an enthusiasm for venturing into the mountains (in Peterson's case, the Wasatch), but he differed from Rydberg in several important ways: as a Mormon convert, he preserved a strong interest in things sacred; as a family member, he was part of a village household economic unit that was similar to the kind he had left behind in Sweden; and as the owner of a business that was in demand in his region, he was interested in making his carpentry shop as successful and efficient as possible through innovations. When Peterson mentions his farm, it is cast as a cooperative venture, but when he mentions his carpentry business, it is cast in a more entrepreneurial light.

Peterson's family suffered a tragic loss in October 1885 when the four youngest of their six children succumbed to diphtheria. Attendant to the severe emotional loss was the loss to the household of the couple's only two sons. Writing a year after this tragedy, Peterson admits to the material support that had been provided by the children: "I have all [of my] time filled up with work. I thought that I would start working the farm but when I lost both my boys it is not going to happen any time soon. I can earn more as a craftsman."[75] Later letters make it apparent that Peterson shifted entirely to carpentry. In autumn 1887 he reports that he has a sawmill to produce lumber and is doing *"mycket Husbyge"* (much house building). He mentions farming in the same letter, but it was other people— *"Folkett her"* (the people here)—who were busy harvesting crops.[76] By 1890, he mentions that he has many workers for his projects, and by 1892, he reports "now I do all of my carpentry with steam power."[77]

In a situation like Peterson's, the camaraderie of fellow workers disappears from the rhetoric of work. Indeed, Rydberg's and Peterson's letters, and the letters of other business and farm owners, lack the sense of brother workers laboring together that is held as a high value in the working-class letters. In this respect, Rydberg's and Peterson's letters resemble the letters of women. Rather than celebrating a brotherhood of workers, they point toward other identities: middle-class, Western, religious, familial, ethnic, and American.

From formulas and proverbial expressions to images and stories, the folk rhetoric of work in the letters of working-class Swedish American men in the Rockies expresses an industrial-era work ethnic. Pet Stred maintains that it "takes real Swedish strength to bear with" the hard work of smelting. This is bragging, but bragging with resignation. The Swedish worker was physically strong enough and mentally determined enough for the tough work of smelting, but that did not mean that Stred valued the work in and of itself. Instead, he valued the ability to do the work. Swedish workers expected a great deal of themselves. Consider, for example, Swanson's taking on the responsibility for not being up to full strength when he went back to work at Argo. He felt almost ashamed of himself to be so weak that his muscles hurt.

There is a subtle difference between the views expressed by Stred and by Swanson and those spoken of by promoters of Swedish America in the press and at the pulpit. The many virtues ascribed to Swedish Americans by the journalist Johan Enander and his fellow writers included "industry"—the value of work for work's sake as a part of the larger enterprise of building industrial America.[78] But the ethic of the Rocky Mountain workers was more pragmatic. Work in and of itself was not enough. Good work had regular hours. Good work was paid sufficiently and regularly. Good work allowed one to stay healthy and whole. Good work was done among one's fellow Swedes.

FIVE

"*I Am Sending Money*"

OLD COUNTRY AND NEW

~∽~

If I leave Rocky Bar! I must travel a considerable distance from here. I am going to try to begin, if possible, the journey home before next Christmas. Be patient about the wait just a little longer, my tenderly beloved Lova! I do not want to work for others—not in Sweden. As long as I have to work for others, I would rather be in America. Meanwhile I can safely assure you that I take setbacks lightly—defy pain and trouble and fear no dangers. I am as determined, stubborn, and persistent as always; because "through persistence you reach the goal" and I am a Nordic son. Son of mother *Svea*.

Leonard Nilsson, 1883, Rocky Bar, Idaho

*T*HESE ARE LEONARD NILSSON'S WORDS to Lovisa Borg, written when he decided he would have to delay his return to Sweden.[1] He had not yet been able to save enough money to set up his own business, and he insisted on reaching that personal goal. Nilsson had experienced cruel masters as a young laborer before traveling to America, and he vowed that he would never again place himself in the power of an abusive boss. Yet Leonard clearly loved Lovisa (whom he calls Lova) and missed her greatly. The endearments in this passage are typical of those found in letter after letter written during Nilsson's stay in America from 1877 to 1884. Even though he was among a minority of Swedes in America who planned to return to Sweden, Nilsson exemplifies the predicament faced by all immigrants and migrants poised between old and new worlds. In their letters, they repeatedly weigh the differences between America and Sweden as they consider where their attachments should lie.

Leonard and Lovisa Nilsson at home with their nephew Bele Broo, after Leonard's return to Sweden. Photograph courtesy of the Swedish Emigrant Institute.

As H. Arnold Barton points out in *A Folk Divided*, the question of national identity and allegiance was complicated by the emergence in America of Swedish Americans as one of the many U.S. ethnic groups. Barton characterizes the immigrants' identification with Swedish America as akin to the kind of loyalty many feel toward an organized nation.[2] Dag Blanck and Orm Øverland's work tells us that nineteenth-century Americans' sense of nation could allow for this ethnic pluralism so long as it was hyphenated—that is, understood as a kind of Americanism.[3] Thus, for the Swede in America, we have to add "ethnicity" as a category of identity. A further complication is a subcategory irrelevant to the surrounding Americans but still evident to the Swedish Americans: one's origin in a particular province within Sweden, such as Jämtland or Halland. According to Ulf Beijbom, institutionalized regional identity emerged much more strongly among Swedish Americans after World War I, but was a vernacular category before that. However, none of these categories acknowledge the familial ties that were foremost for most immigrants.[4]

This situation was further complicated for Swedes heading to the Rocky Mountain West, where Swedish American institutions had a marginal existence, often shading into panethnic Scandinavian-Americanness. Examining their place in nation and ethnicity, Swedes of the West had a variety of claims they could make. It in fact becomes very difficult to separate politics and economics from culture and familial ties as we read letters that use the labels *American* or *Swedish*, or that refer to the old country and the new nation. This chapter examines the immigrant letter writers' explicit use of national/ethnic labels, as well as the existence of implicit references, through image and story, to national, ethnic, and familial connections.

Nilsson was a reader of the Swedish poet Esaias Tegnér. In his letters, he quotes, for example, from Tegnér's *Fritiof's Saga*.[5] His reference to Svea is an allusion to Tegnér's prize-winning 1811 poem "Svea," in which the Swedish nation is personified and celebrated in a female figure who appears as part of a Nordic pantheon:

And Svea sits on her throne upon the mountain,
with a crown of stars about her golden hair.
She gazes down quietly in the summer evening;
her renown spreads newborn throughout the world.[6]

This view of Rocky Bar, Idaho, where Leonard Nilsson worked as a mine laborer, dates from before 1884. Photograph courtesy of the Idaho State Historical Society, 1037-20.

Jan Hecker-Stampehl characterizes the poem and the image as part of an early nineteenth-century movement in Sweden that equated national character with race and racial history, seeking to rebuild a sense of Swedish national pride after the Finnish War of 1808–1809 and during the formation of the constitution of 1809. If Nilsson was a "son of mother Svea," he consented to an identity based on the idea of biological descent from the Svear, the central Swedish group understood to be ancestors of the Swedish people. The Svear were figured as strong seafaring folk, noble and egalitarian, and they were presumed to have lived in a pre-Christian state of freedom akin to a democracy.[7]

Nilsson's letter reads as though he imagines himself a Viking, girding his loins in preparation for battle—in his case, a psychological battle with continued loneliness as he faced even longer separation from Lovisa. Like a warrior, Nilsson claims to be brave in the face of fear and pain, persevering in his purpose, determined and stubborn. We can imagine some frustration on Lovisa's part when she received this declaration. Oh no, she must have thought, how many more years? When will he be satisfied?

To be a "son of . . . Svea" was, on the one hand, to possess certain characteristics. For Nilsson, these were positive values that, as a liberal freethinker, he embraced as he considered his eventual return to Sweden. Upon his return, he intended to be part of the modern Sweden that was emerging in forms such as workers' associations. On the other hand, to be a son was also to have been nurtured. The nation was a parent, old and revered, but perhaps legitimately left behind. These ambiguities emerge frequently in the writings of the Western immigrants. Epithets such as *gamla landet* (the old country) can be read as having an affectionate and nostalgic tone that places Sweden in the past, but that also indicates the kind of condescension sometimes demonstrated toward a parent.

The epithets for Sweden pair adjectives and nouns that have shadings of meaning. Sweden can be personified as *Svea*, as Nilsson demonstrates, or it can be referred to as *landet*, meaning the country or nation of Sweden, here translated as *country*. An alternative, of course, is simply to use the name *Sverige* (Sweden). Another usage is *jorden*, referring to the soil or earth of Sweden, here translated as *soil*. Finally, *hemmet* (home) is a metonym for Sweden that is usually not linked with adjectives to create an epithet. *Svea*, *landet*, and *Sverige* have a much more political, patriotic connotation, while *jorden* and *hemmet* can stand for smaller units of land reflecting familial or regional bonds.

Several modifiers can be joined with these nouns to characterize one's relationship to Sweden: *fäderne* (ancestors), *fader* (father), *moder* (mother), *födelse* (birth), and *foster* (native). *Fader* and *moder* are similar to *Svea* in personifying Sweden, but they suggest an even closer relationship, through both nature and nurture. *Födelse* similarly represents as familial one's connection to Sweden. *Fäderne* and *foster* suggest a more generalized racial identity claim. These modifiers can be seen as falling along a scale, from those identifying a more personal view of nationality to those claiming a more distant, abstract relationship: from *moder, fader,* and *födelse*, to *fäderne*, to *foster*.

Epithets for Sweden also typically include qualitative adjectives such as *gammal* (old), *kära* (dear), *älskade* (beloved), *hem* (home), *fattiga* (poor, in an economic sense), and a variety of others. While these are generally used affectionately, they also can carry condescending or outright derogatory connotations. *Kära* and *älskade* are the most positive of these modifiers. As endearments, they are often used to address people at home as well as to characterize the homeland. Only occasionally does a correspondent use such an endearment ironically. Given twentieth-century Swedes' enthusiasm for the fiftieth birthday and subsequent birthdays, one might expect *gammal* to connote reverence. But this celebratory attitude toward age was only just emerging during the period that Swedes were coming to the Rockies.[8] Thus, rather than necessarily being positive, *gammal* suggests a combination of outmodedness and affection. *Fattiga* can be used condescendingly at the same time that it suggests concern for those at home in Sweden. These modifiers also can be arranged along a scale, from those most positive and personally affectionate, to those least positive and more distancing: *älskade* to *kära* to *hem* to *gammal* to *fattiga*.

The letter writers in the West demonstrate considerable flexibility in using pairings of modifiers and nouns to produce epithets for Sweden. However, two pairings are by far the most common: *fosterlandet* and *gamla landet*, which could be used in both positive and negative contexts. For instance, P. J. Johnson uses *fosterlandet* when he writes in a 1914 letter after a trip home, "Everything is so glorious and beautiful in the native country." He hopes that he will be able to travel home every year.[9] And John A. Leonard uses *gamla landet* in an 1881 letter when he comments he cannot complain about his work as a mine laborer in Silver Camp, where he is healthy, well fed, and well clothed, and where he is not subjected to servitude "as often conditions were in the old country."[10]

The prevalence of these two epithets may have been reinforced by the Swedish American press, which commonly used both *fosterlandet* and *gamla landet*. The journalist Johan Person, for example, uses both phrases when he devotes a chapter of his 1912 book *Svensk-Amerikanska Studier* (Swedish American studies) to *Den Nya Fosterlandskärleken* (the new love of native country). Person maintains that, like religious converts, newcomers to America were America's most fervent patriots, and the interest they retained in Sweden was "a nostalgic interest in 'the old country.'"[11] Person argues for a Swedish American stance toward Sweden that distances the old country. His choice of *fosterlandet* and *gamla landet* is appropriate to his point. Of the range of choices available, *native, country,* and *old* are among the more abstract and distancing. They cast a more remote sense of relationship than does the phrase used by Nilsson when he embraces *modren Svea*.

Country, native, and *old* dominate the rhetoric of Swedish immigration, but letter writers do not restrict themselves to these words alone. Indeed, many writers in the West create their own variations on epithets for Sweden. To do so, they use two main strategies: choosing alternative modifiers, and piling modifier upon modifier to create long and redundant phrases. *Bästa* is an alternative to the more positive *kära, älskade,* and *hem*. Also very positive, while adding the idea of Sweden's Nordic location and history, are *Nordens* (the North's) and *midnattssolens* (the midnight sun's). Alternatives to the ambiguous *gammal* are *föråldrade* (old-fashioned) and *lilla* (little or even insignificant). Alternatives to the more negative *fattiga* are *stackars* (poor in ability and general well-being), *främmande* (strange or foreign), and *träldomens* (bondage's; that is, Sweden as a country of bondage).

Piling up these adjectives in sometimes quite long phrases, writers effectively use redundancy to emphasize their views. A very positive view of Sweden is expressed by Fritz Lindborg, who was living in Helena, Montana, in 1888: "our beloved native-soil, old Svea."[12] A negative view is expressed by John Renström when he personifies Sweden by addressing her as "O, du stackars Sverige" in an 1892 letter objecting to Sweden's military conscription: "O, you poor Sweden and stupid thick-headed authorities who cannot understand that this is a burdensome duty. . . . they will follow old habits and overwhelm poor little Sweden [*det lilla fattiga Sverige*] with more debt."[13] In fact, few letter writers who use epithets limit themselves simply to *fosterlandet* and *gamla landet*. Instead, they demonstrate a playful flexibility in constructing phrases that express more than these two relatively neutral ones.

Epithets are less common among women writers. In the sample of letters from the Rockies, I have located two women who use epithets: Anna Olson, writing in 1889, refers to Sweden as *gamla landet*; and Brita Lisa Matsdotter, writing in 1907, refers to *dett fattiga Sverje* (poor Sweden).[14] However, women do frequently use the metonymic *hemma* (at home), which is a more personal, concrete, and geographically focused way of viewing Sweden. Emma Hallberg writes to her parents, "you say that it is warm at home."[15] Clara Jeppsson writes, "Everything is so unlike home in Sweden."[16] Hallberg and Jeppsson use the idea of home in an ambiguous sense. It is clear they mean a larger area than just the farm or village in which their correspondents live, but how large an area is vague. The boundaries of "home" could extend to the whole nation or be limited to part of a province. While this metonymic reference is very common among women writers, it is not an exclusively female usage.

In addition to epithets, characterizations of the Old World are occasionally distilled into particular, evocative images. One such image is that of Svea as used by Nilsson. Later immigrants who owned Swedish American publisher Engberg-Holmberg's 1891 edition of Tegnér's "Svea" could see the goddess-like figure illustrated as a statuesque and stalwart young woman with a sword in her right hand and a shield in her left, her long hair streaming in the wind, and a helmet with a star atop her head. She wears not armor but a simple short-sleeved dress; nevertheless, her wrist guards show she is ready for battle. Flowing out of the clouds at her feet are winged Viking warriors. In this illustration, the qualities associated with Sweden include steadfastness and courage, virtues espoused as Swedish not just by nationalist Swedes but also by leaders of Swedish America who, although they might distance themselves from the old country, were beginning to express the idea of ethnically Swedish virtues during Nilsson's time in America.[17]

Another way of casting this female image of Sweden is more specifically domestic: as a sweetheart or a mother waiting at home. This woman-at-home image has the static quality of a tableau or a photograph created out of a combination of memory and imagination. It is similar to the image of sweethearts and mothers used in Swedish emigrant ballads; for example, in the 1877 broadside "O, Swerge!" (O, Sweden!): "How could I forget the country where I was born, / Where my dear mother cradled me so sweetly."[18] This is distilled nostalgia. In letters, this female image is cast in more personal and realistic terms and with a less saccharin tone.

Nilsson's memories and imaginings of his faithful Lovisa are touching examples. In an 1882 letter, Nilsson remembers the Christmas when he realized how much he loves Lovisa: "I well remember how I at times was in the kitchen and worked—I was supposed to be second in command [literally, vice host]. I remember how I became bewildered every time I met Lova's eyes."[19] Nilsson imagines what Lovisa would be doing at a given time of day; after a hard day of work, for example: "I imagine I see you, how you stand in the pantry by the kitchen or also at the stove . . . working." Nilsson projects this image into the future, hoping that some-day Lovisa will be working not at the Söderköping hotel where she is currently employed, but "at your own stove in your own home."[20]

Lovisa in the kitchen presents a decidedly domestic image, but one that is still realistic. Charles Flodin uses a similarly domestic tableau of his childhood sweetheart, who in his case did not wait for him. Flodin traveled home to Sweden and met Sofia before returning to Colorado to write this reflection, in which he places her on a bench gazing out the window:

> Lucky Petrus he came in the nick of time to save Sofia from mo-notony. I felt as if a gloom had come over me when I saw Sofi at Manuel's place in Skäremo and my thoughts went: Sofi poor Sofi here you are now (on Sundays when there is no service in either one of the churches) from one bench in the cottage across the floor to the other looking out through the window thoughtfully. What does she see yes in the distance, far away, her youthful love, having unintentionally tied the knot with someone else.[21]

Both Nilsson and Flodin have a poetic flair. Nilsson was influenced by his reading of Tegnér and the Swedish American poets; Flodin was more influenced by spoken language. In both cases, the image of a woman waiting at home reflects the conflicting feelings of homesickness and freedom that many immigrants felt on having left their homeland.

As in "O, Swerge!" the image of the woman at home could focus on a mother rather than a sweetheart. Clara Jeppsson uses the image of her mother busying herself to take care of her children: "When I remind myself of the time when we used to travel home and stayed home for a few days, I can remember so well how mother used to be up in the morning to have everything in order and how she always put out the best for us, then I wish that I were home again."[22] Jeppsson, like Nilsson, creates an image of woman as caregiver. Whether personified as Mother Svea or cast much more specifically as a memory of one's mother in the kitchen, the overarching metaphor for the nation is a domestic place, a home in which one had been nurtured or a home to which one might return.

Visits home evoke another image in the letters, that of placing one's foot on or treading on the soil of the old country. Writing to his brother Olaf in 1884 from Custer, Idaho, Bengt Olson Brodin admits he does not know whether he "once again could get to set foot on the dear native-soil."[23] Fritz Lindborg similarly writes in 1888 from Helena, Montana, to his *broder* Nils that he expects when Nils has received his letter, "you tread our beloved native-soil, old Svea."[24] The image evokes the tactile sense of physical contact with home.

Used by Charles Flodin, a similar expression becomes evocative of the disappointments such a trip could bring: "Falkenberg ... will be my disembarkation next time when my expensive [dyra] native country's soil will have the honor to kiss my American *number eight shoes*."[25] In this line, Flodin cleverly inverts the meaning of the metaphor. For Brodin and Lindborg, it would be a pleasure to tread the soil of the old country again. For Flodin, it is the soil of the old country that has the honor of contact with his American shoes. Flodin also plays with the epithetical *dyra fosterland* (dear native country). This was a common phrase in Flodin's day, but he uses it humorously in the middle of a diatribe about the expense of a recent trip through Gothenburg. Throughout his letter, written to another bilingual immigrant, Flodin makes frequent, self-consciously playful code shifts to English. In this context, *dyra fosterland* can be read as a Swenglish pun: *dyra* can be used to mean dear, in the sense of being valued, but it also means expensive.

The immigrants' commentary on nationality is necessarily dual. Explicit comments about Sweden are embedded in the context of comments about American surroundings, implying a comparison even when America is not explicitly labeled with epithets of its own. While Brodin muses over the possibility of setting foot on native soil, he later in the same letter notes that "this is the most varied country I believe exists,"[26] referring to fluctuations in the western American economy. Lindborg's reference to "beloved native-soil" appears in the context of a letter denigrating Helena as "the worst gambling hole on the face of [the] earth."[27] For Flodin, who characterizes his home village in Sweden as "like a graveyard,"[28] his location in Colorado was perhaps not much better, as he wrote in the midst of a blizzard, complaining that he had been snowed in for two weeks. John A. Leonard evaluates his working conditions in America as generally positive in a letter in which he writes about poor working conditions at home. These attitudes toward Sweden are mixed, as they would be toward a parent whom one had left.

If Sweden is the old home where one had been nurtured and to which some would return, the formulaic language about America focuses on its political and economic systems. The immigrant letter writers use epithets for America sparingly. When they do, they nearly always refer to America using *land* (country), and the most frequent modifier is *fritt* (free), yielding the epithet "a free country." A sprinkling of alternative modifying words and phrases characterizes America with superlatives; for example, "the best country on earth for the poor."[29] More personally and soberly, Peter Peterson writes that America could be a "country where their children might be able to be part of a better nation."[30] This is a comparative statement in which Peterson suggests that such a future is not possible in Sweden, which he calls "a country of bondage." He hopes to tempt his friend Jonas Danielson to visit America, where Danielson and his family would see that "we live in a country that is not so bad."[31] Whatever the degree of enthusiasm for America, the nation is characterized by "freedom," and rather than being old or outmoded, it is a place of the future, a land that promises both political and economic freedom.

The epithets in the letters do not personify America in the same way that Sweden could be personified as Svea, or mother, or father. Personifications of America that were commonly used in the Swedish American press find their way into the letters only sparingly. One such personification was the idea of America as the immigrant's bride—in other words, a chosen partner for whom one had left one's parents.[32] I have identified no instances of this metaphor in the letters from the Rockies that I have examined.

Another metaphor in Swedish American journalism imagines the relationship between the immigrant and his or her new adoptive "parent," America. For example, Johan Person calls America "adoptivlandet" (the adoptive country).[33] There is one instance in which a letter writer, John A. Leonard, uses this metaphor—in the phrase "our free adopted native country."[34] Leonard uses this phrase in a passage where his concern is about the bad character of those who have freely chosen America as their home, poorly behaved immigrants who had been admonished in articles Leonard had read in a Swedish American newspaper. His use of the metaphor recognizes that the immigrant, not America, chooses the adoption.

America is also figured as a place to which one could develop a potentially dangerous physical attraction: a "taste" or even a "fever." One could become "America sick." Clara Jeppsson comments that "you struggle during the dog-years" (the first hard years of immigration) in America, but eventually, after learning English and becoming adjusted to American customs, immigrants can adapt, "so perhaps they have gotten a taste for America."[35] Aron W. Johnson predicts that he "will become America sick" if he returns to Sweden to join his sweetheart, Anna.[36] Whether they should settle in Sweden or America dominates their correspondence between 1901 and 1905. Johnson, who had achieved some success as a sheep rancher in the Rawlins, Wyoming, area, was reluctant to leave "Wyoming's *sagebrush* prairie,"[37] but Anna refused simply to forget him and yet also refused to come to America. When Johnson writes to her in 1903, "I like America and you Sweden,"[38] he is close to a decision to return. When he finally does return, his friend, O. M. Johnson of Rawlins, modifies the typical opening formula in a letter to Aron: "thanks for the warmly welcome letter . . . in which I see that you are alive and well, although I see that you have begun to get the America Sickness, as I believed [would happen]."[39] O. M. hopes that Anna will relent and that Aron can return to America with his family.

John Renström writes to a friend in 1892 that he feels lucky he has remedied his own America fever by emigrating. He is happy in his new nation, but he is not naive in his pro-Americanism: "That doesn't mean that I boast of America or of myself, for this country is not as some believe, that here you can slice gold with 'knives' and stamp your own coins and that pork roasts run around with a knife and fork in their backs ready for anyone to cut a piece and stick it in their mouths."[40] On the contrary, says Renström, one does have to work in America. But workers have better conditions and pay is better: "In these ways this country is better than the old, and another thing, America is a free country in all senses."[41]

Renström describes a utopian image of America common to many immigrant groups. Folklorist Luisa Del Giudice calls this image part of an "imagined state" in which "the peasant merely wishes to live as the lord is perceived to live: idle and well fed."[42] These utopian images often are expressed as foods that are desired by the lower class because they are too expensive for ordinary fare. For the Italian immigrants studied by Del Giudice, the utopian image was a cheese mountain and rivers running with wine.[43]

For the Swedes, a pork roast complete with cutlery is an appropriate equivalent. In Snorri Sturluson's *The Younger Edda*, a miraculous boar, boiled day after day, provides sustenance to human visitors.[44] An even closer parallel was available to the immigrants in contemporary folksong. This example, collected from a Swedish sailor in 1900, features miraculous fowl: "Chickens and ducks rain down / Cooked geese and yet more / fly in onto the table / with a knife and fork in their thigh."[45] The Norwegian popular song "Oleana" presents a similar image: "little roasted piggies / rush about the city streets / inquiring so politely / if a slice of ham you'd like to eat."[46] A Swedish popular song, "Chikago," boasts that "Chicago is such a big city / there are so many horses, there are so many cows / there are such fat pigs and oxen, I believe / and all kinds of livestock animals because there I have a brother."[47] The idea of fabulous gastronomic bounty also appears as "pie in the sky" in Swedish immigrant and unionist Joe Hill's "In the Sweet Bye and Bye."[48] Significantly, like Joe Hill, Renström both invokes this imagery and questions it; his use of the rhetoric of immigration resembles Flodin's inversion of the setting-foot-on-the-soil-of-the-old-country commonplace. Both Renström and Flodin were aware of common wisdom about Sweden and America, and both use the vernacular formulas and images to question that common wisdom.

The "gastronomic utopian"[49] image of readily available food draws attention to the economic differences between Sweden and America as perceived by many of the immigrants. Sweden was not just the old and dear country that had fostered them. As already noted, Sweden was sometimes seen as *fattigt* and *stackars*. Both adjectives can be translated into English as *poor*, with the first referring more to financial poverty, and the second referring more generally to one's state of being. For the first condition, an immigrant could not send walking pork roasts across the ocean, even had they existed. Nor, as Renström notes, was money available for the taking. Here Renström uses another commonplace, identified by Johan Person as a saying that one could hear daily in America at the turn of the century: *skära guld med täljknifvar* (to "slice gold with a knife").[50] But, as with the pork roast, Renström invokes the image in order to deny it.

Most immigrants acted on the perceived poverty of those at home by sending money if they could. Some variation on "I am sending money" is a formula encountered as frequently as formulas for greeting family members. Often these words are used in the opening and closing sections of the letters, which suggests that sending money had as much ceremonial as practical import. Even more ceremonial are the many passages in which correspondents represent the act of sending money through their apologies for not being able to do so. Numerous letters include statements like Andreas Reed's, written from Boulder, Colorado, in 1884: "Greet Brother Salemon, I will do right by him, I will send a little money soon now, this is the reason that I have not written, I have not had money to send."[51] Another example can be found in a letter from Elin Pehrson, writing from Denver in 1897: "I have thought I should send her [Elin's mother] a little [money] but we are such a large family and [have] so much to buy."[52]

For the second condition of impoverishment, poverty of spirit, letter writing itself, along with the inclusion of enclosed photographs and pressed flowers, sought to ease the minds and hearts of those across the Atlantic. In fact, many of the apologies for not sending money are stated in a manner similar to Andreas Reed's, equating the act of sending money with the act of writing, with the lack of either action being seen as important and requiring an apology. Money, letters, and enclosures served as metonyms for the continuing ties of family and friendship.

Regular correspondence was a significant token of familial connection, but correspondents were often delinquent in following through on that obligation. It is difficult, of course, for us to know the real reasons for delinquency in letter writing. They could include the sheer difficulty of producing written text if one's literacy was marginal, as was true of some of the immigrants. For those who quickly adopted English as a main language, that difficulty was compounded. This may have been true in the case of Brita Lisa Matsdotter of Salt Lake City. Having been delinquent in fulfilling the obligation of sending letters and money, Matsdotter reestablished contact with her in-laws, probably her brother's wife, and explained her social lapse through storytelling:

> I have often thought about writing. I got a letter from my
> brother many years ago, I believe it is seven years ago, but I
> never answered. He said that he had 5 boys, my thought was
> to delay writing until I could send them 5 dollars, one for each.
> But then we began to build a house, so that took all of the money
> we could scrape together, but now we are out of debt and have a
> nice home, glory be to God. But how it grieved me when I found
> out that Lars was dead, that I never even answered his letter. But
> now I want to make good to you [on my former intentions] and
> send 5 dollars, one for each boy, but you may also use them for
> necessities.[53]

By turning her lapse into a story, Matsdotter dramatizes the consequences of her inaction. The story's hesitations, with its repetitions of *but*, are like her repeated, hesitant intentions to write. Not having answered the letter from her brother immediately, she left the matter until, with his death, no answer would be possible. Moreover, the absence of the letter parallels the earlier act of emigration itself, the initial sundering from her family that presaged the final separation of death. Matsdotter's story has an implicit moral: the need for continued contact between the old and new worlds.

In Matsdotter's story, the immigrant letter is elevated to the status of a narrative motif, and we perceive that letters can represent the power of literacy itself. The letter motif is found also in the Swedish emigrant ballad "En Visa Jag Diktat" (A song I composed), in which an emigrant plans the writing of "a letter and a greeting," and in "En Ny Amerika-Visa" (A new America-song), in which a letter bears the sad news that a sweetheart has married another man.[54] Other immigrant groups also used the motif of letters written home. For example, folklorist Robert B. Klymatz has documented the importance of the letter in folksongs of Ukrainian immigrants in Canada. In the Ukrainian songs, letters act as motifs, but they also can be personified: "For when the letter is not paid for / It goes and wanders (aimlessly), / But if a letter is paid for, / Then it searches for me."[55] Personification of letters is not a figure of speech that I have found in the letters from Swedish writers, but it is nevertheless very clear how highly valued letters were. The formula *det kärkomna bref* (the warmly welcome letter), which we have already noted in O. M. Johnson's letter to Aron W. Johnson, appears regularly as a part of the opening formula in which letters are acknowledged. In one of her later letters, Clara Jeppsson notes with satisfaction the sheer number of letters she has received from her family: "It is altogether a fine collection of letters, this bundle, which can be pleasant to look through again."[56]

In addition to the letters themselves, the enclosures in letters were also metonyms for the personal contact that correspondents hoped to maintain. Probably the most common letter enclosure was a photograph. Writing from Morrison, Colorado, in 1880, Peter F. Erlandson promises to send a photograph of himself and his buddy taken during their journey westward.[57] Writing from Denver in 1889, Anna Olson thanks her cousin Elna Lundberg for sending a photograph, assuring her, "you have not changed much." Olson apologizes for not being able to reciprocate with a photograph of her own, but promises she will send a photograph with her next letter.[58] Bernhard Rydberg frequently sent photographs to his mother documenting his trips into the mountains near Red Lodge, Montana.

These tokens of contact might also include pressed leaves or flowers sent from Sweden. On one occasion, Lovisa Borg sent Leonard Nilsson a rose leaf, and on another occasion, she sent a rose flower. The rose flower was sent on the occasion of Leonard's name day—the day on which the Swedish calendar recognizes the name Leonard, and those named Leonard receive small presents.[59] The name-day occasion would not have been known by Nilsson's coworkers, none of whom were Swedish, so to Leonard the gift represented an important continuance of Swedish custom.

Occasions like name days were important times for correspondents to renew and maintain contact. Of most importance was Christmas, a time when family and friends assembled in Sweden and when the immigrants most missed those they had left. Christmas is recognized frequently in the letters through a simple formula, *god jul,* meaning "[Have a] good Christmas." Unlike name days, Christmas was observed in America, but not in the same fashion as in Sweden. In Sweden, the holiday was a several-day event, during which workers enjoyed time off, housewives cleaned and decorated their homes, and a festive table was laden with traditional foods, especially baked goods. As discussed in chapter 4, much of this festivity was missing from American life. Thus, the importance of Christmas to the Swedish immigrants was often marked in letters through comments on the lack of time off from work and the lack of festivities. Combined with the commonplace greeting *god jul,* the letter writers' complaints present Christmas as a metonym for Sweden and the familial ties there.

Considering the importance of Christmas, one would expect the letters to contain many images and stories about the holiday. However, this is not the case. An unusual example from Gottfrid Johnson, who spent the Christmas of 1914 on a farm in La Jara, Colorado, provides us with the context missing from the more typically terse *god jul:*

> I will try to describe my Christmas here and I can first of all say that this was my first Christmas *without* "lutfisk o gröt"[60] [and] at the same time the most joyless. Christmas Eve day arrived with sunny and clear weather but all the same I felt so lost and unfamiliar with everything and no happiness came over me that the joyous holiday was approaching. Most around here do not observe the holidays, seldom or never Sunday even. Uncle had bought a load of hay and we drove hay the whole day and my thoughts dwelt stubbornly on times past. When we finally were done with the work and came in, after all aunt had put up some Christmas decorations and that was like a warm breath of air from the blessed past [literally, "the Eden of memories"]. The floors were washed and a white tablecloth on the table but no sign of the old Christmas food was present. The supper consisted of potatoes and pan-fried ham and cranberry jam, coffee, butter, bread, and honey. The same evening the Sunday school in LaJara had its Christmas

celebration and to remind ourselves that it was Christmas after all, we went down there. The week before I was up in the mountains after a load of wood, and I brought down a large Christmas tree. On Christmas Day I put it in a base and Aunt Stiv and I decorated it in the morning while uncle was out checking on his stock that he has now grazing 5 or 6 miles north of here. He appears to find this a nice holiday job and even today [New Year's Day] he is up there.[61]

Even the festivities available to Johnson in LaJara, which included a church celebration, were incomplete. The floor had been washed, a Christmas tradition in rural Sweden, and the table had the traditional white tablecloth, but the baked goods, baked ham, and fish dishes one might expect were missing. Perhaps most important are the events that Johnson places at the beginning and end of his story, that he had to work and that the family was incomplete on Christmas Day. This concern brackets the missing domestic tokens of Christmas. In Johnson's letter, we sense how Christmas came to serve as one of the important symbols of Swedishness among Swedes in America.[62]

Gottfrid Johnson had been in America at least since 1911 when he lived in Nebraska. It must have been there, within a more established concentration of Swedes, that he was able to enjoy his *lutfisk* and *gröt*. In the West, he seems to have experienced a second wave of adjustment to America, though like most of the Western writers, he does not use the common expression for a period of adjustment, *hundår* (dog years). This metaphor for the initial years of struggle in America was common among Midwestern Swedes, but in the letters of Western Swedes I have seen it only in Clara Jeppsson's writing, where she uses the expression to talk about the experience of immigrants in general. The Rocky Mountain letter writers were, however, very much aware of the problem of adjustment to American customs and language. It was a struggle worth telling stories about. For Charles Flodin, this was the point of a story about a greenhorn:

It was when we were in Gothenburg on our way back to America I befriended two guys [literally, "two salmon"] from Småland, one had been home over the summer *before* and the other was an old cattle trader from Ljungby. Talkative men, both were jolly without being on the make. The cattle trader had *lots of money*, you should have seen him in Hull, Liverpool, New York, Chicago and altogether how surprised he was and taken with everything he saw. And in Chicago you should have seen and heard him when he talked with Patron Lindgren with his cap in his hand. He was a *smart man*, anyway when talking about Småland, but in foreign affairs he was lost.[63]

Flodin uses the hat-in-hand image to emphasize that the greenhorn from Småland was not just naive in his enthusiastic response to everything he saw, but he also had no sense of how one was supposed to act in America. As chapter 4 illustrated, the common wisdom was that one did *not* have to stand hat in hand when addressing someone in authority. Flodin concludes his story at this point, having set up dramatic tension. Along with Flodin, the reader has to wonder what happened to this wealthy, naive immigrant after Flodin parted company with him in Chicago. We have to hope that he adjusted to American ways.

These passages from Johnson, Jeppsson, and Flodin point to the process of change the immigrants had to endure. In so doing, did they perceive themselves as becoming hyphenated Americans? The idea of a "Swedish America" and "Swedish Americans" was created during this era in part by the literati—clergy, journalists, teachers, and writers—within the Swedish population in the United States. The term *Svensk-Amerika* (Swedish America) was first used by Johan Person in 1900.[64] As conceived by the literati, Swedish America had both cultural and geographical components. It was a community that shared language and culture, a common Swedish history, and a common experience in America. During the era that the Swedish immigrants were coming into the West, the cultural symbols of Swedish America were being selected and intensified through various institutional efforts, especially the efforts of churches.[65] The Christmas celebrations missed by Gottfrid Johnson were similar to those sponsored by many Swedish churches; the summertime Midsommar celebrations were typically celebrated by secular organizations. Between 1900 and 1917, these and other observances, such as St. Lucia Day, "became established rituals of Swedish America," according to H. Arnold Barton.[66] Dag Blanck points also to the way in which Swedish Americans such as writer Johan Enander used the idea of Swedish contributions to American history as a way of defining and anchoring Swedish America.[67]

But Swedish America was also the clustering of Swedish immigrants in certain regions of the United States, especially in the upper Midwest. Blanck calculates that earlier in the migration from Sweden, in 1870, 75 percent of Swedish Americans lived in the upper Midwest. By 1910 that region still held over half of the Swedish American population.[68] In the West, there were Swedish ethnic enclaves, located in Denver, Salt Lake City, and scattered towns of the Rockies, as described in chapter 3.

As Gottfrid Johnson experienced when he moved from Nebraska to southern Colorado, the Swedish American networks and nodes in the northern Rockies were relatively weak and small compared to those in the Midwest. From the prospect of the Rocky Mountains, we find that the relationship between the individual Swedish immigrant and the larger concept of Swedish America was at best a vaguely expressed relationship. As they comment on the Swedish population among which they dwell, the letter writers most commonly note, "here in the village are many Swedish folk,"[69] not "Swedish Americans." Moreover, some of the writers undercut the unity of the Swedish population, suggesting that for them no unified Swedish America exists.

Even though several letter writers comment on the presence of fellow Swedes, I have as yet located only one use of the term *Swedish American*, and it stands out as having a non-American context. Charles Flodin, writing from Rico, Colorado, in 1895, comments to his *broder* Anders Abrahamsson, who has moved home to Sweden, "I assume that there must be many Swedish Americans there at home in Drägved . . . so that you have what I might call a little 'United States.'"[70] Flodin uses the label *Swedish Americans* not for those Swedes living in America, but for those who have moved back to Sweden. The label is a necessity if he is to be able to clearly distinguish the returnees both from the Americans and from the Swedes who never ventured abroad. This is not Swedish America in the sense used by Johan Person.

Instead of *Swedish America* in the sense of a nation within a nation, what we find represented in the Western letters is a vague sense of the welcome presence of fellow Swedes in the West. For example, August Johansson and Clara Jeppsson, writing respectively in 1891 and 1911, comment that it was agreeable to live in Denver, where they were in touch with many other Swedish immigrants. Johansson was a newcomer to Denver in 1891, when he enthusiastically wrote home to a younger brother, listing by name the friends and relatives he had visited in just the first few days of being in the city, where, he generally observes, there are "many Swedish."[71] For Jeppsson, the Swedish community provided churches where she could meet fellow Swedish speakers and contacts that helped her find employment.[72] When Jeppsson and her husband left the Denver area for LaJara, she missed the presence of fellow Swedes: "Mostly Mormons and Mexicans live here. Here we are only 4 Swedes. The other two are Värmlanders."[73]

In LaJara, Jeppsson experienced many forms of otherness, based on religion, ethnicity, and even Swedish region. Mormons were a distinctive religious group uniting multiple nationalities and ethnicities in a Western region they called Zion. Mexicans gradually became an ethnic minority group through United States expansion; America had acquired the northern portion of Mexican territory about sixty years earlier. For Jeppsson, even the category *Swedish* was complicated by the immigrants' having come from various provincial groups. Herself from the southern tip of Sweden, in Skåne, she may have found the Swedish dialect of a Värmlander difficult to understand.[74] In multireligious, multiethnic LaJara, Jeppsson missed the Swedes of Denver.

The Denver area is mentioned by a few of the letter writers as a travel destination that offered contact with fellow Swedes. For John A. Leonard, it was a welcome circumstance to have many Swedes living in Longmont, Colorado, which he visited in 1883 while taking a break from his mining work. He proudly reports that he was able to stop in Denver to hear Christina Nilsson sing at the opera house. She had, according to Leonard, declared from the balcony of her hotel, "'I am happy to have been born Swedish, and I have never had to be ashamed of my *country name*.' (=Swedish name)."[75]

The two main nodes for the Rocky Mountain Swedish population, Denver and Salt Lake City, developed ethnic institutions that made religious and secular events available. As noted in chapter 3, though, we can question the depth of involvement in such organizations by the working-class Westerners. The *julfest* and *julgran* (Christmas tree) are mentioned by one writer other than Gottfrid Johnson—John M. Swanson of Denver in 1903.[76] Midsommar is mentioned, but mainly as a seasonal designation rather than a holiday, and only by two correspondents, in 1904.[77] I have located no mention of St. Lucia Day.

Moreover, in areas outside of Denver, when clusters of Swedes were apparent, they did not necessarily constitute a population given to creating institutions that would unify the Swedes. Leonard traveled from Silver Camp, New Mexico, to visit the Denver area. As he explains in a letter to his sister in 1881, he saw New Mexico as a territory to which civilization had not yet spread. The Swedish workers were mostly freethinkers, he comments, and they did not support churches, but rather saloons, dance houses, and theaters. The closest Swedish church was in Denver. Perhaps it is no wonder that Edward Wiberg, writing in 1882, saw the many Swedes working for the railroads near Bozeman, Montana, as a business opportunity: there was no Swedish saloon. He wrote to his brother Charles, who was in Stillwater, Minnesota, to ask for money to help with setting up such a business.[78]

Informal familial networks were perhaps as important as and more extensive in their reach than the Swedish institutions; these networks included Sweden as a node. A letter from Jacob Lundquist sent to a sister who had recently returned to Sweden is illustrative. For Lundquist, the important nodes where there were Swedish contacts were Denver, where he was located; Sweden, where his sister had moved; Froid, Montana, where they had both previously lived and where friends and relations lived; and Leadville, Colorado, where they had friends who had relocated from Froid.

In a four-page letter, Lundquist performs the masterful feat of reporting news from each of these localities. In Denver, the weather is good, tourist excursions into the mountains have begun, President Harrison is expected, and the Swedish Lutheran church building is completed. In Leadville, friends have heard of the death of a mother, and another family has a new baby. In Froid, a friend "big across as lengthwise poor little thing almost like a wandering barrel" has finally given birth, two farmers have finished the work necessary to "prove up" on their homesteads, another friend is suffering the visit of "the crankiest old maid they had ever seen," a woman has killed herself with a self-inflicted gunshot wound, and "your great doctor" has fled town with the sheriff hard on her heels to arrest her. In Sweden, Lundquist imagines, his sister will be "in the midst of a great jubilee surrounded by all those who are so dear to us."[79] Conveyed through pithy, humorous description, the scenes of Lundquist's letter unite all these places and people. In this way, his letter creates an informal family-based network that served as an alternative to the institutionalized Swedish America of the press and the churches.

As discussed in chapter 3, in parts of the northern Rockies the nodes and networks for Swedish immigrants were so small and weak that Swedes forged ethnic institutions with those from other Scandinavian countries. This was especially true in Montana and Utah. The letters from those states similarly use panethnic categories. Writers comment on the qualities of the Scandinavians in comparison to other immigrant groups, particularly in work settings. In a letter from Allhambra, Montana, in 1890, Elias Myrholm expresses these contacts as a hierarchy of ethnicities involved in the Montana labor pool: "The native (Yankee) Americans are the worst here in America; those who have invented in the area of mechanics are immigrants Englishmen, Germans, and Scandinavians. Scandinavians and foremost the Swedes are generally recognized to be America's best workers."[80] He of course saw himself as part of this select group. Myrholm makes a complex ethnic- and class-based claim here: Scandinavian and Swedish and working class. Pet Stred makes a similarly positive ethnic claim when he refers to the "Swedish strength" required of him in his smelting work.[81] In Mormon Utah, Peter Peterson also perceived workers as members of larger panethnic groups, but he was not as complimentary toward the Scandinavians as Myrholm was. As quoted in chapter 3, Peterson preferred the work of those whom he terms "Americans."[82] Although expressed from a boss's viewpoint rather than a worker's, Peterson's larger claim is similar to Flodin's point in his story about the naive greenhorn. Peterson felt that Scandinavian workers clung to their old ways and that it was necessary for them to change when they came to America.

Some writers complicated matters by differentiating divisions within the Swedish population. As already noted, Clara Jeppsson calls the two other LaJara Swedes *Värmlanders*. Peter Peterson comments on there being no other "Jemtleningar" (people from the province of Jämtland) in his area of Utah.[83] Charles Flodin notes that his greenhorn is from Småland; Effie Peterson specifies that her husband was born in that same province.[84] And Carl Boline reports to his mother that there were many "halländingar" (people from the province of Halland) in Leadville.[85] These perceptions of regional distinctions challenged the idea of Swedish America, as did the use of the larger category of *Scandinavian*.

This variety of national, ethnic, familial, panethnic, and regional designations indicates that the idea of Swedish America was weak among the Swedish population coming into the Rocky Mountain West beginning in the 1880s. We simply do not see the letter writers labeling and characterizing Swedish Americans in the very explicit way that the Swedish American leaders did. Nor is Swedish America represented in the same kinds of very expressive epithets, metonyms and metaphors, images, and stories that are used to express ideas about the national entities *Sweden* and *America*. Also lacking from the Western letters are claims about Swedish contributions to American history, which were an important basis for the idea of Swedish America that Dag Blanck has documented among the Midwestern congregations of the Augustana Synod.[86]

On the other hand, the writers devote considerable attention to the issue of nationality. The Swedish and American nations and the immigrants' relationship to nationhood are aptly expressed in the letters from the Rockies. *Nation* is a difficult abstraction. The letter writers render the abstract approachable and understandable by using images that are vivid, concrete, and tangible, and often presented in domestic settings. An immigrant's shoes touching the earth, a woman cooking at the stove, a pork roast freely offering its savory meat, a goddess with sword in hand, a letter sitting unanswered, a young man decorating a Christmas tree with his aunt: these images evoke sensual responses that abstractions like "freedom" cannot. The writers also playfully elaborate on the usual epithets and invert the usual images, making them fresh while also questioning them.

Even so, this was an indirect discourse about nationality in which few were willing to make the boldly explicit kind of claim made by Leonard Nilsson: "*I am* a son of mother *Svea*." Nilsson, an avid reader of the free-thinking Swedish American writers in the Chicago *Svenska Amerikanaren*, expresses a strong pull to Swedish America that is not evident in the correspondence of the rest of the Western letter writers, who more typically indicate their ambivalence to nationality and ethnicity by characterizing the nations but not themselves. The letter writers question received notions of nation: Some of the ideas of the press were left unused by the letter writers; some of the images available in vernacular expression were questioned even as they were employed. They largely ignore hyphenated ethnicity, which was not a solution for their condition of suspension between Sweden and America. Instead, the writers emphasize the family as a mediating and unifying institution. In this, the letters contrast with the Swedish American press and other social institutions, which we know actively promoted ethnic symbols that were perhaps not embraced by ordinary immigrants.

SIX

"Out West"

IDENTIFYING WITH A NEW REGION

꙳꙳

I am beginning to become accustomed to the heat, and we are all
like redskins, so if I come home that way I am afraid that I will
never be allowed to stay indoors.

Hjalmar Johnsson, 1917, Camp Cody, New Mexico

𝑊 RITING FROM CAMP CODY, New Mexico, in 1917, while he was
training with the U.S. Army and anticipating engagement in the
Great War in Europe, Hjalmar Johnsson figures his adaptation to New
Mexico as a transformation into an American Indian.[1] He goes on to ask
that he be forgiven for joking, but his jest communicates something more
than humor. Hjalmar felt changed by the West, turned into something
new that he characterizes as indigenous by citing the popular image of the
American Indian: supposedly red skinned, living outdoors, and stoical in
the extremes of Western climate.

By claiming to have become an American Indian, Hjalmar draws on a
Western image that dated much earlier than the World War I era. What
Western historians have labeled the "myth of the West" had its roots in
accounts of Daniel Boone as a pathfinder and James Fenimore Cooper's
novels of the eastern frontier.[2] It began to be expressed as a code in the
earliest of the Western dime novels during the 1840s, and became more
specifically linked with the cattle-ranching West during the 1880s. By the
late nineteenth century, a distillation of the images associated with the myth
of the West was available in two cultural artifacts: the Western novel
and the Wild West show. As characterized by historian David Hamilton
Murdoch, the resulting image of the West included "the lone hero [pitted]

often as not on behalf of the community, against enemies who impede 'progress'—the land itself, Indians, criminals and those who would abuse power.... [The Western] affirms the values of individualism, self-reliance and the democratic impulse."[3]

The myth of the West, then, portrays the region as a frontier, a border at which those coming into the region from the East met the wilderness. In the Western novel, this view of the West was developed through particular characters, actions, and landscapes, including the scout and the cowboy, plots incorporating pathfinding and run-ins with outlaws or American Indians, and the rather vague backdrop of a landscape that contrasted barren, rugged mountains with idyllic meadowland. In all of these images, the West is a liminal place, where civilization meets the wild and primitive and is transformed or renewed.[4] For American studies scholar Richard Slotkin, this image is essentially violent, begun in eastern America's earliest tales of contact between American Indians and the British.[5]

As the new Western historians point out, this image of the West defines the region in a limited way, as only the outer limit of the westward movement of eastern Americans, rather than as a place where peoples converged from all directions.[6] Ironically, the east-to-west portion of settlement history has been told even by recent historians with a focus on the *Anglo*-American role. The non-Anglophone European immigrants' participation in the history of the West and in the framing of a Western myth has received less attention.

This Anglo focus leaves out an important part of the story. As Ulf Jonas Björk has demonstrated in his study of the American Indian story in Sweden, the Wild West image was available in the Swedish press nearly simultaneously with its currency in North America. Swedish readers admired James Fenimore Cooper's work, and they also had available translations from Cooper's imitators on the Continent.[7] By the turn of the century, a Swedish publication calling itself *Vilda Vestern* (The Wild West) was offering Swedish readers tales of Buffalo Bill and Texas Jack in dime-novel format.[8] These publications conveyed an ambiguous view of the American Indian: sometimes as a noble savage whose ways one might want to imitate; sometimes as a violent enemy. Johnsson's claim "we are all like redskins" could have positive or negative connotations.

The Swedish fascination with the American West continues into the

The myth of the West was formulated even as Swedish immigrants came into the Rockies, in images like this posed photograph from 1901–2 of gold panning at Nelson Gulch, Montana. The photograph was used as a model for a mural in the state capitol. Photograph courtesy of the Denver Public Library, Western History Collection, Dan Dutro, photographer, call number X-60187.

twenty-first century with such cultural movements as the Swedish Indian clubs, groups who gather to reenact their vision of American Indian life, as noted by American studies scholar Gunlög Fur.[9] Two twentieth-century Swedish-language novels set in Colorado mining country exemplify the Swedes' enduring fascination with the West. The first, *Guldgrävarna* (The prospectors), written by Nebraskan Leonard Strömberg and published in Uppsala, Sweden, in 1923, includes among its characters Svensk Erik, who helps two greenhorns learn how to prospect and mine at Cripple Creek, Colorado. The second, *Colorado Avenue*, written by Lars Sund in 1991, focuses on the much more realistic story of a Swedish-Finnish boarding-house owner and her husband, a Swedish union organizer, in Telluride, Colorado. The novel depicts, through storytelling sessions on the boarding-house veranda, the workers and how they've been influenced by the myth of the West:

> They tell about prospectors who made fantastic gold strikes and became wealthy overnight. And about clever con men who cheated the gold miners out of their mines at the poker table. And about grizzly bears and wolves. And about human vultures, desperados and gunmen like the young Billy the Kid and Jesse James and Butch Cassidy, who once robbed the bank here in Telluride.[10]

Both these fictional works avail themselves of the stuff of Western myth: gold prospecting, gambling, and facing dangerous animals and men, all of which portray the West as a dangerous place where one could be transformed.

But the constellation of mythic images and their use in narrative is never a single message simply passed along and passively received. Cultural myth is more nuanced. A good example is found in Øverland's work exploring myths that developed specifically within immigrant communities as a way of making a rhetorical claim on the group's part in shaping American history and culture. He points to "homemaking myths" of foundation, blood sacrifice, ideological gifts, and ethnic heroes. An immigrant's claim to being a Westerner can be seen as a variation on Øverland's first homemaking myth, foundation, in which immigrants lay claim to the place where they find themselves by saying, in essence, "we were here first or at least as early as you were."[11]

This is the sense with which we can interpret Hjalmar Johnsson's words. Johnsson imagines himself as "going native," and through association with American Indians lays claim to being not just an American but an indigenous Westerner, transformed by the region into a rugged individual who is at home in the new region. This is one aspect of going native, as defined by Shari M. Huhndorf, using "noble Indian life" as "a means of escaping a degenerate and corrupt white world.... By adopting Indian ways, the socially alienated character uncovers his own 'true' identity and redeems European-American society."[12] The claim is similar to the one portrayed, for example, in Teddy Roosevelt's celebrated transformation from Easterner to Western rancher and big game hunter;[13] however, Johnsson's claim is not just regional but more specifically indigenous.

Another of the Swedish letter writers uses this same image of going native. Bernhard Rydberg of Red Lodge, Montana, was an enthusiastic outdoorsman who describes many adventures in the Montana mountains at the turn of the century. On Sundays, he relates, "I am almost always out in the countryside, and to go there is both good and healthy and so I usually take a bath in the river and run about like an Indian."[14] He explains that the water in Rock Creek, where he bathes, is very fresh and cold, having melted from the snow-clad mountains above; hence the need for activity after bathing.

In reality, these men's self-descriptions were something of a pose. Johnsson was training as a soldier in an era well beyond American Indian battles, and Rydberg suffered bouts of ill health.[15] His life was, in fact, town-centered. He was a business owner in Red Lodge, and he maintained an active social life that included events at the Elks Lodge. His time in the mountains was purely recreational.

Johnsson's and Rydberg's use of the American Indian image is a positive interpretation of the idea of going native, as if to say that the West transformed them into healthier, more resilient beings. The image is part of a nuanced myth of the West that incorporates, as we shall see later in this chapter, a number of values outside those more violent and confrontational images promoted in the Western novel and the Wild West show, although the latter ideas are also present in Swedish letters.

Johnsson and Rydberg imagine themselves as American Indians rather than cowboys. Other significant images associated with the West by Swedish writers are the Western landscape, especially its mountains; characters such as the prospector, the pathfinder, the outlaw, the innocent maiden, and the vigilante; and scenes such as the holdup, the gathering around a campfire, the journey through a mountain pass, and the discovery of gold.

The Western landscape strongly impressed the Swedes who traveled there. The region and its landscapes dominate the earliest reports of letter writers as they first arrived in the Rockies, expressing in commonplace language that they see the region as liminal, a place on the border between civilized and uncivilized space, between farmland and wilderness. We see this imagined geographical placement of the region in the letter writers' use of locational prepositions. Most commonly, the letter writers place the West *ute* (out), signifying that the region was far away from more central and more significant places.

John A. Leonard writes in 1887 that he is "out among the wild mountains" in Kingston, New Mexico. He suggests that having been in the West quite some time (in his case, at least since 1881) had consequences, made one become "more negligent and nonchalant in fulfilling the obligations of friendship to relatives in your home place."[16] Working on railroad construction in Helena, Montana, in 1891, John Reed planned to stay "out here in the West until this railroad track is done."[17] In 1892 Jacob Lundquist expresses how much he and his brother miss their sister Ellen since her return to Sweden: "We two poor creatures out here in the far West will miss her more than we can say."[18] In 1893 Anni Dickson found herself "out in Colorado," where she was unhappy about both the rugged terrain and the people—even the Swedes, who were "stuck-up."[19] Aron W. Johnson had a much more positive experience in Wyoming, where he enjoyed the expanse of desert lands "out away from the railroad."[20] Bernhard Rydberg writes that he is "out in the West" in 1906. Ruing that he might not be in Montana much longer, he planned a trip to revisit some of the mountainous countryside.[21]

Not only was the West imagined as outside of the settled world, it was also *upp* (up) for those settlers located in the most mountainous parts of the region. Hjalmar Johnsson perceived that he was "up in the Colorado mountains" when he reached the West in 1917.[22] Several times throughout his letters, Rydberg describes his travels "up among the Rocky Mountains."[23] Like Rydberg, Peter Peterson and Olof Larsson expressed the idea they were "among" (*ibland*) or "in the midst of" (*emellan*) the mountains, as if isolated by mountainous barriers on all sides.[24]

Whether understood as out, up, or among the mountains, the West was far away from the eastern portions of America that were more familiar to the Swedish audience for the letters. The writers tell their Swedish relatives that what could be easily found in the East, such as rail travel, was nonexistent in parts of the West. Aron W. Johnson, who from 1893 to 1905 owned a sheep ranch near Wamsutter, Wyoming, tried repeatedly to explain to his fiancée Anna how far he was from ready transportation and mail service: "I am so far away from the railroad that I cannot write as regularly as you wish."[25]

A few of the writers emphasize a view of the West as distant and isolated from the East by using the epithet cited above from Jacob Lundquist: "the far West." Lundquist wrote in both Swedish and English to two of his sisters, one of whom had lived for many years in America before returning to Sweden. In a letter written in Swedish, he carefully translates the epithet as "*fjerran* West."[26] Swan Smith also uses this epithet in a letter written from Idaho Springs, Colorado.[27]

The more common modifier for the West emphasizes its lack of civilization and its remoteness. For most of the writers, the West is "wild." As we have seen, this term for the West was current in Sweden in such publications as *Vilda Vestern*. Aron W. Johnsson reminds Anna, who apparently had complained again about not receiving letters often enough, "I am in the Wild West. I have now 5 Swedish miles [31¼ English miles, or 50 kilometers] out to the nearest railroad station and I cannot come any closer for 2 months."[28] In another letter to Anna, Aron calls Wyoming *wildmarken* (the wild domain). But he goes on to attempt to quell her apprehensions about the wildness of the West: "Beloved friend, you should not worry so much about me. We are doing fairly well here."[29]

For others, the West was a "wild country." "This is a wild country," J. Edward Wiberg writes from Bozeman, Montana, to his brother. "I would like to see you come up here, but you are better off down there, because there you don't always have to walk around with a revolver in your pocket."[30] Charles Flodin also uses the phrase "wild country," to refer to the area outside of Dolores, Colorado, where he was working.[31] The mountains were also characterized as wild, as in John A. Leonard's already-quoted phrase "out among the wild mountains."

The West's wildness stands in contrast not just to civilization, but also to agrarian values. For Clara Jeppsson, who brought rural values to her judgment of the West, the terrain had proven either too alkaline or too easily leached of nutrients to be of any use for agriculture. The abandoned farmland in LaJara was not just wild but also a "waste."[32]

This view of the West as remote and wild is encapsulated in one particular image: the mountains. Mountains are mentioned by most letter writers and are emphasized by some writers in letter after letter. This is not at all surprising, given that most of the Swedes who came to the northern Rockies approached from the east. Those entering Montana, Colorado, or Wyoming would have experienced a view of the front range rising 5,000 or more feet above the plains. Those living in the mountains would have also experienced the thin air at elevations over 10,000 feet, in places like Leadville, Colorado. Added to this impressive height and elevation was the Rockies' ruggedness, with a good portion of stone spine above alpine tree level, making the Western mountains decidedly different from any mountains the immigrants would have seen in Sweden or in the eastern United States.

These distinctive features of the Western mountains allowed writers to use the image of mountains both metonymically, as a part for the whole, and metaphorically, using physical features to represent certain qualities associated with the West. As a part of the whole, mountains receive frequent mention as a location for the writer, especially when the writer has recently relocated to the West and writes to family and friends in Sweden specifying the new location as "up in the Rockies." When John A. Leonard moved to Leadville, Colorado, from Kirkland, Illinois, in 1881, he wrote to his brother-in-law in Sweden, "When you first glance at this letter you will discover that I have moved to another place here in this country, 1500 eng. [English] miles west of Chicago to the mountain country of Colorado."[33]

Metonymically, the image of mountains can be used to stand for the entire region. Writing that one is "up in the Rockies" or "up in the mountains" can mean "I am here in this mountainous region, the West." However, there is a second sense in which the same phrase was employed: it was used more specifically to recognize that the West was not an indivisible whole, that there were rural-urban divisions within the West. "Up in the mountains" can mean a location within the West that is away from town. Thus, Charles Flodin tells his friend Anders in an 1895 letter: "Last summer I was in the mountains and prospecting."[34] Similarly, August Peterson writes that he is "here among mountains and hills"[35] doing railroad construction in Montana, and Charles M. Bloomberg of Leadville, Colorado, writes that his mining work has taken him away from home "up in the mountains."[36]

If one was up in the mountains away from town, the mountains could be perceived as a barrier to both communication and transportation. We have already seen that Peter Peterson and Olof Larsson saw themselves as surrounded by mountains. Bengt Olson Brodin comments on the practical effects, as several feet of snow in 1884 meant that "we can hardly get the mail out here to the mountains."[37] The postal service, agriculture, a smelter, a carpentry shop: however positively or negatively conceived, these are the trappings of settled urban society. By repeatedly using the image of mountains, the letter writers evoke their distance from society: from Western centers like Denver, or the eastern United States, or Sweden.

In this more specifically located mountain West, "up in the mountains" conveys physical distance and separation from a locus of activity. While Flodin's prospecting would have presented a more isolated situation, August Peterson and Charles M. Bloomberg were apparently part of work crews, but in all cases these men were isolated from town life, and in Bloomberg's case, his family as well. They were all happy to return from the mountains.

On the other hand, town-bound workers like Bernhard Rydberg intentionally made the opposite pilgrimage, seeking out the natural beauty and resources of the mountains as participants in the beginnings of a Western recreational movement. Peter Peterson of Gunnison, Utah, and John Swanson of Denver also left town and traveled "up in the mountains" in pursuit of recreation. During summer months, Peterson left his carpentry work and his farm fields to enjoy the coolness of the Wasatch Mountains, to which he could easily travel from his home in the valley:

> I want to tell you that I was up in the mountains some time ago. It is so pretty that you cannot describe it. The grass is so [thick] that you can barely get through it and [everywhere] flowers. The cattle can barely be sighted for the grass. There is nearly an endless expanse that is only forest and grass and whoever can take whatever they want, there is so much.[38]

In this passage, Peterson expresses the beauty of the nearby mountains and his perception of the abundance of natural resources available in the Wasatch, resources he viewed as freely available to his community.

During a time when he had several days free from work, John M. Swanson of Denver enjoyed a trip to Cripple Creek, where the clean air contrasted with the sulfurous smoke he was exposed to daily at the Argo smelter:

> You can imagine that it feels good for someone . . . [who works
> exposed to smelting fumes to be able to] feel like a real human
> being. The first days we went out to the parks around Denver and
> then we traveled to a town called Cripple Creek. It lies high up in
> the mountains.[39]

During another layoff from work, Swanson enjoyed a summer with many
fishing trips: "I have had such a good time this summer so I have never
had such a good time. . . . Peter Jonson visits us often, we have fished
many times this summer."[40]

These writers equate "up in the mountains" with being away from
work in a pleasant and relaxing place where nature offers up her bounty;
their journey was a pilgrimage seeking what could not be found in town.
In this usage, the image of mountains represents more than just geographical distance. It represents emotional distance as well, serving as a metaphor for the barrier of distance separating the writer from a more heavily
populated environment. Even as a locational index, then, the mountain
image presents us with a system of reference that is more nuanced than a
simple one-to-one identification of mountains equal West.

The splendor of the Rockies makes phrases such as "up in the mountains" sound like bland commonplaces, but the correspondents also use
the mountains to represent several qualities that they set up in opposition to urban society. In so doing, the writers bring the mountains to
life for their readers. For different writers the mountains are variously
beautiful, troublingly unfamiliar, wild and dangerous, isolated, salubrious, bountiful, or inspirational. Anni Dickson, who traveled in 1893 to
Red Cliff, Colorado, near present-day Aspen, was especially troubled by
the mountainous terrain that surrounded her there, as if there were "no
end to them."[41] For her, the landscape was nothing like Sweden, and "not
beautiful."[42] As much as John M. Swanson relished his fishing trips, he
found the mountains frightening. The mining town of Cripple Creek is
a 110-mile trip from Denver. In 1906, Swanson and his party could reach
the town via a railway route that would today merit the label *scenic*: "It is
frightening to see, on one side [of the train] you can see [a] many thousand feet high mountain wall and on the other side of the train you see
several thousand feet down into the valley."[43]

But Dickson's and Swanson's responses are unusual. Most of the im-

The railroads linking Colorado's mining communities wound through steep canyons. This is the Florence and Cripple Creek Railroad at Phantom Canyon, 1895. Photograph courtesy of the Denver Public Library, Western History Collection, call number X-22240.

migrants perceived the mountains' ruggedness as beautiful. In Leadville, Colorado, John A. Leonard recognized the mountains' differences from the gentle agricultural land of the East while also appreciating the mountains: "There is no farmland here in sight, only sky-high mountains and hills everywhere, which are partly populated by old pine forest."[44] Bernhard Rydberg frequently visited the mountains near Red Lodge, Montana, for "the glorious view, the majestic mountains."[45]

Some writers emphasize aesthetic reactions to the mountains through figures of speech or through narratives, using the mountains as a setting. Charles Flodin anthropomorphizes the landscape in a long narrative about a prospecting trip into the central Idaho mountains near the town of Warren, Idaho, which experienced a rush late in the gold-mining era. Flodin traveled into this isolated and rugged area in 1890 with a Civil War veteran and prospector. During their journey, the mountains presented a tremendous impasse to travel, but Flodin and his companion, whom he calls *Kaptenen* (the Captain), were rewarded not by a gold strike but by the view:

> And over mountains, valleys, wind-felled trees, creeks, and marshes we went but our toil and trouble were well rewarded. Here our admiring gaze met the prettiest view I have ever laid eyes on. You could see a meadow with rich, natural foliage where the wild grass reached a height of many feet. The surroundings of high, majestic mountains, melancholy and gloomy, gazed down on the smiling valley. And to make the picture more complete, in the heart of it the aforementioned river, like an artery slow and quiet, flowed giving life to the whole.[46]

Flodin goes beyond describing scenic beauty to associate other qualities with the mountainous terrain. The mountains are beautiful but also melancholy. They are majestic and gloomy, contrasting with the green valley below. For other writers, the mountains could even be exotic. Bernhard Rydberg compares them to the Alps of Switzerland and the pyramids of Egypt.[47] John A. Leonard compares them to the abode of Tegnér's giants:

> In this wild mountain area you live, like Tegnér says about the Giant [*Jätten*]: I live in the halls of the mountain, deep below the earth, where Odin's eye can never reach with his beam etc.—because many people work several hundred feet under ground by a light.[48]

A significant quality that the immigrants assign to the mountains and to the West in general is salubrity. During this period of time, the Western climate was perceived as healthy because of its clear air and sunshine, and places like Denver marketed themselves to attract tubercular and asthmatic patients.[49] The Swedish immigrants express this same perception of the region. Rydberg felt that his Sunday rides out into the countryside and his dips in cold mountain water were "both good and healthy." He traveled to a health resort northwest of Red Lodge, Montana, the Hunter's Hot Springs, and in 1901 reports to his mother that "there is a wonderful hot sulfur spring here that comes up out of the ground and the water is quite boiling. Strangely enough. We drink the warm sulfur water and bathe in it.... I think it is fun ... and besides it does a person much good."[50]

Victor A. Hallquist had moved West seeking better health, and for a time the region met his expectations. In 1897 he writes to his father: "I want to tell you now how I have been since I came to Colorado. Then I have become completely well, I am now as thick and fat as when I left Sweden and strong—I work every day."[51] Living in Leadville, Colorado, Johan Håkansson claims a similar health transformation: "I have been so well since I came to the mountains that you would not recognize me when you see me again, for I am so fat and hale that you [will] not believe it."[52] Both men's comments reflect a nineteenth-century image of healthiness, using the term *tjock* (thick). To be fat or stout was a sign of health and wealth. Hence, we see the expression *tjock och fet* (thick and fat) used very positively by the letter writers.

Another image further enhances the perception of the mountains as bountiful, isolated, mysterious, and covered with *eviga snö* (everlasting snow). Viewing nature as a resource, Peter Peterson emphasizes that the snowpack up in the mountains will provide summer water. He writes: "Up in the mountains is much snow, and that is riches for Utah because then we get water for the summer."[53] For Charles Flodin, as we earlier saw with Bengt Olson Brodin, the snow could be isolating. Flodin complains of a snowstorm during which he had to don snowshoes in order to get to the post office, and even then ended up sliding there on his buttocks.[54] Writing during July from Bozeman, Montana, J. Edward Wiberg marvels that "up on the mountain some miles farther up lies snow as cold as the coldest winter."[55]

The beauty and mystery of the mountains also evoked a religious response from the letter writers. Leonard Nilsson used his mountain walks as a substitute for the kind of spiritual renewal that others would have sought from church services:

> The summer is warm; over the mountains and the valleys, the sun shines, giving life and warmth to all of nature. It is so beautiful and glorious everywhere. When I get up onto some of the nearby mountains, with their extensive views, then I am really myself. Then I forget the adversities you have to fight now and then; I am

seized with admiration—delighted by the life heard around me
and everything in my sight is harmony.[56]

According to Nilsson, "the church that is called nature"[57] is his solace in
his loneliness and longing for Lovisa and in his isolation from Swedish
society. It is there he finds harmony.

Thus, a cluster of interrelated qualities is associated with the image of
the mountains, presenting us with a sense of how the Swedish immigrants
perceived the Western region. At the heart of the immigrant response is
the nineteenth-century aesthetic of the sublime, in which nature was depicted as having the power to awe with its dramatic contrasts of scale,
of beauty and wildness, and of scenes of gentle nurturing grass against
jagged peaks, like the Idaho valley described by Flodin. By the time that
these Swedish immigrants came to the West, the region had already been
interpreted as sublime through the well-known canvases of the German-
trained artist Albert Bierstadt, who painted mountain scenes of Yosemite
and the Rockies during the 1860s.[58]

The formulas and images used by the immigrants to describe the West
produce a mixed view, neither entirely glowing nor entirely negative. A
couple of images used by the writers bring this mixed response into focus:
fireplace or campfire scenes and firearms. These are contrasting images,
with the former signifying companionable male communities formed in
the midst of wilderness, and the latter signifying the ever-present threat
of violence. Leonard Nilsson describes for Lovisa Borg a charming scene:
"the warming fire, which with its cheering sparks, and crackle, lifts my
spirits a little bit, as I sit alone in my little cabin."[59] But Nilsson sits alone
at his fire; he uses the image to suggest the potential for companionship
that was missing from his circumstances. A writer who experienced companionship around a campfire was Bernhard Rydberg, who valued David
Smethurst's company during the many trips they took into the country
around Red Lodge, Montana. Describing one such trip, Rydberg writes
that after supper they sat around their campfire smoking cigarettes, telling
stories, and singing. Rydberg demonstrates his self-conscious enjoyment
of this Western scene by reflecting that it was all "quite Romantic."[60]

Balancing these scenes that suggest the possibility of establishing peaceful, albeit all-male, communities in the West are those in which the image
of firearms suggests the ever-present possibility of violence. As Edward J.

Wiberg tells his brother, perhaps he shouldn't move West; where his brother is in the Midwest, he does not have to carry a gun with him wherever he goes. The sight of firearms must have been striking to the immigrants. John A. Leonard writes of New Mexico in 1881:

> Here there is little or no cultivation and settlement. It is not a state yet, only a so-called territory, that means that the land here is wild and free for whoever to take and settle, no governor and no state laws that protect the individual, rather he has himself to protect himself and his weapons are—rifles and revolvers, objects which are every man's constant companions.[61]

Leonard makes the contrast clear: the possibility of settlement versus the possibility of violence. Both are present in the West, but they are out of balance.

In a few of the letters, the writers go beyond using commonplace language and briefly citing images to develop stories that dramatize their experience in the West. In earlier chapters we viewed storytelling in response to work and nationality, and we will encounter a few examples of stories in response to religious experience in chapter 7. But the Western region especially inspired storytelling by the letter writers.

Two accounts of killings illustrate the range of story development, from brief mention in which as few as two actions are sequenced, to more fully developed storytelling with a sequence of actions that are structured to impart a theme. In the first example, Olof Larsson writes in 1906 from Kellogg, Idaho, that "among the news that I have to tell you is that Blekings Claes, who served at Nels Person No. 9 [a farm address in Sweden] was shot and killed by a policeman in a bar in Wallace Idaho this fall."[62] A brief account like this one leaves the reader with numerous questions: Why was Claes shot? Had he been involved in a crime? Was there an altercation with another bar patron? Who else was present? What were his last words? Why was he in Wallace, Idaho? Larsson, however, does not develop this episode into a meaningful story.

By contrast, Victor A. Hallquist's stories provide much fuller narratives. In 1900 he writes to his brother Johan: "this is not a nice place [Denver] because here are daily accidents and murders. Most murderers go free."[63] He goes on to tell a gruesomely violent tale:

An 18-year-old Negro took a 14-year-old girl when she was driving
to the post office with a letter, he forced her off the buggy with a
knife, then he raped her. When she began to scream, he cut her in
the legs, then he stabbed her with the knife in the chest. The knife
was not big enough so he had hard work to kill her. He burned his
shirt in order not to be discovered. When the horse had waited
for a while, he turned around and went home. The father's name is
Foster, probably a Scandinavian, immediately went back along the
road and found his daughter a little from the road near death. She
was an only child. She lived 3 hours, all that she said was "mama
here I am."

They set bloodhounds after the murderer, tracked [and] found
him in Denver. 3 days later at the jail he confessed that he had
murdered her and thought that he would not be discovered. He
begged for forgiveness and his father and brother pled for him but
the so-called authorities abandoned him to the people. 700 people
were gathered and at the same place that he killed the girl they
set up an iron rail and bound him. Near it then they had a vote
over whether they should burn him or hang him, but the majority
voted to burn him. He stood there from 3 till 5 o'clock, during that
time he begged the people to forgive him and begged them to hang
him. He prayed to God to forgive him and prayed to God for the
people that they not fall into such a great sin. The Salvation Army
spoke with him about God. At 5 o'clock the father of the girl lit
the fire and they burned him until he died and then burned up
his body. *Such is the life here.*[64]

Such was life in the West as Hallquist perceived it: a godless place of violence. Hallquist does not comment on the obvious racial issues raised by
this accusation against a black boy for a crime against a white girl, and his
lynching by a white crowd. He does, however, appear to be offended both
by the crime itself and by the ethics of vigilante justice. He devotes attention to each through detailed description. First, he describes the girl's abduction at knifepoint, and blow-by-blow, her death; second, he describes
the detection and abduction of the boy, and the suspenseful vote over his

fate, conducted within his hearing. Near death, each victim speaks for herself/himself: the girl calling to her mother, and the boy to his God.

A devout Baptist, Hallquist emphasizes the Christlike image of the boy bound to a rail, praying not just for himself but also for the people who plan to commit the sin of killing him. He uses religious language for the idea of forgiveness—*förlåtelse*—repeating the word three times, and he uses *att be* (to pray) for the boy's and his family members' pleas, as well as for the boy's prayers. Additionally, Hallquist emphasizes the idea of the victims' last words, quoting the girl and paraphrasing the boy, whose sentiments would have been important to Hallquist as proof of the boy's salvation. This is a theme we will see again in Hallquist's religious story-telling, in chapter 7.

The Christlike image of the boy bound to a rail was available to Hallquist in an illustration run in the *Denver Times*, which reported on the event on November 17, 1900. The lynching received wide coverage in the Denver press. The young man, John Preston Porter Jr., who was sixteen years old rather than eighteen, had been detained by the Denver police on circumstantial evidence. After four days in jail and threats of lynching his father and brother as well as himself, the boy confessed to having raped and killed Louise Frost (not Foster, and age twelve, not fourteen). As Hallquist describes, Porter was burned to death near the scene of the crime. The incident was decried in the national press.[65]

Undoubtedly, Hallquist heard about this lynching, and perhaps he read of it in the local English-language newspapers (it did not appear in Denver's *Svenska Korrespondenten*), but the lapses in accuracy of specific details, as they were reported in the press, suggest that he wrote from memory. Hallquist crafts the events into a compelling story in which his main theme—this is not a nice place—is illustrated by violent acts, especially by the violence of lynching. Here and elsewhere, Hallquist structures his storytelling in parallel sections. In this case, the two-part structure places the main actors in corresponding positions. In the first half of the story, the boy is the perpetrator of violence and the girl the victim; in the second, the mob is the perpetrator of violence and the boy the victim. Through these parallels, Hallquist implies that both the girl and the boy can be seen as victims of Western violence, and he raises the possibility of the boy's innocence. He also implies that the crime committed by the lynchers is not really justice, but rather is equivalent to the crimes of rape and murder.

Hallquist is one of a few letter writers, all of them men, who tend to use narratives frequently in their letters. Although we cannot know whether these men were storytellers in their daily lives, we can suspect so, based on the evidence in the letters, in which these men demonstrate a regular tendency to narrate experience rather than to merely report it. We can call these men "epistolary raconteurs," and they include several letter writers already quoted in this chapter and in previous chapters: Leonard Nilsson, Charles Flodin, and Bernhard Rydberg, who were single men living in mining camps or towns; Victor A. Hallquist and Peter Peterson, who were deeply religious men, both carpenters, married, and living, respectively, in a city and in a Mormon village; John M. Swanson, who was a Denverite and a smelter worker; and Gottfrid Johnson, who was a laborer on his uncle and aunt's southern Colorado ranch. All except Flodin and Johnson mention reading newspapers and poetry; Hallquist and Peterson also mention reading the Bible and the Book of Mormon. As with the repertoires of oral storytellers, their repertoires of epistolary stories focus on different concerns that reflect each man's interests, but all of them write at least a few stories reflecting on the Western region.

Their view of the West is as mixed as that of the formulas and images already discussed. They express an awe and appreciation of the beauty of their surroundings, but they also deal with the serious issues of crime and physical danger. Their anecdotes and personal-experience stories emphasize misfortune and adventure, expressing the dangers that they perceived in the Western region, dangers that offset positive traits like salubrity. Because a shift into narrative is a marker of the significance of a subject, we can see the presence of these stories about the West as indicating the storytellers' view that the region was dangerous territory.

Misfortune stories set in the West range from accounts of startling current events to personal accounts of the deaths of close relatives. Whatever the scale, location, or degree of personal knowledge, these stories share a message of potential danger. A boy is trampled by an elephant from a visiting circus; an avalanche kills a group of hikers; a miner dies from gas released in a mine; illness takes the life of a beloved wife or mother. Perhaps most unpredictable is crime: a trusted physician has to flee town,

accused of a nameless crime; a bank is robbed; a respected Mormon em-
bezzles money. These incidents are dramatic enough to move writers to
tell stories.

The story of the respected Mormon who embezzled money was reported by Gottfrid Johnson, who wrote to his parents and siblings in 1914
from La Jara, Colorado:

> folks around here are in an uproar about a slender man by the
> name of Cristenson, a leader in the Mormon church and also a
> cashier in a bank, and he has embezzled significant sums they say
> 100,000 from the bank and the church and particularly how he
> cleaned out many of his religious friends, after which he ran away,
> he was caught down in Texas and is expected to come home soon
> and many seem to want to lynch him.[66]

As with nearly all of the misfortune stories, this story is an anecdote
rather than a personal-experience story. As third-person narratives, anecdotes have by definition a more detached tone, and the dangers narrated
are hypothetical. Nonetheless, the overall effect is a sense of anxiety about
the West and, more specifically, about one's ability to remain out of danger, whole and healthy, while living in the region.

Hallquist was especially concerned about danger in the West. He saw
himself as having traveled to "the far west,"[67] and although religious sentiments, family news, and news of the Swedish population in Denver takes
up most of his letters, his writing is also peppered with references to the
gold mines and anecdotes about crime. In 1898 he wrote to his brother:

> I can also tell you that many have been murdered here in Denver
> last week 3 pharmacies and one jewelry *store* were *robbed.* Murder-
> ers always have a revolver in each hand, one stays outside and one
> goes in, when he gets in he orders hands up. Those who do not
> raise their hands immediately will get shot, then he orders them
> to go out with him behind the *store* with the hands up. Then
> he orders them to stand together, then he takes the revolver in
> one hand and holds it pointed at them, with the other hand he
> picks their pockets, then he orders them to turn around or to sit

down while he walks away. There is no point in saying anything or putting your hands down because then it is all over. A Swede has been murdered in Denver, the police have not been able to catch anybody but they have now gotten bloodhounds to track with and more police have been sent here.[68]

For Hallquist, this was not just a colorful local incident; rather, it directly involved Denver's Swedish American community, since one of the victims was Swedish.[69] Hallquist offers the anecdote, then, as evidence not just of the wildness of the West but also of the Swedish community's part in confronting that wildness.

Stories of adventure feature excursions into the mountainous land surrounding the towns where the correspondents had settled. These trips might be for recreation, as in Bernhard Rydberg's accounts, or for prospecting, which was Charles Flodin's preoccupation. The stories celebrate the Western landscape as both beautiful and awe inspiring, but their tone shifts toward the sober and serious at points where they acknowledge that alongside beautiful views the landscape poses inherent dangers. To a certain extent, these stories overlap with the misfortune stories in their concern with potential mishaps: mountain roads are steep and winding, a rich vein of ore might be too high in the mountains to be extracted, revisiting a mine left abandoned might require days of travel through uncharted territory, a fishing trip might be interrupted by a spectacular thunderstorm.

In the middle of a letter to his mother written in 1901, in which we experience a shift from a humorous mood to one that is more troubled, Rydberg tells the tale of the fishing trip interrupted by a thunderstorm. He begins by stating that he has sent his mother photographs from a camping trip he took to a place twenty-five miles from Red Lodge:

> The place we wanted to go to is a spot high up in the mountains with many lakes, and a very beautiful place. It is cold up there even in the summer and the mountaintops are covered with snow. It is almost like the Alps in Switzerland. We each had a saddle horse and I rode "Rex." . . . We had a tent with us. We had four mules for our things and provisions and one of them we called the "brewery" and that mule had the most responsible position because she had the honor of bearing the beer and spirits.[70]

Rydberg and his friend Smethurst fished, hiked, and admired the view. After their supper of fish, ham, English plum pudding, and other delicacies, the two men sat around their campfire. As Rydberg continues his tale to his mother, he whisks the reader from this peaceful sociable scene to the sublime experience of a mountain thunderstorm:

> One night there was such a terrible thunderstorm and as it was
> high up among the mountains, we were nearly up in the heart
> of the storm, so lightning flashed and crashed and thundered as
> though the earth would go to pieces. It was the most frightening
> thunder I have heard. Sometimes during the lightning flashes
> we could see the lake and the mountains with forests and it was
> beautiful, but almost scary.[71]

Adventure stories like Rydberg's are personal-experience stories, and as first-person accounts they have much more immediacy than the anecdotal misfortune stories. When they include dangers like a thunderstorm, the reader experiences with the writer the uncertainties of the Western environment, even if she has never heard thunder echoing around a mountain cirque.

Charles Flodin's letters include a combination of his personal experiences and several anecdotes about the Captain. According to Flodin, this colorful character had been rich,

> but now he is poor as a church mouse [literally, church rat]. A
> woman whom he had married destroyed the whole lot, he claimed,
> also she went so far in diabolical immodesty as to attempt to take
> his life by poisoning the old man's coffee. He got a good dose. But
> was tough and lived through it. So now he is afraid of Calicos
> [women].[72]

Flodin and the Captain's journey into the mountains between Boise and Warren, Idaho, took them to an area where the Captain and four others had sought gold in 1865, "though the Indians in that area were restless. And [the party] had to flee from them." Their 1890 return to the area was "through ancient forests and over rivers, ice, and snow-covered mountains. Many miles we had to clear a way for ourselves and the horses with axes."

The journey concluded with their finding "both gold and adventure. But in the absence of water we could never profit" from the discovery. That is, working the deposits was not feasible without plentiful water for placering or hydraulics.[73] Flodin portrays himself and the Captain as pathfinders and prospectors up against the American Indians and nature itself, and his anecdotes take on the flavor of legends current in his era: the Lady Bluebeard story of a woman who kills her husbands, and the lost-mine stories about an elusive, very rich lode.[74]

During his early years in Montana, Rydberg also portrays himself as a pathfinder. Rydberg did much of his riding and hiking with Smethurst. On one occasion, they came upon a waterfall and lake that were unidentified, and they named them Lake Rydberg and David's Falls. They photographed their "discovery," making certain that the local newspaper knew of it. They also reproduced some of their photographs on postcards— among the several such frontier-themed postcards that Rydberg sent to his mother. Rydberg brags to his mother that the lake and waterfall are on the Montana map with the names that he and Smethurst gave them.[75]

Images sent home in photographs and postcards augment the letters' many references to the Wild West. Rydberg's photographs were candid, but it was also possible to send one's relatives studio photographs in which one posed as a Westerner, standing in a saloon; dressed in hat, kerchief, chaps, and gun belt; and brandishing firearms, lasso, knife, and beer bottle. Waldemar Holmberg posed with his buddies in just such a studio photograph. Posted above the bar are signs that make the message explicit: "Wild West Bar," "Hello Pard," and "Check your guns."[76]

The letter collections and enclosed photographs establish that many of the Swedish immigrants were aware of the myth of the West. But beyond awareness, some of the immigrants were avid participants, casting themselves as pathfinders in the Wild West. They emphasized the dangers of the region over other concerns, and herein lies a major theme in the body of folk expression contained within the letters, one potentially instructive to historians of the Swedish immigration to the West. The stories of adventure and mishap work to efface distinctions between the Swedish immigrant and other Westerners. By saying they were "out in the Wild West" or "like redskins," the Swedish immigrants could lay claim to being part of the frontier, "in on" a defining moment in American history, and perhaps a little dangerous themselves.

This regional myth of foundation makes the stories of Swedish letter writers very like the English-language stories gathered by folklorist Barbara Allen Bogart in her collection *In Place*, in which storytellers portray themselves as changing through contact with the Western environment by developing what they call "grit." As we have seen in preceding chapters, the Swedish immigrants to the West could cite multiple sources of change as they adapted to the American milieu, not just to the region. But, grittiness, going native, being out West, and being up in the Rockies were important parts of the mix.

SEVEN

"God's Good Gift"

RELIGIOUS LANGUAGE IN THE ROCKY MOUNTAIN LETTERS

❧

The Lord be with you and help you. I now through a few lines
want to let you know that I am healthy to the moment of writing
this, the Lord be praised, and I wish you the same good [gift]
which the Lord with his great grace gives us poor sinners and
[He] does not remove his helping hand from us, but always
stands prepared and willing to help us.

Peter Anderson, 1889, Cheyenne, Wyoming

WITH THESE WORDS, Peter Anderson addressed his aunt and uncle
in an 1889 letter written from Cheyenne, Wyoming.[1] Anderson's
use of religious formulas stands out as unusual within the letter collections from the Rocky Mountain West. He is one among a minority of
the correspondents who weave religious language into the letters or who
include religious issues in the contents. About one-quarter of the letter
writers devote attention to religion in some way, but only fourteen of those
writers use the kind of formulaic language displayed in Anderson's letter.
For these writers, religion was very important, significant enough to be
expressed as an orientation in addition to the categories we have already
examined: class and occupation, nation and ethnicity, and region. It is appropriate, then, to devote a chapter to this minority group, the roughly
one in five of the writers who use pious language in their letters.

Anderson's religious language is based in the Church of Sweden's
Lutheran liturgy. During Anderson's era, the expression *Herren vare med
eder* (may the Lord be with you) was sung by pastors of this denomination, to which the congregation answered *Med dig vare ock Herren!*[2] A

literal translation of this response is "With you also may the Lord be!" but we could render it more familiar to twenty-first-century American Lutherans as "And also with you."

This apostolic greeting appears throughout the New Testament; for example, in 2 Thessalonians 3:16: "The Lord be with you all."[3] It is still commonly used by Lutheran and other Protestant groups and among Catholics, along with the New Testament formula "Peace be with you," Jesus's greeting to his disciples (John 20:21). Current-day Lutherans will recognize "Peace be with you" as part of the Lutheran communion service, into which it was adopted in 1978. We find this phrase used during this much earlier period in a few of the immigrant letters from the Rockies.[4]

We might guess, on the basis of Peter Anderson's use of language from Lutheran liturgy, that he was a member of an Augustana Evangelical Lutheran congregation. However, as for most who wrote about religion at the time, Anderson's church affiliation is conjectural. In Cheyenne, Wyoming, an Evangelical Lutheran congregation was founded in 1884, but membership records from 1889 no longer exist, and no Peter Anderson appears in later membership registries.[5] It is entirely possible he was a passive attendee or was just passing through town. Not only were many of the working-class immigrants itinerants, but many who only occasionally attended church were not communicants, and therefore were not listed in membership registries and in congregational statistics.[6]

Generally, less than one-quarter of Swedish immigrants to the United States became members of a church group. Immigrants who were free-thinkers or who had struggled with the oversight of the Church of Sweden enjoyed the freedom of being able to choose church membership or to choose not to join a church at all.[7] Some expressed open hostility. One such freethinker was Leonard Nilsson, who favorably compares religious freedom in the United States to the "earthly majesty with God's blessing" that he experienced in Sweden, where life was dominated by the interwoven authority of the monarchy and the Church of Sweden.[8]

Not surprisingly, Nilsson values secular achievements in his letters: "progressive thinking in all areas, inventive and earnest. In Europe you can never even dream about the enormous progress that characterizes this country."[9] For spiritual renewal, Nilsson turned to nature: "There lies a book open for my eyes, a book of silver, written by 'God's hand' without unreasonable propositions, without contradictions, without untruthful stories. You do not need to know Greek, Hebrew, and Latin to study it; you need no Priests or Proselytes to thank for it. It is open to all."[10] Nilsson's orientation is secular here, yet ironically he is in agreement with those believers who challenged the Church of Sweden's authority and claimed the right and responsibility to interpret the Bible themselves, as "readers."

Like Nilsson, a majority of those Swedes who moved westward were freethinkers unlikely to join churches or to express themselves with religious commonplaces. Cultural geographers describe much of the general Western population as unchurched, and they characterize the religious groups that did exist as diverse and small. Historian Michael Quinn points to fragmentation and balkanization as typical of Western religious groups. The religious settlers who converged on the Rockies were fragmented into numerous sects. Where there were concentrations of fellow believers, religious-ethnic enclaves formed.[11]

For missionaries coming into the West, the male-dominant, working-class, and often itinerant population posed a frustrating challenge, particularly outside of centers like Denver. Congregations were small and far-flung, forcing clergy to travel long distances. Free Church missionary Anders August Anderson's travels through the West make his reminiscences, *Tjugu År i Vilda Västern* (Twenty years in the Wild West), read like a travelogue, in which one finds, for example, excellent descriptions of everyday conditions on Montana ranches juxtaposed with information about missionary activities.

During one winter in the early 1890s, Anderson traveled across Montana. He traveled from the Black Hills of the Dakotas to Miles City in eastern Montana by horse; to Livingston by train, with a forty-mile side trip south to Paradise Valley, near Yellowstone Park; to Helena by train; back to Miles City; and back to the Black Hills by horse. Anderson wraps up a description of this journey of about 1,200 miles by stating: "The condition of the roads was rough, but it began to thaw and we came safely back after a six or seven weeks' absence. [In the segments traveled by horse we] didn't spend any nights sleeping outside, but stayed at '*Cattle Ranches,*' as they call these farms or places, where the large horse- or stock-raising companies have their cowherds (*cowboys*)."[12] Anderson's dedication to missionary work strikes us as we read of the long distances he traveled in winter weather and on rough roads.

The Augustana Evangelical Lutheran Synod made slow progress in its efforts to establish congregations in the Rocky Mountain West. The first congregation listed in the synod's annual reports was the Augustana church established in Denver in 1878. That congregation grew slowly until the 1890s, when the city and its region began to experience more rapid growth. By 1915, at 545 communicants, the Denver church was by far the largest Evangelical Lutheran congregation in the Rockies, and the only Augustana Synod church with more than 300 members. The Denver congregation benefited from the long and continuous services of pastor G. A. Brandelle, who had been in Denver since 1883.

Much more typical was the situation of congregations like those in Boulder and Loveland, with thirty-six and eighty-three communicants respectively, both served during 1909 by A. M. Broleen, who traveled the forty miles between communities; or of the congregations in Idaho Falls (forty communicants), nearby Shelley (fourteen), and Payette (twenty), all served during 1904 by Utah Mission District pastor Charles E. Bengtson, who would have traveled 330 miles between Idaho Falls and Payette; or of

This view of the Swedish Lutheran Church at Twenty-third and Court Place in Denver depicts the building sometime during the first two decades of the twentieth century. Photograph courtesy of the Denver Public Library, Western History Collection, L. D. Regnier, photographer, call number X-25560.

the several Wyoming, Idaho, and Utah congregations reported as having vacant pastoral positions in 1910: Cheyenne, Rock Springs, Coeur d'Alene, Blackfoot, Ogden, Bingham (southwest of Salt Lake City), and Park City.[13] Of course, the Utah and southeastern Idaho region posed special problems to missionaries, since the Mormon church dominated the area.

Clergy of various faiths reported their frustrations. The Swedish Evangelical Mission Covenant missionaries attempting to preach in Montana were thwarted by the lack of a stable, supportive population. Karl A. Olsson, in his history of the Mission Covenanters, notes that "the little chapels must have seemed . . . like insubstantial rafts tossed on a limitless ocean." He cites the example of A. Gustafson, ministering to a Butte congregation in 1901, who declared that Butte was "a nest of Satan filled with sin and shame."[14] A. P. Nelson explained as partly economic the difficulty in establishing meetings in the mining towns of Montana: "the mine work is variable, sometimes up and sometimes down, so people's livings are also unstable."[15] The Baptists had difficulty even in Denver, where, according to Adolf Olson, "the discord of the church and the lack of a sufficiently enthusiastic gain in the membership created a sense of futility in the faithful preacher [Axel Tjernlund]," who resigned in 1900.[16]

In Cheyenne, Wyoming, where Peter Anderson was located, a series of Evangelical Lutheran pastors visited to serve the small group. In 1889 the Nebraska Conference president visited, but "he was not favorably impressed with the field, and he deemed it absolutely inadvisable to make Cheyenne the headquarters for . . . mission work in western Nebraska and Wyoming."[17] Two years later, according to Nebraska Conference history, the congregation still had only twelve members.[18]

These statistics and anecdotes make Denver's Augustana congregation look very successful, and indeed the Augustana Synod Lutherans commanded the greatest share of Swedish Americans who attended or joined churches nationwide: in 1920, about 70 percent of the total of Lutherans, Baptists, Methodists, Mission Covenant church members, and members of Free churches.[19] But a comparison of churchgoers to the total Swedish population puts the Augustana Synod's apparent success in perspective: the 834 communicants, children, and affiliated nonmembers of the two Augustana congregations in Denver formed less than 19 percent of the 4,500 Swedish-born individuals reported in the 1910 census for Denver County.[20]

Quinn suggests that the religious among the Swedish Westerners might represent a particular socioeconomic category.[21] Unfortunately, for the letter writers it is very difficult to follow up on this interesting suggestion. As we have seen with Peter Anderson, not only is the church membership of any one writer very difficult to trace, but also most of those writing about religion cannot be easily identified with respect to social class. Even their particular religious orientation is vague, as discernible from their use of pious rhetoric.

The information that is available is only suggestive. Among the religiously inclined in our sample are those letter writers who were most settled as long-term residents of towns and who were married and raising families. While the writers were mainly from the working class, a few who were especially involved in religious institutions had their own small businesses and can perhaps be seen as middle class, or as aspiring to middle-class status, although they certainly had financial struggles. Men and women are equally balanced in this small Western sample of religious writers.

The letter writers using religious language include Victor A. Hallquist and Anna Hallquist. The couple met at a Baptist church in Boston that held Swedish-language services. Victor had grown up in a pietistic family that had broken with the Church of Sweden.[22] The Hallquists' move westward was prompted by Victor's ill health, one of the many times he suffered illness during his life. In Denver, Victor worked as a carpenter on many projects, including construction of the Swedish Baptist church building. He reports having attended one of Dwight L. Moody's sermons in Denver in 1898 (see appendix). Both Victor's and Anna's letters interpret their experiences within a religious framework.[23]

An interesting parallel to the Hallquists is Peter Peterson. Also a carpenter, Peterson was a Mormon convert who emigrated with his family. In Gunnison, Utah, Peterson was responsible for work on numerous houses and church buildings. And as a faithful church member, he refers to religious principles, though much less frequently than do the Hallquists.[24]

Others who employ religious language include Charles M. Bloomberg, a mine worker in Leadville, Colorado, who wrote on behalf of his wife and children; Jonas Anderson, a retired Denverite who wrote to a brother to reestablish family contacts; John M. Swanson, a married smelter worker in Denver who was a member of the Augustana Synod church;[25] Ola Svenson, head of a family of Mormon converts; and Nils Trulsson, a Mormon convert who wrote to his sweetheart hoping to convince her to convert and to travel to Utah so that they could marry. We know less about other letter writers: Peter F. Erlandson, John Hedin, Genny Andersson, Anna Olson, Charles H. Anderson, and Karna Anderson. But those whose biographies can be deciphered suggest that being settled with a family, regular employment, and perhaps middle-class status or middle-class aspirations were conditions connected to religious activity.

All these writers were Protestant Christians. Raised in a time when being a Swedish citizen also required baptism in the Church of Sweden, they grew up in a culture steeped in Lutheranism. Moreover, if they had departed to join the Baptist or Mormon or Methodist or Swedish Mission Covenant church, they retained language, imagery, and ideas that were Lutheran-based. The Church of Sweden had already, by the time the emigration began, been touched by pietism, and that heritage influenced all the Swedish Protestants in America. Pietism emphasizes the individual's relationship to God, not just through church services but also in daily life, and the individual's personal access to Bible reading and the responsibility for personal conversion, without needing clerical intermediaries or interpreters such as pastors or priests. In Sweden, an early phase of pietism had been incorporated into the Church of Sweden through new hymns that were adapted from a combination of American gospel ideas and Swedish folk tunes. A selection of Swedish folk tunes reappeared in America in the Augustana Synod's 1892 hymnal *Hemlandssånger*.[26] But pietism also encouraged the emerging practice of private Bible study and of holding meetings separately from the Church of Sweden, outside priestly authority.

Among Swedish American churches, several differences over the nature of atonement and the roles of liturgy and baptism were deeply significant to believers. But when we consider issues like the function of religious language in letter writing, the divisions among Evangelical Lutheran, Evangelical Mission Covenant, Free Church, Baptist, Methodist, and Mormon beliefs are less important than what they had in common—the foundation of Protestant Christianity. Letter writers, regardless of their denomination, use pious formulaic expressions in the openings and closings of their letters. They employ images and themes to convey abstract religious principles. They testify and witness to their belief. They sermonize and tell stories with religious morals. In this, their practice is very similar to that of the New England pietistic writers studied by Maria Elizabeth Erling. Erling finds:

The Swedish Lutheran Church choir, Salt Lake City, posed at the altar during Eastertide, 1908. Photograph courtesy of Utah State Historical Society; all rights reserved; Harry Shipler, photographer.

The religious language New Englanders used when they corresponded with friends and family in Sweden did not differ markedly from that used by [Swedish Mission Covenant president] David Nyvall, even though it is clear from their letters that they did not belong to Nyvall's denomination. Swedish Baptists expressed themselves in much the same way as did David Nyvall's Mission Friend Covenanters or devout Augustana Synod Lutherans.[27]

Peter Anderson's religious greeting "The Lord be with you" is often employed within the opening and closing sections of letters, elevating these already ceremonial sections to the status of ritual. Openings and closings become sacred spaces in which relatives separated by an ocean can share their religious beliefs and experiences. Anderson uses the formula immediately after his salutation to his relatives. Ola Svenson, in a letter to his sister, incorporates similar language into the salutation itself: "Dearly beloved sister, live well, the Lord be with you."[28] Nils Trulsson begins a letter to his sweetheart Elna Andersson with thanks for her letter; he continues, "I wish that these lines might meet you and your mother and Nills in the same condition [and] that you all might live a devout life in the presence of our heavenly father."[29]

While Anderson's language suggests that he was Lutheran, Svenson and Trulsson were both Mormon converts. It is interesting, then, to see that Svenson uses the Lutheran-based formula but that Trulsson reinterprets it. Trulsson shifts from *Herren* (the Lord) to *himmelske fader* (a translation of the Mormon term for deity, "heavenly father"), and he uses "live . . . in the presence of" instead of the liturgical "be with you." At the same time, Trulsson preserves the general idea of the Lutheran greeting and positions it similarly in his letter. His letter attempts to create a sacred space in which he and Elna can meet, if only she will accept the Mormon "heavenly father."

Anna Olson and Charles M. Bloomberg use the Pauline variation of this phrase, "Peace be with you." In a letter to his relatives, Bloomberg begins "God's peace be with you all! Is my dearest wish."[30] Anna Olson plays with the placement of this phrase. Even before her greeting, Olson writes at the top of her first page, "God's merciful grace and peace be with you."[31] This variation on "the Lord be with you" reflects Bloomberg's and Olson's apparently pietistic religious view. God's merciful grace (*nåd*) and peace (*frid*) are certainly ideas present in Lutheran liturgy, even preceding "Peace be with you" as part of the Lutheran communion service, but here they receive special emphasis in letters in which both writers take on a tone of testifying by prominently espousing religious belief or a tone of witnessing by connecting testimony to the evidence of personal experience.[32] Anna Olson demonstrates that she is testifying by placing her statement of faith at the top of the first page, outside the generic form in a space of its own. Bloomberg provides the evidence that his mother is still alive at age seventy-seven: "Mama will be 77 years old the 16th of next month, and that is an advanced age, yes may God be with her and help her!"[33]

As we have seen in previous chapters, the closing sections of letters generally have the function of sending greetings to friends and acquaintances, and wishing for their continued well-being. When religious language is used in the closing, this section of the letter is elevated in status and tone, in this case functioning like a benediction. Spiritual and physical well-being are wished for the recipients, and God is invoked as the agent for continued well-being. As with a benediction at the end of a church service, this leave-taking is intended to have agency outside the bounds of the letter itself, at least until another letter is received. Charles M. Bloomberg ends one of his letters with a benedictory statement just before his signature: "May God be with us all is my Heartfelt Wish."[34] Jonas Anderson closes his letter to his brother: "Before ending this I [wish that] the Great Almighty Majesty, Protector and Ruler, may protect all that dwells on the Earth and over the Earth!!!"[35]

Religious language pervades the letters of Anna Hallquist and Victor A. Hallquist, including Victor's closing lines. In writing to his elderly father, Victor expresses concern that family members still in Sweden should help his father in his old age. But for Victor, God was ultimately looking after his father: "I hope that Johan and Emil see to you, through *God* everything is possible, he has given me health again and if we trust in him we shall not come to disgrace."[36] In the last letter we have from Victor, written when he was bedridden, a more general benedictory statement to his brother is found: "May we all meet in Jesus's house, by grace we are saved / God's peace be with you."[37] Even though Victor had enjoyed a couple weeks of better health, these lines written under his signature, possibly the last lines he wrote to his brother, serve as a parting blessing. Here he employs a theme of heavenly reunion, found also in the writing of Erling's pietistic Swedish Americans of New England.[38]

Reinforcing the liturgy-like religious formulas of these letters are imagery and themes that also bear the general influence of Protestant Christianity. The most common of these is the "gift of God" theme, employed specifically in reference to health. Health as a gift of God appears frequently as part of the opening sections of letters by writers who use religious language. The pairing reinforces what we have concluded in earlier chapters, that health was very important to the immigrants, but it also indicates a particular way of looking at deity and health. Possessing good health was a gift from God, but it was also a transitory state, something that one could not count on. Repetitions of "thanks be to God" for good health function all in one as acknowledgments, praiseful thanks, and petitions. In Ola Svenson's letter to his sister, he says in his opening section: "Now I want to take up the pen and write you a few lines and let you know how I am, I am well and things are going well and I wish the same,

God's good gift, to you."[39] Similarly, Charles H. Anderson writes that he is healthy, "which is a great loan from a good and merciful God."[40]

During Victor A. Hallquist's bouts of illness, including the kidney disease that took his life, he never neglects to thank God for health. "I have had health and work and that is a great gift of God," he writes in 1897.[41] In 1904 Victor was ill in bed, having suffered months of illness. He had been told by his doctor that there was not much hope for him. But at the time that he wrote, Victor had been feeling better for a couple of weeks, "so God in his goodness lets me get well one more time."[42] Although Victor's prognosis was not good, his death came at the hands of an incompetent physician, who removed Victor's one healthy kidney, rather than the diseased one, in a 1905 operation. After Victor's death, Anna became the family correspondent to Victor's family in Sweden, writing in a vein very similar to his, "the Lord be praised we are all well and it is a great gift that we cannot thank God enough for, he has helped me during this sorrowful year."[43]

The "gift of God" theme appears throughout the Bible's Old and New testaments, although as the writer of I Corinthians 12 makes clear, the physical gift of bodily health is not necessarily the only or most important of God's gifts; rather, one should "earnestly desire the higher gifts" (verse 31), such as the wisdom to teach. From the New Testament point of view, the greatest gift is the "free gift of God" of Romans 6:23: "eternal life." As used in the immigrants' letters, the idea of health as a gift of God is a more concrete way of expressing a personal relationship to a deity. The theme takes on the physicality of Ecclesiastes 3:13: "It is God's gift to man that every one should eat and drink and take pleasure in all his toil."

Peter Anderson focuses the abstract ideas in his letter with an image, God's hands, which are for him "helping hands," for whose continued guidance he prays. The image of God's hands is, of course, found throughout the Old Testament, in which they are often the hands of an angry God punishing the enemies of the Hebrews. But Anderson's use of God's hands is a more benevolent image of God's providence. More closely parallel to Anderson's use of the metonym is Psalms 119:173: "Your hand will be my help, for I have chosen your commandments."[44] The same idea appears in the Augustana confirmation hymn "In Your Name I Have Been Baptized," in which God is besought to "guide me always with your hand!"[45]

The image of God's hands was enough of a commonplace in Swedish culture that we even see the freethinker Leonard Nilsson using it when he describes the "book" of nature as "written by 'God's hand.'" Nilsson places the expression in quotation marks, a practice he uses throughout his letters to mark common expressions, proverbs, and quotations. Here he means not only to mark the expression as one that is commonly heard, but also to mark his figurative use of the expression. He may have believed that God is the creator of the book of nature, and that nature is a source of truthful inspiration, but he questions the value of the other book, the Bible, which he sees as written by fallible human beings.

The image of eyes is also found in the letters. Anna Olson uses the metonym of God's eyes when she writes in reference to the status of Swedes in America, "we are all equal in God's eyes."[46] Again, the image derives from biblical scripture. In Psalms 33:18, God's eyes are on humankind: "Behold, the Lord's eye is on those who fear him, on those who hope for his merciful grace."[47] Human eyes appear metonymically too. For human beings, the eyes are the gate to the soul, and the opening of eyes represents revelation of truth or recognition of deity, as in Luke 24:31: "their eyes were opened and they recognized him." This image is used by Peter Anderson in his opening passage, when he writes, "So shall our eyes one time be opened and transfigured."[48]

Olson uses another image that was very important to the religious groups most touched by pietism, the purifying blood of Jesus: "It is good to have your sins forgiven and be purged [or cleansed] in Jesus's blood."[49] The reference here is directly to Lutheran liturgy: "Jesu Kristi, Guds Sons, blod renar oss från all synd" (Jesus Christ, God's Son's, blood purges us from all sin).[50] *Jesus blod* also appears in many Moravian-influenced hymns intended for Lent, in which blood is graphically described as running from the body of Jesus. Take, for instance, number 65 in *Hemlandssånger,* in which is described "the water, the blood, which flows from the wounds in your side," or number 69, "I revere Jesus's blood; it is my salvation [literally, cleansing river]."[51]

The image of home—so important in passages where the immigrant writers consider their relationship to Swedish nationality—also appears in the letters from religious writers as an image for heaven or eternal life. When Victor A. Hallquist's father died, he was anxious to know the details from his brother. "You say that you believe he has gone home," Victor writes (meaning that his father has gone on to the reward of eternal life). "I am happy about that."[52] Karna Anderson pulls in the theme of pilgrimage when she uses the image of home: "when we come home someday, though, we shall see why it has been so [why suffering exists]; then shall no pilgrim regret what he has suffered here."[53]

Lutheranism, and Christianity generally, employs a bounty of imagery and themes. From these the Western writers made the most concrete and personal choices—heaven as a home, Jesus's blood as cleansing, God's watching eyes, divine revelation as opening the believer's eyes, pilgrimage, and heavenly reunion. These images and themes have also been identified by Erling in the letters of Swedish immigrants living in New England during the same period, and many of them date to earlier use in Swedish pietistic groups.[54] As Erling points out, the ideas of pilgrimage and reunion had special application for the immigrants; she finds these images emphasized in the writing of the New Englanders. Erling's larger sample of pietistic writers in New England also reveals the use of a few images and themes that I have not seen tapped by the Western writers: Jesus as friend, Jesus as bridegroom, Jesus's wounds (not just his blood), the heart of the converted, and captivity.[55] In the letters from the West, though, one theme not noted by Erling appears more frequently than any other theme; it is the most concrete and compelling image used by these writers to express the active presence of deity in the everyday world: the idea of health as a gift from God. The concreteness and intimacy of the images chosen by the Western writers exemplifies Jay P. Dolan's generalization about immigrant religion, that "the God of nineteenth-century immigrants was a personal God who was in close touch with the people."[56]

The examples of religious language cited thus far bear a close relationship to oral forms, some more influenced by pietism than others but all familiar either from daily use, in a more pietistic household, or weekly use, during church services. Among the forms mentioned, such as benediction and petitions, testimony is a prominent category. Testimony is a public avowal of belief. In Lutheranism this is represented in the creed, a set piece recited as part of the service, which in many ways parallels the Catholic mass and its credo. In less formal settings and especially among the more pietistic groups, testimony can emphasize particular aspects of the creed, especially Jesus's sacrifice. For these groups, testimony also exists outside of church services; it is a matter of everyday practice to testify to faith in the course of conversation or of letter writing.

The beginning of Peter Anderson's letter is an extended example of testimony of faith. This is a very unusual way to begin a letter, practiced by only two other letter writers, Karna Anderson and Genny Andersson.

The letters of all three of these Andersons (who apparently were unrelated) begin with an extended testimony and then make a clear break from pious language to secular language and content, the shift in language marking distinct sections of their letters. In Peter Anderson's letter, the first one-and-a-half pages are devoted to testimony using the formal, liturgical *we*:

> And that we only understood God's goodness, what it actually is,
> but for that we are too limited because we see no more than our
> mortal eyes can comprehend and therein lies the problem. But the
> Lord must in his merciful grace help us safely through this evil
> world. So shall our eyes in time be opened and transfigured and
> we shall in our salvation know God as he is.[57]

As mentioned earlier, the image of human eyes being opened to a larger truth is biblical. Here, Peter Anderson uses the image to testify to his own faith that Christian salvation will result in opening humanity to a better existence whose qualities are so mysterious that one cannot, in one's mortal state, comprehend them. But Anderson is not proselytizing, nor is he witnessing by providing examples from his personal experience. Nothing in the passage suggests that Anderson thinks his audience—his aunt and uncle—would not simply accept what he writes. The passage remains merely extended testimony of faith, grounded in the authority of biblical language. Thus, Anderson uses the beginning of his letter as a sacred space in which a creed is being "recited."

Anderson then leaves an empty line. The space sets off his testimony from the remainder of the letter, as does the accompanying shift in tone and subject. The tone comes partly from Anderson's sudden use of the informal you (*du*):

> I will now say to you Aunt a heartfelt thanks for the welcome let-
> ter that I received from you 25 July, where I was happy to see that
> you were well. But I must ask you to forgive me for the delay in
> answering you.[58]

Anderson then turns to the usual subject following such an opener, his labor in the coal works in Cheyenne. It is as if Peter Anderson begins his letter twice over; in the second opener he reenters the secular, everyday world of work.

Another instance of extended testimony at the beginning of a letter is found in a letter written August 19, 1904, by Karna Anderson of Troy, Idaho. Anderson does use an ordinary opening format, beginning her letter with a return address, date, and salutation—"My dearly beloved childhood friend and playmate Gunilla"—followed by the greeting "God's peace."[59] The latter phrase is a bridge to a nearly three-and-a-half-page testimony of faith that opens with a creed-like statement:

> *He* was wounded for *our* transgressions, and beaten for *our* misdeeds: was chastised, was raised up so that *we* should have *peace.* Heartfelt heavenly *peace! peace, peace!* That Jesus can give, thanks be to have this *peace* that is more valuable than all the world.[60]

At the end of her testimony, Anderson shifts abruptly from pious language to the kind of content more ordinarily encountered in the letters: "Now at last something about my family." The remainder of her letter is much more true to form, inquiring after relatives and wishing her friend good health.[61]

A similar testimonial opener with very little in the way of greeting appears in a December 1, 1887, letter from Genny Andersson of Helena, Montana. Andersson begins her letter to her parents in English, without even a salutation: "Khristians carol sveetly. Up till day an sing tis the happy birthday of our Holy kring Haste ve then to greet Him." She continues through the first one-and-a-half pages of her letter with what she calls a "reading for Christmas."[62] The text is a Christmas carol, written by nineteenth-century English hymn writer William Chatterton Dix, which Andersson writes out apparently from memory. Andersson includes the first two verses, and then continues with verses of another carol, concluding, "far and near the tings tell hov the Lord to earth did come ring and tell, Angels." She then abruptly, without a paragraph break or punctuation, shifts to Swedish and to secular concerns, writing, "I can let you know that I am on my own."[63] Andersson's "recitation" here acts as a testimony of faith at Christmastime, but it also seems to represent a means of showing off her growing ability to understand English. Later in her letter, Andersson tells her parents, "I can speak well now."[64]

We can make a distinction between mere testimony, a statement of personal faith, and more complex testimony that includes witnessing. Witnessing cites personal experience, often in the form of narrative, to provide evidence supporting belief. Including a personal experience story within a testimony implies not only that the speaker holds certain beliefs, because of his or her experience, but also that the audience listening to the witness should share those beliefs. Witnessing is a form of proselytizing.

Elaine Lawless's study of oral testimony in Pentecostal groups of the latter half of the twentieth century has described a five-part format for testimony that includes witnessing: introduction, metanarrational device, narrative, explication, and conclusion.[65] The introduction sets forth the point of faith for which the speaker wants to offer witness. The metanarrational device is a statement such as "I want to tell you about," which warns listeners to expect a shift to storytelling; it is a statement about storytelling itself rather than a part of the story. Explication is an explanation of how the story applies to the point of faith. The conclusion tends to repeat the testimony offered in the introduction; these two parts of the testimonial form draw most heavily on formulaic language. Oral testimony that includes stories of witnessing tends to require all these parts so that listeners can stay on track. Written testimony can be briefer. We have already seen a very brief example of witnessing in Charles M. Bloomberg's letter that offers his elderly mother's continued health as experiential evidence of God's grace.

Karna Anderson's letter parallels oral testimony more closely than does Bloomberg's brief reference to his mother's health. We've seen that Anderson begins with a creed-like statement setting forth the theme of thankfulness for "God's peace." Later in her letter, she moves to her own experience, shifting to past tense and providing the metanarrational line (lined out here using Lawless's method):

[I] thought about

and then the narrative:

how much better off I have been
certainly I have suffered too sometimes
but then I have been able to leave the bed from time to time,

and my *heart* was filled with thanks and praise to *the Lord*
who has been so good to me
and I prayed that *he* might bless you doubly

then moving to explication:

his ways are so strange we understand so little of his undertakings
    among us
but we know that for those who *love the Lord* everything works
    out for the best.

Anderson continues her explication of her personal experience by writing the passage already quoted, "when we come home . . . then shall no pilgrim regret," developing the themes of providence, pilgrimage, and reunion by comparing human plight to that of a pilgrim who will someday come home and attain understanding. She concludes by bidding her friend to pray for her and by returning to the theme of thankfulness for Jesus's sacrifice on behalf of humankind.[66]

Even in this lengthy testimony, Anderson employs personal experience sparingly, with much less development than we have seen in chapters 4 and 6 in narrative used to convey the dangers of work, for example, or the wildness of the West. But the tendency to tell stories is not a matter of thematic material so much as an expression of the talents and preferences of the writer. Victor A. Hallquist, who enjoyed expressing the dangers of the West through storytelling, is even more eloquent when telling stories with a religious theme. Hallquist's letter to his brother Johan on the event of their father's death employs the overall shape of testimony with a fully developed embedded narrative. Hallquist focuses on the themes of leave-taking, last words, and reunion. His introduction of these religious themes is dialogic. He refers to statements his brother wrote to him, following up with comments of his own, in which he makes it evident that his brother's letter was not informative enough:

Since he died on a Sunday, [I] presume that you were all home;
you say that he was sick for 3 weeks but you do not say anything
about his last words, what he said himself. You say that you believe
that he has gone home and I am happy about that.[67]

After introducing the important themes of loved ones being parted at death and of the deceased's last words, which would provide important evidence of salvation, Hallquist shifts to past tense, alerting the reader to expect a story, and he provides a metanarrational statement:

> I have thought a lot about my home and Father and also my mother.

He begins his narrative midsentence:

> who bade me pray to God for her at her deathbed. I remember so well I read chapter 14 of John: Let not your hearts be troubled Believe in God and believe also in me.—and prayed to God for her and her face beamed with happiness and the last she said to me was that I should Live for Jesus and that she wished to speak with Emil [another brother].[68]

This deathbed scene with his mother is offered as a consoling substitute for what Hallquist has missed by his absence at his father's deathbed. Hallquist moves on to offer a second narrative, in which the theme of last words is developed further and he finds further consolation:

> I never forget the last words that my Father said to me at Sponhult's Smithy: if I never get to see you here again Victor, then I wish to meet you in Jesus's house when we are both in the grave.[69]

Hallquist draws a compelling parallel between the deathbed scene with his mother and the scene of his departure from Sweden as an emigrant, with the last words of his mother paralleled with the parting words of his father. Lacking the consolation of his father's last words at his deathbed, Hallquist offers the parting words at the smithy as a substitute.

The thematic structure is tripartite as Hallquist moves back in time: missing last words at his father's deathbed, last words at his mother's deathbed, and last words from his father on Hallquist's emigration from Sweden. Hallquist's storytelling uses connotative structure. The third instance of the theme is the most powerful, and it provides closure for the incompleteness of the theme in its first development. The parallel structure equates emigration with death, and for both, the pain of separation is resolved through the religious theme of reunion in heaven.

Hallquist moves on to an explication that explores the consequences of his father's death:

> Both father and mother have now ended their earthly life full of many sorrows and lived to an old age and in *older* days they have become saved—But we have been called in our youth during the great time of awakening when many million became converted to God and a greater responsibility rests on us than our parents because Jesus says that we shall become the light of the world.[70]

Hallquist's explication explores the idea of being an orphan. Accepting the fact that his generation is now the eldest, he feels new responsibilities. His parents were converted in their old age, but he and his siblings have the advantage of having been raised as—apparently—Baptists. The older generation has departed, leaving them with the responsibility to testify and witness and to convert others. Like Jesus in John 8:12, the new generation will become "the light of the world."[71] Victor concludes with a benediction-like hope for his generation:

> May God help us all when we become old so we can say that we shall be saved through Jesus's blood.[72]

These final lines of the letter subtly return to the idea of last words, answering the implied question "What will we be able to say on our deathbeds?"

This blend of testimony and witnessing takes up nearly the entirety of Hallquist's letter to his brother. In it we see him move from grief through reminiscence of past departures and last words, to the consolation of reunion, to the awareness of his responsibility to take up the torch from the last generation, and finally to a sense of rededication, ending with a prayer for his generation's future salvation. The stories of deathbeds and leave-taking bring these themes into sharp focus.

Also embedded within the religious letters is another form that originates in spoken language, the sermon. Although none of the letter writers were ordained, the practice of lay preaching in Mormonism encouraged the LDS writers to consider their letters as a genre that could be used to encourage conversion. They frequently shift from an ordinary tone conveying information and personal contact to a more didactic, persuasive mode of sermonizing. This use of letters varied. Peter Peterson wrote to a friend who was apparently not Mormon but whom he did not explicitly attempt to convert. Peterson turns to religious themes in only one unusual letter. Nils Trulsson, on the other hand, hoped to convert his sweetheart. His letters take up religious beliefs briefly but do not develop them as thoroughly as Ola Svenson's letters do. Svenson wrote to a sister whom he hoped to convert. His letters read like extended sermons.

Svenson and his wife Johanna had emigrated from Sweden in 1882, traveling with their three children, all less than five years old.[73] By 1884 the family was established in Jordan, Utah, near Salt Lake City. From 1884 through 1887 Svenson sent proselytizing letters to his sister, hoping that even if she were to stay in Sweden, she would allow herself to be baptized as a Mormon. Like the introduction to Victor A. Hallquist's "last words" narrative, Svenson's letters are dialogic. He responds to a series of points that he cites from a letter he received from his sister, a letter-writing strategy that he employs with both the secular and the religious content. Svenson attempts to answer his sister's assertions point by point, using a combination of Mormon belief and biblical authority.

Svenson's letter dated March 11, 1886, sets forth an interesting series of arguments. The letter begins with a page of secular news in which Svenson thanks his sister for her letter and informs her about his family's situation in Jordan. Then, using the idea of a dialogue, he shifts to a long middle section concerning religious belief:

> You mentioned the loan and that you thought I had paid it in full,
> which I had, but it was either the bank men in Sweden or here
> that stole it, where I do not know. You say that if you received
> the Holy Spirit then it would be easier to understand the Holy
> Scripture and that is a truth. But I am going to tell you. . . .[74]

Svenson continues with this pattern: you say that; I can tell you this. He answers Maria's concerns about the connection between "receiving" the Holy Spirit, the Pentecostal religious experience of rebirth, and the ability to understand the Bible as follows:

you cannot receive it [the Holy Spirit] without experiencing the laying on of hands from a servant of the Lord who is clad with God's pastoral garb who puts his hands on your head bringing [you] the Holy Spirit's gift, which you can find in Acts of the Apostles chapter 8.[75]

Svenson refers here to the desire of the apostles at Jerusalem who had not been present to experience the Holy Spirit on the day of Pentecost to "receive the Holy Spirit; for it had not yet fallen on any of them, but they had only been baptized [by water]." According to Acts of the Apostles 8, Peter and John "laid their hands on them and they received the Holy Spirit." In Mormon belief, the LDS church as an institution represents a renewal of the early Christian communities of the Acts of the Apostles. One of the early apostolic practices—the laying on of hands—is performed by those men who have achieved a priestly status in the church. The laying on of hands is seen as having sacred power, including healing and investiture with the Holy Spirit.[76]

Svenson continues his letter with a series of similar arguments, citing the New Testament books of James, John, and Hebrews as authorities. It seems clear that he was a "reader" influenced by Swedish pietism who read the Bible with the point of view that he could understand what he read without priestly guidance. Svenson also applies this idea to his and his sister's writing by drawing an analogy between their letters and the epistles. Reading the epistles, then, should be as transparent as reading one of his sister's letters. He says to his sister:

You need to do precisely what the Scripture tells you and not what the clergy preaches because they say that they are explaining it but that is a falsification and not an explanation. You can understand that yourself, that it does not mean anything different than what is written. Because when you write to me you write what you mean. And consider the fact that all the Epistles in the New Testament are letters from the Apostles to the Christian congregations and they wrote what they wanted the people to do and live by and not because there could be another explanation. All other interpretations and explanations are simply a falsification from the evil spirit.[77]

Svenson expresses the pietistic view that a believer could have direct access to biblical text, and he assumes its meaning is transparent. He and his sister "write what [they] mean," as the apostles must also have done.

The letter writers in the Rockies who used religious language drew on the formal oral forms of liturgy, hymns, and sermons, and the less formal forms of testimony and storytelling. They also had the model of the apostles' letters, a model that combined with pietism to suggest they could use their letters to perform lay preaching. Denying priestly authority, a writer like Ola Svenson transgresses on territory reserved for the clergy in Swedish Lutheranism.

This transgression is apparent throughout the religious letters, as the letter writers create their own sacred space in which they offer each other the pious language of liturgy. "The Lord be with you," offered by each writer in turn, in letter after letter, is inherently pietistic in its assumption that worship can occur outside the bounds of church services. So, too, are lay benedictions, testimonies, and sermons. This was a special use of letter writing that more self-consciously advanced a personal position on identity than did the letters written to express class, nationality, ethnicity, and regionalism.

An Epistle-like use of the letter genre imbues the religious letters with a sober tone that may be surprising to twenty-first-century readers who are more familiar with the current-day Upper Midwest Lutheran fondness for self-deprecating humor.[78] We have seen humor and playfulness when the Rocky Mountain letter writers turned to secular issues of nationality, ethnicity, and region, but these religious writers take no such license with their subject matter. The themes of providence, pilgrimage, and reunion; the imagery of God's hands and Jesus's blood; the stories of departure and last words; and the analogy between the Epistles and the immigrants' own letters are developed by these writers in all seriousness. There is no room for levity in the sacred spaces created in their letters. What these writers do share with the more secular writers is their ability to express difficult abstractions concretely and personally through compelling imagery and story.

EIGHT

Identity, Genre, Meaning

WHAT WE LEARN FROM READING VERNACULAR LETTERS

❦

I have a Scotsman as a coworker in *the shop*, he is a good smith
and horseshoer; we are working on sleds now. I wish that you all
were here instead of in Sweden. Then we could all work together
and do much better than you have it in Sweden. . . . I just brought
home *some* lutefisk this evening. I wish that I could come home at
Christmas and have a little of Mama's good lutefisk and porridge.
I certainly remember how good the food is that Mama usually
cooks. I am trying sometimes to teach Jessie to cook like Mama
usually does.

John Peterson, 1910, McCall, Idaho

*E*XPRESSING HOW MUCH HE MISSES HIS FAMILY and the Swedish
Christmas season, John Peterson wrote an unusually long, eight-page
letter home in December 1910.[1] Peterson and his wife Jessie lived on a
farm seven miles from McCall, Idaho, where she was a schoolteacher and
he a blacksmith. They made the trip into town every day by horse, probably by horse-drawn sled during the snowy season. In his letter, Peterson
explains he is just back home from a long trip to Colorado, where he
helped one of his in-laws with a land transaction. He wanted to see the
land for himself before paying for it, because "there are so many such
companies nowadays in the country that just swindle and deceive people,
[they] advertise everywhere that the land is spacious and rich."[2]

John Peterson expresses connections to those around him and those
left behind in Sweden; his affiliations were multiple. He had a Scottish

157

American work companion with whom he enjoyed a prosperous black-smithing business. He lived in an Americanized household into which he had been unsuccessful in introducing the Swedish foods he remembered from his youth. Hence, Peterson especially missed the traditions associated with Christmas, the good foods prepared for the Christmas table. How-ever, in McCall, where there was a small Nordic population, he was able to obtain lutefisk. Having lutefisk at Christmastime had become a marker of Swedish-Americanness for him. So, too, might have been his work with sleds. McCall was becoming, and still is, a center for Nordic recreational ac-tivities such as sledding and skiing. Finally, Peterson writes with awareness that he is no longer a greenhorn in the West, where many were out to de-ceive newcomers. In his letter, then, he quickly expresses his understanding of a kaleidoscope of occupational, national, ethnic, and regional issues.

Is it accurate to identify John Peterson as Swedish American when Swedish heritage is only one of several affinities he expresses in his writ-ing? He seems to have been as much a blacksmith, a fellow worker, a busi-ness owner, a farmer, a husband, an American, a son and brother, a Swede, and a Westerner. He does not label himself as any of these, yet his letter establishes indirect claims on all of them at once.

Throughout the bulk of the immigrant letters, we have met individu-als like Peterson—Swedish writers who express themselves as related to various cultural groups surrounding them, not all of which were ethnic or national. The epithets and formulas, metaphors and images, and stories and embedded subgenres of the letters express an orientation to fellow workers, to fellow Westerners, or to fellow believers. The letters can be read as self-presentations created always with multiple concerns in mind. In this respect, the letters are like autobiography, a genre that Jerome Bruner has said "involves not only the construction of self, but also a con-struction of one's culture."[3] Just as selves constructed in autobiography can be multiple, letters can express multiple self-identities and cultural group identities.

For folklorists, identities are most convincingly expressed through participation. It has become axiomatic in American folklore studies that individuals can belong to a number of folk groups, through which they establish not ascribed identities but identities claimed through cultural participation.[4] Barre Toelken sees depth and breadth of participation as a key to determining these claimed identities:

How is a person said to be a member of a Serbian American folk group: by having a Serbian name and learning to dance the *kolo* in college or by participating fully in the ongoing vernacular traditions of an American Serbian community? Obviously, the latter.[5]

As noted in chapter 1, folklorist Sandra Dolby Stahl has systematized the idea of folk-group participation and its relationship to individual identity claims. Her study of personal experience stories has found that storytellers express their orientation to particular groups through their storytelling. Admitting that the number of actual folk groups would be infinite, Stahl suggests eight broad categories that can be used to analyze any one person's patterns of group participation. Within each category, by creating the divisions "primary" and "secondary," Stahl recognizes that participation can vary. Primary participation is direct, personal engagement in a group, while secondary is more passive, involving an awareness of a group's folklore as part of one's shared heritage.

We can use Stahl's "folk group categories significant in the formation and expression of individual identity"[6] to analyze John Peterson's group affiliations. He establishes his primary interaction with occupation through comradeship with a coworker, with family through his relationship with Jessie, with ethnicity through his attempts to teach Jessie to cook and through his purchase of lutefisk, with place through his claim of being savvy to land dealing in the West, and with social networks through his attempt to convince his relatives to better their economic status by emigrating from Sweden. Some of these interactions are reinforced secondarily. Peterson demonstrates an awareness of ethnic heritage, for example, through his comments on the lack of foods appropriate at Christmastime. His writing provides no evidence for strong affiliations based on age, sex, or religion.

Peterson's letter reminds us that identity claims are rarely simple and singular. His letter demonstrates how individuals can forge mixed identities that emphasize certain of Stahl's folk group categories over others. Orm Øverland has described another example of mixed identity in the letters of Norwegian immigrant Jacob Hansen Hilton. During his time in New Mexico in the 1880s, Hilton expresses himself as a male white Westerner. He describes the community in which he lived, Socorro, as entirely male. According to Øverland, in Hilton's accounts, "there seem to be neither women nor children."[7] Hilton also explicitly claims to be part of a "white" society that is superior to the Apaches, and he states outright his aversion to Easterners, who were too sympathetic to the American Indians. Hilton's letters demonstrate his primary participation in groups based on his sex, his location in the West, and his perception that he is racially white. This last category, race, combines elements of Stahl's ethnic and social network categories. In nineteenth-century America, perceptions of race overlapped with perceptions of shared culture and language, but race also was an ideology embedded in social networks.[8]

Among the Swedish letter writers are several who, like Øverland's Norwegian correspondent Hilton, express an affinity with the West, and for whom we have evidence of direct participation in all-male regional activities. We met these men in chapter 6. Each of them emphasizes a different mixture of affiliations, but they all express themselves as male Westerners. They portray themselves as active in the environment with other men. They prospected, explored, and fished in the mountains, or ran cattle on the range, activities that are coded in American culture as masculine.

Consider, for example, Bernhard Rydberg, who explored the Montana mountains with David Smethurst, photographing scenery for Rydberg's mother. Or Charles Flodin, who explored the central Idaho mountains with the Captain, pushing his way through rugged territory where the views were spectacular but the terrain nearly impassable. Or Aron W. Johnson, who, with the help of his brothers, drove cattle on the open range of Wyoming, where he experienced expanses of high desert with brisk weather that he considered possibly dangerous for his Anna, who was awaiting him in Sweden. Or, finally, John M. Swanson, who teamed up with another Swedish American man to fish in the mountains near Denver, taking the trip up to Cripple Creek via a railway line with a frighteningly sheer drop-off.

These men enjoyed the companionship of other men as they explored their corner of the West. But were they enamored with a specifically masculine West? Were they also claiming whiteness? Those affinities are less clear than in Hilton's case. All these writers emphasize the beauty of the West over the potential violence of its inhabitants, with whom they had no primary interaction. And they do not label themselves explicitly as part of a "white" society, as did Hilton. They note their affiliations with male groups, but these are not simple masculinist claims. Swanson values his fellow male workers not so much as Westerners but rather as workers. Rydberg values Smethurst's companionship during camping trips, but with Smethurst he also participated in the social networks of local politics and fraternal clubs. Of all of the writers, Flodin strikes the most masculinist pose when he describes his adventures with a Civil War veteran. This is partly accounted for by his correspondent, Anders Abrahamsson, whom he addresses as "brother." Flodin had known Abrahamsson since boyhood, and they had emigrated together. On the other hand, Rydberg, Swanson, and Johnson wrote to correspondents who were outsiders to the male West: Rydberg to his mother; Swanson to his parents; and Johnson to his fiancée.

Other categories—social networks, religion, occupation, and ethnicity— moderated the masculine side of regional affiliation for these men. Bernhard Rydberg and Aron W. Johnson, who owned their own businesses, had middle-class, entrepreneurial interests. Rydberg participated in local, nonethnic fraternal organizations and in a Montana militia group, organizations that anchored small-town, middle-class society. Swanson was a churchgoer who eventually joined a Swedish Lutheran church in Denver. And although he does not describe any specific union activities, Swanson expresses a strong concern for the condition of workers.

Some writers express place as a secondary category, a category influencing them through general awareness rather than primary participation. Leonard Nilsson, for example, wrote many letters describing his hikes into the mountains, which he appreciated for their beauty and solitude. But Nilsson's groups of primary participation show him to have had a great deal in common with Rydberg. His social networks included the local I.O.O.F. (Independent Order of Odd Fellows). He aspired to the middle-class status that Rydberg had attained, yet he still maintained an interest in the local workers' group he had belonged to in Sweden. His affiliations also included ethnicity. Although he did not interact with other Swedes in Rocky Bar, Idaho, Nilsson read the Swedish American papers, and he is one of the few writers to label himself as Swedish.

Two other writers who were fascinated with the West, though for quite different reasons, also do not portray themselves as manly adventurers. Peter Peterson writes with an awareness of Utah as Zion, a Western region where the Mormons sought to establish a utopian society based in

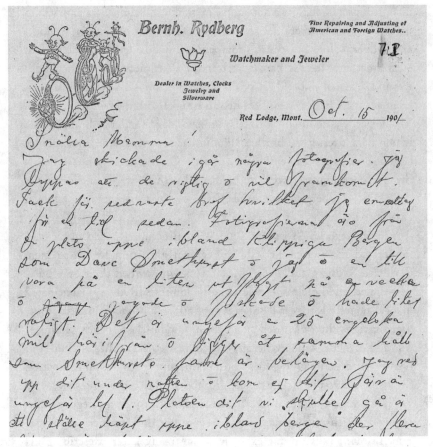

Bernhard Rydberg wrote to his mother on stationery that featured fantastical creatures balancing on rolling rings. Image courtesy of the Swedish Emigrant Institute.

LDS belief. However, Peterson's primary participation was through his occupation as a carpenter, his immediate family (which was also an economic unit), his religious group, and his middle-class social network. The latter two categories especially guided his impulse to write as a booster for Utah, attempting to convince Jonas Danielson that he would find a better future there if only he would emigrate. Victor A. Hallquist was also strongly guided by his active participation in a religious group. His Baptist faith, augmented by strong familial ties, provides a framework for his writings about the region's violence. Rather than embrace the region's ethos, as Flodin does, Hallquist judges the West as uncivilized and un-Christian.

Three other male writers demonstrated the primary importance of religious groups through their active participation. The letters of John E. Jernberg of Moscow, Idaho, frequently mention attending Lutheran services, participating in Christmas celebrations, and reading Swedish American newspapers. For Jernberg, religion and ethnicity were the primary categories. The letters of Ola Svenson and Nils Trulsson, both Mormon converts, focus so closely on religious issues that we see little evidence of their participation in any of the other categories.

While the West and religion were categories of affiliation that were very important for many of the male writers, another combination of categories—family, sex, and age—emerges as important in the writing of women. Like Flodin's letters to Abrahamsson, Clara Jeppsson's letters to her sister establish a relationship based on sex and age as she corresponds with a woman of the same generation within her family. With her sister, Jeppsson shares concerns about family members, scenes from her childhood, and news of her pregnancy. Jeppsson's letters also evidence some involvement in the local Denver community of Swedish Americans. She attended church, for example, admitting that it was not so much for worship as for meeting fellow Swedish Americans, and she obtained work via her contacts there. Anni Dickson's categories of participation similarly placed familial connections at the center of her much more isolated life in Red Cliff, Colorado. She lived with a member of her generation, a sister. But she did not mingle outside of home because she had not mastered English and, as she perceived the situation, the Swedish population in Red Cliff considered themselves to be of higher social status.

Familial connections were also of importance to Emma Hallberg and Ida Sandberg, sisters who lived in Denver within just a few blocks of each other and of their brother, John M. Swanson. Their letters frequently mention the comings and goings among the three households of the siblings, their spouses, and their children. When John's wife Tilda died, the letters provide ample evidence of sisterly support. Ethnic and religious connections probably were also of importance to Emma and Ida, as well as their location in Denver, but these are not emphasized in their letters.[9]

Just as the myth of the West promoted a masculine image of the region, creating for some of the male writers a strong gender- and place-based identity, the nineteenth-century cult of domesticity promoted an ethos by which women were associated in the popular imagination with family, home, education, and the arts. We have seen this image expressed by the immigrants of both sexes in the image of the woman at home in Sweden. The primary participation of the women, as evidenced in their letters, supports the idea that this ethos held weight for the Swedish immigrant women, as several of them forged mixed identities based on sex, family, and age.

We can easily document, then, the letter writers' participation in and awareness of a mixture of groups and of heritage traditions. But is mixed identity the same as blended identity? Øverland interprets Hilton's "white, Western, and American" identity as an inseparable unity: "This male identity is trinitarian, not only in the sense that it is composed of three elements, but in the sense that the three elements are inseparably one."[10] It is perhaps less clear that such a unity was created by our Swedish writers, but we can say that the process of participation in groups was not entirely idiosyncratic or random.

The Western historians Cronon, Miles, and Gitlin agree that ethnicity and regionalism can be blended: "Once ethnic difference expressed itself geographically—and frontier processes made this almost inevitable—it could evolve and reproduce a personal sense of selfhood that was both ethnic and regional at the same time."[11] We can more precisely say that when blended identity is espoused by many, as a claimed and participatory category, and when it is also recognized from without, as an ascribed label, blended identity becomes a whole in which it is difficult to perceive the parts. Such a blending might be true, for example, of Jeppsson, Swanson, Hallberg, and Sandberg, who found themselves in a localized Swedish American community in Denver. Similarly, Charles Flodin might have recognized himself as a Western Swedish American. And Peterson, while he self-consciously promotes Utah and Mormonism, still demonstrates an awareness that he lived among fellow Scandinavians, making him a Scandinavian Mormon.

None of the Swedish writers make an explicit claim that they have become Westerners in the bold way that Nilsson claims he is a "son of mother *Svea*," but their descendants came to see themselves as Westerners. The label masks other categories, such as ethnicity, race, and sex, to unify Westerners within a regional culture. If not within the first generation, by the second and later generations, Swedish Americans in the West were participating, for example, in the folk traditions of horsemanship and

First- and second-generation Swedish Americans gathered for an elegant picnic at New Sweden, Idaho. The photograph dates from the early twentieth century, probably within the first decade. Photograph courtesy of David A. Sealander; preserved and gifted to Sealander by Anna Margaret Nygaard Cobb.

saddle making; in the regional masculinist and individualistic ideology embodied in the image of the cowboy; and in regional political issues such as the Sagebrush Rebellion's attempts to establish state rights to federally managed public lands. These have become Western tradition, ideology, and political issues that focus the energies of the people of the region, whatever their origin.

An example of regionalism masking a blended identity that includes ethnicity is found in the New Sweden, Idaho, local history *After Fifty Years*, written in 1941 by a committee headed by Charles E. Anderson. This is a very well-told, accurate, and well-researched local history, in which the authors identify those who traveled to Idaho in the 1890s, mostly by rail, as Oregon Trail pioneers, eliding their Swedish origins.[12] In 1994, when the community of New Sweden celebrated its centennial, there was in the United States more enthusiasm for ethnicity, and the community had thus rediscovered its Swedish heritage. However, the pioneer idea was still prominent at the centennial as well. The souvenirs one could purchase included bright-blue feed caps with yellow lettering that read "New Sweden Centennial / 1894–1994." If one did not recognize blue and yellow as the distinctive colors of the Swedish flag, the Swedish connection would be apparent only in the community's name. One could also purchase a coffee mug with a logo that included drawings of a covered wagon, labeled "Yesterday 1894," and of a John Deere tractor, labeled "Today 1994." The community's rural Western character was thus emphasized as much as its Swedishness.

Like "Westerner," the label "Mormon" also can be used to mask the ethnic components of blended identity, and in the multiethnic population of nineteenth-century Utah, there were clearly reasons to do so. The LDS church felt it needed to unify its diverse population under a religious umbrella and to have its people set aside other bases for shared culture. This is why Svenson's and Trulsson's letters are so one-dimensional, expressing little in the way of orientation to place, social networks outside the Mormon church, ethnic groups, or groups based on sex or age.

The immigrant letters reveal that becoming a Westerner or a Mormon was not a simple process. Identity for these Swedish immigrants was a very complex matter, complicated by the often combined processes of migration, including westward movement within America, naturalization, enculturation, economic mobility, and religious conversion. It was perhaps a natural impulse to eventually claim one main category over all others as one struggled through changes of location, nationality, culture, economic status, and religious belief, grasping one strong focus amid the confusion of cultural affiliations.

Writing the letters was one means of establishing that focus. The letter writers grapple with difficult abstractions such as nationality by representing them concretely, through imagery, storytelling, and other vernacular, oral-based forms. This is where the expressive eloquence of the letters lies. In the many examples throughout the preceding chapters, we have seen how the vernacular epistolary tradition of the Swedish immigrants renders identity physically, through the senses. Through the immigrant letters, we see and feel, and occasionally hear, taste, and smell, their experiences.

The letter genre's organization and its formulas embody the customary social visits that immigrants could no longer make. The overall organization of letters, moving from the situation of the writer in America to that of the reader in Sweden, mimics in thought the movement of the letter itself across the Atlantic. At a finer level, the dialogic strategy used by many writers embodies the turn-taking of conversation or argument. The formulas for letter greetings and closings, phrases like "thanks for the letter" and "I am alive and well," evoke the customary greetings, well-wishing, and giving of thanks that one would experience during an actual visit to a Swedish household.

Formulas and epithets are employed too, to convey the letter writers' principal concerns. From writer after writer, we hear "I work every day," "I am sending money," "I will tread the soil of the old country again," "I am out in the Wild West," and "may the Lord be with you"—formulas and epithets that embody issues surrounding change or stagnation in socioeconomic status, migration to a new nation, westward movement within the United States, and religious practice or conversion. The issues represented in formulaic language are brought to life for us through metaphorical and metonymic imagery. We are unlikely to forget the way that John M. Swanson describes his body as though he were a worn-out machine that was ready to be scrapped by the Argo smelter. Or Leonard Nilsson's description of Lovisa Borg as she worked in the kitchen at Christmastime, he the shy helper embarrassed every time their eyes met. Or Bernhard Rydberg's descriptions of jumping around after his dips in glacial streams. Or the way Victor A. Hallquist, as he lies in his sickbed, describes his fragile hold on health as a gift from God.

Through images like these, we experience the immigrants' identity claims directly, as if through our own person. We feel Swanson's fatigue from work, and we understand the constellation of related worker issues. We see Lovisa meeting our eyes, and we feel Leonard's homesickness for the nation left behind and all that it represents. We feel the chill of Rydberg's mountain dips, along with his excitement about being in a beautiful yet harsh and potentially dangerous new region. We feel Hallquist's reprieve from pain, and we understand his belief in a God who is present and active in the world.

The writers' use of forms from oral tradition elevates their writing above ordinary language and intensifies their message. When we encounter a proverbial expression, a sermon, testimony, or storytelling, we recognize these embedded genres as special modes of discourse. Like the "once upon a time" of an oral performance, the beginnings of these embedded genres are cues to us, indicating that we need to read the passage differently from how we read the preceding sentences. Leonard Nilsson puts "going at rocks" in quotation marks to alert us that he is playing with figurative language. John M. Swanson writes "perhaps you have heard" to signal that he is beginning a story about his brother-in-law's injury. Gottfrid Johnson writes "I will try to describe" to signal the beginning of a narrative of his Christmas in LaJara, Colorado. Ola Svenson writes "You say that if you received the Holy Spirit" to signal the beginning of a dialogic sermon. Karna Anderson writes "I thought about how much better favored I have been" to mark the beginning of witnessing within her testimony of faith. In each of these instances, we know we have entered new aesthetic territory.

Within that territory, the writers catch our attention through strategies of expression that derive from orality: wordplay such as punning and manipulation of proverbial expressions, clustering and contrasting of images and ideas, characterization and plotting, and the use of connotative structures. In the preceding chapters, we met a few masters of this vernacular epistolarity, writers whose letters are dense with such strategies. Charles Flodin puns with the Swedish *dyra*, inverts the image of treading the soil of the old country, and relates his personal experience as a series of stories in which he and those around him are cast in roles reflecting traditional motifs. His letters display a bitter and poignant wit when reflecting on Sweden, but enthusiasm when describing the West. Leonard Nilsson playfully takes the Swedish expression "going at rocks" literally, and describes sublime images of the West and tableaux based on his memories of Lovisa. His letters express his deep love for her and his homesickness for Sweden. Bernhard Rydberg tells stories of adventures in which he casts himself as an explorer, discovering and naming geographical features, enjoying male companionship around the campfire, and braving a lightning storm. He clusters these images of Western life with the ideas of the West as salubrious and sublime. His letters reflect enthusiasm for the Wild West that contrasts with his small-town life as a watchmaker and Elks Club member. Victor A. Hallquist demonstrates perhaps the most effective storytelling in his doubling and tripling of narrative sequences to juxtapose characters, actions, and themes, always within a religious worldview. Hallquist's stories of the John Preston Porter Jr. lynching and of Hallquist's father's last words move us to ponder racist violence and the question of the afterlife more deeply than if he had attempted expositions on those themes.

Throughout the letters, we see writers employing a basic meaning-making strategy that also derives from orality. Meaning is immanent. A narrative motif or an image means more than is apparent from its immediate context in a letter because it is able to refer, or allude, to a larger folk tradition or popular mythology shared by writer and reader. The formula "I am alive and well" refers to a broad cultural concern about health and well-being. The image of standing hat in hand refers to the popular mythology of America as a place of equal social standing and economic opportunity. The narrative theme of last words at a deathbed refers to the pietistic Christian concern over whether a relative's soul has indeed been saved. An embedded genre like Flodin's personal experience stories about his adventures as a prospector refers to the existence of traditional story-telling sessions for those of the culture who can meet face-to-face. The associational organization of letters like Emma Hallberg's refers to the existence of women's conversational groups. And a letter in and of itself refers to the relationship between writer and sender. At every level, this metonymic process of meaning-making renders the letters powerfully expressive.

Spending time with Swedish immigrant letters teaches us several lessons. The first is a corrective lesson about the complexities of ethnic identity. Picking up a letter like John Peterson's, we might hope to find traces of Swedish American ethnicity. We are not entirely disappointed, because Peterson does let us know that a Swedish Christmas should include certain foods. But if that is all we come away with, we have read Peterson's letter as if it were one-dimensional, missing the other identifications that were important to him.

Another lesson concerns immigrant history in the West. If Western historians and Scandinavianists were naively to take at face value the identity claims of the descendants of Western immigrants, we would find ourselves accepting the idea of Swedish assimilation to American culture without detecting the identity mixing and blending that occurred early in the immigration experience. We might also overlook the degree to which Western history is immigration history, and to which Western regional identity is a mixed identity created by the immigrants as well as the Easterners who moved westward. Westering was a process in which the Swedes and other European immigrants were equal partners with the "Americans."

We learn, too, about the letters themselves as a kind of vernacular text. Far from being clichéd and uninformative, the immigrant letters are an expressive form that rewards our reading if we are willing to bring to these texts the tools of the folklorist alongside the tools of literary, historical, and linguistic scholars. The communal aesthetic of the immigrant letter responds to a reading that looks for qualities derived from orality: formula, parataxis, connotative structure, and immanent meaning. Immigrant letters respond to a reading that sets any one immigrant letter beside other letter texts by the same and other writers. Immigrant letters respond to a reading that places a letter in the context of its writer's participation in numerous folk groups. The letters respond to a reading that brings to the text an understanding of the oral genres and folk customs employed by their writers.

Folklorists can see in the study of immigrant letters a validation of recent work in interpreting folk texts. Foley's *immanent art* is very similar to Stahl's idea of allusions and Toelken's idea of multivalent metaphors. Examining epic, personal experience story, and ballad, each of these folklorists sees individual performances as able to tap into implicit meanings that lie outside the text itself in the shared culture of performer and audience. That we find a similar process in a vernacular written form suggests how broadly applicable their insights are. They and the other scholars of their era—the latter two decades of the twentieth century—have been working toward what folklorists could embrace as a "unified field theory" of vernacular textual interpretation, the kind of theory that Alan Dundes sees as needed in folklore studies.[13]

Folklorists studying historical materials such as personal letters are in a peculiar position. We are nonparticipant observers, but we are hidden ones. Reading texts from the past, we miss the direct fieldwork experience, but we do not influence the production of the text itself. That has already occurred through the selecting and collecting activities of letter recipients and archivists. We are ever outsiders peeking in on a shared cultural experience. With historians, we share the tasks of reconstructing the context for a letter based on internal clues and external evidence. With literary scholars, we share the frustration that we will never be able to meet Leonard Nilsson or Charles Flodin, Emma Hallberg or Clara Jeppsson, as much as their letters have delighted and intrigued us.

Stahl writes of the personal experience story: "the narrative itself creates a literary world in which shared culture draws attention to itself and to the intimacy it represents."[14] Letter writing functions in a very similar fashion, creating a shared space for the writer and reader in which the terms of their shared culture and personal experience are inscribed self-consciously, often redundantly, but allowing for only a partial reading by outsiders. So Flodin can tell his friend Abrahamsson stories about his Gothenburg visit in a letter in which many of the references are so intimate that we grasp only part of his meaning. Or Johan Håkansson can tell his wife that he has become "thick and fat," assuming she will know what he means based on her knowledge of his personal health history and of the expression's positive connotations. Or Peter Anderson can write a religious testimony to his aunt, assuming that his creation of a sacred space at the beginning of his letter will be acceptable to her.

Perhaps this is one of the most important insights we can gain from a reading of the immigrant letter as folklore: that our interpretation will always be partial. We can only partially reconstruct Clara Jeppsson's life as a Denver housemaid, her relationship with her absent husband, her relationships with her sisters, the community that she moved to in LaJara, her experience of Swedish American church services, her experience of her first pregnancy, and her socioeconomic aspirations. What we have in her letters and the few ancillary sources are mere traces.

But following the traces as they lead us through Jeppsson's letters and on into other letter collections where we find similar formulas and themes is well worth doing. There are few genres available to us for the folk culture of the past, most of them the mute genres of material culture: painted chests, quilts, photo albums, or folk house plans. Even a legend or a folk ballad known to have existed in an earlier era represents only the moment of its collection, usually decades later than the era we are interested in studying. As a verbal genre, the personal letter offers us a unique opportunity to read vernacular texts from the past, as performed in the past, and to reconstruct the worldviews they express.

The Letter Writers and Twenty Letters

Translations by Christina Johansson

~~~

*T*HE LETTER WRITERS are arranged here alphabetically by last name. Because most of the immigrants changed their names and also were often inconsistent in the spellings of these new names, the names that appear here and throughout the book are those that they eventually came to use in their later correspondence. John A. Leonard, for example, was Johan Andersson in Sweden, but he emigrated as J. A. Lennartz. He signed his first few letters from Illinois and Colorado as J. A. Lennartz, but he eventually signed his letters as John A. Leonard, which is how he is referred to here.

Points of birth or origin can be traced for some but not all of the letter writers. These are provided using parish and/or town names and the regional divisions known as *landskap* (provinces). The *landskap* are traditional divisions that were occasionally used by the writers to indicate regional affiliations. In cases where it would be impossible to trace the parish records without knowing the more recent *län* (county name), the *län* is provided in the notes. The number of letters from each correspondent is the number of letters written specifically from the Rocky Mountain West, dated between 1880 and 1917, and included in this study. In several cases, other letters exist that were written before and after those dates or from states outside the region of the Rocky Mountain West.

Following twenty biographical sketches are letters translated into American English. These translations are by Christina Johansson, head of archives at the Swenson Swedish Immigration Research Center, Augustana College, Rock Island, Illinois. Johansson is a native Swedish speaker

SWEDEN

LAPPLAND

NORRBOTTEN

VÄSTERBOTTEN

· Föllinge

ÅNGERMANLAND

JÄMTLAND

HÄRJEDALEN

MEDELPAD   Junsele
· Sundsvall

HÄLSINGLAND

DALARNA

Lima ·   GÄSTRIKLAND
· Svärdsjö
· Äppelbo

UPPLAND

VÄRMLAND   VÄSTMANLAND   · Uppsala

· Lysvik   · Karlstad
· Örebro   Stockholm ·
Gällersta   SÖDERMANLAND
NÄRKE

DALSLAND

Kimstad
Motala ·   Söderköping
Hjo ·   Linköping ·
Hudene   ÖSTERGÖTLAND
BOHUSLÄN   VÄSTERGÖTLAND

Göteborg ·   Jönköping ·   GOTLAND
Håcksvik ·

HALLAND   SMÅLAND

Falkenberg ·   Ljungby   · Växjö   Köping
· Vislanda   Nybro ·
Kalmar   ÖLAND

Hässleholm   · Kyrkhult   BLEKINGE
Ignaberga ·
· Brännestad
SKÅNE   · Genarp
· Malmö

Sweden, noting the regional provinces and communities
where the Rocky Mountain immigrants were born.
Map by GIS TReC, Idaho State University.

and is also familiar with nineteenth-century Swedish manuscripts and their challenges as regards handwriting, spelling, and idiom. After her first draft of each letter, we discussed the translation line by line and resolved issues about meaning, fluency, diction, and so on. Our goal was to capture the writing style and literacy level of each letter writer, rendering each translation very close to the original manuscript in diction, grammatical construction, punctuation, and paragraphing. Scholars of immigrant letters have recently become concerned with editorial practices that omit the most formulaic portions of letters, especially their formulaic opening and closing passages. They also have been concerned with translations that render letters as though their writers were fluent in the original language, producing what David A. Gerber calls "a homogenized, deindividualized 'representative' voice that belongs to no one in particular—except perhaps the editor."[1] This is just what we hoped to avoid.

While it would be a very difficult task to render translations with all of the misspellings and ungrammatical expressions of the originals, we have attempted to render awkward Swedish in awkward English and more eloquent Swedish in fluent English. We have also attempted to render a low level of diction in Swedish with very simple, Anglo Saxon–based word choice in English, and a high level of diction in Swedish with a similarly elevated, Latinate word choice in English. Where a correspondent uses formulaic expressions, we have rendered those expressions as formulas rather than taking the literacy-informed approach of seeking innovative phrasing. Hence, readers should be able to gain a sense of formula use throughout the collections and to detect a difference between the prose of, for example, Johan Håkansson and Leonard Nilsson.

Word choice is a very difficult matter in any translation effort. Many of the discussions between Johansson and me involved the choice of just the right English word to convey as precisely as possible the full connotation of a Swedish word. Even simple words like *trevlig* encompass meanings that are not entirely conveyed by the main choices in English: nice, jolly, fun, pleasant. Another example is *man*, meaning *one*. *Man* is a common word in Swedish, with less formality than the English *one*. Especially in American English, *one* is a formal and relatively uncommon usage. *You* was our choice, but that translation probably renders some passages a bit too informal. Added to these difficulties are the social differences between nineteenth-century Sweden and the United States. When a

Swedish immigrant working as a saloonkeeper explains to his Swedish letter readers that he is a *källarmästare,* how are we to translate this term? Working in a saloon is a low-status position in the United States; being a *källarmästare* is much higher status, more like being the manager of a restaurant. Our choice *manager of a tavern* only approximates the actual meaning.

False starts that are crossed out are not included in the translations. Such passages are very rare in the letter collections. Writers typically produced manuscripts that show little evidence of rereading and correction. Most of the letters are free of paragraphing, and many use punctuation very lightly. Ola Svenson's letters, for example, read as though they are each a single, exceedingly long sentence. In such situations, we have added commas and periods to suggest our sense of where there are natural divisions between thoughts. These were introduced through an oral process of editing: Johansson read the letter manuscripts aloud to seek the pauses that would occur in speech. We recognize, of course, that any such editorial process remains conjectural, but this oral process was used to honor the oral-derived quality of the letters. Through indentation, we have made a modest attempt at suggesting the way in which lines were laid out on the pages of the original manuscripts. Unless otherwise explained in editorial comments, italics indicate passages where correspondents use English or Swedish English words and phrases. Brackets are used to provide explanations or augmentations of some of the more obscure passages and to provide examples of Swedish English. For example, when Victor A. Hallquist uses the Swedish English *storet* in his letter, we have provided the translation *the store* and placed his Swedish English usage in brackets immediately following the translation.

We are very grateful to Larry E. Scott, professor of Scandinavian studies at Augustana College, for assistance with Charles Flodin's letter and with nineteenth-century idioms in other letters, and to David M. Gustafson, PhD candidate in church history at Linköping University, for his assistance with Ola Svenson's religious language.

Anderson, Charles H.
1889
Limon, Colorado
One letter

Charles H. Anderson wrote in 1889 from Limon, Colorado, to Hanna Gustafson in Minneapolis. This isolated letter reveals his dilemma: he wanted to be able to propose to Hanna but felt that he was too poor. His very tentative proposal instead was that she travel to Colorado to work as a cook, and wait until 1891 to marry him. He wrote knowing that the offer would not be tempting to her and that it would be likely she followed her intent to move to Texas. This letter underscores the connection between money and marriage.

Anderson, Jonas
1906–7
Denver, Colorado
Three letters

Jonas Anderson wrote letters during 1906 and 1907 to reestablish contact with his brother Nils in Västra Torsås, south of Vislanda in Småland. Jonas was living in Denver with one of his sons, the owner of a music store. In 1907 he turned eighty, and his 1907 letters reflect on age and the need to maintain a family network.

Anderson, Karna
1904
Troy, Idaho
One letter

Karna (Mrs. J.) Anderson wrote from Troy, Idaho, in 1904, heading her letter "Troy Lumber & Mfg. Co." She wrote to a childhood friend living in Skärsnäs, in Skåne. Anderson's letter is unusual in that the first half consists of a religious testimony. The second half imparts family and domestic news and her feelings about being in touch with an old friend, who had apparently surprised her with a letter. A search of Latah County Historical Society collections has turned up no trace of a Karna Anderson or a Mrs. J. Anderson.

Anderson, Otto
1903
Butte, Montana
One letter

In 1903 Otto Anderson wrote from Butte, Montana, to a friend in Minnesota to offer him books that he had left behind there. Anderson also sent his friend a poem. This isolated letter is unusual in representing the upper-class Swedish American. Anderson was a traveling correspondent for the Minneapolis newspaper *Svenska Folkets Tidning* between 1899 and 1911; he used the pen names Otto and Viftare (wanderer) for his reports from various locations. Reports from the Montana cities of Great Falls, Helena, Butte, and Anaconda appeared during the summer of 1903.[2]

Anderson, Peter
1889
Cheyenne, Wyoming
One letter

Only one letter survives from Peter Anderson, sent from Cheyenne, Wyoming, in 1889.[3] Anderson had emigrated from Skåne, according to the donor of his letter, seeking adventure and fortune. He soon broke off correspondence with his family, even though in his letter of 1889 he considered returning to Sweden from the "rain-free land" of Wyoming.[4]

Andersson, Genny
1887
Helena, Montana
One letter

Genny Andersson wrote a Christmas letter to her sister and parents from Helena, Montana, on December 1, 1887. The isolated letter provides no clues as to her age, marital state, or point of origin in Sweden. Andersson's letter is unusual in that there is no greeting. Instead she launches, in heavily Swedish-influenced English, into a "Christians carol," a Christmas carol written partly by William Chatterton Dix. Then, partway through the letter, she shifts to Swedish and begins the format that one would ordinarily expect, commenting on her progress in learning English and on purchases she had made in New York, and wishing her relatives and friends a happy Christmas.

Bloomberg, Charles M.
1910–13
Leadville, Colorado
Five letters

Charles M. Bloomberg, originally Carl Johannesson, wrote letters to his mother, sister, and in-laws in Stenbrohult, Småland. Bloomberg was married and had at least two school-age daughters, Hellen and Jenni. His letters included news about their progress in learning English and other more general family details.

Boline, Carl
1915–17
Leadville and Romley, Colorado
Six letters

Carl Boline wrote letters to his mother from the mining towns of Romley (southeast of Aspen) and Leadville, Colorado, between 1915 and 1917. He had moved from Chicago to Leadville to find work. Boline expressed a desire to travel home, but delayed travel because of the war in Europe.

Borg, Oskar
1884
Vienna, Idaho
One letter

Oskar Borg,[5] or Oscar Frederik Borg, was born in 1857 at Kärna, near the city of Linköping in Östergötland.[6] He was a foundry worker before traveling in 1880 or 1881 to the United States, where he eventually found mine work in the Wood River, Idaho, mining region. The brother of Leonard Nilsson's fiancée, Lovisa, Oskar wrote two surviving letters to Lovisa: from Arkansas in 1881, and from Vienna, Idaho, in 1884. According to Nilsson, he also corresponded frequently with Oskar, but those letters do not survive in the Nilsson collection. Oskar's letters mention his concerns about American women and marriage, the poor economy, the multiethnic population in the West, and card playing. (See also Leonard Nilsson in this appendix.)

Brodin, Bengt Olson

1883–84
Custer, Idaho
Three letters

Bengt Olson Brodin wrote in 1884 from Custer, Idaho, to his brother Olaf in Sweden to describe the birth of his son. Brodin had not been with his wife for the birth; she had stayed behind in San Francisco, where she and Brodin felt there were better doctors available.[7] Originally named Bengt Olofsson, Brodin was born in Kyrkhult parish, Blekinge, in 1850. He emigrated in 1868. He first worked in Galesberg, Illinois, where three of his brothers located, and then in San Francisco, where he worked in a horse stable. He married his wife Emma, also a Swedish immigrant, in 1879. Brodin's sojourn in Custer was brief, only a couple of years from 1883 to 1884. There he was a laborer, probably a miner. In 1884 he returned to his family in San Francisco, and succumbed to pneumonia later that year.[8]

Dahlgren, Emma

1912
Texas Ridge, Idaho
One letter

In 1912 Emma Dahlgren[9] wrote from Texas Ridge, near Deary, Idaho, to her cousin John R. Johnson (see John R. Johnson in this appendix), inviting him to the wedding of their uncle, Mike Knutson, of Kendrick, south of Troy and Deary, Idaho. Writing October 31, Dahlgren dated her letter "Hallow'een." Her Swedish was heavily influenced by English.

Dickson, Anni

1893
Red Cliff, Colorado
Seven letters

Anni Dickson wrote several letters in 1893 to her friend Carl Israelsson of Pigeon Cove, Massachusetts. Dickson related her adjustments to the mining community of Red Cliff and to the limited social life available there. She was living with her sister, who gave birth to a baby during Dickson's stay. By the end of the letter collection, Dickson had begun studying English. There is no indication that the friendship between Dickson and Israelsson blossomed into a closer relationship. In the following sample, Dickson explains how her lack of ability to speak and read English restricted her studies and her social life. Her affection for and hopes regarding Carl are apparent.[10]

Red Cliff the 1st of November 1893

When a sigh
is heard faintly
by no friend
it's like the dove
who flies toward the sky.[11]

Dear friend Carl during a peaceful evening I do not find more pleasure than to write you my dear friend. And of all, I have to thank you for the letter I received a few days ago, which was welcome. I thought you had forgotten me, but now I see that you have not done that yet. I see that you are in good health and doing well, which is nice to hear. I also have to tell you the same. I hear that you are going to attend school which I will do too here. There are two English schools; I am going to one [of them]. I will begin as soon as my sister is well, she just had a baby 14 days ago, so she is not recovered yet, but as soon as she is well I will begin school. I am going to study music but I have to learn how to read [musical notation] first. I play the organ every day but I cannot read English notes so I will learn that, but it will be fairly expensive to take the exam. It costs about 50 cents per hour but learning comes easily to me. So [do] you think that there is a point for me to study? Also I see that you have bought yourself a horse and *buggy [buggi]*. If I will go and visit you this spring I hope I can go in it. But I get to go in a *buggy* here sometimes also. You say that you have lots of fun and dance; here they dance as well, but I have only attended one dance since I came here. As long as I cannot speak I do not want to go places because there are no Swedes here and I never hear a Swedish word during the days. My sisters speak English all the time and now I am beginning to be able to speak [English]. You say there are [literally, "you are"] many Swedes [where you are]; it is fun to be in such places with [many] Swedes. I am thinking about going to Chicago in the spring. You can certainly come and see me in the spring; then I can go *back [bäck]* with you. It would be nice to see you, you say that you have wished many times that I was where you are. You must believe that I have too. Here are many boys that like me because Swedish girls are highly regarded here, but I do not like any of them because I am not intending to stay out here. And I wish that you, my dear Carl, will not forget me. It is nice to receive letters from you, now I have not delayed my answer, and I hope that you my dear Carl do not take too long in replying either. Also I wish that you do not forget [to send me] a picture when you take one. Now I am too tired to sit up, it is 11 at night and I have been standing and ironing the entire day, but I will end my simple letter to you for this time with many dear greetings from me to you and your brother.

Anni Dickson

When I see and consider about how much fun we have had in the time that already has passed then my heart fills with tears and sorrow becomes my lot.

Write soon my dear friend good night to you now I am going to bed.

Erickson, Nils
1884
Fort Craig, New Mexico
Two letters

Nils Erickson wrote letters entirely in the form of poems to his sweetheart Emelia [Emmy] Sofia Peterson, who by 1891 had married him. Nils served in the U.S. cavalry at Fort Craig, New Mexico (south of Socorro), where the couple met. Emelia was a housekeeper for the commanding officer's family. She had earlier worked as a household cook in Colorado Springs.

Erlandson, Peter F.

1880–81
Morrison, Colorado
Three letters

Peter F. (Fredric) Erlandson, born in Köping on Öland, 1855, emigrated in 1873.[12] By 1880, he had traveled from the eastern United States to Colorado, where he wrote from Morrison, Colorado, in 1880 and 1881. Only three letters survive. They testify to Erlandson's growing emotional distance from family and friends in Sweden, and to his having been tempted to the West by the idea that money could be made by prospecting. Characterizing the Utes as a barrier to mining, Erlandson is one of the few writers to mention American Indians.

Flodin, Charles

1886–95
Monarch, Ouray, Dolores, and Rico, Colorado
Eleven letters

Charles Flodin, or Karl Leonard Flodin, was born in 1858. At the time of his emigration in 1882, he was working as a miller at Håcksvik in Västergötland.[13] In the United States, Flodin worked in Michigan, Wisconsin, and Minnesota before moving to Colorado sometime between 1884 and 1886, when his first letters from the West were sent. In Colorado he did railroad and mining labor, but he also traveled widely to prospect for gold. His letters continued through 1895. They were written to a friend, Anders Abrahamsson, who spent several years in the Upper Midwest, beginning in 1882, but who returned to Sweden in 1889.[14] Flodin addressed Abrahamsson as *broder* (brother), but there is no evidence in parish records that they were related.

Flodin wrote colorful letters in which he recounts his travels to seek gold, describing the mountainous Western terrain and the people he met. Among immigration letters that have been preserved in archives, Flodin's are unusually earthy in language and content. The following sample was written after a visit to Sweden, and displays Flodin's attitudes toward women, Sweden, and America. Italicized passages exhibit Flodin's frequent code switching to English expressions.[15]

Charles Flodin begins a letter to his buddy Anders exclaiming over the depth of the snow at Madonna Camp. Image courtesy of the Swedish Emigrant Institute.

Madonna Camp Jan. 28 [1888?]

Brother Anders!

Your letter of the 16th this month I picked up on Monday. God, God, for a walk in snow above the knees. We have been snowed in for over two weeks now and it continues to storm and snow, you have never seen a snowstorm in the Rocky Mountains? Good! May the Lord bless you from seeing such. Oh, I am doing fairly well as long as it storms because the only thing there is to do is to tend to my horses and others, besides I usually stay in bed until 8 or 9 in the mornings. The only thing that is hard for me to solve is the monotony, can you imagine being snowed in and have nothing to do. If the weather gets really God-damned awful—I walk to *town* on snowshoes or also, as the last time, on my butt when it so happens. Say Anders, are you really going home this spring? It will be a *picnic* for you until you get to Gothenburg, when you would wish the devil would take the entire crowd of city folks, because many suffer with America fever there and you would wish that you had never set foot on the damned pier in Gothenburg. I have *spent [spendt]* more *money* in that damned hole than she is worth, lock, stock, and barrel.[16] No, Falkenberg there is a city to come ashore. That will be my disembarkation next time when my expensive *[dyra]*[17] native country's soil will have the honor to kiss my American *number eight shoes [No eight shoez]*. And then there is another thing, if you would want a nice girl as a bed warmer it costs 20 crowns. Is that not the height of rudeness. *As "anyhow"* she was sweet that child of Satan of Norwegian *descent [descend]*, oh my A. *I never can forget*. It was when we were in Gothenburg on our way back to America I befriended two guys [literally, two salmon] from Småland, one had been home over the summer *before* and the other was an old cattle trader from Ljungby. Talkative men, both were jolly without being on the make. The cattle trader had *lots of money*, you should have seen him in Hull, Liverpool, New York, Chicago and altogether how surprised he was and taken with everything he saw. And in Chicago you should have seen and heard him when he talked with Patron Lindgren with his cap in his hand. He was a *smart man*, anyway when talking about Småland, but in foreign affairs he was lost. Seriously are you thinking about staying home and giving up traveling. *"Settle [Cattle]* at home *and children"* or only *"pay a visit"*? Say Anders if you marry remember that your first born should be my godson or daughter *how at ever it is*. But I do not want to carry a scream-ing child to the baptism. I could mention a girl by name that would be perfectly suitable to *raise [resa] Young ones after but I will be quiet*, so per-haps you want to pass by inns [visit taverns to meet other women]. But make no mistake, if I come home and she is free and available, then, yes, I do not know [what would happen]. You are so wise to go home during the spring, had I known as much as I do now, in '84 I would have waited until the weather [got better]. I . When. . . .[18]

You speak of them getting married at home and, yes, that can be good for some people, as the old lady says.

Lucky Petrus he came in the nick of time to save Sofia from monotony. I felt as if a gloom had come over me when I saw Sofi at Manuel's place in Skäremo and my thoughts went: Sofi poor Sofi here you are now (on Sundays when there is no service in either one of the churches) from one bench in the cottage across the floor to the other looking out through the window thoughtfully. What does she see yes in the distance, far away, her youthful love, having unintentionally tied the knot with someone else. You shall see Anders how depressed you will be when you get out to Skäremo. I thought my chest would *burst*. Just like a *"graveyard."* The only one who followed me a bit to the big road was Edvard from Skäremo. Then I walked home myself through the high forest which was so well known from days you yourself perhaps love to think about for a while. If Anders at least had been home I thought then I would have let the devil take the rest. *Yes*, and *here* I was, and went to bed just like a pig.

Good *brother* Anders Calle *might* come sometime in the future, but when only time will tell.

Have a good trip if you decide to go. Greet the Pettersson brothers, [tell them] that I am sorry from my heart about the loss of their brother. You are much greeted brother Anders from

Charles

Håkansson, Johan
1888–89
Leadville and Florissant, Colorado
Eight letters

Johan Håkansson worked in Leadville, Colorado, during the years 1888 and 1889, sending letters and money home to his wife Britta and their children, who were in Sweden. Throughout his letters, Håkansson writes about returning to Sweden, so he is best considered a part of the labor migration—that is, an emigrant who never intended to become an immigrant. According to information provided by the donor of Håkansson's letters, Håkansson was born in 1858, left Virestad, southwest of Vislanda in Småland, for America in 1886,[31] spent some time in Chicago, and returned to Sweden in 1889.

Håkansson's letters contain mostly expressions of longing for his wife and family and concern that she should write and that she had received the money he had sent her. He worked in a smelter, describing the work as hard, tiring, and hot; however, he considered the location, up in the mountains, to have improved his health. On the other hand, he worried that his wife might not recognize him on return, so he sent her photographs, commenting that he had become an old man. The following letter is typically brief and focused on family relationships and work.[32]

Leadville August 16th 1888
Dear wife and children

I want to write you a few lines and let you know that I have good health to the moment of writing this and I wish the same good condition for you, health. Today I am sending money, it is 152 kr 13 öre which you will receive. You can lend it to brother for his loan that he asked me about a long time ago. I am sending you more, in time you can take out a promissory note on Bengt, that is best. I do not work now during the day because the machine is broken. I will find out in a couple of weeks if they need [me]. I have worked constantly for 6 months so you can imagine that I am tired so I was happy when it came to an end. They are beginning to fix the machine. You should write as soon as you receive this letter so I will get to know how things are at home this summer. [It] has begun to get cold during the nights so we will soon have winter. I am wondering if the money I sent last has reached you. Write about that when you write. I have no news to tell you this time. [It is] so quiet here, greet all my relatives at home from me, with love from me Joh Håkansson.

Finally, [please] care for my children, greetings from your faithful husband, wishes

Joh Håkansson.
Leadville

Hall, A. P.
1905
Logan, Utah
One letter

In 1905 A. P. Hall wrote to his brother Jöns P. Hall of Lyngsjö in Skåne about how an inheritance should be divided among the six siblings, five of whom had immigrated to Utah and Colorado. A brother, Nels, had died, and in his final illness was nursed by his sister Hanna, but her inheritance was disputed by Nels's former wife. A. P. argued for equal division. A. P. wrote from Logan, where he was visiting family members for Christmas. (See also Ellen H. Mohr and Hanna [Hall] in this appendix.)

[Hall], Hanna
1906
Logan, Utah
One letter

A sister of Ellen H. Mohr and A. P. Hall, Hanna[19] wrote in 1906 from Logan, Utah, regarding how an inheritance on the death of their father should be apportioned among the six siblings, five of whom were in the western United States. Hanna was the most literate of the three siblings. (See also Ellen H. Mohr and A. P. Hall in this appendix.)

Hallberg, Emma
1891–1917
Denver, Colorado
Nine letters

Emma Hallberg[20] emigrated to America in 1890 to join her brother, John M. Swanson. With John and her sister Ida, who joined them in 1893, they formed a close-knit family, with homes located close to one another in the Denver neighborhood now known as Sunnyside, northwest of the downtown area. (See also John M. Swanson and Albert and Ida Sandberg in this appendix.) The fourth and youngest sibling, Anna Lovisa, who died in 1892, and their parents remained in Virestad, southwest of Vislanda in Småland. Emma, John, and Ida wrote regularly to them.

Emma was Emma Kristina Svensdotter, born in 1870 in Virestad.[21] In Denver, she married Olof Hallberg, a laborer.[22] Her letters concern domestic news of births and deaths, the health and well-being of family members, her children's schooling, and family trips to the mountains. The following example is typical.[23]

Denver September 1, 1902

Dear parents

I now have to thank you for the greetings I received. I am happy that you are in good health and which we also have up to the moment of writing [this]. I have thought about writing so many times but it always gets so late so I think now it is such a long time ago since I received a letter from you. I see in your letter that you have lots of rain back home. It is sad that people cannot get their fall [farm] chores done and that the crops are not mature, but we hope that it has become better now. Here we have had a fairly beautiful summer, there were three large hailstorms in the early part of the summer, but since then it has been beautiful. I can tell you that I have so many beautiful flowers this summer. So we have never had that many. It would have been nice if you could have come to see us, have you been to Kengsleboda [Kängsleboda, a village in the parish of Virestad] this summer or have they [relatives] been home at times? I think that the girls could go home and visit sometimes. They do not stay in touch at all. Bengt and Axel want to come here. Hallberg says that he could probably find them work if they were here. *Then [Twen]* we hear that Lina has written home and she is just like her old self. We have heard that she begged from you your gold ring last time she was home, we think that at least she could let you hold on to what you have. When you needed it, she did not give you much either, now she could help you a bit if she understood it. She ought to be ashamed of herself. Have you heard what Betty's boy is doing or if he is as great as she brags. Betty is certainly a nice girl so she is worthy a good man. Tomorrow the second all English schools will begin then I am going to bring Semmi there and see if she can begin she might not be old enough, but she will be next month so it is just a month difference. The schoolhouse is located on our street so it is not further than from your cottage to the well. They go just half a day at first.

I am wondering if you have any hens now, I have quite a few so if you were here I would give you a few eggs sometimes. We have about 40 hens big and small then we have bought a cow so I can give Ida milk now and another lady *[Fru]* it gave 5 qv [1qv = 0.375 liter] of milk per day now and it is going to have a calf in December so if that works we will have lots of milk for Christmas. She usually gives 4 pitchers per day and we got it cheap: 45 dollars and it is worth 65 to 60 dollars. I have to end here because you are probably tired of reading my rambling. Good-bye for this time signed by your daughter Emma Hallberg and the children send their best.

Blenda sends her greetings to you, she says that she shall send you a picture of the boys. We are going there sometime this week. They were here about three weeks ago.

Hallquist, Anna
1904–6
Denver, Colorado
Two letters

Anna Hallquist[24] and her husband, Victor, moved to Denver from Boston in 1896. Anna (née Olson), born in 1868, met Victor at the Tremont Temple Church in Boston, where Swedish parishioners held separate meetings. The couple married and began a family, eventually moving to Denver. When Victor became very ill with kidney disease in 1904, Anna wrote to her in-laws in Sweden. When Victor died in 1906, Anna was left with a house and money from an insurance policy, but she also took in laundry to support the family of six. (See also Victor A. Hallquist and Victor Hallquist Jr. in this appendix.)

Hallquist, Victor, Jr.
1898
Denver, Colorado
One letter

Victor Hallquist Jr.[25] was born to Anna and Victor A. Hallquist in 1891, while they were living in Boston. He moved with his family to Denver in 1896. In 1898, when he was in second grade, he wrote a letter in English to his Uncle Johan, translated into Swedish by his father. When Victor's father died in 1905, Victor Jr. took on work to help his mother support the family. (See also Victor A. Hallquist and Anna Hallquist in this appendix.)

Hallquist, Victor A.
1897–1904
Denver, Colorado
Six letters

Victor Hallquist[26] was born in the city of Jönköping in 1865, and emigrated from Småland to the Boston area as a carpenter. By 1889 he was active in a Baptist congregation there. In Boston, Victor suffered from poor health and was eventually urged to try treatment at the Phipps Sanatorium in Denver. Moving there in 1896, Victor experienced improved health. He found work as a house carpenter and was responsible for construction of numerous houses and the Emmanuel Baptist Church. His letters to his brother Johan provide detailed descriptions of the houses he and his family occupied. He also told stories about local crimes. Victor became very ill again in 1904, this time with kidney disease. After one unsuccessful operation, in 1905 he again went under the knife for removal of the diseased kidney. The doctor removed the wrong kidney, and Victor died on the operating table. The following letter is from 1898, a much happier time, when Victor was healthy and had enjoyed a recent visit to Denver by the evangelist Dwight L. Moody.[27] (See also Anna Hallquist and Victor Hallquist Jr. in this appendix.)

Denver the 27th of Nov 98

Brother Johan

I want to briefly write to tell you how we are doing here in the far west.
We have good health all of us, I am just like I was when I left Sweden
healthy and strong. Anna is healthy! Victor is in school and he is doing
well with writing and reading, Ruth, Harold, Esther are home keeping
Mama busy. I have to tell you that we have not had any rain this summer in Colorado so all of the harvest is destroyed, it has been so dry that
the irrigation has dried out in most places, in September and October
we saw lightning hitting the sky far up in the mountains but no clouds in
our sight so we had [no] water on this side rather it all fell to the west of
us. So food is very expensive and job opportunities appear to be getting
scarcer. I also have to tell you that Dwight Moody [Dwiet Moddey] the
world-renowned evangelist as well as a singer whose name is Jakob has
been in Denver for 2 weeks. They have held 2 meetings per day and a big
revival has been here. He preached in various churches, but the first time
he appeared the hall was packed and the *street [streetet]* outside the hall
the biggest in Denver [was also packed]. The governor sat on the platform
and [there was] police protection in every door and Jakob sang Sankey's
Songs. Sankey [gospel hymnist Ira David Sankey] was not along. The
meeting was for men only, no women were there because it was just like
that.[28] So he held special meetings for women. His first text was what you
sow is what you reap. The first thing he said was that he was sent by God
and what he says comes from God and he does not need police protection.
He spoke against ungodly living, as well as saloons and gambling houses,
he argued that those were the worst evils in Denver and that they were to
blame for many murders and crimes and he appealed to the governor for
support. Then he presented "The One Jesus Loves, That One He Seeks"[29]
and when the meeting was over you could almost see tears in most eyes.
The next day the newspaper was blaming Moody and wrote lies that he
had $100 per day and that he preached for money, but they corrected this
later. Moody was happy about that and he said during the next meeting
that when you meet Satan with the truth he always fights back and he
prayed to God for them.

I can also tell you that many have been murdered here in Denver,
last week 3 pharmacies and one jewelry *store [stor]* were *robbed [robbat]*.

Murderers always have a revolver in each hand, one stays outside and one goes in, when he gets in he orders hands up. Those who do not raise their hands immediately will get shot, then he orders them to go out with him behind the *store [storet]* with the hands up. Then he orders them to stand together, then he takes the revolver in one hand and holds it pointed at them, with the other hand he picks their pockets, then he orders them to turn around or to sit down while he walks away. There is no point in saying anything or putting your hands down because then it is all over. A Swede has been murdered in Denver, the police have not been able to catch anybody but they have now gotten bloodhounds to track with and more police have been sent here. I now want to send you dear regards from all of us and wish you a Merry Christmas. Greet everybody we know, greet aunt at Lilengen, greet Lina and my half brothers. I am wondering how they are getting by. I [can]not send a Christmas present because I am in difficult circumstances myself. Greet Emil and his family, greet Malen and their family.

A dear greeting to you all signed by your friend Brother Victor.

Address 4582 Arlington St.
    North Highland
    Denver Colo.

Hedin, John
1889
Helena, Montana
One letter

John Hedin,[30] or Johannes Hedin, was born in 1867 and emigrated in 1889, writing back to a brother in Sweden upon his arrival in Helena, Montana, where he lived with a brother and one other Swedish immigrant and worked on a city waterline. His comparisons of Sweden and America focus on economic differences and the status of workers. English-speaking ability, he notes, is very important in the West. Hedin was originally from Lima in Dalarna.

Jeppsson, Clara
1911–12
Denver and LaJara, Colorado
Fourteen letters

Clara Jeppsson wrote to her sister Sigrid from Denver and from LaJara, Colorado, during 1911 and 1912. Clara had come to the United States in 1910 to join another sister, Ida, who lived in California. By August of that year, she was married to Johan. In 1911 the couple moved to Denver to seek better work, but what they found kept them apart, with Clara working as a maid in the city, and Johan working as a laborer on a farm outside the city. In LaJara they were able to live together. After their time in Colorado, the inventory of Clara's letters shows that she returned to Sweden from 1913 to 1915, and then lived in Kansas and California. Jeppsson's letters emphasize family relationships and news, but she also offers descriptions of Denver and its advantages for a Swedish woman. The following letter was written while Jeppsson was still separated from her husband. It was part of an extended discussion with her sister over the situation of their brother, Axel.[33]

Denver the 31st of July, 1911

Dear Sister!

Thank you for the letter that I received the 29th of this month. It was sad information about Axel, who would have thought anything like that a few years ago. It sounded as if he was keen on traveling when we were there, but I took it to be a joke.

I do not think that he will come over because of his bad eyes, so it is almost madness to leave without consulting a doctor. Another thing is, what he will do here, this place is so full of male workers so there are many who have been here for many years who are without jobs. If it had been next year or after the presidential election. It is so easy to say that they will take any job when they are still in Sweden, but they do not understand what it is like to work in America. If he comes here he will be attending a hard school [learning the hard way] and he will see things he never could have imagined. I am wondering if he has perhaps thought about going down into the mines or out in the forest, which is not exactly the worst work there is, and working on Sundays and every day year around. Johan works on a farm 150 miles from Denver and there he has to work on Sundays too. But now uncle has sold his house and is ready to build a new one and then Johan can work there unless he prefers to stay on the farm. If you yourself do not have any work to offer friends and family [as a newcomer] you cannot expect to find anything in these bad times. When we came to Denver, Johan was trying to get in with a wagon factory here in the city and uncle who is an old Denverite went with him and he received a half promise and he was asked to come back again, but the next time he went it was a definite no. [Returning to Axel's case] I also think there is some problem with finances and therefore there are of course disagreements between them, if they have lived together for fifteen sixteen years why can they not continue to do so now. But as you say there is nothing you can do about it, rather things will have to run their course. If he comes here, which I seriously doubt, he will have the same experience as most everybody else.

It is a long time ago since I heard from Ida and I have not sent her any letter even though I have one already written. She is out in California's snowy mountains with her people so I think that she has cool [weather] just like us. Otherwise, it has been very hot in America. Here in Denver it is not at all warm and we are receiving a fair amount of rain. I do not want to tell Ida about Axel's personal dealings because I am afraid that she will send him all the money she has.

I do not have much to tell otherwise, I work at the same place as before and when I am off I often go to City Park which is only a few minutes away so that I can lie in my bed and hear the music. I have made acquaintances with a few other Swedes here. Most of the Swedes you meet here are well-off if not rich. A man from the province of Skåne [Skåning] who owns a laundry service here. I got to know them because the wife suddenly fell ill and they needed somebody to care for the children and I was recommended by another Swedish woman, so I stayed there for a few days. That was before I took this place. I hope that I soon will have my dear man [gubbe] here again because it is more enjoyable when he is here.

The address on the letter was wrong, but I do not know if I gave you the wrong address or if you forgot the name on the street. I will write the correct address below for you. I did not get around to writing to mother for her birthday, and that I have gone around and regretted for many days but it is too late now but I will write to her soon anyway. You should send my greetings to her and everybody at home and kindest regards to you and Lindblad. kindly Clara.

My address is: Mrs. Clara Jeppson
           c/o Mrs. Stuggis 1776 Williams St.
           Denver Col.

Ida's address is
           c/o Mrs Tevis Fallack
           Lake Tahoe Cal.

Jernberg, John E.

1912–17
Moscow, Idaho
Eleven letters

John E. Jernberg,[34] christened Johan Erik, was born in 1857; his family emigrated to the United States in 1882 from the parish Svärdsjö in Dalarna.[35] In the Midwest, he married another Swedish immigrant, and he farmed at Geddes, South Dakota. In 1912 Jernberg auctioned his farm and moved with his family to the vicinity of Moscow, Idaho. Jernberg describes their new location as one-and-a-half miles outside Moscow, still close enough to the town to be active in the Swedish Lutheran church. He and his wife, Anna M., were still farming on rural route 5 near Moscow in 1922.[36] In 1927 Jernberg moved to Spokane, Washington, where he died one year later. Jernberg's letters contain many details about his farming and about church functions. He also expresses his desire that neither Sweden nor the United States become involved in a senseless war in Europe.

Johansson, August

1891
Denver, Colorado
One letter

August Johansson wrote from Denver in 1891, describing the sea passage via Liverpool and the Swedish American community in Denver. He wrote to a younger brother, which may be why his letter is very detailed in describing such things as the elevators in Denver department stores and the city's cable cars. August refers to a Sofi with whom he traveled, perhaps his wife.

Johansson, Peter J.
1891
Great Falls, Monarch, and Neihart, Montana
Five letters

Peter J. Johansson was an itinerant railroad worker who traveled through Montana during 1891, writing from Great Falls, Monarch, and Neihart to his brother in Sweden. Johansson had two brothers in Sweden: Johannes Petersson, married with at least one son, and Emil, who was ill in a Stockholm hospital during 1891. Johansson sent money home to both brothers, his nephew, and his father, even though his work was intermittent and prices were high in the West. Prior to his employment in Montana, Johansson had worked in railroad construction in Niagara and Fort Buford, North Dakota, as part of contract labor crews. He described the sleeping and food arrangements that were part of the contract in Montana. The crew included a least a few other Swedes and a Norwegian. The letter collection allows us to trace Johansson's path westward from Montana to Washington and California, and by 1904 to the Yukon. In the following letter, written from Neihart in 1891, Johansson expressed concerns about work and money.[37]

Neihart, Mont, 27 July 1891

Brother Johannes!

Thank you for the letter I received from you 14 days ago, I see that you are in good health and doing well even though times are rough in Stockholm, but I hope that you now have begun to work at your old place and then you have a steady income. Times here in the west are the same as last summer, nothing to brag about but not the worst. I do not know what we are going to earn here for the job we are doing now, but the last [job] got only 2 dollars in excess of daily wages. I think that we are earning a bit more here because we have [a] 1500 (meter) *yard* mountain in this job, but we have had to purchase rock blaster tools [perhaps percussion caps] for about 5 per dollar. I think that we will finish here in a month, but I will most likely stay here until (the rails) the railway is finished, which it will be in the end of September [at least] that is what I am thinking now. We are now 5 men who are companions 4 Swedes and 1 Norwegian. I do not know if I am going to stay here in Montana until the winter. Because here [it] is very difficult with jobs during the winters, nearly impossible to get anything. The contractor whom I work for is intending to travel to the Pacific coast 6 to 700 miles farther west this coming winter, either I will follow him or I will go to Minnesota I think.

You asked me if I thought there would be any point in you coming here, but I should tell you that it is best that you stay where you are. Because you know what you have, but not what you might get here. Because here in the west you have to travel a lot and that takes both time and money. So those who are married and have a family in such a place [have a hard time]. As in Stockholm money is needed [all the time]. [Just] as I had to go through this past winter almost three months without a job and if you do not have any money then you are out in the cold. The month of June was very rainy here, so we were unable to work a lot because we are up here in a high mountain area called Bell Mountain and it rains a lot here in the spring, but now the weather is beautiful. I received a letter from home a few weeks ago and I heard that they are very poor and that [they] do not have the strength to work and you can imagine how the prospects are in Småland for a poor man whose strength is starting to fail him. I am therefore intending to send him some money, which I hope that you can exchange and send (mine) yes our old father. I do not have the time to write more because I am going to town to get myself some money. That is a paycheck for the last job. Greet Amalia and Albin so much from me signed by your brother

Peter J. Johansson
Neihart, Mont.
N. Amerika

Magnuson is sending his regards. I am sending 20 dollars and of that I give your oldest son Albin, his name is, 10 crowns which I want you to save for him in the bank. Perhaps that will amount to something in the future for him. The rest I want you to be so good to send father

P.J. Johansson

Johnson, Aron W.

1901–5
Wamsutter and Rawlins, Wyoming
Twenty letters

Aron W. Johnson,[38] known as Aron Wilhelm Johansson in Sweden, was born in 1871 in Madesjö, near Nybro in Småland. In 1893 he emigrated to North America, the same year that his sister Adelina emigrated. They were followed by their brothers, Carl Gottfrid in 1894 and Amandus Elof in 1896.[39] Johnson became a sheep rancher in Wyoming, running, according to family tradition, over 7,000 head. His letters to his fiancée, Anna, who lived in Nybro, Småland, ask her again and again to consider joining him in America. When she refuses, he agrees to return, even though it will make him "America sick." Johnson moved back to Sweden in 1905, selling his business, which had been valued at $7,980 in the county tax assessment for that year. He was able to purchase a farm (*gård*) near Kalmar and to marry Anna, but the sale of his Wyoming ranch at a distance resulted in protracted issues with the new owner, from whom it was difficult to obtain payment. (See also Fabian Johnson, O. M. Johnson, and Adelina Reinhold in this appendix.) The following letter was one among many in which Aron alternately chided Anna and pleaded with her to join him in America.[40]

Rawling Wyo
Sept. 10 1903

Beloved friend thank you for the letter which I received from you yesterday in which I see that you had written as early as the 12th of August, that will be in 2 days a month ago since you wrote. I was in town a couple of weeks ago but then your letter had not arrived so therefore I did not get around to writing you. I am happy to hear that you are healthy which I am too. Dear Anna you say that you are unsure of whether I want to leave you or come home you shall never think that I want to leave you I will probably never become that sleazy.

If any leaving will become an issue then it will be your fault, we could have been together a long time ago if you had wanted to come here. You must believe that I have small circumstances here since you think it would be so dangerous to come here. I would like to please you, if I could sell my sheep even though no good times await me in Sweden. I do not like Sweden's long mandatory military service. To come from the most free nation on earth and go under Swedish military snobs an entire year is too much for my sense of pride to digest. I have no prospects of getting out of it with the exception of the first two years when I can stay in Sweden as an American citizen if I do not want to own any property, which is not something I must [do] because you can. But then I will let go of my sheep this fall or spring and do what you say whatever might happen. But if I cannot sell out, could you not come here if I send you some money to pay for your farm before you travel here or do I absolutely have to come back for this to happen. If I am forced to stay here and you cannot accept my suggestions it would be the only way to act properly toward you. I am sorry Anna but I did not think that you had such low thoughts about me in such a way. I see that A. Sjöstrand is married to Anna Johnson from Tjukehall [Tjukahall, a village in Madesjö parish]? I never could have thought that she would take such a joker. But he had, to put it mildly good luck. I am sorry about my forgetfulness and not remembering that they had gotten engaged, that I had totally forgotten. [I] see also that the Lundquist woman has gotten herself a soldier, that was also fresh news to me because I have not received or written to them. All my Swedish news is from you. You are the only one who writes to me from Sweden. I have written one letter to Adrian but I have not received any answer. [I] hope that you forgive my nosiness in the last letter I sometimes get depressed when I see how impossible it is to get you from Sweden

Many dear regards to you from me

Respectfully A. A. Johnson
L Box 332 Rawling Wyo
North America

Johnson, Fabian
1907
Wamsutter, Wyoming
One letter

Fabian Johnson[41] addressed Aron W. Johnson as "brother" when he wrote to him after Aron's return to Sweden, sending him news of his work and a subscription to the Chicago newspaper *Svenska Amerikanaren.* However, there is no evidence that Fabian and Aron were related. (See also Aron W. Johnson, O. M. Johnson, and Adelina Reinhold in this appendix.)

Johnson, Gottfrid
1914–15
La Jara, Colorado
Two letters

Gottfrid Johnson wrote from La Jara, Colorado, during 1914 and 1915, when he was there working on an uncle's ranch. Not much can be gleaned regarding Gottfrid's personal history, but his letters are interesting for their descriptions of Christmas, of work on the ranch, and of a local crime perpetrated by a Mormon. Gottfrid's first letters were from Nebraska in 1911. By 1914 he was working in Colorado, and after a brief return to Nebraska during 1918 and 1919, he lived in Colorado through the 1960s. His letters were directed to relatives in Skåne.

Johnson, John R.
1905–6
Moscow, Idaho
Two letters

John R. Johnson, listed in the Äppelbo, Dalarna, parish records as Johan Johansson Rööds, was born in 1876, and left for the United States in 1893, destined for Minneapolis.[42] Johnson wrote to his family in Sweden in 1898 from Wisconsin, and in 1905 and 1906 from Moscow, Idaho. In 1908 he moved farther west, to Langley, Washington, where he bought farmland. Johnson died in 1947. In his letters from Moscow, Johnson comments on the dissolution of the Swedish-Norwegian union. A main concern in his letters is the economics of purchasing land. Johnson received letters from his cousins living in the Pacific Northwest, including Emma Dahlgren of Texas Ridge (an area of Swedish settlement near Deary, Idaho). (See Emma Dahlgren in this appendix.)

Johnson, O. M.
1906–11
Rawlins, Wyoming
Four letters

O. M. Johnson,[43] perhaps a relative of Aron W. Johnson, wrote to Aron from Rawlins, Wyoming, imparting news of the Swedish community that Aron had left. A year after Aron's return to Sweden, O. M. comments that Aron had become "America sick," as O. M. had predicted he would. (See also Aron W. Johnson, Fabian Johnson, and Adelina Reinhold in this appendix.)

Johnson, P. J.
1915–16
Rawlins, Wyoming
Two letters

P. J. Johnson of Rawlins, Wyoming, wrote in 1914 and 1915 to a friend, Lars Bergstrom, in Lysvik, Värmland. Johnson and his family had made a trip back to Sweden in 1914, and he commented on how welcome it was to see friends and family again. Johnson was a wholesale distributor of alcoholic beverages; he used his company letterhead for his letters.

Johnson, P. N.
1902
Victor, Colorado
One letter

An acquaintance of August Peterson, P. N. Johnson[44] wrote to Peterson's correspondent, Hjalmar, in 1902 to relate the circumstances of Peterson's death in a mine and the plans for his burial. (See August Peterson.)

Johnson, Victor
1908
Unionville, Montana
One letter

Victor Johnson wrote in 1908 from Unionville, Montana, near Helena, where he worked in a mine. He and his family had just returned from a visit to his sister and in-laws in Sweden, and he wrote to assure their Swedish relatives of their safe return and of his having returned to work. The return to America reinforced his view of America as a free land where workers had a higher status than in Sweden. Johnson was one of four brothers who had left Sweden; two lived in Montana and two in Brooklyn. In the following letter, Johnson informs his relatives of his family's return to Montana, and he reflects on American-Swedish differences.[45]

Unionville Mont 11 December 1908

Dear sister and brother-in-law Bergström I now have to write to let you know that we [are] happily and safely back in Montana again. We left Sweden as you know and we had a fairly fast and good trip. I wrote to Norramåla when I was in New York and told them that I did not meet Fritz because I heard that he had gone to Panama so if you hear from him would you let me know his address. I began to work right away when I arrived in Helena in a mine that I have worked in before. It is where Oscar works, it is only 4 English miles from Helena but we live here and Oscar *boards [boardar]* with us. I *had* some days off but now there is work every day so I don't know if there will be time to be off on Christmas Day so there is no time to contemplate anything. I think that it is going to be fine to work during the winter then I will have to see what spring will bring if everything goes well. Then I have to tell you what the trip was like and the trip itself was fine but we had too much of it because after we left Norramåla then we went to Östergötland for a month and then Stockholm and Örebro and all over. And Östergötland is beautiful but everything is too reserved in Sweden so there I did not [feel] like I can say what I think and as soon as I set foot on American soil everything felt so free and spacious again. You can walk around freely and be yourself and you do not have to stand with your hat in your hand in front of wooden characters with badges in their caps or a big fat belly or anything like that. I do not want to speak ill of Sweden but it certainly is an old, old-fashioned society, a poor country with much of its population unaware of their values as human beings. The minister and police shall think for the entire parish, the king for the entire nation and the people believe them as Israel's children believed in Moses' law. I have to wish you all a happy and joyous Christmas and I wish that you are all enjoying good health just like we are. I am wondering what the weather is like in Sweden. I thought it started to seem unstable before we left so there was a big difference when we arrived west of the Nordic Sea. Here we have a little snow now and [it is] like winter and we have had a few cold days. I have not heard anything from David since I came here, but Oskar was here visiting before we came back and they were doing well I will probably hear from him soon I imagine. I will end with many greetings to all of you from us greet the ones in Norramåla. I am wondering how things are there and imagine the preparations for Christmas if it was not this far I would send a box of apples because here we have *plenty*. In Sweden I paid 30 öre for one, here 20 kilo for 1 dollar. I hope I will receive an answer from you when you get an opportunity and get to know how you are doing and what is going on etc. the address is as before

Victor Johnson
Helena
Montana
Box 112

Julia sends special greetings to Amanda and the boys

Johnsson, Hjalmar
1917–18
Nederland, Colorado, and Camp Cody, New Mexico
Two letters

During 1917 and 1918, while he was a mine laborer in Nederland, Colorado, and preparing for military service in Camp Cody, New Mexico (at present-day Deming, in the southwest corner of New Mexico), Hjalmar Johnsson wrote letters to his father, Ola Johnsson, in Sverkedal, a farm near the village of Arkelstorp in Oppmanna parish, east of Hässleholm in Skåne. Johnsson signed his name Hjalmar even though he said he went by Swan H. Olson while in the military. Hjalmar's letters indicate that by 1914 he had emigrated and was working in Nebraska.

Larsson, Olof
1904–6
Kellogg, Idaho
Four letters

Olof Larsson was an itinerant worker who traveled to the United States in 1902 via Copenhagen and Liverpool. His work in America included farm labor, mining, and construction. During 1902 and 1903 he worked in Illinois, Minnesota, and North Dakota. He spent 1904 through 1906 in Kellogg, Idaho, where he did various kinds of mine work, including logging timbers to shore up the mine tunnels, and laboring at a stamp mill. He moved on from Idaho to the Pacific coastal states. His correspondence eventually dwindled, and he lost track of his parents, finding out about their deaths years after the fact. Larsson's letters from Idaho reveal his notion that one could become wealthy in the mines, an idea that his own life story contradicted. In the following letter, Larsson described the wealth to be had in the Idaho mountains.[46]

Kellog July 29th 1904

Dear parents!

Heartfelt thanks for the letter I received from you a while back, which I have not until now gotten around to reply to. I am alive and well and I like it fairly well here in the west among the mountains, because here are hills that are almost worse than those you have at home in Vånga. But the hills are good to have because they have Gold, Silver and lead, almost all over in them. There are also lots of people camping out everywhere in the mountains during the summers looking for it. Some that are lucky can also [just] stumble on it. There is a Danish boy here that has been offered 1 million dollars for his share if he is willing to sell it to a *mining company*, but he makes more if he works for himself. He has now an income of 18,000 dollars per month, which is a good monthly income to have. Others spend most of their lives looking without finding anything. Now

I have to ask how things are at home and how the crops are doing these days. I saw in a paper that you had frost all over northern Skåne the night of midsummer, we had the same here.

I do not have anything else to say this time but end here with many dear regards to you all back home.

Signed by your son Olaf
Address Kellog Idaho

Leonard, John A.
1881–1916
Leadville, Longmont, and Boulder, Colorado, and Silver Camp,
Lake Valley, and Kingston, New Mexico
Nine letters

John A. Leonard, or Johan Andersson, was born in 1854.[47] He emigrated as J. A. Lennartz in 1880, going first to Kirkland, Illinois, where he boarded with a farmer for whom he worked. By April 1881 he had made his way to Leadville, Colorado, and taken up work as a miner. He became an itinerant worker, writing from Leadville, Longmont, and Boulder, Colorado, and Silver Camp, Lake Valley, and Kingston, New Mexico (the locations of Silver Camp and Lake Valley are uncertain). By 1916 he was sixty-two, crippled with rheumatism, and working for his room and board at Lund's Hotel, a Swedish hotel run by John Wahlgren in Boulder.[48] Even though he reported being in a great deal of pain, he tallied his life experiences as having more joy than sorrow. Leonard is an articulate writer who explicitly interprets his experiences through Western motifs and Swedish values. In the following letter, Leonard describes his trip from Illinois to Colorado, and compares his new surroundings in the Rocky Mountains to the Swedish poet Tegnér's treatment of Nordic myth.[49]

Leadville 16 April 1881
Johan Andersson
Lennart

My dear Friend!

When you first glance at this letter you will discover that I have moved to another place here in this country, 1500 eng. [English] miles west of

Chicago to the mountain country of Colorado and the city of Leadville, where I am presently in the company of B.J. Magnusson from Granhult and other acquaintances. On account of this trip I have not wanted to reply to your letter because I have not had an address to give. Your letter dated the 10th of February, stamped in Liatorp the 3/3 [March 3] and received in Kirkland the 24th of March has consequently been on the way for a long time so it is not all my neglect. You cannot imagine how happy I get when I see letters from you, because they are always filled with fun and interesting details. The 1st of April I gathered my things and left P. Paulsson and walked to Chicago, which took me 4 hours. I stayed there until noon on the 5th, then I continued my trip night and day until 9.00 a.m. on the 8th when I arrived in the city of Leadville. I passed through the states of Illinois, Iowa, and Nebraska on the Union Pacific railroad. We went over the large rivers Missouri, Mississippi, as well as the Platte *river [rifver]*. In Nebraska we traveled over an immense flat countryside that was neither settled nor cultivated at all, but excellent land; it took us an entire day to travel through this flat land although the train kept a speed of 40 (eng) miles per hour. This land is used for cattle range and since there is not usually winter and snow there, the animals remain outdoors year-round, but this past winter thousands of animals have perished on these plains due to the unusually cold winter. Even though the snow is now gone, I was able to witness myself the abundance of dead cattle, at times up to 5 or 6 in a pile. By the city Cheney [Cheiney], I got off for Denver and then to [this] place. The railway compartments are as nice here as 1st class in Sweden. Sleep and restaurant compartments are available on each train if you wish to use it and want to pay extra for it. The trip here from Chicago cost 40 dollars. I paid P. Paulsson 2 dollars per week for 4 months. The two weeks when I was most ill I paid 4 dollars per week. The doctor charged 20 dollars and that was especially cheap for the 10 visits he paid me. The city of Leadville is a large enough town, some areas very well built, but on the outskirts lie the most unassuming houses I have ever seen. There is no farmland here in sight, only sky-high mountains and hills everywhere, which are partly populated by old pine forest. In this wild mountain area you live, like Tegnér says about the Giant *[Jätten]*: I live in the halls of the mountain, deep below the earth, where Odin's eye can never reach with his beam etc.—because many people work several hundred feet under ground by a light. The city is located 11,000 feet above sea level, but the top of the highest mountains are 19,000 feet. We do not have any snow here with the exception of the mountaintops. The majority of the laborers here do not have any work yet. B.J. Magni from Granhult asks [me] to send greetings. We live well and enjoy ourselves, your friend

J. A. Lennartz

P.S. Aug. Johnsson stays at P. Paulson's until further notice. All acquaintances in "DkalbsCo" [DeKalb County] were all *right [reite]* when I left them. This evening we get to have a little dance [*polska*] with some other happy souls. Greetings in abundance to everyone in Qvarnatorp and various relatives and friends, whom I never have forgotten.

I wonder why Brita Olson never has time to answer my letter, which I sent last autumn. Tell my Father too, that I never write to anyone unless they delight me with a return greeting and kindly answer my letters that I send.

Lindborg, Fritz
1888
Helena, Montana
One letter

Fritz Lindborg may be the Frits Alexius Lindborg born in Hjo, Västergötland, who emigrated in 1882.[50] In the following letter, Lindborg writes from Helena, Montana, to a close male friend who planned a trip home, apparently to marry. Lindborg describes Helena as a place where gambling flourished and prices were high. Lindborg had traveled to the West with gold fever, but by 1888 was thinking of acquiring farmland instead of prospecting. The many passages italicized in this letter indicate Lindborg's frequent code switching from Swedish to English.[51]

Helena Montana the 9th of December 88

Honored brother Nils!

Thank you kindly for the letter of the 10th this past month in which I find that you are intending to make a long trip. So I assume that when you receive this you tread our beloved native soil, old *Svea*. Hope your trip went well and that you are doing well and are safe on land in Skåne [Skaune] and I wish that your stay there, if it is long or short, may altogether become pleasant. Naturally there is no reason to assume the opposite. I also have to wish you a Happy New Year, a rich, beautiful and kind fiancée etc.

We have had very beautiful weather here, but who knows how long that might last, but they say that the winter here is not especially long.

In the spring I am thinking about the possibility of taking land, if I cannot realize that idea, I will try my luck with gold digging, as you know Montana is rich in gold and silver, they stumbled upon some gold quartz here in the middle of the street a few days ago, which with *assaying* proved to be very rich.

The entire valley where Helena is located has been worked over *and old timers say that they got [från] 10 dollars a day here at that time, so that shows they were striking [where stricking] it rich when they paid that price.*

I know another thing that would pay to have here and that is a few hundred hens (or say a thousand) because eggs are very expensive here. Now they cost 60 cents a dozen and in the summer they go no lower than 30 cents. *"but talk is cheap [sheap]" but to be sure I know what I would do if I had the money here in the West is many thing[s] to do what would pay good if only a person had the dust* [the gold dust] *this town is the worst gambling hole on* [the] *face of the earth I guess [guss], soon after I came here I went [whent] in to such a place and lost about ten dol. and you may bet I walk long way around them after that.* Now you shall be kind and write to me now and then so I will find out how you are and if you are coming back to the U.S.A., [Here I] end with many heartfelt greetings your true friend

Fritz Lindborg

My address:
34 Pine Street
Helena
Montana

Lundquist, Jacob
1891–92
Denver, Colorado
Four letters

During 1891 and 1892, Jacob Lundquist wrote to his sisters in Sweden regarding the engagement of one of them, Ellen, who had been living with him and their brother Nils in the United States but had returned to Sweden in 1891. Lundquist's letters are full of advice for Ellen, even though he was a bachelor. He worried particularly that her "soldier" would not be careful with alcohol or would fight wars at home as well as abroad. In the midst of this advice, Lundquist provides news of the Swedish American communities where Jacob, Nils, and Ellen had lived: Froid, Montana, where Ellen still owned land; and Leadville and Julesburg, Colorado. Lundquist also wrote to his sister Anna. According to the donor of the letters, Lundquist was born in 1855 in Sandby, just west of Hässleholm in Skåne, and had tried several kinds of work in Sweden before emigrating in 1879. Nils followed him in 1882. The brothers worked together as farm laborers in Nebraska and in Turlock, California. Jacob finally returned to Sweden a few years after Nils's death in 1927, and settled in Hässleholm. A remarkable feature of Jacob's letters to Ellen is that he wrote them in fluent English, while he wrote to Anna in Swedish.

Matsdotter, Brita Lisa
1907
Salt Lake City, Utah
One letter

Brita Lisa Matsdotter,[52] born in 1857, had traveled in 1881 from Lima, in Dalarna, to North America, and wrote in 1907 from Salt Lake City to a sister-in-law on the event of her brother's death. She hadn't written to Sweden in response to her brother's letter, written years earlier. Matsdotter sent a portrait taken to celebrate her fiftieth birthday, and she reported on the careers of her children. She had no regrets for having left "poor Sweden" and no plans to revisit the country. Although Matsdotter doesn't say she is a Mormon convert, she uses a pious greeting in her letter. Brita Lisa Matsdotter was this correspondent's name upon emigration and before marriage. Her name in the United States is unknown.

Mohr, Ellen H.
1905
Logan, Utah
One letter

Ellen H. Mohr,[53] originally Elna, of Logan, Utah, was one of three siblings who in 1905 and 1906 wrote to their brother Jöns P. Hall of Lyngsjö in Skåne. Their letters were prompted by issues over division of an inheritance. In addition to explaining her ideas about how the money should be divided among the siblings, Ellen explained to her brother how difficult it was for her to write in Swedish, and provided some news about her and their sister Hanna's children. (See also A. P. Hall and Hanna [Hall] in this appendix.)

Myrholm, Elias
1890
Alhambra, Montana
One letter

Elias Myrholm wrote in 1890 from Alhambra, Montana (south of Helena), to his parents. Myrholm worked hewing railroad ties. He had worked previously in the Dakota Territory. His letter is interesting for his evaluation of the immigrants among whom he worked, including an assessment of which immigrant groups were better workers and which worse. According to Myrholm, the worst of all were the Yankees. Myrholm was born in 1862 in Vallen, near Junsele, in Medelpad; he emigrated in 1889.[54]

Nilson, O.
1889
Pleasant Grove, Utah
One letter

When writing in 1889 from Pleasant Grove, Utah, to in-laws in Sweden, O. Nilson[55] had been in America for many years and had lost touch with the family. Hence, Nilson inquired whether a sister was dead.

Nilsson, Leonard
1879–84
Rocky Bar and Bullion, Idaho
Forty-six letters

Nils Leonard Nilsson[56] was born in 1855 in Kimstad, Östergötland, the son of a crofter (in Swedish, *torpare*, a peasant farmer who rented rather than owned his land and house).[57] In his reminiscences, Nilsson reported that he had left home at age fourteen and did hard physical labor for bosses who were abusive. In 1877 Nilsson traveled to the United States, working first in Illinois and Wisconsin before moving to Rocky Bar, Idaho, in 1879. He worked there and in Bullion (southeast of Vienna) as a mine laborer, eventually saving enough money to return in 1884 to Söderköping, where he became a brewer running his own business and then ultimately a homeowner, achieving his ambition of being self-employed.[58]

Nilsson wrote to his fiancée, Lovisa Borg, and to a friend, Johan Westerberg. To Westerberg he wrote of politics, workers' unions, and business management. To Lovisa he wrote tender love letters. The son of a crofter, he was educated by the local priest, who rated his reading and Bible knowledge highly. Nilsson read Swedish American newspapers and literature. The collection of his letters includes a poetry scrapbook assembled from newspaper clippings. His letters are beautifully written. In the following example from May 22, 1880, he tells Lovisa about walking in the mountains, and he considers the relative merits of settling in America versus Sweden.[59] (See also Oscar Borg.)

Rocky Bar, Idaho Terr U.S. of America 22/5 1880
Precious lovely Lovisa,

Clear, warm and radiant shines the sun down on the now green valleys. All of nature is breathing the rejuvenating forces of spring. The trees are clad in summer garb. The rivers ripple swiftly. The birds send their chirping as offerings to nature's lord. Everything is beautiful and lovely. Flora's children are beginning to open their mouths. The Old Man [*Gubben Bore*] appears seriously to have disappeared from this place. Hard, bitter and barbaric he has been so no one will ask him to return—No, go your

One of Leonard Nilsson's many letters to his precious Lovisa. Image courtesy of the Swedish Emigrant Institute.

way—old soul—you have brought us enough worries "in this corner be-tween the mountains"—the sky-high.

[I] have just now returned from a little walk up in the mountains to enjoy the grand, wonderful and vast view and to breathe in the fresh mountain air. From there I gazed unintentionally toward—Northeast—I thought "certainly I can see far away now—several miles are within my field of vision: but what would I like to give [to be to closer to you]? If I could see my 'native country.' Had I had wings like the birds—on to her I would hurry so—to my adorable Lova!" In the fantasy world I hurried carried by thoughts on swift wings over to you—I sank into dreams—about our future Lovisa.

Light and smiling it appeared to me; may reality likewise turn out the same my Lova! Then what do we care about all the evil and unfairness that exists to such large degree, on this planet which is called—the earth—where so many are forced to fight for their existence—where so many sighs are produced by distressed souls, so much sorrow is heard and so many tears are flowing—where so much violence, injustice and tyranny is practiced: but within these gloomy issues. . . . We have many bright things also and it is unhealthy to see everything from the dark side of life—. Let us return up to the mountaintop where I just sat and admired the beauty of nature, dreamt about you and our future—

I was awoken from my sweet dream, finally, by a flapping eagle, close by me, which swooped upward majestically. I decided then to walk down to my unpretentious home (cabin), to let my feelings flow, from sending you a few lines, my lovely Lovisa.

Have you received my previous letters? There are a few of them. What are your thoughts on the proposal I put forward in my last letter? Consider it carefully for yourself, and let me know your decision and thoughts about it. I consider this your decision now because I will then arrange my plans. In other words, that is if you have courage and desire to travel over here. Then I will naturally arrange my personal dealings accordingly. But as I said in my last letter "your wish is my command" in this respect—say that I should come, then I will do that.

Although I do not know how soon that can happen. Though you are dearer to me than anything else on this earth. Therefore I will obey you. If you were here I would be content, happy and satisfied. I do not mean here in this place—no that will not be suitable. Nature here is certainly divinely beautiful: but these are wild sparsely populated areas almost unpopulated: only the mining camps and a few gold diggers here and there. So in this area, I do not want to live for any long period of time, least of all take my little Lova here. Rather I would choose a more populated and "civilized" place. Say whatever you want about the United States of North America. It is a free country—No earthly majesty with God's blessing. Progressive thinking in all areas, inventive and earnest. In Europe you can never even dream about the enormous progress that characterizes this country. More equality and much more.

My favorite occupation is farming, but I am also considering trying a smaller business in a small town. Yet to become a free man with land—

that is the jewel of all things, but at home in Sweden I will probably never be capable of becoming a farmer: but in America it is easier. Dear Lovisa, answer my proposals soon that I have stated in this and in the previous letter. I want to meet your wishes, because you are too dear to me and I would not want you to make any sacrifice too difficult. To separate from your parents and siblings against your own will, I am only asking you a question, answer it my love.

I am just recollecting that it is now three years ago since I saw your lovely happy visage. It was the 22 of May 1877 that I said my last good-bye to you and Söderköping. That moment was significant to me. How well I recall in my memory that afternoon when we sat conversing in the sitting room outside the "parlor." Oh such lovely: but painful hours were those, many words we exchanged then about my future destiny, about my hopes for happiness in America and return and much more. My dreams and hopes were too bold and convoluted and they have not been realized and shall, most likely not be either. But a good experience, a memorable, life lesson, I have learned from the journey and the stay here in America, useful for the future. And our good-bye Lova! On the hill above the dockside—as there were too many present, who could not sense the feelings we have for each other, this perhaps appeared cold for the uninformed: but I caught a meaningful glimpse from your faithful eyes, sent you a similar in return, jumped up on the wagon—just in the same moment as I felt my self-control was close to failing. With a shaky and anxious voice I said—drive. My heart felt as if it would burst. It is this evening now three years ago since then. How much longer will it be before we see each other?? I am going to stop traveling and try to save more. I think it was bad to come here [to the western United States]; the trip was too expensive.

What news from Söderköping? Greetings to your brother Per Joh and his better half as well as the young ones, Ida and others. Many dear regards to my lovely treasure and ditto kisses. Write soon to your honest and faithful Leonard.

Olson, Anna
1889
Denver, Colorado
One letter

Anna Olson wrote to a cousin in the parish of Ignaberga, Skåne, after having traveled west to Denver in 1889. Her letter celebrated her cousin's religious conversion, apparently to an evangelical Christian position. Anna had found work in Denver and was impressed with its Swedish American population and churches. Anna may be the Anna W. Olson listed as living at 370 South Franklin Street in the 1910 *Svenska Adresskalendern*.

Olson, Bengta
1911
Midvale, Utah
One letter

Bengta Olson[60] wrote to her brother and her in-laws with family news. She mentioned that a Mormon missionary had visited her brother. Bengta may have been the spouse of Ole Olsson (see Ole Olsson in this appendix).

Olson, Nils
1897–1900
Kalispell, Montana, and Orofino, Idaho
Two letters

Nils Olson worked for a time in Nebraska farming with his brother Ole, but he took on railroad construction work and moved westward with the construction. In 1897 he wrote from Kalispell, Montana, and in 1900 from Orofino, Idaho, at which point we lose track of him. By that time he had turned again to farming, and his letter to his brother Johan in Fredskog (probably the name of a farm) in the parish of Farstorp, just north of Hässleholm in Skåne, dwells on the poor farm economy and the fact that Orofino had not blossomed into a railroad town, as had been hoped.

Olson, Pit
1887
Granite, Colorado
One letter

Pit Olson[61] wrote in 1887 from Granite, Colorado, a community near Leadville. He had set himself up in business by purchasing mules with three partners, one of them John Renström, who was recovering from an eye illness or injury. They were working in the woods, perhaps logging. Both were Lima, Dalarna, emigrants. (See also John Renström in this appendix.)

Olsson, Ole
1914
Midvale, Utah
One letter

Ole Olsson wrote very briefly to his in-laws with family news and greetings. Ole may have been the spouse of Bengta Olson (see Bengta Olson in this appendix).

Pearson, Nels
1907–12
Coeur d'Alene, Cottonwood, Twin Lakes, and Bovill, Idaho
Four letters

A series of letters from Nels Pearson survives to document his time in the Pacific Northwest and in the Upper Midwest. Four letters, dating from 1907 to 1912, represent his travels through northern Idaho doing itinerant work as a logger and railroad construction worker; he wrote from Coeur d'Alene, Cottonwood, Twin Lakes (a logging camp close to Spokane, Washington), and Bovill (northeast of Deary). Pearson appears in parish records as Nils Pehrsson, born in 1876. His father was a farmer (*åbo*—a farmer who didn't own his land) who by 1889 had gained ownership of his farmland (had become an *ägare*) in Farstorp, a parish just north of Hässleholm in Skåne. In 1894, at age eighteen, Pearson emigrated from Farstorp to America.[62] He was preceded by his brother Hilding and two sisters, Annette and Alma.

Pearson wrote from his various work locations to Annette, or "Annie," and to Hilding, both of whom lived in Minneapolis. His letters to Hilding continued after Hilding's return in 1913 to the family farm to care for their ailing father after the death of their sister Hulda, the eldest child, who had stayed in the old country. Pearson's letters focus on his work and the pay he received for it. After doing itinerant work for a decade, in the late 1910s he homesteaded in South Dakota, where he was forced to supplement his income with coal mining and handyman work.

Pedersen, Ole
1904–6
Downey, Idaho
Four letters

According to family legend, as related by his granddaughter, Vega Tränefors, Ole Pedersen was born in 1856 in Svelvik, Norway, a town on the Oslo Fjord. In the late 1870s he moved to Timrå, Sweden, just north of Sundsvall in Medelpad. There he married and began a family, but in 1891 he traveled to America without his wife and four surviving children, the youngest of whom was two years old. Pedersen worked a homestead in the Downey, Idaho, area. None of his family chose to follow him there. He eventually became a Mormon convert, moved to Salt Lake City, married again, and started a family with his second wife.[63] Four letters and fragments exist from 1904 to 1906, when Pedersen wrote to his son from Downey, describing his farm, recommending that his son avoid alcohol and tobacco, and encouraging him and the rest of the family to consider joining him in America.

Pehrson, Elin
1896–97
Denver, Colorado
Three letters

In 1896 and 1897 Elin Pehrson wrote letters from Denver, Colorado, to a cousin in Vislanda, Småland. Information about Elin is purely internal to the letters themselves, in which she dwells on the death of an elderly relative, her illness and the illnesses of her children, the time that has passed since her departure from Sweden, and the lack of letters from her family there. Amid these issues, she considers the question: Where is home?

Peterson, August

1900–1902
Gem and Burke, Idaho, and Victor, Colorado
Four letters

In 1886, at age nineteen, August Peterson (originally Petersson) left his home in Blädinge, west of Växjö in Småland, to emigrate to America.[64] He worked in Minnesota, served in the U.S. military as an infantryman at Fort Keogh (near present-day Miles City in eastern Montana) and at Fort Leavenworth, Kansas, returned briefly to Sweden in the mid-1890s, and then moved to the western United States to work as a mine laborer in Idaho and Colorado from 1900 to 1902. His letters report many enjoyable celebrations with fellow Swedish Americans in Denver and Victor, Colorado, and in Gem, Idaho; he wrote from Gem and Burke, both northeast of Wallace. In 1902 Peterson succumbed to gas in a mine shaft at Victor. The following letter was written during Peterson's time in Gem, where he enjoyed the company of a few fellow immigrants.[65]

Gem Idaho June 13th 1900

Esteemed nephew Hjalmar

Your letter I have received a long time ago. [It is] nice to get some news now and then. I am doing well [and] wish you all the same. I live with Walter Ehneberg and that is excellent. [I] work every day or rather every night. I have had the night shift for an entire month because half of the workers have been laid off for a couple of weeks due to necessary repairs that must be done. Fritiof, he has gone to Burke about three miles from here so I have not seen him for a while. Per Nelson, he has begun to work again and is healthy now. We have a superbly beautiful summer just like home but you hardly hear a single bird singing———

Among Swedish news that I saw in a newspaper a while ago, which was sad, [I noticed that it must] have been Carl from Klackaregården that had taken his life by hanging himself. If that is the case I imagine it is her fault who stood *bride* not too long ago. *I know.* I now have to end, wish you all good health and well-being.

Greetings to sister Ingrid and brother-in-law. Is Hilma still home? Let me know when you write.

You yourself are kindly greeted from August Peterson.

I had thought about going to Alaska about a month ago but then I thought I had traveled enough for a while so it will not be this summer.

When you write again *send* my exit permit or *Utflyttningsbetyg* because I think that [it] is unnecessary to be registered in two places and I have to pay taxes here and if you have to do that there then that is all too good. If you cannot get it I will write to the King myself and let him know that I am just as well an American Citizen.

Fulfill my request.
Respectfully,
Aug.

Peterson, Effie
1914
Denver, Colorado
Two letters

Two Christmas letters from 1914 survive from Effie (Mrs. J. A.) Peterson's residence in Denver that she shared with her husband, a railroad boiler man, and their young son. Effie's focus was on family relationships, illnesses, deaths, and raising her son. She found Swedish difficult to write, and wondered whether her relatives could understand her letters.

Peterson, John
1909–11
Canon City, Colorado, and McCall, Idaho
Four letters

John Peterson wrote to his brother in 1909, recounting his travels with his wife Jessie through Iowa and Kansas to Canon City, Colorado, where they had an orchard. This letter provides an interesting account of the couple's trip through the Midwest, stopping to visit a factory in Red Oak, Iowa, and their reaction to the scenic countryside of Colorado. Peterson stated their intent to move farther west, perhaps seeking a homestead in Oregon. In later letters written to his father, Erik Johan Petersson, a master blacksmith at Gällersta in Närke, it becomes apparent that he and Jessie instead took up a farm near McCall, Idaho, also establishing a blacksmith shop in town, where Jessie taught school. Peterson's letters express his worry over his father's continuing to do hard labor even though he is old and ill. He and Jessie consider moving to Sweden, but he also hopes that family members will consider moving to McCall, where he believes they can quickly and comfortably establish themselves.

Peterson, Maria
1889–99
Gunnison, Utah
Two letters

Maria Peterson[66] was the eldest daughter of Peter and Dortha Peterson, Mormon converts who had immigrated to Utah in 1878, establishing themselves in Gunnison, in the Sanpete Valley, where many Scandinavian converts located. Maria, born in Sweden, studied Swedish, and to practice her skills, she wrote letters to Maria, daughter of Jonas Danielson, who was her father's regular correspondent.

Peterson, Peter
1883–1907
Gunnison and Salt Lake City, Utah
Fifteen letters

Peter Peterson wrote letters for his family. On the Swedish side of the exchange was another father representing his family, Jonas Danielson of Föllinge (apparently Peterson's home parish) in Jämtland. Peterson was born in 1846 in Sweden; his wife Dortha was born the same year. They married in Sweden before traveling to Utah in 1878. It is likely that they had converted to Mormonism in Sweden prior to emigration.[67]

Peterson established himself as a carpenter and a farmer, but he notes that his carpentry work earns him more income than the farming. His carpentry work apparently included both a shop, in which he had employees working for him, and a house-building business. By 1902 he had devised furniture designs that he patented, but his attempts to establish a factory may have gone astray. By 1907 he had moved to Salt Lake City and was working in someone else's factory.

By 1900 the Petersons had been married twenty-eight years. The couple lost four children in 1886 to diphtheria, and then lost one more a year later, leaving them with only their eldest child, Maria (see Maria Peterson in this appendix). At least four more children were born to the Petersons after 1887. In his letters, Peterson writes very few words on Mormon belief, instead imparting family news to his friend. He was convinced that Utah was the best place on earth, and was especially pleased that the area where he settled in Gunnison, Sanpete Valley, had numerous Swedish and other Scandinavian converts. Describing these advantages, he hoped to tempt his friend to move to Utah. The following letter, written in 1902, displays Peterson's fascination with inventions and his enthusiasm over the Utah environment.[68]

Gunneson the 25th of March 1902

Jonas Danielson and family

Your lines have reached us. It is nice to hear from you, and not the least to hear from your girl. She is probably as wise as the portrait shows, and the other 2 do not look so bad either. I see that you are delivering the mail still. I wonder how I would cope in Föllinge now if I would go there. It would be different to eat the thin bread after having for such a long time cut slices of thick wheat bread, but I am thinking that I would like to see Föllinge one more time. I think that I will get less busy in the future and perhaps more money. Yesterday, I received a letter from the Patent Office regarding getting a patent on my new kitchen table. As soon as I can I will get it manufactured in different furniture factories and they will pay me a certain amount per table. The factories here in America are full of new inventions. A few weeks ago there was a Swede close by Salt Lake City who received a patent on a new kind of trap that catches larger and smaller pests, and he sold the patent for 25,000 dollars but I am [not] so foolish that I wanted to sell my patent for $25,000, if I can get more or less for it I do not know yet. The wheel that I was telling you about is getting closer to being complete, and that will be the only one in the world of its kind, and it looks like it is going to be a useful thing, it will become a perpetual motion machine. You will hear more about it in the future. The times here are nothing to complain about, and it looks like we are going to get a good harvest because lots of snow is falling in the mountains right now. When there is much snow in the mountains we can be assured of a steady stream of water throughout the entire summer, because we can never trust the rain here so you can see that it is not difficult to save the hay here. If some of you only could see, how big the difference is between here and Jämtland then there would be many more here. I do not mean to say that you can live without work here either, but there is a difference and it is not a small one. I am going to send newspapers. I hope that you will not forget to write, Härman I do not think will live long since his lungs are gone.

Greetings to all P. Peterson

I write so seldom that this is probably difficult to read.

Petterson, Gust
1916
Missoula, Montana
One letter

Gust Petterson, or Johan August Petersson, of Missoula, Montana, dictated the letter he sent to his sister and in-laws in 1916, helped in its writing by a Swedish American acquaintance who may also have translated for him. Petterson may be the Johan August Petersson born in 1861 who emigrated in 1881, at age twenty, from Aneboda, northwest of Växjö in Småland. Petterson's letter is very spare, mainly serving as a means of maintaining familial contact rather than imparting news.

Reed, Andreas
1884
Boulder, Colorado
One letter

Andreas Reed (Svensson) was in Boulder, Colorado, in 1884, when he wrote home to his brother Carl, commenting on the poor American economy but the growth of nearby Denver. By 1884 Reed had been away from

Sweden for thirty-two years. He was born in Hudene, Västergötland, in 1833.[69] By 1884 he and his wife had three children, the eldest of whom was teaching in Denver. Reed's Swedish exhibits significant confusion with English, and the opening and closing segments of his letter are oddly formal, suggesting the influence of letter-writing manuals.

Reed, John

1891
Helena, Montana
One letter

John Reed wrote in 1891 from Helena, Montana, to his brother and parents in Vislanda, Småland. Because he had not heard from his family, he worried that they had forgotten him. He worked in the forest, logging, and lived with two other workers, but anticipated moving on to do railroad work.

Reinhold, Adelina

1910–11
Denver, Colorado
Two letters

Adelina Reinhold[70] left Sweden in 1893, the same year as did her brother, Aron W. Johnson. Adelina was born in 1869 in Madesjö, near Nybro in Småland.[71] She apparently married in America, settling in Denver, from where she sent Aron news of her family after his return to Sweden. (See also Aron W. Johnson, Fabian Johnson, and O. M. Johnson in this appendix.)

Renström, John

1892–1901
Spring Gulch (or Gulch), Colorado
Two letters

John Renström[72] worked during the 1890s as a saloonkeeper in a place he called variously Spring Gulch or Gulch, from where two letters survive, dating 1892 and 1901. His letters comment extensively on differences between America and Sweden. By 1901 he had married and was able to offer advice to a friend in Sweden who wished to emigrate. Renström had come from Lima, in Dalarna, as early as 1887, when he was mentioned as a business partner in a letter written by Pit Olson, also from Lima. (See also Pit Olson in this appendix.)

Rydberg, Bernhard

1900–1905
Red Lodge and Hunter's Hot Springs, Montana
Ten letters

Bernhard Rydberg wrote to his mother, father, and sister Amelie from Red Lodge, Montana, where he was a jeweler, and from Hunter's Hot Springs (northwest of Red Lodge). Rydberg was born in 1870 in the city of Motala in Östergötland.[73] He first left Sweden in 1889, having learned watchmaking. After a four-year stay in Chicago, he moved to Billings, Montana, where he worked two years as a clock inspector for the Northern Pacific Railroad Company. From Billings, he moved to Red Lodge, Montana, setting up his own watch and jewelry shop.[74] In the 1900 U.S. census, Rydberg appeared as a bachelor living in a boardinghouse in Red Lodge. He was by then a naturalized citizen able to speak, read, and write English.[75] Those skills are well attested in the newspaper columns he wrote for the *Carbon County Democrat* under the pen name Benedictus. From the late 1890s through 1906 he spent his leisure time exploring the countryside with an English immigrant, David Smethurst, and participating in the local Elks Lodge and militia. He also ran for office, unsuccessfully, on the Democratic, Labor, and People's tickets.[76]

In 1905 Rydberg declared that he would return to Sweden to marry a cousin, Emma Franzén. They lived in Motala, where Emma bore two girls, one in 1908 and the other in 1910. Rydberg returned to Red Lodge in 1912, reestablishing his jewelry business there, and Emma and their children emigrated in 1916. A boy and another girl were born to the couple in Montana. Rydberg died of a sudden illness in 1929.[77]

Rydberg wrote lengthy, detailed, and enthusiastic descriptions of his life in Red Lodge. In the following example, written during his bachelor years, he describes to his mother a dance.[78]

March 20 1901

Dear Mama!

Thank you for the letter that I received a few days ago. I am doing fairly
well now although I have been sick for a little while with the influenza [*La
Grippe*], but am better now. Sometimes it is of course fun, other times
boring, just like any place. A while ago, we had a nice event in any case. It
was a big ball and banquet or nicer dinner arranged by "*The Elks*" or the
Moose Lodge. This lodge attracts the most successful people in the community. Only one lodge of this kind can exist in each city even in those
with many thousands of inhabitants.—When *they* are hosting an event
everybody knows that it will be grandiose. It has been the talk for many
weeks and all seamstresses and tailors have been busy day and night. The
ladies came in full evening dresses, which have décolleté with support
e.g., almost like court dresses. Almost all the men wore tuxedo suits and
I and many others had to order a full evening dress—tuxedo with special
starched shirts, black leather shoes, and silk handkerchiefs for the chest
pocket, a few other small items and also top hats. I looked nice that evening and now I have all those things, but it cost like crazy. I took a lady
to the event, but would have preferred somebody else although she was
elegant like a little princess. We had very nice music and it was a very
elegant gathering of people, the ladies with fine outfits and almost all the
men in tuxedos and fully cut vests and if there had been a few in uniforms
there then you could I thought [imagine] that it was a court ball. We had
of course also elegant printed programs—

At about 11 o'clock the electrical light went out and all the members
of the Order gathered in a half circle in the middle of the room and went
through one of our rituals which consisted of a greeting or a reminder of
"our missing brothers both dead and alive" on land or at sea and this appeared to make a deep impression on the invited guests. Then the light
came back and the party continued until 12:30 a.m. when we all left the
ballroom and went to the lodge hall where an elegant supper awaited us.
The hall was decorated with draperies in the order's colors, white and
purple, with large natural stuffed elk heads hanging along the walls. They
had once been real live four-footed elks that had been running around
the forests here. Besides it was decorated with flowers and greenery along

with many other decorations. The tables were stepped and decorated with flowers *etc*. The dinner was delicious and the first thing we had was oysters served on the shells but broken so we wouldn't have to bother with that ourselves. Besides that we had chicken, turkey, bouillon, salads and other things. Dessert and cake with exotic fruits. Then we also had claret—punch, which is a type of wine. Then we of course had some good coffee too. When we had filled up and had everything we wanted, the speaker of the lodge gave a talk and many speeches proceeded and they were all comical, each and every one was there to amuse themselves. Then there were some members of the Order that were dressed in special uniforms, like police constables, with the purpose of collecting fines from dutiful members present. First many names were called out and among those were Mr. Rydberg and Mr. Smethurst, and several others and they were asked to stand up. Thereafter we were informed that since we had dared to be so insolent and come to the event as bachelors when there are so many nice girls in the neighborhood, we were to be fined $5.00 each.—After that many other names were read and they were asked to stand up. They received a lesson and were reminded that they had been shameless enough to catch several ladies and made them their wives and been shameless enough to marry and they were all fined $5.00 each. Then there were those who were asked to stand up and fined for being bald. Others were fined because they had not shown up for the party. Each and everybody had to pay a fine and nobody was exempted. One was ordered a fine because his life was too good and another because his was fairly good, but he could have done better. The fines were of course intended to cover the costs. The supper lasted for several hours and afterward we went up to the ballroom again and continued the festivities and I did not get home until after 5:00 in the morning. Then I and David Smethurst went over to the hotel and sat there and smoked a cigar and talked with several others. I came home at ½ 7:00 [6:30] in the morning and at that point I did not think there was any point in going to bed so I changed out of my elegant ball wear and got out my riding boots and put on my clothes, and went out and saddled up and went for a morning ride instead. It was a bit chilly. Had some breakfast at 9:00 and then I went to the store and opened up. Most of the other night birds slept during the day, but I did not go to bed until XI o'clock in the evening. So I live well, a little too fast I imagine, but you might as well do that and have some fun while alive. There is no point in making life long, boring and dismal. That is only foolish, you do not live to have a boring life. You are alive to be as happy as possible—The ones who go through life bored certainly have a screw loose.—Tonight there is a ball at an organization here. The members are not just anybody and I expect that we will use our new suits and top hats.—I have been asked to become a Mason and when I can afford it I will also become a Mason.—This past Sunday afternoon there was a little event sponsored by another lodge I belong to and have belonged to for many years, namely the Knights of Pythias. We had speeches, music, and song Light supper with beer *etc.* and it was a lively afternoon. The store is doing fairly well, but it is still slow after Christmas, but I hope the summer will be better. Our winter has been really beautiful and it has not been very cold at all and almost nice and warm the entire time. I am invited to this and that and get out so I should not feel so lonely and if anybody *ought* to be happy it is me, but I wish I *could* feel more content. My health is a bit better, but it is so boring to sit still so much.—Greetings to everybody I know. Shall write to Amelie soon.

Bernhard

Sandberg, Albert
1898
Denver, Colorado
One letter

Albert Sandberg of Denver, Colorado, married Ida Svensdotter sometime before March 31, 1898, when he penned a letter to Ida's parents in which he expressed his hope that if America went to war with Spain it would be for idealistic reasons. He also commented on hard economic times. He described himself as working for a company that dealt with railway sleeping cars.[79] By 1906, according to one of Ida Sandberg's letters, the Sandberg family was doing well enough that they were able to purchase a new home for $2,000.[80] At least three children were born to Ida and Albert. (See also Emma Hallberg, Ida Sandberg, and John M. Swanson in this appendix.)

Sandberg, Ida

1900–1906
Denver, Colorado
Seven letters

Ida Sandberg,[81] originally Ida Svensdotter, was born in 1873 in Virestad, southwest of Vislanda in Småland. She was the last of three siblings to emigrate to America, joining her brother John M. Swanson and her sister Emma Hallberg in 1893 in Denver, Colorado. A fourth sibling, Anna Lovisa, died the year before Ida left Sweden.[82] In Denver, Ida married Albert Sandberg. In 1921 Ida and two of her children, son Sandford Theodore, born September 4, 1905, and daughter Helen Maria, born February 7, 1913, were recorded in the membership registry of the Denver Lutheran church.[83]

The letters of John, Emma, and Ida, written to their parents in Virestad, depict a close relationship among the three Denver households (see also Emma Hallberg, Albert Sandberg, and John M. Swanson in this appendix). Ida's letters emphasize her domestic environment and family news and relationships, including her thoughts on motherhood after the birth of a son in 1900, as detailed in the following letter.[84]

Denver March 30th 1900

Dear kind parents

After a long delay I now with much joy want to answer your kind letter which we received a long time ago. The reason for the delay is that we have been waiting for news, which you might already have heard. I can with great happiness report that on March 1, we had a little boy, which all went happily and well. I had thought about telling you that we were expecting another young one, but thought I [would] wait until next [time; that is, until the baby was born]. I wish that you could see the child, he is growing and doing really well. Besides we are healthy up to the date of writing this, and I am happy to have it all over. We had the same Doctor as last time then we had an English *nurse [nörs]*. She stayed here for 2 weeks. It is expensive to have children in this country. Doctor and care besides, but I can never understand how everything could work out at home at such an occasion. Poor womenfolk they must have been half dead from pain. How is everything at home, I hope that these *simple* lines will meet you in good health. I hear in Emma's letter that you have had a gathering for the women. That is more than I have had, I have been home so much during this long nine month period so I am almost afraid of people. The reason is that I have felt more or less nauseous the entire time. I have not been to brother's since the end of September.

The boy will be 1 month this coming Sunday, it is shameful that it has taken this long [to write you]. The two first weeks I was mostly in bed and after that I have had some acquaintances visiting me, almost every afternoon so it seems like time has passed so quickly. It is nice that the boy is so good, of course he takes time to care for, but he sleeps very well all night. Albert thinks that it is the only child worthy of living he takes such pleasure in him. Everybody thought it was so small when it was born they guessed and thought it weighed 6 pounds [*skålpund*], but it has grown amazingly. I have to say for my sake that it was not small to give birth to. Say it is incredibly hard to give [birth]. I do not think that [it] is harder [to] die than to give birth to a child. I got sick Wednesday night at 1 and I gave birth to the child Thursday evening at 5. Anything more about this I do not need to mention because I do know that you know it all. But I am happy that it is all over. I have lots more to tell but do not have the time. We soon want to write a few lines again. I hope that you can overlook the delay in writing and sloppiness. The boy is waking up so I have to get him. Give Mrs. Westerlund my best, she must hurry for our child's baptismal, everybody says that the boy looks like his father with dark hair and dark blue eyes, but then comes who is his papa?[85] Well if he is still doing well at 5–6 months old you will be able to see all of him in a picture.

Good-bye I hope that you will write immediately.

The nurse charged 10 dollars per week and the doctor 20, but it is all paid and forgotten. It is expensive to live.

The Hallbergs are all healthy. It was 7 years ago since [I] traveled here. Albert sends his best.

Smith, Swan
1899–1907
Wallace, Idaho, and Idaho Springs, Colorado
Three letters

Smith, Mrs. Swan
One undated fragment

Swan Smith's collection of letters dating from 1899 to 1907 includes an undated fragment from his wife, whose name is uncertain. The fragmentary nature of the entire collection makes it difficult to establish much about Swan and his wife. He apparently served in the U.S. military, mined in Wallace, Idaho, and was a mine worker in Idaho Springs, Colorado. His attempts to work his own mine claims were limited by lack of capital. He was, by report of his wife, very tired from the hard mine labor that he had to do in order to support the family. At the time of her letter, they had a two-year-old boy. The letters written home were to parents and a sister Anna in the Fjälkestad parish in Skåne.

Stred, Pet
1891
Bay Horse, Idaho
One letter

Pet Stred wrote from Bay Horse (northeast of Custer) in 1891 that he was working in a smelter, hard work that required real "Swedish strength." He noted the lack of women and churches in the region and the great difficulty faced by workers who did not know any English. Unfortunately, only one letter survives from this informative correspondent.

Svenson, Ola
1882–1915
West Jordan, South Jordan, and Sandy, Utah, and Afton, Wyoming
Ten letters

Ola Svenson was the letter writer for his family as they sent news from Utah and Wyoming back to his siblings and parents in Sweden. Svenson was born in 1848 in Genarp parish, Skåne, where his name was recorded as Ola Svensson. He and Johanna Håkansdotter, born 1856, married in 1877. In June 1882 Ola, Johanna, and their three children—Anna (four), Jöns (three), and Hans (one)—left Genarp for North America.[86] After a rough sea voyage, they made their way to West Jordan, Utah, south of Salt Lake City, and then lived in various communities in the vicinity of Salt Lake City. By 1911 they had moved to Afton, Wyoming. Ola had been a crofter in the parish of Genarp. In Utah he first found work at a silver smelter. According to a relative, the couple had eleven more children after emigrating. Son Hans, who changed his name to Henry, returned to Sweden as a Mormon missionary.[87]

Religion is the dominant topic in Svenson's letters. In more than one letter he sermonizes to his sister Maria about the basis for Mormon belief, including a disclaimer about polygamy. They had converted to Mormonism, Svenson writes, but that did not mean he would become a polygamist. Svenson uses the middle segment of his letters for lay preaching, and his typical opening formula includes religious language.

We chose to translate the following letter, written to Svenson's sister Maria, for its very interesting content, even though the copy at the Swedish Emigrant Institute is incomplete. In the letter, Svenson describes at length a few Mormon beliefs as he understood them: "laying on of hands" (*handpåläggande*) as a means of receiving the Holy Ghost; the existence of a newly discovered sacred book (the Book of Mormon), written by a previously unrecognized prophet; and rebaptism into this new faith. Svenson capitalizes most of the words in his letters; here we have used standard English capitalization to render the text more readable.[88]

West Jordan 11th March 1886

Maria Svenson dear compassionate sister live now and always well. The Lord be with you. I would now like to sit down and write you a few lines and let you know how we are doing. I can tell you that we all have our good health, God's invaluable gift, up to the moment of writing this and we wish you the same in the future. I now have to thank you for the welcome letter we received from you the ninth of March in which we hear that both you and Helena are in good health and that you are doing well with your work which pleases. And I can also tell you that we are doing well here, but I can tell you that we have neither maid nor farmhand. That would cost me too much because I have had much debt to repay from our journey here and then we were devoid of everything when we got here so I have not yet become debt-free. So we have not had the opportunity or been able to afford any servant here but it is not like in Sweden. The women do not brew and they do not bake large batches, rather they bake every day with the exception of the Sunday and they do not spin or weave, but my wife spins wool for socks for us. But otherwise I buy finished fabric and I have bought her an excellent sewing machine so it is quick for her to make clothes. And with other things I have to help her sometimes and my clothes I buy ready-made. You mentioned the loan and that you thought I had paid it in full, which I had, but it was either the bank men in Sweden or here that stole it, where I do not know. You say that if you received the Holy Spirit then it would be easier to understand the Holy Scripture and that is a truth. But I am going to tell you that you cannot receive it without experiencing the laying on of hands from a servant of the Lord who is clad with God's pastoral garb who puts his hands on your head bringing [you] the Holy Spirit's gift, which you can find in Acts of the Apostles chapter 8. You say that when you read the Old Testament things do not make sense to you but the New Testament you understand a little better. But I am going to tell you to believe in the Scripture is the first thing you need to do in order to receive knowledge from it and secondly, you need to do precisely what the Scripture tells you and not what the clergy preaches because they say that they are explaining it but that is a falsification and not an explanation. You can understand that yourself, that it does not mean anything different than what is written. Because when you write to me you write what you mean. And consider the fact that all the Epistles in the New Testament are letters from the Apostles to the Christian congregations and they wrote what they wanted the people to do and live by and not because there could be another explanation. All other interpretations and explanations are simply a falsification from the evil spirit which has large influence among the children of humankind on earth. [text missing]

… and become baptized in Jesus's name for forgiveness of your sins, and to receive the laying on of hands for the Holy Spirit's gift, then you will also fully understand about the words in the scriptures both the New and Old Testament. The Apostle James [Jacob] says in his Epistle in the first chapter if anybody is lacking wisdom he can pray to God who willingly gives and if you are lacking knowledge then fall on your knees while by yourself, call for heaven and pray from the honesty of your heart, not from a prayer book because that is only a lesson, but pray for what your heart is telling you when you are kneeling down to pray and if you cannot pray more than a few words they will be more powerful and influential for the heavenly God than a long prayer from a prayer book and you want to get more strength to pray for each time [you do it]. You say furthermore that there are so many teachings so you cannot know what you shall believe. Therefore you shall take the word in the Scripture, as a guiding rule and only the sect that teaches the people to act properly according to the word of the Scripture only that is the correct teaching because here are many false faiths but there will be even more because there shall be six. . . . [text missing]

. . . man is great. But you say that you cannot find any place in the Bible that they should be called Mormons and this is true but you do not find anywhere in the Bible that they should be called Lutherans either, yet you are a Lutheran. And the name Mormon is not a name that we ourselves have assumed rather it is a name the other people have given us. We have a book that was written about four hundred years after Christ's death by a prophet whose name was Mormon and therefore because we believe and do what is written in this book they call us Mormons. But we have not taken any other name but the same as Christ's apostles and the first Christians. They called themselves saints and the people of Israel were [also] called saints at that time when they lived by God's commandments and laws and we call ourselves the Latter Day Saints and that people nowadays think is too much that a man or a woman could [be seen] as holy [saintly, sanctified] but it is written in the Scripture that you shall be holy because I am holy the Lord your good God. Here we can see that it is each and everyone's duty [that] you live so that you can become holy and this [is] what we learn in Jesus Christ's Church of the Latter Day Saints, that we shall live and conduct ourselves as holy and if we do not do so, then we will sooner or later be excommunicated from the Holy Communion. You say furthermore that you desire to be baptized but then you cannot remain in Sweden. Yes you could very well, many people have been baptized by the Lord's servants who have had to stay in Sweden for several years and some their entire life but they have nevertheless felt more happy and at peace than they were before they were baptized and you cannot possibly mean that . . . [missing text]

I could write much more about Luther's religion and its content in Luther's days, but what I doubt is that you would not read it [I doubt that you would read it] and I do not want to write because you might think I would lie to you. You write furthermore that Kersti Motfred thinks that it is not right that people are baptized [as adults] but she stated, as so many others, that people can be born again without being baptized. I want to ask: How can people be so stupid and think that when they cannot find even the smallest evidence for this in the Bible, not one single word proves this, how can they then believe that. When they think that it is impossible to be born again in any other way than through water and the spirit. Admit [it] they can find so many clear evidences for this in the Bible. Read the third chapter by the Evangelist John. There you can find what Jesus said to Nicodemus when Nicodemus asked him how a person might be born again. I also want to ask you [whether you have] read chapter 6 in the Epistles to the Hebrews? You can find it in verses 8, 5, 6 what they say about sinning against the Holy Spirit.

I can also greet you from Johannes' brothers. They are doing well. They have just come home to us from their work in the silver mines. We have also received a letter from her sisters they are also doing well. Merlin Else [an unusual name in Swedish] is doing miserably.

Now I do not have anything else to write about for this time and lastly you are greeted sincerely from us.

Signed kindly by your brother Ola Svensson

When you write next time let me know how our brother Jöns Svensson is doing. I also think that it would be nice if brother-in-law Per Jönsson would write us a little letter.

Swanson, John M.

1891–1911
Denver, Colorado
Twenty-four letters

John M. Swanson, originally Johan Magnus Svensson, was born in 1863 in Virestad, southwest of Vislanda in Småland. He was the first of three siblings to emigrate to America and settle in Denver, Colorado; they ultimately located their families close to one another in the city and made frequent visits to each other's households throughout the week. (See also Emma Hallberg, Albert Sandberg, and Ida Sandberg in this appendix.) The fourth and youngest sibling, Anna Lovisa, remained in Sweden; she died in 1892.[89]

Swanson traveled to America in 1888. He worked at the Argo smelter doing work that was difficult and dirty but that sustained a comfortable economic position for him and his wife, Tilda, whom he married in 1891.[90] Swanson and his sisters wrote letters home to their parents. The letters depict a close-knit family that took an active interest in each other's children, participated in church activities, stayed in touch with friends in other Colorado communities, and supported each other after the death of Tilda in 1908, during Swanson's second marriage (to a Swedish American named Josephine, in 1910), and after Swanson's death in 1912, at age forty-eight.[91] Amid these events, Swanson joined the Swedish Lutheran church in Denver in 1909.[92]

A consistent concern throughout the letters is the American economy, which was, according to this family, not much better than what they had left behind in Sweden. In the following letter, which Swanson wrote to his parents in 1894, Swanson comments on how hard his work is and the difficulty of obtaining any other kind of work. He also describes a fishing trip he took with friends.[93]

Denver 3 Sep 1894

I will now again have to send you a few lines to let you know that we are in good health and are doing well as usual. I also have to thank you for your letter we received a week ago in which we see that you are in good health and that considering the circumstances are doing well, which makes us happy to hear. I also have to tell you that it is as usual bad times here, but we [take] one day at a time now like before. I have begun to work now, so I am thinking that everything will become the way it was. I have been home now for such a long time that it has become old too. I have gotten so big and fat and I have never been this fat any time. I have had such a good time this summer so I have never had such a good time. I can tell you that we went out fishing yesterday it was Anders Johan and Peter the Carpenter [*Snickare*] from Bäckkhult and I. We had a nice time, we got lots of fish. Peter Jonson visits us often we have fished many times this summer. I also have to tell you that Anders Johan is leaving with his family. He has gotten another place to work. I can barely tell you how, but he is going to look after a house and a yard and a few horses for a rich old man [*gubbe*] and that will be a good place. It is for the same old man that Elna Hörlin worked for so she has actually gotten them the place. They are moving tomorrow, it is pretty far from here. It is called Salida, Kansas so Anders Johan has quit his work at the smelter today. It is so hard to work at the smelter, there is no wonder that some people quit if they can, but it is hard to get anything else. Peter Nilson from Degersnäs went back to Sweden a week ago so if you meet him you have to ask about us. I have even heard that there has been an auction on the farm in Tvetaryd. I am wondering how it went, or if there was something for you. I hear the other it is lost.[94] Emma and Ida send their best to you, they were here yesterday. They are healthy and work as usual, finally you are greeted by your son and your daughter-in-law

Johan and Tilda Swanson

Greet everybody in Röckla from us, Carl and Maina were here yesterday, greet also Magnus Jonson and Elna from us and Pär and aunt.

We sent you a picture of our house last time and I hope that you have received it now.
Tilda she thanks you for her letter.

Trulsson, Nils
1882–86
Peoa, Utah
Ten letters

Nils Trulsson wrote several letters to Elna Andersson during his time in Peoa, Utah, attempting to convince her to convert to Mormonism and to join him in Utah. His letters include protests that he does not plan to become a polygamist and that the Mormons are good people. Apparently he was successful in his plea. In June 1886 he sent Elna a ticket for passage and gave her instructions regarding the voyage, which she was to take via Copenhagen.

The collection of Trulsson's letters includes a few sent to Elna from Brännestad, in Skåne, before his emigration via Copenhagen. It is possible that he was originally from Brännestad, which was a parish that saw many Mormon converts.[95]

Wall, Oscar
1906
Butte, Montana
One letter

According to the donor of this collection, Oscar Wall was born in 1878 and traveled via Liverpool to the United States in 1902. In the following letter from 1906, Wall writes to his mother from Butte, Montana. His letter consists mostly of a plea for letters in response to those he had sent previously.[96]

Butte 10/18 1906

Dear mother and siblings

Thousand thanks for the letter that I received today, in which I see that you are alive and well. I am healthy as well, I have had good luck ever since I came here to this country. I have had good health the entire time, which is the best of all. I see in the letter that you have gotten a letter from aunt and she is in Seattle [Caeattle] and that you would like to go there. That would probably be nice for you to come here to this country, but I do not want to say anything, you have to do what you think is right. How is it going with Anna's legal proceedings? Did she win or lose? Can you send aunt's address? I am wondering how father is doing, have you had any letter from him. I would like to write him. Is Martin working at the Sugar factory or Mårten's? Where do they live? How much did you pay for Taningsberg, or how much did you get for the house? You have to excuse me for asking so much, but I like to know a few things about the old country.

I do not have time to write more this time but many thousands dear regards to you mother

Sincerely
your son and brother
Oscar Wall
58 East Park Street
Butte
Montana
Write soon

Wiberg, J. Edward
1882
Bozeman, Montana
Two letters

J. Edward Wiberg was during 1882 a railroad construction worker in Bozeman, Montana. Because of the proximity of the Yellowstone geysers and hot springs and the construction of a railroad through the region, Wiberg thought that the area would quickly become populated. He hoped to establish a saloon that would cater to Swedish workers, and he wrote to a brother Charles, living in Stillwater, Minnesota, for a loan to begin the venture. By 1887 Wiberg had relocated to Bismarck, (now North) Dakota.

Notes

Preface

1. Luebke, "Introduction," vii.
2. Dag Blanck, in discussion with the author, 25 January 2006.
3. Limerick, *Something in the Soil*, 19.
4. Limerick, "Making the Most of Words," 183.

1. Vernacular Writing

1. Clara Jeppsson to her sister Sigrid, 6 March 1912, letter 35. "Jag sätter mig strax att skrifva till dig ty det är så många tankar och känslor som kommer då jag erhåller bref men som jag inte kan hålla fast länge därför vill jag hälst nedskrifva dem strax om jag kan, det får i alla fall bli så godt jag kan."
2. Barton, *Letters from the Promised Land*, 4.
3. Ibid., 4–5.
4. Zempel, *In Their Own Words*, xii.
5. Ibid., xiii.
6. Beauchamp, "The Persona and the Real Woman—A Case Study," 42. Hanna Snellman considers this methodological issue from the point of view of ethnology in her essay "Was It Actually So?"
7. Clara Jeppsson to her sister Sigrid, 13 October 1911, letter 27. "Som du här ser har jag nu lemnat Denver.... Vi äro så tillsammans igen på en farm men det är den skillnaden att jag denna gång har mitt eget hus." For this random example, I simply turned to the collection on my desk at the moment and drew a letter from the middle of the stack.
8. Ibid. "Det inte är stort, det innehåller nämligen endast 2 rum, så kan jag emellanåt göra några timmar arbete för basen här men det är inte mycket förtjänst. Johan har 50 doll. i mån och så har vi fri bostad."
9. Ibid. "Regnade det också som himlen var öppen och alla vägar voro fulla af vatten."
10. Ibid. "Men han lefver fattigare än en fattighusgubbe i Sverige. Han är ogift och han gör själf allt sitt husarbete såväl som sitt farmarbete."
11. Øverland, "Learning to Read Immigrant Letters," 216.
12. Clara Jeppsson to her sister Sigrid, 23 August 1911, letter 25. "Johan har stannat

på farmen så jag tänker kanske att jag också går dit det kan sparas mera om vi lefver på landet." Similar phrasing appears in letters 23, 24, and 28.

13. Clara Jeppsson to her sister Sigrid, 11 January 1912, letter 30. "Jag endast vill förtjäna pengar så att jag kan komma hem." The theme of saving or gathering (*skrapa*) together money appears in letters 23, 25, 28, 29, 31, 33, 34, and 35, usually figured as an impediment to their desires, especially the desire to travel home to Sweden.

14. Clara Jeppsson to her sister Sigrid, 29 September 1911, letter 26. "Så svalnar väll kärleken snart då pengarna är slut och de få taga ihop med att arbeta så det svider i ryggen."

15. Clara Jeppsson to her sister Sigrid, 19 November 1911, letter 29. "Kanske de kommit att tänka på huru mycket pengar du skrapat tillhopa för dem."

16. Clara Jeppsson to her sister Sigrid, 13 October 1911, letter 27. "Som du här ser"; "jag har fått bref från"; and "du får nu hälsa mor och alla från oss."

17. These are the epithets as translated by Foley in *Immanent Art*.

18. Foley, "Word-Power, Performance, and Tradition," 286.

19. Ong, *Orality and Literacy*, 61.

20. Foley, *How to Read an Oral Poem*, 50–53.

21. Dégh, "Two Letters from Home," 808.

22. Ibid., 812.

23. Klymasz, "The Letter in Canadian Ukrainian Folklore," 54.

24. Mieder, "'Now I Sit Like a Rabbit in the Pepper,'" 35–36.

25. Jason, "Literature, Letters, Verbal Texts," 227.

26. Chain letters have also received much study. One Swedish example is Palmenfelt, "Bryt Ej Kedjan!" However, the chain letter differs significantly from the more flexible personal letter in its slight variability and rigid rules for transmission.

27. Øverland, "Learning to Read Immigrant Letters," 210–11.

28. Øverland, "Becoming White in 1881," "Norwegian Texans Tell Their Story in Letters, 1843–1884," and "Religion and Church in Early Immigrant Letters."

29. Altman, *Epistolarity: Approaches to a Form*, 186–87.

30. Dolan, "The Immigrants and Their Gods," 69.

31. Gerber, "Forming a Transnational Narrative," paragraph 17.

32. Gerber, *Authors of Their Lives*, 192.

33. Gerber, "Epistolary Ethics," 18.

34. Gerber, "Epistolary Ethics," 11–16; Gerber, *Authors of Their Lives*, 101.

35. Stahl, *Literary Folkloristics and the Personal Narrative*, 35.

36. Ibid., 41.

37. Oring, "On the Concepts of Folklore," 17–18.

38. Examining Swedish-American letter manuals, Carl Isaacson agrees that the manuals were not necessarily used, but instead represent an attempt on the part of upper-class Swedish immigrants to improve the language use of their lower-class counterparts (229–30).

39. *Fullständig Svensk-Engelsk Bref- och Formulärbok*, 21.

40. Lönnkvist, *Allt-Omfattande Svensk-Amerikansk Uppslagsbok*, 312.

41. Culley, "Women's Vernacular Literature," 9–10.

42. Blegen, *Land of Their Choice*, viii.

43. Foley, *Immanent Art*, 107.

44. Ibid.

45. Toelken, *Morning Dew and Roses*.

46. Allen, "Personal Experience Narratives," 242; and Kalčik, ". . . like Ann's Gyne-cologist or the Time I Was Almost Raped," 7.

47. "Someone who knocks on your door for no apparent reason" or "Someone who knocks on your door and asks you what you believe." I heard the first of these responses from a Unitarian Universalist as an oral joke, but both versions are also available at http://stoney.sb.org/uujokes.html.

48. Attebery, *Building with Logs*.

49. See, for example, Blegen, *Land of Their Choice*, xiii. Fitzpatrick comments on this pattern of editing, *Oceans of Consolation*, 20–21.

50. Beauchamp, "The Persona and the Real Woman—A Case Study," 42.

51. Clara Jeppsson to her sister Sigrid, 10 April 1912, letter 34. "Tack för ditt bref som jag erhöll i dag." Similar phrasing appears at the beginnings of letters 24, 26, 28, 29, 30, and 35.

52. "Som du här ser har jag nu," as already quoted in note 7 for this chapter. Similar phrasing appears at the beginning of letter 22.

53. Clara Jeppsson to her sister Sigrid, 23 August 1911, letter 25. "Jag fick bref från Axel i förra veckan."

54. Clara Jeppsson to her sister Sigrid, 29 September 1911, letter 26, "Jag vill nu sluta"; 13 October 1911, letter 27, "Skrif snart"; 13 June 1911, letter 23, "Jag har inte mera att skrifva denna gången," "Kära hälsningar."

55. Øverland, "Learning to Read Immigrant Letters," 214.

56. Clara Jeppsson to her sister Sigrid, 10 April 1912, letter 34. "Men det är inte endast det som gör att jag önskar resa hem. Jag kan väl lika gärna tala om att er [ni?] väntar en arfvinge." *Arvinge* is still used in Sweden as an affectionate way of referring to a baby as it is developing in the womb.

2. "Thanks for the Letter"

1. John A. Leonard to his brother-in-law D. Lungcrantz, 11 May 1884, letter 7. "Mycken, outsägligt mycken varm och hjärtlig tacksägelse för den kära skrifvelse jag erhöll den 3je April. Huru glad blef jag ej, då jag än en gång—utan att förvänta—fick emottaga ett bref från dig, fullt af nyheter och vicktigare tilldragelser, som ägt rum i min hemort på senare tiden."

2. Bakhtin, "The Problem of Speech Genres," 60. The linguist Patrizia Viola agrees that informal letters "are constituted by the presence of features used in oral discourse" (164).

3. Bakhtin, "The Problem of Speech Genres," 62–67.

4. Toelken, *The Dynamics of Folklore*, 40–41.

5. John M. Swanson to his parents, 1 October 1911, folder B, letter 13. "Älskade Förälldrar, Tack för edra mycket kärkomna bref som vi har bekommit. Det gläder oss mycke att höra att ni har någorlunda hälsan och mår efter omständigheter godt. Jag får efven nämna att vi mår alla godt här så vi har mycke att tacka gud före, både hemma och borta, att vi har varit skonade ifrån alla olyckor till kropp och själ."

6. Toelken, *The Dynamics of Folklore*, 137.

7. Nels Pearson to his sister Annie, 30 November 1908, letter 11. "Det är så längesedan jag hörde något ifrån dig så jag vill låta dig få några rader och låta dig veta huru jag är, så du vet att jag lefver och har helsan och arbetar, som vanligt."

8. Frykman and Löfgren, *Culture Builders*, 144–50.

9. Allwood, "Are There Swedish Patterns of Communication?" section 4.3.1 (iii). *Tack för sist* (thanks for past times) and *Tack för trevligt sällskap* (thanks for pleasant company) are cited as Swedish American sayings in Williamson and Williamson, 14.

10. The phrase *jag lever och har hälsan* is so common in Swedish immigrant letters that the Swenson Swedish Immigration Research Center used it as the title for its 2004 conference on immigrant letters. Papers from the conference are available in the *Swedish-American Historical Quarterly* 56, nos. 2–3 (2005).

11. Frykman and Löfgren, *Culture Builders*, 174–77; quotation page, 177.

12. Emma Hallberg to her parents, 19 June 1891, John M. Swanson Collection, folder C, letter 1. "Må nu och alltid vel är min dagliga önskan."

13. Emma Hallberg to her parents, 27 February 1912, John M. Swanson Collection, folder B, letter 14. "Må nu och altid vel är min dagliga önskan. Efwen beder jag eder att stå wid gott mod och lesa detta Sorgsna bref hvilket ni nog kan förmoda hvad det inne holler."

14. Bernhard Rydberg to his mother, 15 October 1901, letter 7. "Jag skickade igår några fotografier. . . . Fotografierna äro från en plats uppe ibland Klippiga Bergen."

15. Leonard Nilsson to Johan Westerberg, 8 August 1880, box 8, folder B, letter 6. "För ditt bref af den 18 siste Juni—hvilkedt till mig anlände den 20 Juli—är jag dig af hela mitt hjerta tacksam."

16. Leonard Nilsson to Lovisa Borg, 8 November 1881, box 8, folder A1, letter 24. "Ack min lilla engel, om du hade kunnat se huru glad, huru förtjust jag blef—då jag den 30 sist oktober hade nöjet och glädjen att, å Postkontort, här i R.B., emottaga ett bref, hvilkedt jag ögonblickeligen igenkände—att det var ifrån min snälla, trogna och tåligt (med en engels tålamod) väntande Lova!"

17. Leonard Nilsson to Lovisa Borg, 22 May 1880, box 8, folder A1, letter 16. "Klart, varmt och strålande skiner solen neder, på den nu grönskande dalsänkningarne. Hela naturen andas vårens lifsförnyande kraft—Träden kläder sig uti sommarskrud. Bäckarne sorla lifligt. Foglarne sänder qvittrande sitt pris till naturens herre—Allt är skönt och härligt. Floras barn börjar öppna sina munnar. Gubben Bore tycker på allvar hafva dragit sin kosa härifrån."

18. Johan Håkansson to his wife Britta and their children, 16 August 1888, letter 6. "I dag sänder jag pängar till dig. . . . jag undra om de pangerna som jag sände sist äro komma till dig skrif om det när du skrifa."

19. Fritz Lindborg to Nils Persson, 9 December 1888, letter 20.

20. Oscar Wall to his mother and siblings, 18 October 1906, letter 2. "Jag har haft tur ända sen jag kom hit till landet. . . . ni får ursäkta för jag fragar efter sa mycket men jag likar vete lite om gamla landet."

21. Johan Håkansson to his wife Britta and their children, 16 August 1888, letter 6. "Du skrifva så fort du for deta brefvet så for jag veta hur det går der hemma i somer har börjar att bli kalt om näterna så har blir snart vinter" (emphasis in English added; see note 18 in this chapter for a continuation of this passage).

22. Fritz Lindborg to Nils Persson, 9 December 1888, letter 20. "Visstelse där . . . måtte i alla blifva angenäm natturligtvis är det ingen orsak att förmoda motsattsen."

23. Oscar Wall to his mother and siblings, 18 October 1906, letter 2. "Har ni haft något bref från honom jag skulle lika skrifva till honom."

24. Emma Hallberg to her parents, 1 September 1902, John M. Swanson Collection, folder C, letter 10. "Rams" (emphasis added in the outlined version).

25. Allen, "Personal Experience Narratives," 237.

26. Emma Hallberg to her parents, 1 September 1902, John M. Swanson Collection, folder C, letter 10. "Vi har sport [spört] att hon tigde i från er er guld ring i sist hon war himma wi tycken att hon kunde min stone låta er hafwa det ni har. Så lenge ni behöfwa det hon gaf er inte mycke heller nu hon kunna hjelpt er lite så om hon förstod det Så borde hon sjemmas."

27. Ibid. "Har ni hört hvad Bettis Pojk gör eller om han är så förnem som hon Skryter. Betty är wist en Snell flicka så hon är verd en god man."

28. "The Kind and Unkind Girls" is Aarne-Thompson tale type 480, a *Märchen* (magical tale) of international distribution.

29. Daun, *Swedish Mentality*, 48.

30. Stahl, *Literary Folkloristics*, 21–24.

31. Dégh, "Folk Narrative," 70.

32. Klymasz, "The Letter in Canadian Ukrainian Folklore," 61.

33. John Hedin to Ole (Olof Larsson), 7 July 1889, Ivar Larsson Collection, 387. "*Fränd and brother* . . . jag kommer ihåg olika platser der vi traflade oss fram med vårt praperti på ryggen."

34. Leonard Nilsson to Johan Westerberg, 22 August 1881, box 8, folder B, letter 9. "Presidenten anlände till Bangården i sällskap med 'Utrikes-Ministern['] Blaine. Just som de—hållande hvarandra under armen—inträdde i wäntsalen af—fyrades tvenne skott bakifrån och den ädle, förträfflige, af hela nationen så afhållne, mannen störtade till golfvet. Den ena kulan gjorde endast ett skrapsår i ena skuldran, men den andra gick igenom ryggens ena sida, söndersplittrade ett refben, gick igenom lefvern och stannade i trakten af ljumsken—den är ännu icke uttagen, icke lyckate ännu."

35. Leonard Nilsson to Johan Westerberg, 1 May 1881, box 8, folder B, letter 8. "Den nuvarande Presidenten har börjat som vedhuggare, varit snickare och nu påstår man att ifrån hyfvelbänken till President-stolen är endast—ett steg."

36. Leonard Nilsson to Lovisa Borg, 16 October 1881, box 8, folder A1, letter 23. "President Garfield afled Måndagen den 19 September. Sörjd af maka och barn,

jemmte (50) femtio millioner medborgare. Det är en Nation som sörjer en folkvald skef. Det är ett land som sörjer en värdig son, som född under torftiga omständigheter. Som ifrån yxan och plogen samt hyfvel bänken, genom egna förtjenster—arbete, flit och förstagsamhet med tillhjelp af goda natur—gåfvor, bragt sig upp till den högsta värdighet som kan ernås i hela werlden—En folkvalld styresman, för werldens rikaste och mäktigaste nation. Dertill den mest upplyste och framåtgående.

Jag sade han är sörjd af maka och barn. Han är äfven sörjd af en 80 årig moder. Den gamla qvinnan har burit honom på sina armar. Hon har sedt honom arbeta hårdt för att försörja henne och yngre syskon. Hon har sedt honom stiga högre och högre tills han slutligen nått höjden—och hon fick se honom falla—ett offer för en lönmördares kula. Lifvet är ändå en gåta—omöjlig att lösa." (I have added paragraph breaks to indicate the parallels between the two sections of Nilsson's eulogy.)

37. Peter Peterson to Jonas Danielson and family, 25 March 1902, letter 19. "För några vickor sedan så var det en Svensk i nerheten af Saltsjöstaden, som fick Pattent på ett nytt slags jern att Fånga storre och mindre Odjur i, och han sållde Patenten för 25,000 Då men jag är så dum att jag ville intet selja min Patent för $25,000."

38. Wolf-Knuts, "Contrasts as a Narrative Technique in Emigrant Accounts," 97.

39. Charles Flodin to Anders Abrahamsson, 9 October 1890, letter 21. "Så till råga på allt efter att vi fortskridit opp en ström vi funno oss själva inkilade ibland höga berg hvar det syntes till oss vid första påseendet ringa utväg annan än den vi kommo in. Men efter två dagars sökande finno vi ändtligen ett pass, genom hvilket vi fortsatte vår mödosamma färd till nästa hinder hvilket representerade sig sjelf i en stor ström som vi hade att slå en brygga öfver på hvilken vi buro våra ting öfver samt sam eller simmade våra hästar. Nu gick allt sin vanliga gång igen till vi hade att krossa en hög bergskedja på höga snödrifvor hvilken var solid nog att upp bära oss och hästar. En gång kom jag nära deran att mista min häst han föll i en bergsklyfta men undkom med några fula skrapor och sår."

40. Ibid. "Genom skog, moras, öfver bäckar och strömmar. Wi funno oss sjelfva på toppen af en hög bergskedja Hvarifrån vi i fjerran urskilde konturerna utaf en grön dal."

41. Ibid. "Två gamla guldsökare."

42. Ibid. "För oss var ej något annat att göra än gå tillbaka hvilket vi gjorde."

43. Toelken, *The Dynamics of Folklore*, 251.

44. Clara Jeppsson to her sister Sigrid, 13 June 1911, letter 23. "Jag har inte mera att skrifva."

45. Blegen, *Land of Their Choice*, xiii.

46. Cited in Beauchamp, "The Persona and the Real Woman—A Case Study," 42.

47. Clara Jeppsson to her sister Sigrid, 13 June 1911, letter 23. "Jag har inte mera att skrifva denna gången utan många hälsningar till Eder alla. Skrif snart och omtala hur det är stäldt hemma i Sverige—om ni har vacker sommar. Hoppas ni alla äro friska och krya. Kära hälsningar Clara."

48. Ibid. "Min adress är."

49. Ibid. "Jag får inte träffa min gubbe på en hel vecka. Det käns."

50. Emma Hallberg to her parents, 1 September 1902, John M. Swanson Collection, folder C, letter 10; Peter J. Johansson to his brother Johannes, 27 July 1891, letter 3; Ola Svenson to his sister Maria, 11 March 1886, letter 6; John A. Leonard to a friend, 16 April 1881, letter 3; and Anni Dickson to Carl Israelsson, 1 November 1893, letter 19.

51. Allwood, "Are There Swedish Patterns of Communication?" section 4.3.1 (iii).

52. Oscar Wall to his mother and siblings, 18 October 1906, letter 2. "Jag har inte tid att skrifva mera denna gång men många tusen kära hälsningar sender jag till eder Mamma."

53. Olof Larsson to his parents, 29 July 1904, letter 15. "Något mera har jag inte att tala om för denna gången utan slutar jag med många hälsningar till eder alla derhemma."

54. Aron W. Johnson to Anna Johanson, 10 September 1903, letter 16. "Många hjartliga hälsningar till dig fran mig."

55. Gerber, "Epistolary Ethics," 15–16.

56. Ibid., 14.

57. Slotkin, Regeneration through Violence, 6.

3. "Here Are Many Swedes"

1. Leonard Nilsson to Lovisa Borg, 27 November 1879, box 8, folder A1, letter 12. "Jag reste genom Mormonernas land (Utah) som de kallar, 'Sion,' och sig sjelfva 'De sista dagarners heliga.'" (I traveled through the Mormon's country [Utah], which they call "Zion," and themselves "The Latter-Day Saints.")

2. John A. Leonard to his sister, 4 December 1881, letter 5. "Indianerna har sitt hemland här såväl som i Arizona." (Indians have their homeland here, as well as in Arizona.")

3. August Johansson to P. Magnus, 13 May 1891, letter 25. "Här är många svarta o många svenskar också." (Here are many blacks and many Swedes also.)

4. Pet Stred to Carl Johannisson, 9 August 1891, letter 4. "Supa och skuta [skjuta] varandra här [hör] till ordningen för dagen här lefves ett ganska vildt lif nogon kyrka eller nogon Dylik platts fins här eke på öfver 100 mil."

5. John M. Swanson to his parents and siblings, 8 December 1891, letter C2. "Ni tror inte att vi har det så vackert som vi har. Spårvagnen går på nästa gata intill så vi kan komma vad [var?] vi vill i Staden för 5 Cent."

6. According to Luebke, in 1900 the percentage of foreign-born residents in the western United States (not including the Great Plains states) was greater than in any eastern region, with the exception of New England (x). Conzen notes that "even in . . . relatively immigrant-poor states [of the West] . . . they [immigrants] significantly exceeded the national average" ("Introduction," 345–46). Quinn comments on religious balkanization in the West as a result of ethnic enclaves ("Religion in the American West," 147). Rooney, Zelinsky, and Louder map the area outside Mormon Utah and southeastern Idaho as generally high in religious diversity (This Remarkable Continent, 183). The ethnic and racial diversity of the West also is noted by several

other scholars; see Barkan's review of this literature ("Turning Turner on His Head?" 59–62, 65–68). Limerick presents convergence as one of her "four 'c's" of Western history (along with conquest, continuity, and complexity; *Something in the Soil,* 18–21).

7. University of Virginia Geospatial and Statistical Data Center. The area that eventually became New Mexico always harbored a much smaller share of the Swedish population, with only 310 Swedish-born residents, or less than 1 percent of the state population, by the 1920 census. See Helge Nelson, *The Swedes and the Swedish Settlements in North America,* 320.

8. Luebke, "Introduction," x–xiii.

9. Helge Nelson, *The Swedes and the Swedish Settlements in North America,* 311.

10. Dag Blanck, in discussion with the author, 25 January 2006.

11. Helge Nelson, *The Swedes and the Swedish Settlements in North America,* 310.

12. County percentages presented throughout this paragraph were retrieved through the University of Virginia Geospatial and Statistical Data Center. See also Helge Nelson, *The Swedes and the Swedish Settlements in North America,* 312–13.

13. Helge Nelson, *The Swedes and the Swedish Settlements in North America,* 320.

14. Ibid., 319.

15. Hallberg, *Swedish Heritage in Wyoming,* 7–8.

16. Carlson, *Northmen Who Went West,* 25–27; Segerhammar, *First Lutheran Church of the Rockies,* 8–10; Helge Nelson, *The Swedes and the Swedish Settlements in North America,* 312–23.

17. See Marshall's demographic study of Swedes in Latah County, Idaho, "Swedish Immigrants to Latah County, Idaho"; and Attebery, "Transplantations of Swedish America in Idaho" and "Being Swedish-American in the Intermountain West." See also Helge Nelson, *The Swedes and the Swedish Settlements in North America,* 320.

18. Hallberg, *Swedish Heritage in Wyoming,* 11; Helge Nelson, *The Swedes and the Swedish Settlements in North America,* 318.

19. Helge Nelson, *The Swedes and the Swedish Settlements in North America,* 318.

20. For example, as documented in Wilson, "Folklore of Utah's Little Scandinavia." See also Helge Nelson, *The Swedes and the Swedish Settlements in North America,* 316; and the sources listed in chapter 3, note 80.

21. Unless otherwise indicated, statistics reported for Swedish immigrants, male and female, are from the United States Senate Reports, Doc. 282, 201–2, 431; United States Bureau, Eleventh Census, 538–9, 550–51, 578–79, 614–15, 626–27; and United States Bureau, Twelfth Census, 236–39, 260–61, 324–27, 396–99, 420–23.

22. Helge Nelson found anecdotal information regarding the good reputation of Swedish carpenters in Denver (*The Swedes and the Swedish Settlements in North America,* 312).

23. United States Senate Reports, Doc. 633, vol. 3, 223–28.

24. Nilsson, "What Do Literacy Rates in the Nineteenth Century Really Signify?" 292.

25. Meinig, *The Shaping of America,* 178–81.

26. Clara Jeppsson to her sister Sigrid, 1911 (no month or day identified), letter 22. "Efter att döma hvad jag sett af Denver så är denna stad vackrare än San Fransisco."

27. Ibid. "Villastil."

28. Ibid.

29. Clara Jeppsson to her sister Sigrid, 1911 (no month or day identified), letter 28. "Jag har fått smak för Denver och därför är det lite svårt för mig att gå tillbaka till en farm igen."

30. Peter Peterson to Jonas Danielson and family, 3 November 1902, letter 20. "Ljusare en Förenade Staternas Huvudstad Washington D.C."

31. *Svenska Adresskalendern,* n.p. "Svenska Denverkoloni."

32. Ibid.

33. University of Virginia Geospatial and Statistical Data Center.

34. Hallberg, "Nineteenth-century Colorado through Swedish Eyes," 121.

35. Ibid., 120.

36. Ibid., 113.

37. Clara Jeppsson to her sister Sigrid, 1911 (no month or day identified), letter 28. "Folket som går i kyrkan här äro väl inte så värst religiosa de gå väl mäst dit för att träffas."

38. *Denver City Directory;* Carlson, *Northmen Who Went West,* 49–58; and Hallberg, "Nineteenth-century Colorado through Swedish Eyes," 125.

39. *Officiellt Referat,* Kansas Conference, Colorado District, 1890 and 1892. Congregations were picked up by city directories well after their establishment. Lutheran congregations were listed for Boulder in the 1901 *Boulder City Directory;* for Longmont in the 1904 *Boulder City and County Directory;* for Pueblo in the 1904 *Pueblo City Directory;* and for Victor in the 1914 *Cripple Creek District Directory.*

40. Swedish Evangelical Free Church Collection, constitution and minutes, box A, pp. 9–11; and *Golden Jubilee,* p. 198.

41. Swedish Evangelical Free Church Collection, Protokoll öfver Svensk Evangeliska Ungdomsföreningen af Denver Colorado (minutes of the Swedish Evangelical Young People's Society of Denver, Colorado), box A, pp. 35, 79, 84; and Swedish Evangelical Free Church Collection, Record of Sewing Auction, 1890–1900, box A.

42. Swedish Evangelical Free Church Collection, minutes, box A, p. 16; and *Golden Jubilee,* pp. 60–61.

43. Clara Jeppsson to her sister Sigrid, 31 July 1911, letter 24. "Välbergade om inte rika."

44. Ibid. "Jag kan ligga i min bädd och höra musiken."

45. Carlson, *Northmen Who Went West,* 47.

46. *Anderson, Petterson och Lundström,* 1898 playbill, 1915 poster, and 1917 program, folder 12, Albert H. Aronson Collection; and Nyårs Soiré (New Year's party), 1914 program, folder 12, Albert H. Aronson Collection.

47. *Värmländingarne,* 1917 play program, folder 12, Albert H. Aronson Collection. Värmländingarne would be people from the Swedish province of Värmland, the point

of origin for many of the immigrants. Along with *Anderson, Petterson och Lundström,*
Värmländingarne was one of the most popular plays in Swedish America; Harvey,
"Performing Ethnicity," 155–56.

48. "Nailing a Lie," "Han är Sysslan Värd" (He is worthy of the office), "Scandinavians to Support Lindsey," clippings in folder 9; "Souvenir Program" for Second
Entertainment and Ball given by the Scandinavian Democratic Club, 30 April 1908,
folder 12; and contract between Swedish American Republican Club and Swedish
Military Band, 13 October 1891, folder 6; all in Albert H. Aronson Collection. There
is a list of organizations in *Svenska Adresskalendern.*

49. Carlson, *Northmen Who Went West,* 48; and the *Denver City Directory.* The
Vasa Order's Denver district lodge was organized in 1911; by 1913, it had overseen
the establishment of lodges in the Colorado towns of Leadville, Telluride, Silverton,
Idaho Springs, Greeley, Colorado Springs, Cripple Creek, Aspen, and Longmont;
and in the Wyoming towns of Rock Springs and Laramie (*Historical Review of Vasa*
Order of America, 1896–1971, 137–38).

50. The Midsommar picnic advertised on 4 June 1891 in the Denver *Svenska*
Korrespondenten claimed to be the eighteenth such event (8).

51. John M. Swanson to his parents, 7 February 1903, letter C11. "Jag ser i tidning-
arna nu att de stackars menniskorna i Norra Sverige äro svårt hemsökta af nöden."

52. Karl W. Bergström to Albert H. Aronson, 4 April 1903 and 12 June and 29 June
1903, Albert H. Aronson Collection, folder 1; and H. Arnold Barton, "The Norrland
Crop Failures of 1902 and the Swedish Americans," 10.

53. "Complete Statement of Relief Fund," 1903, Albert H. Aronson Collection,
folder 1.

54. *Svenska Korrespondenten,* 19 April 1894, 4.

55. Ibid., 23 August 1900, 5.

56. Ibid.

57. Ibid., 29 March 1894, 4.

58. Hallberg, "Nineteenth-century Colorado through Swedish Eyes," 114.

59. Gernes, "Recasting the Culture of Ephemera," 111.

60. Clara Jeppsson to unknown recipient, n.d., letter 31. "Jag skall sända ett tid-
ningsurklipp af den Svenska tidning vi har här. Du kan där se de olika meningar som
invandrare här [har] om America o Sverige. Men många kan man inte rätta sig efter
ty de som har lämnat Sverige för 20 eller 30 år bedömer Sverige efter den tiden och
kunna inte begripa att Sverige gått framåt så väl som America."

61. Clara Jeppsson to her sister Sigrid, 10 April 1912, letter 34.

62. In his article "Folkets Röst," Ulf Jonas Björk studied the emergence of letter-
to-the-editor columns in the Swedish-language press. Barbro Klein studied letters to
the editor in the Chicago *Svenska Amerikanaren Tribunen* (The Swedish American
tribune) from a much later period, 1966–68.

63. Klein, "Folkets Röst," 89.

64. *Svenska Korrespondenten* (Denver), 5 February 1891, 5. "Vi vilja skrifva."

65. Ibid., 26 March 1891, 5. "Jag vill sända tidningen en liten helsning." Klein finds

that her sample of letters from the 1960s can be seen as having formal and stylistic conventions sufficient to mark them as a genre (89).

66. Hallberg, "Nineteenth-century Colorado through Swedish Eyes," 127–29.

67. Ibid., 120. Hallberg also identifies one Swedish language newspaper in Cripple Creek, published for a year, *Svenska Cripple Creek Posten* (Cripple Creek Swedish post). No issues survive; Hallberg, "Nineteenth-century Colorado through Swedish Eyes," 122.

68. "Svensk-Amerikanska Western," n.d., clipping from *Svensk-Amerikanska Western* (The Swedish American West), Albert H. Aronson Collection, folder 9. "Vår förste vice-konsul"; "hjälpte inviga dem i Västerns mysterier."

69. Hallberg, "Nineteenth-century Colorado through Swedish Eyes," 120; and "After 70 Years," *Western News* (Denver), 26 June 1958, 1.

70. "Svensk-Amerikanska Western," n.d.; and Carlson, 14. Wærnér's career is described in Skarstedt, *Våra Penn-Fäktare*, 186–93. Wærnér served at the Denver paper from November 1889 to November 1891.

71. *Svensk-Amerikanska Western* (Denver), 28 March 1901, 1. In an undated holograph, one of the owners, A. H. Aronson, suggested that the paper was in financial difficulty when Newton took it over; Albert H. Aronson Collection, folder 3.

72. Anna Stina, *Svenska Korrespondenten* (Denver), 25 June 1891, 4. "En liten vacker svensk kyrka finnes äfven här och den lär vara den högst belägna kyrka på jorden. Kyrkan i fråga begagnas äfven af norrmännen, och jag har hört att ledsamt nog densamma är orsak till mycken split och tvedrägt svenskar och norrmän emellan här på platsen. Det är illa och häfdar visst inte skandinavernas anseende hos amerikaner och folk af andra nationer, hvilka äro här bosatta."

73. Hallberg, "Nineteenth-century Colorado through Swedish Eyes," 124.

74. Lindquist, "Swedish American Pseudonyms," 151.

75. Lindgren, "The Swedes Come to Utah," 23; and Lund, "Out of the Swan's Nest," 94–95.

76. Mulder, "Mormons from Scandinavia, 1850–1900." Varying accounts of the sea passage and the trip across the plains can be found in Larn and in Martin. The migration through Hull, England, is studied in Woods and Evans.

77. Mulder, "Mormons from Scandinavia, 1850–1900," 229, 235, 241.

78. Lindgren, "The Swedes Come to Utah," 15.

79. Mulder, "Utah's Ugly Ducklings," 234–35.

80. Kenneth Bjork, "A Covenant Folk, with Scandinavian Colorings," 213; Poulsen, "Folk Material Culture of the Sanpete-Sevier Area"; Wilson, "Folklore of Utah's Little Scandinavia"; Rice, "Spring City"; Carter, "Building Zion" and "North European Horizontal Log Construction in the Sanpete-Sevier Valleys"; Lund, "Out of the Swan's Nest"; Mulder, "Mother Tongue, 'Skandinavisme,' and 'the Swedish Insurrection' in Utah," 16, and *Homeward to Zion*, 196; and Polson, "The Swedes in Grantsville, Utah, 1860–1900." Nearly half (forty of ninety-one) of the families recorded in the 1880 U.S. census for St. Charles, Idaho, had at least one Scandinavian-born parent; twenty-two families included at least one Swedish-born parent.

81. Mulder, "Mother Tongue, 'Skandinavisme,' and 'the Swedish Insurrection' in Utah," 15, 19.

82. Peter Peterson to Jonas Danielson and family, 27 September 1886, letter 7.

83. Mulder, "Utah's Ugly Ducklings," 240–41.

84. Mulder, *Homeward to Zion*, 210.

85. Peter Peterson to Jonas Danielson and family, 3 November 1902, letter 20. "Saltsjöstaden liger vid sidan af bergett och det är bygd så högt upp i Bergsluttningen som kan låt sig göra, Springvatten brukas öfver hela staden, i Husena och att bevattna gräs och Blomster anleggningar."

86. Kenneth Bjork, "A Covenant Folk, with Scandinavian Colorings," 214. Lund also notes this trend, "Out of the Swan's Nest," 82. A good example of Swedish enculturation to a Mormon American cultural position can be found in Larson, *The Education of a Second Generation Swede*, in which Larson labels himself a Swede, but provides very few examples of Swedish tradition.

87. Peter Peterson to Jonas Danielson, 6 November 1899, letter 17. "Jag vet många goda arbetare både från Swerge och Norge och Danmar[k], deras veg att arbeta är intet antaglig förr en de har varitt her bra lenge och dett är många som intet kan legga bort sin gamla lans vana jag vill namna en af de mest simpla tingen at slå in en spån spik så kan man höra om det är en Skandenavien eller en Amerikkan en Skandinav så hör man 5 eller 6 slag och en Amerikkan så hör man intet mera en ett slag."

88. Kenneth Bjork, "A Covenant Folk, with Scandinavian Colorings," 215.

89. Mulder, "Mother Tongue, 'Skandinavisme,' and 'the Swedish Insurrection' in Utah," 11.

90. Kenneth Bjork, "A Covenant Folk, with Scandinavian Colorings," 215–20.

91. Mulder, *Homeward to Zion*, 264–66.

92. *Fyrbåken* existed in 1895 and may not have had more than two issues; *Salt Lake Bladet* was published by the Lutherans beginning in 1902, and extant issues date through 1911. Setterdahl, 30.

93. Peter Peterson to Jonas Danielson and family, 25 March 1902, letter 19.

94. Mulder, *Homeward to Zion*, 252. Rydman's career is also described by Ernest L. Olson.

95. Lund, "Out of the Swan's Nest," 99–103.

96. *Tomtar* are supernatural beings found in the household, sometimes mischievous and sometimes helpful, similar to the English brownies. They are often associated with Christmas.

97. Ernest L. Olson, "Otto Rydman, Satirist," 70. See, for example, *Utah Korrespondenten* (Salt Lake City), 16 March 1893, 7.

98. *Utah Korrespondenten* (Salt Lake City), 13 April 1893, 2. "Hvad slags materialer var satan gjord, att han kunde tåla 2,000 gånger mera hetta än diamanten förutan att smälta?"

99. *Utah Korrespondenten* (Salt Lake City), 22 June 1893, 4; 10 May 1894, 1; 23 August 1894, 4; 5 June 1896, 4; and 18 March 1898, 1.

100. *Utah Korrespondenten* (Salt Lake City), 2 August 1894, 4. "Undertecknad anhåller härmed ödmjukligen att dessa rader måtte få inflyta uti eder tidning med anledning af hr Nilsons skrifvelse i förra numret. Jag tror att alla som hafva insändt något i tidningen om missförhållandet med de skandinaviska mötena vilja och kunna stå för detsamma utan någons ursäkt och mellankomst." Literally translated, *måtte få inflyta uti* means "may flow out."

101. Ernest L. Olson, "Otto Rydman, Satirist," 69–70.

102. *Utah Korrespondenten* (Salt Lake City), 26 June 1896, 1. "Det var en man, men det var ingen man. Han gick på en väg, men det var ingen väg. Han hittade ett ting, men det var ingenting. Hade han sett det, så hade han inte tagit upp det; men förr att han inte såg det, så tog han upp det. Hur kan detta förklaras?"

103. *Utah Korrespondenten* (Salt Lake City), 3 July 1896, 4. "Mannen var en pojke. Vägen var en skogsstig. Föremålet, som han hittade, var ett nötskal. Han trodde det var an hel nöt, men hade van [han?] sett att det blott var ett skal, hade han ej tagit upp det."

104. Klein also finds folklore genres within reader letters, but notes, quite appropriately, that folkloric study of such letters would be limited were we to look only for embedded genres (88–89).

105. Ernest L. Olson, "Otto Rydman, Satirist," 38–39, 55.

106. *Utah Korrespondenten* (Salt Lake City), 12 June 1896, 4.

107. "Two Popular Scandinavian Plays," 5 March 1900.

108. *Montana Posten* (Helena), 15 August 1891, 1. Gothic type was used for a longer time in Norway than in Sweden, a practice that was continued by Norwegian American newspapers.

109. *Montana Tidende og Skandinav* (Butte), 9 February 1894, 1.

110. *Montana Posten* (Helena), 23 February 1893, 2.

111. *Montana Posten* (Helena), 22 June 1893, 4. "Firas med mer än vanlig ståt bland alla svenskar i Amerika."

112. *Butte City Directory*, 83.

113. *Historical Review of Vasa Order of America, 1896–1971*, 152.

114. *Montana Posten* (Helena), 18 May 1893, 2; 25 May 1893, 3; 20 July 1893, 1. "Alle Skandinaver var paa Benene og deltog i Festen."

115. *Bergs-Väktaren* (Helena), October 1898, 3; December 1898, 3.

116. *Butte City Directory*, 70–71.

117. *Helena City Directory*, 71–72.

118. *Montana Posten* (Helena), 23 February 1893, 1. "Ferskt og salt kjød. Den eneste skandinaviske Slagterbutik i Helena."

119. *Montana Posten* (Helena), 23 February 1893, 2. "Den eneste skandinaviske Dentist i Byen"; "Skandinaviske Pharmacopea"; "skandinaviske Farmaceut."

120. *Montana Posten* (Helena), 29 June 1893, 1.

121. Setterdahl, 31. Extant issues begin with the 31 August 1910 publication. The paper included news items from Troy, Wallace, and Coeur d'Alene, Idaho.

122. Olof Larsson to his parents, 17 June 1905, letter 16. "Jag ser i tidningarne di har haft lite krångel mellan Sverige och Norge."

123. John R. Johnson to his parents and siblings, 11 August 1905, no letter number.

124. Undated correspondence from Leonard Nilsson to Lovisa Borg, box 8, folder A1, letter 27.

125. Swenson Swedish Immigration Research Center, Swedish American Church Records in North America, S-334, S-333, S-337, S-458, S-338, S-336, S-335, S-459, and B-124. See also Attebery, "'Transplantations of Swedish America in Idaho"'; Marshall, "Swedish Immigrants to Latah County, Idaho"; and Reed, "Latah County's Scandinavians."

126. Hallberg, *Swedish Heritage in Wyoming,* 9, 12–16.

4. "I Work Every Day"

1. Pet Stred to Carl Johannisson, 9 August 1891, letter 4. "Jag är frisk och arbetar och knogar lite för varje dag men jag har varit sjuk, eke så att jag varit sängligande, men jag var mycke dålig för nogra dagar sedan men är nu fult frisk igen. Jag har arbetat med varjehanda arbeten i somar. En tid arbetade jag vid en väg som skulle byggas. En månad arbetade jag för Farmare och nu arbetar jag vid en smälta där de smällter mallmen som tages utt af Grufvarna. Dätt är ett hårt arbete och fodras verkligen äkta Svenska krafter för att kunna stå utt med dätt. Arbetet är mycke styft och så är dätt varmt som i ett visst *ställe* [emphasis in original]. Jag vet inte hur länge jag komer att stå här när jag trötnar blir dätt att försöka med nogonting ennat Dänn som är ung och oerfaren bör försöka allt."

2. So universal is the topic of work that those few who do not mention it represent special cases. For instance, they wrote with a specific purpose in mind, or they were too young yet to be working. Karna Anderson and Genny Andersson wrote letters in which religious testimony was the main focus. Otto Anderson wrote offering a book collection to a friend. Emma Dahlgren invited a relative to a wedding. O. Nilson attempted to reestablish contact with relatives, and A. P. Hall attempted to settle an inheritance. Two correspondents, Maria Peterson and Victor Hallquist Jr., were children at the time of their letter writing—in Maria's case, to a friend she barely remembered; in Victor's case, to an uncle he had not met.

3. Peter F. Erlandson to his sister Ida Deurell, 30 January 1880, letter 1. "Jag har arbetat stadit."

4. Johan Håkansson to his wife and children, 21 November [188?], letter 9. "Jag har arbetat varje dag."

5. Charles M. Bloomberg to his mother, 3 December 1910, letter 1. "Jag arbetar för hvarje dag, och min lilla käring hon har så mycke att bestyra med att vaska och laga mat."

6. Carl Boline to his relatives, 24 February 1915, letter 6. "Jag arbetar var dag söndag som måndag."

7. John M. Swanson to his parents and siblings, 8 December 1891, letter C2. "Så nu önskar jag att vi fingo beholla vår helsa och att jag kunde arbeta, så hoppas jag att allting skall gå bra för oss."

8. See Sinor's study of the uses of diaries by women, *The Extraordinary Work of Ordinary Writing*, 155.

9. Ida Sandberg to her parents, 12 March 1906, John M. Swanson Collection, letter C15. "Jag har sytt så den lila har 9 eller 10 vita klänningar san [samt] undertjortlar samt kopa [kåpa]."

10. Ibid. "Albert sender serskillt sin helsning till er bada, han arbetar förvarje dag som förr."

11. Bengta Olson to her brother and in-laws, 23 June 1911, letter 2. "Hon har nu arbetat på en plats i öfer 2 år o hon har for ett års tid haft 7 dollar i veckan."

12. Pet Stred to Carl Johannisson, 9 August 1891, letter 4. "Här är i dätt hela ganska Dåliga tider för närvarande här i Landet och mycke svårt att få nogot arbete."

13. Daun, *Swedish Mentality*, 200.

14. Nils-Arvid Bringéus describes the extended Swedish Christmas season in *Årets Festseder*.

15. Daun, *Swedish Mentality*, 200. See also Frykman and Löfgren, *Culture Builders*, 15–19.

16. Frykman and Löfgren, *Culture Builders*, 24–26.

17. Roediger and Foner, *Our Own Time*, x.

18. Frykman and Löfgren, *Culture Builders*, 188, 190–92.

19. Leonard Nilsson to Johan Westerberg, 4 January 1881, box 8, folder B, letter 7. "För mig har julen varit rätt dyster. Jag har icke märkt att det varit jul alls. Endast sedt det genom 'almanackan.'"

20. Victor Johnson to his sister Amanda and in-law E. G. Bergström, 11 December 1908, letter 2. "Jag had några dagar fritt men nu går det var dag så jag vet ej om det blir tid att få fritt juldagen."

21. Sinor, *The Extraordinary Work of Ordinary Writing*, 172, 154–55.

22. Peter F. Erlandson to his sister, 30 January 1880, letter 1. "Jag erholler emellan 7 och 8 kronor om dagen."

23. Olof Larsson to his parents, 22 February 1904, letter 14. "3 till 3.50 om dagen och ändå inte arbeta hardt."

24. Swan Smith to his parents and siblings, 24 July 1906, letter 5. "Man får nog arbeta hårdt men betalningen är temligen *good* när jag arbetar för daglön har jag i allmänhet (3.50) 3 doller 50 cent om dagen stundum lite mera men så kostar det också at lefva."

25. Peter J. Johansson to his brother Johannes, 18 January 1891, letter 1. "Vi fick dagpenningen nedsat i December till 1 dol 50 Cent och så betala 50 Cent i veckan mer för maten så då blef det ej så mycket till venster [vinster] för den månaden."

26. Peter J. Johansson to his brother Johannes, 27 July 1891, letter 3. "Jag vet ej hvad vi kommer att fortjena här på det arbetet som vi nu håller på med men det förra gick endast till extra dagpenning som är 2 dol. Jag tror nog att vi förtjena

något mera här ty vi har 1500 (meter) *yard* berg i detta arbetet, men vi har och måst köpa bergsprängare verktyger för Cir. 5 P. Dol. Jag tänker att vi bli färdiga här om en månad." Walter Cameron describes the process used before compressed air drilling: hand drilling, stick dynamite, and percussion caps attached by wire to batteries (74).

27. Charles H. Anderson to Hanna Gustafson, 14 October 1889, letter 1. "Du sager att ni har litet betalt, och jag tror att det är så *al öfver*. Flickor här har från 2 till 4 Do i Veckan för god kokerska men de får arbeta hårdt." *Al öfver* appears to be a Swedish-English expression.

28. Anna Olson to her cousin Elna Lundberg, 30 March 1889, letter 4. "Jag . . . har en ricktigt bra plats jag har samma sorts arbete som jag hade i Topeka har betaldt 20 dollars i månaden."

29. Elin Pehrson to her cousin Maria, 13 May 1896, letter 3. "Det är för dyrt för oss att ha Piga, hon har nu 25 doll i månaden, så för flickor är det bra här om di är starka och orka arbeta."

30. John Renström to P. Björling, 31 December 1892, letter C7, 117–20. Quote from John Renström to P. Björling, 1901, letter C17, 163. "Min ide är då, att han stannar hemma öfver wintern ty det är ganska kalt på sjön denna tiden på året och en annan sak är det, att det är bättre att få arbete på vår sidan för en som får börja på med utsides arbete tills man lärer något Engelsk och sedan om han skulle vilja gå in och arbeta i grufvan, då kan man få arbete när som helst."

31. Clara Jeppsson to her sister Sigrid, 11 January 1912, letter 30. "Det är bättre för honom att stanna i Sverige då det är så dåliga tider här."

32. Clara Jeppsson to her sister Sigrid, 31 July 1911, letter 24. "Det är så öfverfullt på manlig arbetskraft så det är många som har varit här i många år som går utan arbete. . . . Jag undrar om han har tänkt sig att kanske han får gå ner i grufvorna eller ut i skogarna som ju inte pricis är det värsta och så arbeta så väl söndagar som alla dagar året rundt."

33. Leonard Nilsson to Lovisa Borg, 14 July 1881, box 8, folder A1, letter 20. "Älskade! Du vill att jag skall upphöra med grufarbete. Du har rätt, det är skadligt för helsan; så jag tänker att snart upphöra dermed. Dock finnes det ingenting annat här i orten. . . . Jag har här 'huggit i sten' och det i ordets fulla mening bokstafligen taladt."

34. Leonard Nilsson to Lovisa Borg, 5 October 1882, box 8, folder A2, letter 31. "Något trött efter att hela dagen hafva 'huggit i sten.'"

35. Leonard Nilsson to Johan Westerberg, 8 August 1880, box 8, folder B, letter 6. "Aflöningen är god 3,50 pr dag. Ja—man borrar och spränger, man gnor och man flänger, man hackar och plockar, man svär och man pockar, man drickar af vatten, sig full,—Allt för den allsmägtiga penningen skull." I have not been able to identify a source for these rhymed couplets. Nilsson may be quoting, or he may be using his own imaginative sense of wordplay. The reference to getting drunk is ambiguous. While Nilsson was not particularly a drinker, he may have meant that water was all that was available for drinking. Or he may have been suggesting the hasty manner in which one would consume water during a hot workday.

36. Ibid. "Malmen uti denna grufa innehåller arsenik, hvilkedt just icke förlänger lifvet."

37. August Peterson to his nephew Hjalmar, 1 February 1900, letter 22. "Jag fått ena fingret skadat på högra handen. Jag kan just nu hålla pennan till att skrifva men jag kan inte arbeta ännu så det har kostat mig (Ja det har det)."

38. Daun, *Swedish Mentality*, 200–201, 209–12.

39. John M. Swanson to his parents, 28 July 1906, letter C17. "Men Som ni kan hända har sport att Hallberg har skadat sin hand. han klämde af tummen på sin venstra hand det hände vid tåget på statjonen der han arbetar han skulle länka vagnarna tillsammans och då fick han tummen emellan så det klamde [klämde] af den det är fyra vickor i qväll sedan det hände. så han måste gå till sjukhuset genast och han var der i två vickor sedan kom han hem. Det är inte riktigt bra ännu men han tänker om ett par vickor att han skall kunna arbeta igen han hade fritt sjukhus och Docktor och han tänker att han skall få lite skade ersättning. Så det var godt att han inte förlorade hela handen."

40. Wells, *Gold Camps and Silver Cities*, 103–4.

41. MacMillan, *Smoke Wars*, 29.

42. August Peterson to his nephew Hjalmar, 1 February 1900, letter 22. "Jag arbetade i Butte City endest en Månad så tankte jag det war best att sluta innan hälsan tog slut. Fritiof slutade några dagar före mig för wärmen och gasen war förfarlig."

43. Johansson to his brother P. Magnus, 13 May 1891, letter 25. "Jag har vatt o sett på dem vid smälten hur det går till o Androws arbete är liksom o stå o röra i en bakugn, malmen är röd som eld o så skall di o röra o vända det så det är rysligt hett."

44. John M. Swanson to his parents, 28 July 1906, letter C17. "Att stå och raka i en het smält Ung och lukta på Svafvel röken."

45. John M. Swanson to his parents, 3 September 1894, letter C4. "Det är nu så hort [hårt] att arbta på smältan så jag undrar inte på någon som slutar om han kan. Men det är hort att få något annat."

46. John M. Swanson to his parents, 2 October 1894, letter C5. "Det var nästan som jag alldrig hade arbetat. Jag blef så öm i händerna och i hela kroppen så jag nästan skemdes för mig sjelf."

47. Fell, *Ores to Metals*, 137, 158, 216.

48. John M. Swanson to his parents, 1 April 1909, letter C20. "För [får] se om ni känner igen mig."

49. Ibid. "Efter hort [hårt] arbete på en Smälta om det vore en maskin af jern och stål skulle den ge vika. och så har efven jag gört."

50. The automata, or mechanical man, and related anxiety about automation became common tropes in popular fiction during the Industrial Revolution. See Franklin, 131–33; and Clute and Nicholls, encyclopedia entries for *androids, automation, machines,* and *robots.*

51. Jameson, *All That Glitters*, 90–91.

52. P. N. Johnson to August Peterson's nephew Hjalmar, 26 March 1902, August

Peterson Collection, letter 27. "Jag vill Underratta dig så långt jag kan om Gust Peterson's hedangång han arbetade i en liten grufva som heder 'Mä Ki' [probably Mackey] han gick på [word illegible] uti kl. 8. om morgonen. han och en kamrat steg på tunnan och blef nedlåten nära 200 fot hvarefter de gaf stoppsignal hvarved de stannade. om några se kunder ringde de 3 gonger hvilket betyder men på tunnan Injenären väntade 4-5 minuter på vidare signal, då han ej erhöll någon tänkte han på den dåliga luften som åfta existerades och försökte hissa upp tunnan men fann den var fast där nere. Då gick förmannen och 3 mera *men* stegarna ned men fannde kunde ej komma på 30 fot nära för gasen skull sedan hadde de till att blåsa komprest luft ned en stund innan de kunde komma till dem. Då de komma dit låg Peterson i tunnan död och hans komrat låg 10 fot nedom död. förmodligen hade hans kamrat stått på tunnan då han ringde och så blifit öfvermägtad af gasen och fallit och taget tunnan med sig af sin langång och så tog den emot timber så den kunde ej blifva hissad det tog ungefär 2 timar från de gick ned till de fick dem upp. Jag var på förhöret och hörde där hur det gick till. Gust var lik sig efter han var död. Man kunde se han ej hade haft några plågor han hade ej varit i Victor länge men var ofta gången och helsade på mig och vi vara alltid goda venner han var här samma kvell som han hade fått Foto från dig." *Tunnan* is a bucket used as a simple mine elevator.

53. In American English, *buddy* is a close equivalent for the idea of a working comrade or (in British) mate. According to the *Dictionary of American Regional English*, *buddy* was used among American miners and military men. Its connotation similarly includes the idea of brotherhood, as it derives from the word *brother*.

54. August Peterson to his nephew Hjalmar, 1 February 1900, letter 22. "Vi reste hit och fick arbete genast treffade Walfrid Chals *and* Gust Ehrneberg Gust är Förman så wi har haft det bra."

55. August Peterson to his family, 18 November 1894, letter 16.

56. John A. Leonard to a friend, 16 April 1881, letter 3.

57. Holmberg, *Hellhole on Earth*, 110–12.

58. For a representative example, see Leonard Nilsson to Johan Westerberg, 4 January 1881, box 8, folder B, letter 7. "Vän & Broder Johan!" Both Nilsson's and Lovisa Borg's families are well documented in the Swedish parish records (see appendix), making it very clear that there was no familial relationship between Leonard and Johan.

59. Fritz Lindborg to his friend Nils Person, 9 December 1888, letter 20. "Heders Broder Nils!" "Den sanne vän."

60. Ulf Jonas Björk suggests that this use of *broder* may have been first used by the upper classes in Sweden (it is found in Carl Michael Bellman's lyrics, for example), and then later adopted by workers. Björk has observed its use in correspondence between Swedish American newspaper editors. Ulf Jonas Björk, personal communication with the author, 28 November 2005. The practice is still common among older men in academic and other institutional settings, and as such is criticized for its tendency to exclude women.

61. Johan Håkansson to his wife Britta and their children, 12 April 1888, letter 4.

"Jag har hälsan och mår bra intill skrifvande stund jag Arbetar på en smälta i Ledville. Jag och Johan i Jedhult så det är trefligt vi har det här vi arbeta till sammans var dag vi arbeta på en *fanis* der är varmt men det gar bra när man blir van vid det jag har arbetat der i 2 manader var dag sa jag har kant [tjänat] lite pänger till dig det behafvar du."

62. Emihamn index, emigration code 1886:1322:2358.

63. Burke points to the gradual development of this limited idea of a classless America during the nineteenth century (*The Conundrum of Class*, 124–32). Swedish Americans' view of America as a place where they could seek both cultural and economic improvement is established in their own statements about emigration; see Lindquist, "Appraisals of Sweden and America by Swedish Emigrants," and Barton, *A Folk Divided*, 114–15, 143.

64. John A. Leonard to his sister, 4 December 1881, letter 5. "Det vara mycket bättre att vara arbetare här i landet än i det gamla." "Ty dels är arbetarn aktad och respekterad . . . man slipper begagna en del högdragna titlar, stryka på foten eller löfta på hatten då man träffar storgubbar och vill tala med dem."

65. Victor Johnson to his sister and brother-in-law, the Bergströms, 11 December 1908, letter 2. "Man kan gå och vara som man vill ogenerad och inte behöver man stå med hatten i hand för trägubber med en knapp i mössan eller en stor isterbuk ellar något dyligt."

66. Edvinsson, "The Demographic Data Base at Umeå University," 240.

67. See the appendix for brief biographies of each of the correspondents.

68. *Husförhörslängder*, Östergötland: Kimstad, 1851–55, entry for Langsäter, within Runstorps.

69. *Husförhörslängder*, Kronoberg: Virestad, 1888–90, p. 559.

70. *Husförhörslängder*, Östergötland: Söderköping, 1885–90, p. 281.

71. John Renström to P. Björling, 31 December 1892, Ivar Larsson Collection, letter C7, 117. "Du frågar hvad jag gör nu för tiden, och vill här låta dig veta. Som du kanhända har hört förut så är jag källarmästare. 'Saloon keeper' på Engelska."

72. Allwood, "Are There Swedish Patterns of Communication?" section 4.2.

73. Bernhard Rydberg to his mother, 20 March 1901, letter 5.

74. In addition to Rydberg's letters, his political attempt is documented in the *Carbon County Democrat* (Red Lodge), 17 October 1900 and 14 November 1900, and his columns appeared in the same paper on 10 and 24 April 1901, and on 15 and 29 May 1901.

75. Peter Peterson to Jonas Danielson and family, 27 September 1886, letter 7. "Jag har alla tider fullt upp med arbete, jag tingte [tänkte] att jag skulle bär ja [börja] att Bruka gården men ner jag mistade Båda mina Pojkar så Blir dett nog intet så hastigt jag kan tjena mera med mitt Handverke."

76. Peter Peterson to Jonas Danielson and family, 3 October 1887, letter 8.

77. Peter Peterson to Jonas Danielson and family, 27 April 1890, letter 12; and Peter Peterson to Jonas Danielson and family, 19 November 1892, letter 14. "Nu gör jag aldt mitt snickeri med ång kraft."

78. Barton, *A Folk Divided*, 64–69.

5. "I Am Sending Money"

1. Leonard Nilsson to Lovisa Borg, 17 January 1883, box 8, folder A2, letter 36. "Om jag lemnar Rocky Bar! Måste jag resa ett ansenligt långt stycke härifrån. Jag skall försöka anträda hemresan—om möjligt före nästa Jul. Blif tålig och sagtmodig uti din väntan ännu en liten tid min ömt, outsägligt, älskade Lova! Jag vill icke arbeta för andra—icke i Sverige. Så länge jag nödgas arbeta för andra, vill jag heldre vara i Amerika. Emellertid kan jag tryggt försäkra dig att jag tager motgångar lätt— trotsar mödor och besvär och fruktar inga faror. Jag är lika beslutsam, envis och ihärdig som alltid; ty 'genom ihärdighet vinnes målet' och jag är en nordens son. Son af modren *Svea.*"

2. Barton, *A Folk Divided*, chapter 5, 59–70.

3. Blanck, *Becoming Swedish-American*, 221; and Øverland, *Immigrant Minds*.

4. Beijbom, "Swedish-American Organizational Life," 66.

5. Leonard Nilsson to Lovisa Borg, 27 July 1881, box 8, folder A1, letter 21. Enthusiasm for Tegnér was not limited to upper-class Swedish immigrants; see Beijbom, "Tegnér and America," 167–72.

6. Tegnér, "Svea," 11. "Och Svea sitter å sin tron på fjällen, / med stjernekronan omkring gullgult hår. / Hon blickar stilla ner i sommarqvällen; / dess rykte nyfödt genom verlden går."

7. Hecker-Stampehl, "Nation-State Formation and Cultural Diversity in Sweden," 1–3; and Kurunmäki, "'National Representation' in Sweden in the Early Nineteenth Century," 9–10. Ethnic claims based on consent and descent are from Sollors, *Beyond Ethnicity*, 6.

8. Frykman and Löfgren identify the celebration of birthdays as originally a middle-class custom, noting that "birthday celebrations . . . only began to be common among the peasantry and the working class around the turn of the century" (*Culture Builders*, 32).

9. P. J. Johnson to Lars Bergstrom, 25 October 1914, letter 2. "Alting är så härrligt och skönt i Fosterlandet."

10. John A. Leonard to David Ljungkrantz, 20 November 1881, letter 4. "Såsom ofta förhållandet var i gamla landet."

11. Person, *Svensk-Amerikanska Studier*, 53.

12. Fritz Lindborg to Nils Persson, 9 December 1888, letter 20. "Vår älskade fösterjord, gamla Svea."

13. John Renström to P. Björling, 31 December 1892, Ivar Larsson Collection, letter C7, 118. "O, du stackars Sverige och dumma tjockhufvade överhet som ej kan inse att detta är en tung pålaga. . . . det skall gå efter gammal vana och öfverlasta det lilla fattiga Sverige med mera skuld."

14. Anna Olson to Elna Lundberg, 30 March 1889, letter 4; and Brita Lisa Matsdotter to her in-laws, 22 November 1907, Ivar Larsson Collection, 369.

15. Emma Hallberg to her parents, 19 June 1891, John M. Swanson Collection, letter C1. "Ni seger att der är varmt der himma."

16. Undated correspondence from Clara Jeppsson to an unknown correspondent, letter 32. "Allting är så olikt hemma i Sverige."

17. Barton, *A Folk Divided*, 66.

18. Wright, *Swedish Emigrant Ballads*, 178. "Hur kan jag wäl förglömma det land der jag blef född, Der som min kära moder mig waggade så sött."

19. Leonard Nilsson to Lovisa Borg, 22 February 1882, box 8, folder A2, letter 26. "Jag minnes väl huru jag stundom var inne i köket och syslade om—jag skulle vara vise värd. Jag minnes hurusom jag blef förvirrad hvarje gång jag mötte Lova's blickar."

20. Leonard Nilsson to Lovisa Borg, 25 January 1880, box 8, folder A1, letter 13. "Jag tycker mig se dig huru du står uti Skafferit innanför köket eller också vid Spiseln .. syslande" (the two-dot ellipsis is Nilsson's punctuation). "Vid egen spisel uti eget bo."

21. Charles Flodin to Anders Abrahamsson, 28 January [1888?], letter 18. "Lyckliga Petrus han kom i grefvens tid och frälste Sofia från enformigheten. Jag tyckte som om en förstämning hade fallit öfver mig när jag såg Sofi hemma till Manuels i Skäremo då gick min tankegång Sofi arma Sofi här går du nu (om söndagarna när det ej är tjenst i någon utaf Kyrkorna.) från den ena bänken i stugan tvärs öfver golvet till den andra ser ut genom fönstret tankfullt hvad ser hon jo i fjerran fjerran sin ungdoms kär bunden med hymnens band oafsiktligt vid en annan."

22. Clara Jeppsson to her sister Sigrid, 11 January 1912, letter 30. "När jag påminna mig den tiden då vi brukade resa hem och stanna hemma några dagar så kan jag så väl påminna mig alls hur mor brukade vara uppe bittada om morgnorna för att ha allt i ordning och hur hon alltid satte fram det bästa för oss då önskar jag att jag vore hemma igen."

23. Bengt Olson Brodin to his brother Olaf, 10 March 1884, letter 20. "Ännu en gång kunde få beträda den kära fosterjorden."

24. Fritz Lindborg to Nils Persson, 9 December 1888, letter 20. "Du beträder vår älskade föstterjord, gamla Svea."

25. Charles Flodin to Anders Abrahamsson, 28 January [1888?], letter 18. "Falkenberg ... will bli min debarkeringsplats härnäst mitt dyra fosterlands jord får den äran att kyssa mina amerikanska No eight shoez."

26. Bengt Olson Brodin to his brother Olaf, 10 March 1884, letter 20. "Här är det mest omväxlande Land jag tror fins."

27. Fritz Lindborg to Nils Persson, 9 December 1888, letter 20. Lindborg's letter slips in and out of Swedish. This phrase is rendered in English. Gambling, drink, and prostitution in the West were anathema to some of the Swedish immigrants. Waldemar Holmberg's reminiscence *Hellhole on Earth* portrays 1909 Telluride, Colorado, as one of the toughest of Western mining towns, a place where fellow immigrants might take advantage of newcomers (72–80).

28. Charles Flodin to Anders Abrahamsson, 28 January [1888?], letter 18. "Som en 'gravyard.'"

29. Aron W. Johnson to Anna Johanson, 21 April 1903, letter 13. "Bästa land på jorden för den fattige."

30. Peter Peterson to Jonas Danielson and family, 3 November 1902, letter 20. "Ett land var deras Barn kan måla ett bettre framtidens Land."

31. Ibid. "Ett träldomens land." "Vi intett bor i så dåligt Land."

32. Björk, "A Swedish-American View of Sweden," 24.

33. Person, *Svensk-Amerikanska Studier*, 53.

34. John A. Leonard to his brother-in-law D. Ljungcrantz, 11 May 1884, letter 7. "Vårt fria adopterade fosterland."

35. Undated correspondence from Clara Jeppsson to an unknown recipient, letter 32. "Man stridt öfver hundåret." "Så kanske de ha fått smak för America."

36. Aron W. Johnson to Anna, 11 July 1903, folder D, letter 15. "Skulle bli America sjuk."

37. Aron W. Johnson to Anna, 7 December 1904, folder D, letter 15. "Wyoming's *sage-brush* praire."

38. Aron W. Johnson to Anna, 11 July 1903, folder D, letter 15. "Jag tycker om America och du om Sverige."

39. O. M. Johnson to Aron W. Johnson, 8 September 1906, folder E, letter 4. "Tack för det kärkomna bref . . . hvar jag ser att du lefver och har hälsan, fast jag ser att du har börjat att få America Sjukan, som jag trodde."

40. John Renström to P. Björling, 31 December 1892, Ivar Larsson Collection, letter C7, 118. "Detta menas ej att jag skryter af Amerika eller af mig själf heller, för detta landet är ej heller som en del tror, att man här kan skära guld med 'täljknifvar' och slå penningar sjelfva och att det springer stekta grisar med gaffel och knif i ryggen här öfverallt i ordning för hvilken som helst att skära af en bit och sticka i munnen."

41. Ibid. "I denna vägen så är detta landet bättre än det gamla, och en annan sak, Amerika är ett *fritt land* i alla hänseende."

42. Del Giudice, "Mountains of Cheese and Rivers of Wine," 41.

43. Ibid., 13–14.

44. I am grateful to Larry E. Scott for suggesting the parallel with Snorri's Edda and with folksong. See Sturluson, *The Younger Edda*, 104: "But however great may be the throng in Valhal, they will get plenty of flesh of the boar Sahrimner. He is boiled every day and is whole again in the evening."

45. Wright, *Swedish Emigrant Ballads*, 37–38. "Höns och änder regna ner / stekta gäss och ännu fler / flyga in på bordet / med kniv och gaffel i låret."

46. *Memories of Snoose Boulevard*, side 2, selection 6; translation by Larry E. Scott. According to the liner notes, the song was "written as early as 1853 by Norwegian newspaper editor Ditmar Meidell."

47. Ibid., side 2, selection 1. "Chikago, Chikago det är en stad så stor / det finns så mycket hästar, det finns så mycket kor / det finns så feta grisar och oxar som jag tror / och alla sorters kreature för där har jag en bror"; translation by Larry E. Scott. The song was written in the 1920s by Swedish comedian Calle Lindström. It also appears on *From Sweden to America*, side 2, selection 4.

48. William Sayers draws a connection to Joe Hill's later use of similar ideas in "In

the Sweet Bye and Bye" ("Joe Hill's *Pie in the Sky* and Swedish Reflexes of the Land of Cockaigne," 332–33).

49. Del Giudice, "Mountains of Cheese and Rivers of Wine," 41.

50. Person, *Svensk-Amerikanska Studier*, 54.

51. Andreas Reed to his brother Carl, 10 May 1884, letter 1. "Helsa Broder Solemon jag ska jöra honon ratt jag skal sänd litte penningar nu snart dett är orsacken att jag intet har skrifvett jag har intet hat [haft] peningar att sända."

52. Elin Pehrson to Maria Jonasson, 19 January 1897, letter 4. "Jag har tänkt jag skulle sändt henne litte men vi är altid stor familj och så mycke att köpa."

53. Brita Lisa Matsdotter to her in-laws, 22 November 1907, Ivar Larsson Collection, 369. "Jag har ofta tenkt att skrifva. Jag fick ett bref av min bror för många år sedan jag tror Dett är 7 år sen men jag svarade ej han sade att han hade 5 pojkar, min tanke var att venta skriva tils jag fick senda dem 5 Daler en för dem var men, så börja vi byga oss ett hem, så dett tog alla pengar vi kunde skrapa ihop, men nu är vi skuldfri samt har ett trefligt hem, ära vare Gud men o vad dett grämde mig ner jag fick se att Lars var död att ej jag ens svara hans bref, men nu vill jag gotgjöra till Dig och senda 5 Daler en för var gosse men du må hafva dem för dätt nödvendigaste kan du förstå."

54. Wright, *Swedish Emigrant Ballads*, 63–66. "Ett brev och en hälsning."

55. Klymatz, "The Letter in Canadian Ukrainian Folklore," 59.

56. Clara Jeppsson to her sister Sigrid, 10 April 1912, letter 34. "Det är allt en fin samling bref den där bundtan som det kan bli roligt att ögona igenom en gång."

57. Peter F. Erlandson to his sister, 30 January 1880, letter 1.

58. Anna Olson to Elna Lundberg, 30 March 1889, letter 4. "Du har icke förändrat dig mycket."

59. Leonard Nilsson to Lovisa Borg, 19 August 1881, box 8, folder A1, letter 22; Leonard Nilsson to Lovisa Borg, 5 October 1882, box 8, folder A2, letter 31.

60. Lingcod that is dried, salted, and boiled, and porridge—both traditional Christmas foods.

61. Gottfrid Johnson to his parents and siblings, 1 January 1915, letter 6. "Jag skal söka skildra min jul här och jag kan på förhand säga att detta var min första jul *utan* 'lutfisk o gröt' på samma gång som den mest glädjelösa. Julaftonsdagen ingick med solsken och klart väder men ändå kände jag mig så bortkommen så främmande för allt och intet lyckades angöra att den glada högtid var i annalkande de flästa haromkring hålla ej någon helg sällan eller aldrig söndag ens. Morbror hade köpt en del hö och vi körde hö hela dagen och mina tankar hängde envist fast vid förflutna tider. När vi äntligen voro slut med arbetet och kommo in hade ändå Moster gjort lite Julagrant och det var som en varm vindfläckt från minnets lustgård. Golven vore tvättade och en vit duk på bordet men intet spår av den gamla julmaten förekom. Kvällsmaten bestod av potatis o stekt skinka och tranbärssylt, kaffe smör bröd o honong. Samma kväll hade söndagsskolan i La Jara sin julfäst och för att giva oss sjelv en erindran om att det ändå var jul gick vi dit ned. Weckan förut var jag uppe i bergen efter ett

lass ved, och jag hämtade då ned en stor julgran juldagsmorgon satte jag den i fot och moster Stiv o jag klädde den på f.m. medan morbror var uppe och sag efter sina krea-tur som han nu har å bete 5 a 6 mil norr härom, han synes tycka detta vara ett trevligt helgdagsarbete och även i dag är han där uppe." Because Johnson drops most of the diacritical marks required in Swedish spelling, rendering his Swedish very difficult to read, we have corrected much of his spelling throughout this passage.

62. Christmas has been emphasized both from a lay point of view and by schol-ars in both Swedish America and Sweden. See, as examples, Berry, "Memories of a Swedish Christmas"; Peterson, "Swedish Christmas in Iowa in 1879"; Esping and Esping, "The Swedish-American Custom of Ljuskrona; Måwe, *Värmlänningar i Nordamerika*, 280–91; Bringéus, *Årets Festseder*; Rehnberg, *Swedish Holidays and An-nual Festivals*, 17–24; and Löfgren, "The Great Christmas Quarrel and Other Swedish Traditions."

63. Charles Flodin to Anders Abrahamsson, 28 January [1888?], letter 18. "Det war när vi voro i Göteborg på återresa till Amerika då jag gjorde bekantskap med två laxar från Småland den ena hade varit hemma öfver sommaren *before* den andra var en gammal oxhandlare från Ljungby. Vitala karlar båda du vet der var munterhet förutom skoj. Oxhandlaren hade *lots of money* du skulle sett honom i Hull Liverpool New York Chicago och alltigenom hur förvånad och betuttad han var öfver allting han såg. Ock så i Chicago du skulle hört och sett honom när han talade vid Patron Lindgren med mössan i handen. Han var en *smart man* innan [?] när Småland kom på fråga men i utrikes affärer var han borta."

64. Beijbom, "The Historiography of Swedish America," 257. Also see Blanck's study of Swedish America, *Becoming Swedish-American*, 29.

65. *Selection* and *intensification* are terms used by Toelken to describe processes frequently used by ethnic groups. See Toelken, "Ethnic Selection and Intensification in the Native American Powwow."

66. Barton, *A Folk Divided*, 211.

67. Blanck, *Becoming Swedish-American*, 204.

68. Ibid., 34–35.

69. Peter Peterson to Jonas Danielson, 20 August 1883, letter 4. "Her i byn är mycke Swenskt folk." Similar comments come from J. Edward Wiberg, John A. Leonard, John Renström, Anna Olson, Elias Myrholm, August Johansson, Ole Pedersen, John M. Swanson, Clara Jeppsson, and John E. Jernberg.

70. Charles Flodin to Anders Abrahamsson, 5 March 1895, letter 23. "Jag antager det måste vara en stor del utaf Svenska Amerikanare der hemma i Drägved . . . så att ni har hvad jag må kalla ett litet 'United States.'"

71. August Johansson to his brother P. Magnus, 13 May 1891, letter 25. "Många svenskar."

72. Clara Jeppsson to her sister Sigrid, 31 July 1911, letter 24.

73. Clara Jeppsson to her sister Sigrid, 25 January 1912, letter 33. "Här lefver mest mormoner och mexikanare. Här äro vi endast 4 svenskar. De två andra äro två värmländingar."

74. That Jeppsson came from Skåne is supposition based on two facts: She returned to Hörja, in Skåne, between 1913 and 1915, after the birth of her first child; and her letters were donated by Sigrid Pålsson of Lund, also in Skåne. Pålsson may have been the sister Sigrid to whom most of the letters were sent.

75. John A. Leonard to D. Ljungcrantz, 3 February 1883, letter 6. "'Jag är glad öfver att vara född Svensk, och jag har aldrig behöft blygas för mitt country-namn' (=svenska namn)." The parenthetical clarification is Leonard's.

76. John M. Swanson to his parents, 27 December 1903, folder C, letter 13.

77. Ida Sandberg to her parents, 1 July 1904, John M. Swanson Collection, folder C, letter 14; and Olof Larsson to his parents, 19 July 1904, letter 15.

78. J. Edward Wiberg to Charles Wiberg, 1 July [1882], letter 22.

79. Jacob Lundquist to his sister Ellen, 9 May 1891, letter 2. Lundquist demonstrates his bilingual competence by writing to Ellen in fluent English, while he writes to other relatives in Swedish.

80. Elias Myrholm to his parents, 7 March 1890, letter 8. "De infödda (Yankes) Amerikanerna äro de sämsta här i Amerika, hvad nytt som har uppfunnits på mekanikens områden så är det av invandrade Engelsmän, Tyskar och Skandinaver. Skandinaverna och förnämligast Svenskarna äro allmänt kända för att vara Amerikas bästa Arbetare."

81. Pet Stred to Carl Johannisson, 9 August 1891, letter 4. "Svenska krafter."

82. Peter Peterson to Jonas Danielson and family, 6 November 1899, letter 17.

83. Peter Peterson to Jonas Danielson and family, 19 November 1892, letter 14.

84. Mrs. Effie Peterson to her cousin Hilda, 18 January 1914, letter 13.

85. Carl Boline to his mother, 28 December 1917, letter 13.

86. Blanck, *Becoming Swedish-American*, 204.

6. "Out West"

1. Hjalmar Johnsson to Martin, 2 August 1918, letter 30. "Jag börjar bli van vid hettan nu, och vi äro alla som rödskin, så om jag kommer hem sådan är jag rädd att jag ej finge [fingo] stanna inomhus . . . ursäkta mitt skoj."

2. The term *myth* in everyday usage can mean a mistaken notion, but I use it here to mean a body of narrative and its accompanying set of values, so powerful in the popular imagination that it takes on a life of its own—that is, influences people's behavior, however true or false it may be.

3. Murdoch, *The American West*, ix.

4. This formula is described in Cawelti, *The Six-Gun Mystique* and *Adventure, Mystery, and Romance*.

5. This point is developed throughout Slotkin, *Regeneration through Violence* and *The Fatal Environment*.

6. Limerick, *Something in the Soil*, 94.

7. Björk, "Stories of America," 510, 522.

8. Björk, "The Dangerous Prairies," 166–68.

9. Fur, "Romantic Relations," 152–56.

10. Sund, *Colorado Avenue*, 89. "De berättar om prospectors som gjort fantastiska guldfynd och blivit förmögna över en natt. Och om smarta skojare som narrat gruvan av guldgrävarna vid pokerbordet. Och om grizzlybjörnar och vargar. Och om mänskliga gamar, desperados och revolvermän som den unge Billy The Kid och Jesse James och Butch Cassidy, som en gång rånade banken här i Telluride."

11. Øverland, *Immigrant Minds, American Identities*, 19.

12. Huhndorf, *Going Native*, 5.

13. Roosevelt's Western career is discussed in numerous sources, including Hine and Faragher, *The American West*, 495–98, and Murdoch, *The American West*, 66–71, who credit G. Edward White's 1968 study, *The Eastern Establishment and the Western Experience*.

14. Bernhard Rydberg to his mother, 30 June 1905, letter 9. "Då är jag nästan alltid ute på landet och att gå dit är både bra och helsosamt och så tager jag vanligen ett bad i floden och springer om kring som en Indian."

15. According to a local newspaper report, Rydberg twice attempted suicide. "Rydberg Took Poison," *Carbon County Democrat* (Red Lodge), 15 May 1901, 1.

16. John A. Leonard to his brother-in-law David Ljungkrantz, 9 August 1887, letter 8. "Ute bland de vilda bergen." "Mera försumlig och likgiltig i att uppfulla vänskapslagarna mot slägtingar i sin hemort."

17. John Reed to his parents and siblings, 25 January 1891, letter 5. "Här ute i vestren tils denna banan blir färdig."

18. Jacob Lundquist to his sister Anna, 16 June 1892, letter 21. "Vi två stackare harute i fjerran West komma att sakna henne mer än vi kan omtala."

19. Anni Dickson to Carl Israelsson, 28 September 1893, letter 17. "Ute i Colorado." "Högfärdiga."

20. Aron W. Johnson to Anna, 11 January 1902, folder D, letter 6. "Ute ifrån jern vägen."

21. Bernhard Rydberg to his mother, 26 July [1906?], letter 12. "Ut i Western."

22. Hjalmar Johnsson to his father, 10 September 1917, letter 29. "Uppe i Colorado Bergen."

23. Bernhard Rydberg to his mother, 15 October 1901, letter 7. "Uppe ibland Klippiga Bergen."

24. Peter Peterson to Jonas Danielson and family, 20 August 1883, letter 4; Olof Larsson to his parents, 29 July 1904, letter 15.

25. Aron W. Johnson to Anna Johanson, 11 January 1902, folder D, letter 6. "Är jag så långt ute ifrån jern vägen så jag kan ej skrifva så regelbundet som du önskar."

26. Jacob Lundquist to his sister Ellen, 15 June 1892, folder D, letter 21; and to his sister Anna, 15 June 1892, folder E, letter 21.

27. Swan Smith to his sister Anna, 14 December 19??, letter 9.

28. Aron W. Johnson to Anna Johanson, 27 October 1903, folder D, letter 17. "Jag är i vilda vestern. Jag har nu 5 svenska mil ut till närmaste jernvägstation och jag kan ej komma nagot närmare på 2 månader."

29. Aron W. Johnson to Anna Johanson, 15 November 1902, letter 11. "Älskade vän du skall ej hafva så stora bekymmer för mig, vi har det ganska bra här."

30. J. Edward Wiberg to his brother, 2 July [1882?], letter 22. "Detta är ett vildt land." "Jag skulle gerna se dig komma upp här men du har det roligare der nere du är för der slipper man gå med revolvern i fickan jemt."

31. Charles Flodin to Anders Abrahamsson, 20 April 1888, letter 20.

32. Undated correspondence from Clara Jeppsson to an unknown correspondent, letter 32. "Öde."

33. John A. Leonard to a friend, 16 April 1881, letter 3. "Wid första påssendet af detta bref finner du, att jag flyttat till annan plats här i landet, 1500 eng. mil vester ut fron Chicago till berglandet Colorado."

34. Charles Flodin to Anders Abrahamsson, 5 March 1895, letter 23. "Förliden sommar var jag i bergerna och sökte mineraler."

35. August Peterson to his nephew Hjalmar, 26 May 1899, letter 21. "Här i bland berg och backer."

36. Charles M. Bloomberg to his mother, sister, and family, 4 September 1913, letter 4. "Uppe i Bergen."

37. Bengt Olson Brodin to his brother Olof, 10 March 1884, letter 20. "Vi kan knappast få Posten fram hit till bergen."

38. Peter Peterson to Jonas Danielson and family, 15 September 1885, letter 6. "Jag will tala om att jag var upp i Bergen en liten tid sen dett är så vakert att man kan intet Beskrifva det greset är så att man kan knappast komma fram för dett och endast blomster Kreaturen syns knappast för greset Der är nästan an endlös widd som är bara skog och gräs och hvem sam helst kan gå taga hvad de vill dett är så myckett." Perhaps Peterson's incoherence in this passage stems from his struggle to describe what is, indeed, an overwhelming sight: a mountain meadow full of wildflowers and tall grass.

39. John M. Swanson to his parents, 28 July 1906, folder C, letter 17. "Ni kan tro att det käns godt för den som är van vid att [work in a smelter] kanner sig lika som en annan menniska. de första dagarna var vi ute i Parkarna här runt Denver och sedan reste vi till en stad som heter Cripple Creek. den ligger högt upp i Bergen."

40. John M. Swanson to his parents, 3 September 1894, folder C, letter 4. "Jag har haft så trefligt i sommar så jag har alldrig haft så trefligt. . . . Peter Jonson kommer till oss ofta vi har fiskat många gånger i sommar."

41. Anni Dickson to Carl Israelsson, 16 May 1893, letter 8. "Ingen ände på dem."

42. Anni Dickson to Carl Israelsson, 28 September 1893, letter 17. "Ej vackert."

43. John M. Swanson to his parents, 28 July 1906, folder C, letter 17. "Det är hemst att se på en sida kan vi se flera tusen fot höga bergväggar och på den andra sidan af tåget ser du flera tusen fot ner i dalen."

44. John A. Leonard to a friend, 16 April 1881, letter 3. "Något jordbruk fins icke häromkring på långa vägar utan idel skyhöga berg och backar till någon del bevuxna med uråldrigatallskog."

45. Bernhard Rydberg to his mother, 30 June 1905, letter 9. "Den härliga utsigten, de majestätiska bergen."

46. Charles Flodin to Anders Abrahamsson, 9 October 1890, letter 21. "Och över berg, dalar, Windfällen, bäckar och moras gick det men våra mödor och svårigheter blefvo väl belönade. Här mötte våra beundrande blickar uttaf det vackraste landskap jag någonsin lagt mina ögon uppå. Der man kunda se en rik naturlig grönskande äng hvar det vilda gräset nådde en höjd utaf flera fot. Omgifven utaf höga majestätiska Berg melankoliskt dystra blickande ned på den leende dalen. Och för att göra tafvlan mera fullständig. I hjertat af den sistnämda Floden, likt en pulsådra sagta och tyst flytande gifvande lif till det hela."

47. Bernhard Rydberg to his mother, 15 October 1901, letter 7.

48. John A. Leonard to a friend, 16 April 1881, letter 3. "I denna hvilda bergstrakt lefver man, liksom Tegnér säger om Jätten: Jag bor i bergets salar, Djupt under jorden, Dit aldrig Odens öga Trängt med sin stråle, etc.—ty man arbetar flera hundra fot under jorden vid ljussken."

49. See Mitman, "Geographies of Hope."

50. Bernhard Rydberg to his mother, 21 May 1901, letter 6. "Det är underbara Varma Svafvel källor här som kommer upp från jorden o Vattnet är aldeles kokkett. Nog är det underligt. Vi dricker varmt svafvelvatten o badar i det. . . . Jag tycker det är roligt . . . och dessutom så gör det en person mycket godt."

51. Victor A. Hallquist to his father, 28 November 1897, letter 26. "Jag vill nu omtala hur jag mår sedan jag kom till Colorado Så har jag blifvit fulkomligt frisk jag är nu lika tjock och fet som när jag lemnade Sveden och stark—Jag arbeta varje dag."

52. Johan Håkansson to his wife Maria and their children, 27 January 1887, letter 2. "Jag har varit så kry sedan jag kom till berjen så du kan inte kena mig igen när du får se mig för jag är så feter och rask så du tror inte det."

53. Peter Peterson to a friend, 14 January 1884, letter 5. "Upp i Bergen är mycken snö, och det är rikedomen för Utah för då får vi vatten om sommaren."

54. Charles Flodin to Anders Abrahamsson, 28 January [1888?], letter 18.

55. J. Edward Wiberg to his brother Charles, 2 July [1882?], letter 22. "Uppe på bergen några mil högre upp ligger snön så kall som den kallaste vinter."

56. Leonard Nilsson to Lovisa Borg, 27 July 1881, letter 21. "Sommaren är varm, öfver höjder och dalgångar, strålar Solen, gifvande lif och värme till hela naturen. Det är så skönt och härligt öfverallt. Då jag kommer upp på någon of dessa häromkring liggande höjder, med deras derifrån vidsträckta utsigter, då är jag riktigt mig sjelf. Jag glömmer då de svårigheter man då och då har att bekämpa, jag intages af beundran—förtjust av lifvet som omkring mig höres och allt är harmoni."

57. Leonard Nilsson to Lovisa Borg, 9 July 1880, letter 17. "Den kyrkan som heter—naturen."

58. Britsch, *Bierstadt and Ludlow*, 3–5, 9–16.

59. Leonard Nilsson to Lovisa Borg, 3 April 1880, letter 14. "Den varmgifvande eldbrasan, hvilken med sitt muntra sprakande, och smattrande, upplifver mig en smula, ensam sitter jag uti min lilla hydda."

60. Bernhard Rydberg to his mother, 15 October 1901, letter 7. "Rigtigt romantiskt."

61. John A. Leonard to his sister, 4 December 1881, letter 5. "Här är lite eller intet odlat och bebygdt. Det är ingen Stat ännu, utan s.k. Teritorie, d.v.s. att landet här är villt och fritt för hvar och en att intaga och bebo, ingen Guvenör och inga Stätlager som skyddar individen, utan han har sjelf till att försvara sig, hvars vapen är—reflan och revolfren, hvilka tingästar är hvar man ständigt följaktiga."

62. Olof Larsson to his parents, 8 April 1906, letter 17. "Bland nyheter får jag tala om för Eder att Blekings Claes som tjenade hos Nels Person no. 9 blef skjuten och dödad af en polis på en krog i Wallace Idaho i höstas."

63. Victor A. Hallquist to his brother Johan, 19 December 1900, letter 29. "Här är ej någon treflig plats för här är nästan daglige olyckor och mord di mäste mördare gå fri." Hallquist's writing is hurried, leaving out diacritical marks, and it is influenced by English and regional Swedish dialect (småländska).

64. Ibid. The paragraphing provided here is an editorial addition to reveal the story's two-part structure. First section: "En 18 års neger tog en 14 års flicka när hon tjörde till post office med ett bref han tvingade henne at gå af buggen med en knif sedan våldtog han henne när hon börja skrika så stack han henne i benen sedan tjörde han knifven i hennes brost knifven var ej stor nog så han hade ett hort arbete att döda henne han brende up sin skjorta för att ej blifva uptackt när hesten hade väntat litet så vände han om och gick hem faderen heter Foster troligen skandinaf tog genast och okte efter vägen och fan sin dotter liten fron vägen närr döt hön var enda barnet hon lefde 3 timmar allt hvad hon sade var mamma här är jag." Second section: "Di satte blod hundar efter mördaren spårade honom fan honom i Denver 3 dagar efter på fängelset—erkände han att att han mördade henne och trode att han ej skulle blifva uptackt han bad om förlåtelse och hans fader och broder bad för honom men myndigheterna lemnade honom till folket 700 parsonor [personer] Samlades och på samma plats der han dödade flickan satte di ned en järnskena och band honom vid den sedan hade di röstning om di skulle bränna honom eller hanga honom men de mäste röstade att bränna honom han stod der från 3 tils 5 oklo. under tiden bad han folket om förlåtelse och bad dem hanga honom han bad Gud om förlåtelse och bad till Gud för folket att de ej faller i so stor synd frälsnings armen talade med honom om gud klockan 5 antande fadren till flickan elden och di stekte honom tills han dog och seden brandi up hans kropp sådan är lifvet har."

65. Stephen J. Leonard, Lynching in Colorado, 1859–1919, 123–25. Both Hallquist's version and the newspaper versions follow what Ronald L. Baker identifies as "the basic recurring pattern in lynchings of blacks by whites," including a black man accused of a crime, lynching by a white mob, and torture/mutilation of the black man. Baker points out that the mob's "primary motivation" is often the "alleged rape of a white woman." Baker, "Ritualized Violence and Local Journalism in the Development of a Lynching Legend," 318.

66. Gottfrid Johnson to his parents and siblings, 1 January 1915, letter 6. "Befolkningen haromkring är förnärvarande mycket upprort över en smärt man vid

namn Cristenson ordförande i mormonkyrkan och tillika kasör i en bank, och har han förskingrat betydliga summor man påstår 100,000 för bank o kyrkan och i synnerhet har han ränsat många av sina trossfränder, varefter han rymde, han blev dock fast nere i Texas och man vantar honom hem snart och många synas hava lust att lynscha honom."

67. Victor A. Hallquist to his brother Johan, 27 November 1898, letter 28. "Fjerran vestren."

68. Ibid. "Jag få äfven om tala att här är många som har blifvit mördade i Denver for liden vicka [förliden vecka] var det 3 Apotek och juvelere [juvelare] *stor* som var *rabbat* mördare har alltid revålfver en i varje hand en stanna utan för och en gor in nar han kommer in så befaller han streck up hender vilken som ej holler up hender ögonblick så sjuter di honom sedan befaller han den gå ut med honom med upstrackta hender i bak *storet* sedan befaller han dem att stalla [ställa] sig till sammans sedan lager han revolfver i en hand holler d recktad mot dem med den andra genom letar han fickorna sedan befaller han dem att vända sig om eller satta sig med han gör det är ej löns att säga något eller ta ned henderna for [för] då är det slut en Svensk har blefvit mördad i denver Polisen har ej kunnat tagit någon annu men di har nu skaffat Blodhundar för att nosa up dem flera extra Poliser har blifvet hitsanda." *Stor, storet,* and *rabbat* appear to be Swedish English for *store* and *robbed.*

69. However, the incident was not reported in the Denver *Svenska Korrespondenten.*

70. Bernhard Rydberg to his mother, 15 October 1901, letter 7. "Platsen dit vi skulle gå är ett ställe högt uppe ibland bergen der flera sjöar äro belägna o en mycket vacker plats. Det är kallt der uppe äfven under sommaren o bergstopparne äro klädda med snö. Det är nästan som Alperna i Schweitz. Vi hade hvar sin sadelhäst o jag red 'Rex' . . . Vi hade ett tält med oss. Vi hade 4 mulåsnor som vi hade vårt bagage o proviant på o vi hade en af dem som vi kallade för 'brygeriet' O den åsnan hade den ansvarsfullaste befattningen ty hon hade äran att bära ölet o spriten."

71. Ibid. "En natt var det en så förfärlig åska o som det var högt uppe i bland bergen varo vi nästan uppe i åskans hemvist så det blixtrade o skrälde o dundrade alldeles som jord klotet skulle ha gått i kras. Det var den mest förfärliga åska jag hört. I bland blixtrade det till o vi kunde se sjön o bergen med skog o det såg skönt, men hemskt ut nästan."

72. Charles Flodin to Anders Abrahamsson, 9 October 1890, letter 21. "Men nu är han fattig som en kyrkråtta. En qvinna som han gifte sig med förstörde hela härligheten påstod han, äfven gick hon så långt i diabolisk oförsynthet som att försöka taga lifvet utaf honom med för gift i Gubbens Kaffe. Han fick en god dosis. Men var seg och lefvde öfver. Så nu är han rädd för Calicås."

73. Ibid. "Då indianerna i den trakten voro oroliga Och måste fly för dem." "Genom Urskogar, floder öfver is och snöbetäckta berg. Många mil vi hade att bana väg för oss och hästar med yxan." "Både guld och äventyr. Men i brist på vatten kunde vi ej tillgodogöra oss."

74. The Lady Bluebeard story is explored by Langlois, "Belle Gunness, the Lady

Bluebeard." The lost-mine motif is N596.3 in Baughman, *Type and Motif Index of the Folktales of England and North America*, 377.

75. Bernhard Rydberg to his mother, 6 October 1905, letter 11. A Rydberg Lake and a Smethurst Lake appear on the Black Pyramid Mountain 7.5-minute topographic map, Montana/Wyoming, U.S. Geological Survey, which maps the area just north of the Montana-Wyoming border and southwest of Red Lodge.

76. Holmberg, *Hellhole on Earth*, 133.

7. "God's Good Gift"

1. Peter Anderson to his aunt and her husband, 7 November 1889, Ola Svenson Collection, letter 1. "Herren vare med eder och hjelpe eder. Jag vill nu genom några få rader låta eder veta att jag eger till Herrens pris hälsan intill skrifvande stund och jag önskar äfven eder detsamma goda som herren i sin stora nåd gifver oss eländige syndare och icke tager sin hjelpande hand ifrån oss utan alltid står med beredd villighet att hjelppa os."

2. *Den Swenska Psalm-Boken*, 34.

3. All biblical quotations are from the Revised Standard Version (New York: Nelson, 1952), checked against the Evangeliska Fosterlands-Stiftelsens edition of 1936.

4. In spite of the precedent in both biblical and nineteenth-century usage, in its ritualized form as "passing the peace," the phrase has not been universally endorsed, especially by old-timers; Danielson, 60. On the other hand, the congregational response "and also with you" has emerged as a self-identifier for Lutherans, even though it is certainly not unique to their services. The phrase has become the basis for insider jokes: "You might be a Lutheran if you're watching *Star Wars* in the theatre and when they say, 'May the force be with you,' [everyone in] the theatre replies, 'and also with you.'"; http://www.oldlutheran.com (accessed 28 September 2005).

5. Sandahl, 351; and Swenson Swedish Immigration Research Center, Swedish American Church Records in North America, microfilm S-615.

6. Granquist, "Swedish Ethnic Denominations," 30.

7. Wentz, *A Basic History of Lutheranism in America*, 186.

8. Leonard Nilsson to Lovisa Borg, 22 May 1880, box 8, folder A1, letter 16. "Jordiskt majestät med Guds nåde."

9. Ibid. "Framåtgående uti allt, Uppfinningsrikt i sanning, man kan icke drömma uti Europa, om det jättelika framåtskridande som utmärker detta Land."

10. Leonard Nilsson to Lovisa Borg, 27 July 1881, box 8, folder A1, letter 21. "Der ligger en bok uppslagen för mina ögon, en bok af silver, skrifven af 'Guds hand' utan oförnuftiga sattser [satser], utan motsägelser, utan lögnaktiga framställningar. Man behöfver ej kunna Grekiska, Hebreiska och Latin för att läsa densamma, man behöfver ej Prester och Proselyter för att tacka densamma. Den är öppen för alla."

11. Quinn, "Religion in the American West," 153–54. See also Rooney, Zelinsky, and Louder, *This Remarkable Continent*, 183.

12. Anders August Anderson, *Tjugu År i Vilda Västern*, 73. "Väglaget var ju svårt,

men det började töa och vi kommo lyckligt tillbaka efter en sex eller sju veckors bortovaro. . . . [Vi] inte lågo ute någon natt, utan stannade på 'Cattle Ranches', som de kalla dessa gårdar eller platser, där de stora häst- och kreatursuppfödarebolagen ha sina koherdar (*cowboys*)."

13. *Protokoll*, 1880–1883; *Officiellt Referat*, 1884–1890; and *Referat*, 1891–1915.

14. Cited in Karl A. Olsson, *By One Spirit*, 467.

15. A. P. Nelson, *Svenska Missionsvännernas Historia i Amerika*, 556. "Grufarbetet är växlande, än upp- och än nedgående, så blir också folkets vistande ostadigt."

16. Adolf Olson, *A Centenary History as Related to the Baptist General Conference of America*, 362.

17. Sandahl, *The Nebraska Conference of the Augustana Synod*, 352.

18. Ibid., 351. In that year, the congregation did not yet appear in the synod's statistical report; hence, this number cannot be confirmed.

19. Granquist, "The Swedish Ethnic Denominations in the United States," 28. Granquist does not factor in the Mormon Swedes.

20. *Referat*, 1910, statistical appendix. The actual percentage of the Swedish-born population who were affiliated with the Augustanans would have been yet smaller, as not all of the Augustana congregation would have been Swedish-born.

21. Quinn, "Religion in the American West," 147, 153–54.

22. Victor A. Hallquist to his brother Johan, 14 August 1898, letter 27.

23. Victor A. Hallquist Collection, "Epilog," item 34; and Björkborg, *Den Första Boken*, 92–117.

24. Peter Peterson Collection.

25. Swenson Swedish Immigration Research Center, Swedish American Church Records in North America, microfilm S-595, roll 2, membership register, 47.

26. Philip J. Anderson, "The Lively Exchange of Religious Ideals between the United States and Sweden during the Nineteenth Century," 34; Granquist, "The Swedish Ethnic Denominations in the United States," 12; Erling, "Crafting an Urban Piety," 62, 80; and Grindal, "The Swedish Tradition," 437.

27. Erling, "Crafting an Urban Piety," 59.

28. Ola Svenson to his sister, 22 July 1882, letter 2. "Ömt Älskade syster Lef väl Herren vare med dig."

29. Nils Trulsson to Elna Andersson, 8 April 1886, letter 25. "Jag önskar att dässa radar mate träfva dig och din moder och Nills med sama förhallande att ni alla mate [måtte] leva ett gudeligt liv inför vår himmelske fader." The use of apostolic greetings worded very similarly to Anderson's is a practice that Erling also makes note of; see Erling, "Crafting an Urban Piety," 85.

30. Charles M. Bloomberg to his mother, sister, and in-laws, 24 August 1912, letter 3. "Guds frid vare Med Eder alla! Är Min Hjertliga Önskan."

31. Anna Olson to Elna Lundberg, 30 March 1889, letter 4. "Guds nåd och frid vare med dig."

32. See, for example, a prayer closely following the singing of *Herren vare med eder*

that incorporates the phrases *gif oss nåd* (give us merciful grace) and *låt oss då få insomna i din frid* (let us rest in your peace). *Den Swenska Psalm-Boken*, 34.

33. Charles M. Bloomberg to his mother, sister, and in-laws, 24 August 1912, letter 3. "Mamma fyller 77 år nu den 16de nästa månad, och det är en hög Ålder, ja Gud var med henne och Hjelpe Henne!"

34. Charles M. Bloomberg to his mother, sister, and family, 4 September 1913, letter 4. "Måtte Gud vara med oss alla är min Hjertliga Önskan."

35. Jonas Anderson to his brother Nils, 19 August 1906, letter 2. "Jag innesluter Eder i den Stora Allsmäktiga Herskaren, Beskyddaren och Regerandas makt hafver öfver allt hvad Aht heter på Jorden och öfver Jorden!!!"

36. Victor A. Hallquist to his father, 28 November 1897, letter 26. "Jag hoppas att Johan o Emil ser till eder för *Gud* är allting möjligt han har gifvit mig hellsan åter och om vi förtrösta på honom så skall vi ej komma på skam."

37. Victor A. Hallquist to his brother Johan, 6 December 1904, letter 32. "Mo [Må] vi alla mötas hos Jesus af nåd ären vi frällste / Guds frid vare med eder."

38. Erling, "Crafting an Urban Piety," 86–87.

39. Ola Svenson to his sister, 22 July 1882, letter 2. "Jag fatta penna i handen och skrifva några få rader till dig och låta dig veta hur jag mår jag har hälsan och mår väl och jag önskar Den samma Guds goda Gåva åt dig."

40. Charles H. Anderson to Hanna Gustafson, 14 October 1889, letter 1. "Ett stort lån af en god och nådig Gud."

41. Victor A. Hallquist to his father, 28 November 1897, letter 26. "Jag har haft hellsa och arbete och dit [det] är en stor Guds gåfva."

42. Victor A. Hallquist to his brother Johan, 6 December 1904, letter 32. "So [Så] Gud Efter sin Godhet låter mig ännu en gång blifva frisk."

43. Anna Hallquist to her in-laws, 20 May 1906, letter 33. "Herren till pris äro vi alla friska och det är en stor gåfva som vi inte nog kan tacka Gud för han har hjelpt mig under detta sorje år."

44. "Din hand vare mig till hjälp, ty jag har utvalt dina befallningar"; from the 1936 Swedish edition.

45. *Den Swenska Psalm-Boken*, 410. "Uti ditt namn jag döpt är vorden." "Håll mig beständigt vid din hand!" The religious theme of providence has been noted among other immigrant groups by Dolan (70).

46. Anna Olson to her cousin Elna Lundberg, 30 March 1889, letter 4. "Alla äro vi lika för Guds ögon."

47. "Se, Herrens öga är vänt till dem som frukta honom, till dem som hoppas på hans nåd"; from the 1936 Swedish edition.

48. Peter Anderson to his aunt and her husband, 7 November 1889, Ola Svenson Collection, letter 1. "Så skall våra ögon en gång öppnas och förklaras."

49. Anna Olson to her cousin Elna Lundberg, 30 March 1889, letter 4. "Det är godt att hafva sina synder förlåtna och vara rentvagen i Jesu blod."

50. *Den Swenska Psalm-Boken*, 33. In turn, this is drawn from I John 1:7.

51. *Hemlandssånger*, 63, 66. "Vattnet, blodet, hvilket går från din stungna sidas sår." "Jag vördar Jesu blod; Det är min reningsflod." See pages 62–93 for other Lenten hymns in which the crucifixion and Jesus's wounds flowing with blood are graphically depicted. Similar imagery appears in Mission Covenant hymns; see, for example, "Kristi Lidande" (Christ suffering) and "Min Blodige Konung" (My bloody king) in *De Ungas Sångbok*, 56–57. The examples provided here from *Hemlandssånger* are not present in the earlier Church of Sweden psalmbook. Selander points out that the theme of the blood and wounds of Jesus was less prominent in Church of Sweden hymnody and was most prominent among groups influenced by Moravian hymnody (272, 282).

52. Victor A. Hallquist to his brother Johan, 14 August 1898, letter 27. "Du säger att du tror att han har gått hem och jag känner mig glad der öfver."

53. Karna Anderson to her friend Gunilla Svensson, 19 August 1904, letter 5. "När vi en gång komma hem då skola vi se hvarför det har varit så, då skall nog ingen pilgrim ångra hvad han lidit här."

54. Erling, "Crafting an Urban Piety," 60, 81–82. Inger Selander identifies the themes of pilgrimage, heavenly home, and the blood and wounds of Jesus in Swedish hymns (*O Hur Saligt att Få Vandra*, 103, 221, 228).

55. Erling, "Crafting an Urban Piety," 60, 63. Many of these themes and images also date to earlier use in Sweden; see Selander, *O Hur Saligt att Få Vandra*, 63–67, 154–55, 180–81, 228.

56. Dolan, "The Immigrants and Their Gods," 70.

57. Peter Anderson to his aunt and her husband, 7 November 1889, Ola Svenson Collection, letter 1. "Oh. att vi blott förstod Guds godhet bådan den i skjelfva verket är men dertill är vi mycket förkortsynta ty vi ser ej mer än vårt naturliga öga kan omfatta och deri ligger felet Men måste herren i sin nåd hjelpa oss lyckeligen igenom denna onda verlden så skall våra ögon en gång öppnas och förklaras och vi skall till vår stora Salighet känna Gud såsom han är."

58. Ibid. "Jag vill Nu säga dig Moster ett hjerteligt tack för det kärkomna bref som jag erhöll ifrån dig den 25/7 deri jag såg till min glädje att ni hade hälsan. Men jag får be om ursäkt för jag har dröjt så länge med svar."

59. Karna Anderson to her friend Gunilla Svensson, 19 August 1904, letter 5. "Min kära älskade barndoms vän och lek kamrat Gunilla." "Guds frid."

60. Ibid. "*Han* blef *särgad* för *våra* överträdelser, och slagen för *våra* missgarningar; nöpsten lades uppå *honom* på det att *vi* skulle hafva *frid*. Härlig himelska *frid! frid, frid!* Som Jesus kan ge, Tänk så godt att äga denna *frid* det är mer värdt än alla värdens [?—last word nearly illegible]."

61. Ibid. "Nu till sist något om min familj."

62. Genny Andersson to her parents, 1 December 1887, letter 5. "Läsning för julen."

63. Ibid. "Jag kan låta eder veta att jag är själ."

64. Ibid. "Jag kan språka got Nu."

65. Lawless, "Shouting for the Lord," 445–49.

66. Karna Anderson to her friend Gunilla Svensson, 19 August 1904, letter 5. "[Jag] tänkte på huru mycket bettre lottat jag har varit nog har jag fått lida också ibland men så har ja väl ändå sluppit Sängen allt emelanåt, och mit *Hjerta* fyldes med tack och lof till *Herren* som varit så god emot mig, och ja bad att *han* måtte välsigna dig dubbelt." "Hans vägar äro så underliga vi förstå så lite af hans handlingsätt med oss, men vi veta att för dem som *älska Herren* samvärker allt till det besta."

67. Victor A. Hallquist to his brother Johan, 14 August 1898, letter 27. "Efter som han dog på en Söndag så var ni väl alla hemma, ni säger att han var sjuk i 3 vecker men ni Säger ej något om hans Sista ord vad han sjelf sade, du Säger att du tror att han har gått hem och jag känner mig glad der öfver."

68. Ibid. "Jag har mycket tänk på mitt hem och Far och äfven min moder som bad mig bedja Gud för henne vid sin dödsbedd. Jag mins så väl jag läste Johannes evangelium 14 cap Eder hjerta vare icke orolig Tro på Gud och tro på mig.—och bad Gud för henne och hennes ansikte Strålade af glädje och det sista hon bad mig var att jag skulle Lefva för Jesus och att hon önskade att tala vid Emil."

69. Ibid. "Jag glömmer alldrig di sista ord som min Far sade till mig vid Sponhults Smedja om jag alldrig for se dig mera har Victor så onska jag att möta dig hos Jesus under det vi grafbåda."

70. Ibid. "Både far och Mor har nu slutat sitt jordiska lif ful af många sorger och lefvat till hög ålder och i *older* dagar har di blifvit frelste—Men vi har blefvit kallade i vår ungdomsdagar under den Stora besökelse tiden då flera milioner blef omvända till Gud och ett Större ansvar vilar på oss än vara föräldrar ty Jesus säger att vi skola varda vardens ljus."

71. John 8:12 actually reads, "Jesus spoke to them, saying, 'I am the light of the world; he who follows me will not walk in darkness, but will have the light of life.'" Hallquist interprets the passage as suggesting that Jesus's followers not only "will have the light of life" but also will be like Jesus—will themselves be "the light of the world."

72. Victor A. Hallquist to his brother Johan, 14 August 1898, letter 27. "Må Gud jelpa oss all när [vi] blifver gamle att vi kunna saga att vi äro frelste för Jesus blod."

73. *Husförhörslängder*, Malmöhus: Genarp, 1881–92, 457.

74. Ola Svenson to his sister Maria, 11 March 1886, letter 6. "Du talar om Wexelen Att Du trode Att jag hade betalt Den fult [fullt] ut Dett hade jag också Men Ditt War Bankherrarne Antingen i Sverge Eller också här som Stal Dem undan jag Wet icke hvilket Du Säger Att Du tror Att om Du undfick Din heliga And Då Skulle Det Blifva Lätt Att förstå Skriften och Dett Är En Sanning Men jag Skall Säga Dig. . . ."

75. Ibid. "Den Kan Du icke Erhålla Den på Annat sätt utan Genom Handpåläggelse Af En herrans Tjenare Som Är bekläd Med Guds Prästadöm Lägger Sina händer på Ditt hufvad för den Heliga Andas Gåfva hvilket Du kan finna i ApostlaGerningarna 8 Cap."

76. Shipps, *Mormonism*, 76.

77. Ola Svenson to his sister Maria Svenson, 11 March 1886, letter 6. He writes, the second thing she needs to do to receive knowledge from Scripture "Är Att Göra Såsom Skriften, ord bokstafligen lärer och icke Såsom Presterna förkunnar Dett Ty

Di Säger Att Di förklarar Dett Men Dett Är En förfalskning Och icke förklaring, Dett kan Du Sjelf Eftertänka Att Dett icke betyder Annerlunda Än der Står Skrifvet Ty Då Du Skrifver bref till Mig Så Skrifver Du hvad Du Menar och Eftertänk Så Att Alla Epistlarne i Nya Testamentet Äro bref ifrån Apostlarne till De Christne församlingarna och Di Skref hvad Di Wille Att folket Skulle Göra och Efterlefva och icke Att Dett Skulle uttydas Annerlunda All Annan förklarning och uttolkning Är blott En förfalskning ifrån Den onde."

78. Discomfort with "passing the peace," for instance, has produced a number of recent Lutheran jokes. Writing in 1986, folklorist Larry Danielson provides the example of a fellow parishioner who says "Have a banana," instead of "Peace be with you," as a form of gentle personal protest against the ritual; Danielson, 60. Among the joke gifts available from OldLutheran.com in 2005 are Pass the Peace Protection kits with latex gloves, and Pass the Peace cards; http://www.oldlutheran.com (accessed 28 September 2005).

8. Identity, Genre, Meaning

1. John Peterson to his father Erik Johan Petersson, 19 December 1910, letter 51. "Jag hafver en Skottländare för kompanjon i *shoppet* han är en god Smed och hästskötare, vi håller på och arbetar på slädar nu. Jag skulle önska att ni alla sammans vore här istället för i Sverige. Då kunde vi alla arbeta tillsammans och göra det bra mycket bättre än vi hafver det i Sverige. . . . Jag just tog hem *som [some]* Lutfisk i qväll. Jag skulle önska att jag kunde vara hemma i jul och få litet utaf Mammas goda Lutfisk och Gröt. Jag kommer allt ihåg huru God mat mamma brukar koka. Jag försöker att lära Jessie ibland att koka som mamma brukar att göra."

2. Ibid. "Det är så många sådana Companin här i Landet nu för tiden som är bara skojare och lurar Folk öfverallt annonserar stort och fint."

3. Bruner, "Self-Making and World-Making," 35. See also Harré on multiplicity of selves created in autobiographical writing, "Metaphysics and Narrative," 62.

4. Oring begins his folklore textbook *Folk Groups and Folklore Genres* with this point, based on Alan Dundes' earlier *The Study of Folklore*; Oring, "On the Concepts of Folklore," 1.

5. Toelken, *The Dynamics of Folklore*, 79.

6. Stahl, *Literary Folkloristics and the Personal Narrative*, 35.

7. Øverland, "Becoming White in 1881," 137.

8. Jacobson, *Whiteness of a Different Color*, 7–11.

9. We know that Ida and her husband Albert were members of the Lutheran Church in Denver; Swenson Swedish Immigration Research Center, Swedish American Church Records in North America, microfilm S-595, roll 2, membership register, 74, 93.

10. Øverland, "Becoming White in 1881," 140.

11. Cronon, Miles, and Gitlin, "Becoming West," 19.

12. Attebery, "Claiming Ethnicity," 25.

13. Dundes, "Folkloristics in the Twenty-first Century," 387.

14. Stahl, *Literary Folkloristics and the Personal Narrative*, 38.

Appendix

1. Gerber, *Authors of Their Lives*, 54.

2. Skarstedt, *Pennfäktare*, 22-23; *Svenska Folkets Tidning*, 24 June 1903, 3; 1 July 1903, 7; 8 July 1903, 8; 15 July 1903, 3.

3. Ola Svenson Collection, letter 1.

4. Staffan Jönsson to "Amerikaminnet," 20 February 1978, in Ola Svenson Collection.

5. Leonard Nilsson Collection, 10:2:8, folder A3, letters 1 and 2.

6. *Husförhörslängder*, Östergötland: Kärna, 1881–85, p. 20.

7. Bengt Olson Brodin Collection, letter 20.

8. Biographical statement in Bengt Olson Brodin Collection.

9. John R. Johnson Collection, letter A1.

10. Anni Dickson Collection, letter 19.

11. "När en suck / sig smyger hörd / af ingen vän den lik / Dufvan flyger den mot himlen."

12. *Husförhörslängder*, Kalmar: Köping, 1872–76, p. 239.

13. *Husförhörslängder*, Älvsborgs: Köping, 1881–90, p. 41.

14. Ibid., p. 34.

15. Charles Flodin Collection, letter 18.

16. "Med både hull och hår"; literally, "with both flesh and hair."

17. *Dyra* can mean valued or expensive. Flodin appears to be using the latter meaning and to be punning on the formula *dyra fosterland* (beloved native country).

18. These incomplete expressions and their punctuation appear in the original letter as given here.

19. A. P. Hall Collection, letter 2.

20. John M. Swanson Collection.

21. *Husförhörslängder*, Kronoberg: Virestad, 1888–90, p. 559.

22. Olof Hallberg appears in *Svenska Adresskalendern* as a laborer living at 4048 Shoshone Street, the return address for Emma's letters.

23. John M. Swanson Collection, folder C, letter 10.

24. Victor A. Hallquist Collection, letters 30 and 33.

25. Victor A. Hallquist Collection, letter 27.

26. The Victor A. Hallquist Collection includes genealogical information, Victor's citizenship papers, a newspaper clipping of a death notice, and an "Epilog" about a search for information about Victor's emigration.

27. Victor A. Hallquist Collection, letter 28.

28. *Svenska Korrespondenten* recorded an incident during Moody's stay in Denver, when a young woman disrupted a meeting, perhaps a reason for the restriction; *Svenska Korrespondenten*, 10 November 1898, 8.

29. This may be "God Is Love," or it may be another of Moody's sermons on the topic of "seeking the lost, rather than the righteous." David Gustafson, personal correspondence with the author, 19 July 2005.

30. Ivar Larsson Collection, pp. 387–88.

31. This is confirmed in the Emihamn index, emigration code 1886:1322:2358.

32. Johan Håkansson Collection, letter 6.

33. Clara Jeppsson Collection, letter 24.

34. The collection includes genealogical information, a broadside advertisement for the 1912 auction in Geddes, and obituaries of Jernberg's death, clipped from the Swedish American newspapers.

35. *Husförhörslängder*, Dalarna: Svärdsjö, 1877–86, p. 270.

36. *Latah County Directory*.

37. Peter J. Johansson Collection, letter 3.

38. The collection includes Johnson's U.S. citizenship certificate, homestead certificates, grazing permits, tax billings, shipping and sales sheets, and other miscellaneous financial papers related to his ranch.

39. *Husförhörslängder*, Kalmar: Madesjö, 1893–94, p. 356.

40. Aron W. Johnson Collection, folder D, letter 16.

41. Aron W. Johnson Collection, folder E, letter 5.

42. Emihamn index, embarkation records, 1893, contract 51:33:1974.

43. Aron W. Johnson Collection, folder E, letters 4, 6, 7, 11.

44. August Peterson Collection, letter 27.

45. Victor Johnson Collection, letter 2.

46. Olof Larsson Collection, letter 15.

47. Nearly all information about Leonard is from the letters themselves and from the donor file, as Johan Andersson is far too common a name for a fruitful search in emigration indexes without having more information to aid the search.

48. *Boulder County Directory*.

49. John A. Leonard Collection, letter 3.

50. Frits Alexius Lindborg is indexed in the Emibas index of parish records, but without a reference complete enough to check the original records.

51. Fritz Lindborg Collection, letter 20.

52. Ivar Larsson Collection, pp. 369–70.

53. A. P. Hall Collection, letter 9.

54. Emihamn index of embarkation records, code 39:273:2362. Myrholm does not turn up in a search of the Emibas index.

55. There is no internal evidence as to the sex of O. Nilson.

56. More about Nilsson is available in Attebery, "A Lonely Guy in Rocky Bar, Idaho."

57. *Husförhörslängder*, Östergötland: Kimstad, 1851–55, entry for Langsäter, within Runstorps.

58. *Husförhörslängder*, Östergötland: Söderköping, 1881–85, pp. 22, 137; *Husför-*

hörslängder, Östergötland: Söderköping, 1885–90, pp. 140, 281; and Idaho Genealogical Society, *Idaho Territory Population Schedules and Mortality Schedules 1880,* 155.

59. Leonard Nilsson Collection, box 8, folder A1, letter 16.

60. Ole Olsson Collection, letter 2.

61. Ivar Larsson Collection, pp. 223–24.

62. *Husförhörslängder,* Kristianstad: Farstorp, 1879–88, p. 355, and *Husförhörslängder,* Kristianstad: Farstorp, 1889–95, pp. 381, 412.

63. Vega Tränefors, "Amerikaminnet," in the Ole Pedersen Collection.

64. Emibas index of Blädinge *husförhörslängder,* Kronobergs län.

65. August Peterson Collection, letter 23.

66. Peter Peterson Collection, letters 11 and 14.

67. With the exception of the U.S. Census of 1900, information about Peterson and his family is all internal to the letters, which are fairly informative. See U.S. Census Bureau, Twelfth Census, Utah, Sanpete County, Gunnison, dwelling 33. In recording property ownership, the 1900 enumerator crossed out F for "farm," writing over it H, for a mortgaged house, suggesting that Peterson was no longer actively farming at that time.

68. Peter Peterson Collection, letter 19.

69. *Husförhörslängder,* Älvsborg: Hudene, 1851–55, p. 61.

70. Aron W. Johnson Collection, folder E, letters 9 and 10.

71. *Husförhörslängder,* Kalmar: Madesjö, 1893–94, p. 356.

72. Ivar Larsson Collection, C7 and 17.

73. *Husförhörslängder,* Östergötland: Motala, 1885–89, p. 392.

74. "Svenska Pionjären Som Ha Gått Hädan," *Svenska Amerikanaren Tribunen* (Chicago), 19 December 1929, 1. Rydberg appeared in the *Minnesota, North and South Dakota, and Montana Gazetteer* of 1900 as a jeweler (2267).

75. U.S. Census Bureau, Twelfth Census, Montana, Carbon County, Red Lodge Township, ED 5 sheet 10, dwelling 202, line 77.

76. Rydberg's political career is documented in the *Carbon County Democrat,* 17 October and 14 November 1900. Rydberg's columns appeared in the *Democrat,* 10 and 24 April 1901, and 15 and 29 May 1901; and in the *Carbon County Gazette,* 26 October 1905. The *Gazette* provided an account of one of his camping trips on 28 September 1905.

77. *Svenska Amerikanaren Tribunen* (Chicago), 19 December 1929, 1; Emibas 2001 index of Motala *husförhörslängder,* 1912–16.

78. Bernhard Rydberg Collection, letter 5.

79. John M. Swanson Collection, folder C, letter 7.

80. Ibid., folder C, letter 16.

81. John M. Swanson Collection, folder B, letters 1–3, folder C, letters 8, 14–16.

82. *Husförhörslängder,* Kronoberg: Virestad, 1892–93, p. 567. Unlike Emma Hallberg and John M. Swanson, Ida and Albert Sandberg do not appear in *Svenska Adresskalendern.*

83. Swedish American Church Records in North America, microfilm S-595, roll 2, membership register, p. 93.

84. John M. Swanson Collection, folder C, letter 8.

85. Our best guess is that Ida is joking, that the identity of the father is certainly her husband.

86. *Husförhörslängder*, Malmöhus: Genarp, 1881–92, p. 457.

87. Staffan Jönsson to "Amerikaminnet," 20 February 1978, in Ola Svenson Collection.

88. Ola Svenson Collection, letter 6.

89. *Husförhörslängder*, Kronoberg: Virestad, 1888–90, p. 559. Swanson also appears in *Svenska Adresskalendern* as a laborer living at 4314 Elati Street.

90. John M. Swanson Collection, folder C, letter 2.

91. *Chicago Svenska Amerikanaren Tribunen*, 7 March 1912.

92. Swenson Swedish Immigration Research Center, Swedish American Church Records in North America, microfilm S-595, roll 2, membership register, p. 47.

93. John M. Swanson Collection, folder C, letter 4.

94. The "it" to which Swanson refers is unclear, probably a reference external to the letter and known by his parents.

95. According to the Emibas index of parish records, a Nils Trulsson was born in Verum, Skåne (Kristianstads län), in 1857, and was a tenant farmer in Sweden who emigrated to the United States in 1880. However, my search through the Verum *husförhörslängder* for that period turned up no Nils Trulsson.

96. Oscar Wall Collection, letter 2.

Bibliography

Abbreviations

BYU   Special Collections, Brigham Young University, Provo, Utah
CHS   Colorado Historical Society, Denver
EI   Swedish Emigrant Institute, Växjö, Sweden
SC   Swenson Swedish Immigration Research Center, Augustana College, Rock
      Island, Ill.

Manuscript Collections

Anderson, Charles H. EI, 10:15:9:A.
Anderson, Jonas. EI, 10:5:6:D.
Anderson, Karna. EI, 10:4:1:A.
Anderson, Otto. EI, 10:9:3, folder C, letter 1.
Andersson, Genny. EI, 9:9:13.
Aronson, Albert H. CHS, Manuscript 1079.
Bloomberg, Charles M. EI, 22:12:1:I.
Boline, Carl. EI, 10:5:8:C.
Brodin, Bengt Olson. EI, 10:2:4:B.
Dickson, Anni, letters in the Carl Israelsson Collection. EI, 22:16:14, letters 8, 11, 14,
    16, 17, 19, 20.
Erickson, Nils. EI, 16:19:13:D.
Erlandson, Peter F. EI, 22:6:16:G.
Flodin, Charles. EI, 22:6:11:C.
Håkansson, Johan. EI, 22:4:2:B.
Hall, A. P. EI, 10:4:1:J.
Hallquist, Victor A. EI, 22:4:14:J.
Husförhörslängder (catechetical registers, on microfilm). EI.
    Älvsborg: Hudene, Håcksvik
    Dalarna: Svärdsjö
    Kalmar: Köping, Madesjö
    Kristianstad: Farstorp, Verum
    Kronoberg: Virestad

Malmöhus: Genarp
Östergötland: Kimstad, Kärna, Motala, Söderköping
Jeppsson, Clara. EI, 10:15:6.
Jernberg, John E. EI, 22:1:13.
Johansson, August. EI, 9:6:10:E.
Johansson, Peter J. EI, 10:6:6:A.
Johnson, Aron W. EI, 29:6:19:D.
Johnson, Gottfrid. EI, 10:16:8:B.
Johnson, John R. EI, 22:8:A.
Johnson, P. J. EI, 10:5:5:J.
Johnson, Victor. EI, 10:3:15:E.
Johnsson, Hjalmar. EI, 10:4:13, letters 29 and 30.
Larsson, Ivar ("Bondas Ivar Larsson's Samlinger för Hembygdsföreningen i Lima, Dalarna"). EI, 10:17:8.
Larsson, Olof. EI, 10:16:18:B.
Leonard, John A. EI, 10:2:17:B.
Lindborg, Fritz. EI, 10:6:2:B.
Lundquist, Jacob. EI, 29:5:8, folder D, letters 2–4, folder E, letter 21.
Myrholm, Elias. EI, 3:10:1:Stenmark 8.
Nilson, O. EI, 10:3:6:H.
Nilsson, Leonard. EI, 10:2.7–9.
Olson, Anna. EI, 10:4:11, folder E, letter 4.
Olson, Nils. EI, 10:11:2:G.
Olsson, Ole. EI, 10:5:19:D.
Pearson, Nels. EI, 22:17:9.
Pedersen, Ole. EI, 10:1:4:I.
Pehrson, Elin. EI, 10:2:16, folder I, letters 3–5.
Peterson, August. EI, 10:2:17:F.
Peterson, Effie. EI, 10:11:2, folder B, letters 13 and 14.
Peterson, John. EI, 15:14:13, folder B, letters 20, 28, 50, 51.
Peterson, Peter. EI, 10:3:3:P.
Petterson, Gust. EI, 16:19:1:A.
Reed, Andreas. EI, 9:2:11, folder E, letter 1.
Reed, John. EI, 10:1:7, folder F, letter 5.
Rydberg, Bernhard. EI, 10:3:2:H.
Smith, Swan. EI, 10:16:18:A.
Stred, Pet. EI, 10:5:15, folder A, letter 4.
Svenson, Ola. EI, 10:1:4:A.
Swanson, John M. EI, 10:2:19:B and C.
Swedish American Church Records in North America (microfilm). SC.
Swedish Evangelical Free Church Manuscript 1540. CHS.
Trulsson, Nils. EI, 22:12:4:C.
"Two Popular Scandinavian Plays," 5 March 1900. BYU.

Wall, Oscar. EI, 29:11:16, folder D, letter 2.
Wiberg, J. Edward. EI, 29:4:13:I.

Primary Sources

Anderson, Anders August. *Tjugu År i Vilda Västern: Erfarenheter och Iakttagelser som Missionär och Församlingslärare.* Minneapolis: Missionstidningens Tryckeri, 1910.
Bergs-Väktaren. Helena, Mont. 1898–99.
Boulder City and County Directory. Boulder, Colo.: W. G. Brown, 1904.
Boulder City Directory. Boulder, Colo.: Daily Herald Press, 1901.
Boulder County Directory. Colorado Springs: R. L. Polk Directory Company, 1916.
Butte City Directory. Butte, Mont.: R. L. Polk, 1905.
Carbon County Democrat. Red Lodge, Mont. 1900–1901.
Carbon County Gazette. Red Lodge, Mont. September and October, 1905.
Cripple Creek District Directory. n.p.: Gazetteer Publishing Co., 1912.
Den Swenska Psalm-Boken af År 1819. Rock Island, Ill.: Augustana Book Concern, [1885].
Den Ungas Sångbok. Chicago: Svenska Evangeliska Missionsförbundet i Amerika, 1914.
Denver City Directory. Denver: Corbett & Ballenger, 1900.
Emibas and Emihamn indices of Swedish emigrant records. EI.
From Sweden to America: Emigrant and Immigrant Songs. Caprice Records, catalog number 2011. 33 rpm.
Fullständig Svensk-Engelsk Bref- och Formulärbok. 9th ed. Chicago: Engberg-Holmberg, 1896.
Fyrbåken. Salt Lake City. October 1895.
Golden Jubilee, Reminiscences of Our Work under God: Swedish Evangelical Free Church of the USA, 1884–1934. [Minneapolis: Swedish Evangelical Free Church of the USA, 1934].
Helena City Directory. Helena, Mont.: R. L. Polk, 1891.
Hemlandssånger. Rock Island, Ill.: Augustana Book Concern, 1892.
Holmberg, Waldemar. *Hellhole on Earth: Timmerskog och Emigrantår.* Skellefteå: Ord & Visor Förlag, 2003.
Idaho Geneological Society, *Idaho Territory Population Schedules and Mortality Schedules 1880.* Boise: Williams Printing, 1976.
Larson, Andrew Karl. *The Education of a Second Generation Swede: An Autobiography.* St. George, Utah: Andrew Karl Larson, 1979.
Latah County Directory. Moscow, Idaho: 1922.
Lönnkvist, Fred. *Allt-Omfattande Svensk-Amerikansk Uppslagsbok.* Philadelphia: John C. Winston, 1895.
Memories of Snoose Boulevard: Songs of the Scandinavian Americans. Olle i Skratthult Project, Stereo Album SP-223. 33 rpm.
Minnesota, North and South Dakota, and Montana Gazetteer and Business Directory, 1900–1901. St. Paul: R. L. Polk, 1900.

Montana Posten. Helena, Mont. 1890, 1893.

Montana Skandinav. Butte, Mont. 26 January 1893.

Montana Tidende og Skandinav. Butte, Mont. 9 February 1894.

Officiellt Referat. Rock Island, Ill.: Augustana Synod, 1884–90.

OldLutheran.com. http://www.oldlutheran.com (accessed 28 September 2005).

Person, Johan. *Svensk-Amerikanska Studier.* Rock Island, Ill.: Augustana Book Concern, 1912.

Protokoll. Rock Island, Ill.: Augustana Synod, 1880–83.

Pueblo City Directory. Pueblo, Colo.: R. L. Polk, 1904.

Referat. Rock Island, Ill.: Augustana Synod, 1891, 1892, 1895, 1900, 1905, 1910, 1915.

Salt Lake Bladet. Salt Lake City. December 1902–January 1903.

Strömberg, Leonard. *Guldgrävarna.* Uppsala, Sweden: J. A. Lindblads, 1923.

Sturluson, Snorri. *The Younger Edda.* Trans. Rasmus B. Anderson. Chicago: S. C. Griggs, 1880.

Sund, Lars. *Colorado Avenue.* Helsingfors: En bok för alla, 1991.

Svensk-Amerikanska Western. Denver. 1901–2.

Svenska Adresskalendern. Denver: Adolf E. Bundsen, 1910.

Svenska Amerikanaren. Chicago. 19 December 1929.

Svenska Amerikanaren Tribunen. Chicago. 7 March 1912, 19 December 1929.

Svenska Folkets Tidning. Minneapolis. June–July 1903.

Svenska Korrespondenten. Denver. 1890–1900.

Svenska Nordvästern. Spokane. 1911–12.

Tegnér, Esaias. "Svea." In *Svea, Samt Karl XII, Sång för Skånska Landtvärnet, Sång för Jämtlands Fältjägare, Skytten, Det Eviga, och Fridsröster,* 3–13. Chicago: Engberg-Holmberg, 1891.

"A Unitarian Universalist Joke." Available from http://stoney.sb.org/uujokes.html (accessed 13 February 2003).

United States Bureau of the Census. *Census Reports,* vol. 16, Eleventh Census of the United States. Washington, D.C.: GPO, 1890.

———. *Census Reports,* vol. 1, Twelfth Census of the United States. Washington, D.C.: GPO, 1900.

———. *Twelfth Census of the United States,* Schedule 1, Population, Montana, Utah. Microfilm.

United States Geological Survey. Black Pyramid Mountain, 7.5 minute series.

United States Senate. *Reports of the Immigration Commission,* Document 282. Occupations of the First and Second Generations of Immigrants in the United States. Washington, D.C.: GPO, 1911.

———. *Reports of the Immigration Commission,* Document 633. Japanese and Other Immigrant Races in the Pacific Coast and Rocky Mountain States. 3 vols. Washington, D.C.: GPO, 1911.

University of Virginia Geospatial and Statistical Data Center. United States Historical Census Data Browser. University of Virginia, 1998. http://fisher.lib.virginia.edu/census/ (accessed 4 March 2003 and 21 July 2005).

Utah Korrespondenten. Salt Lake City. 1890–1900.

Western News. Denver. 26 June 1958.

Secondary Sources

Allen, Barbara. "Personal Experience Narratives: Use and Meaning in Interaction." In *Folk Groups and Folklore Genres: A Reader,* ed. Elliott Oring, 236–43. Logan: Utah State University Press, 1989.

———. *See also* Bogart, Barbara Allen.

Allwood, Jens. "Are There Swedish Patterns of Communication?" In *Cultural Acceptance of CSCW in Japan & Nordic Countries,* ed. H. Tamura, 90–120. Kyoto, Japan: Kyoto Institute of Technology, 1999. Available at www.ling.gu.se/~jens/publications/docs076-100/087.pdf (accessed 14 February 2007).

Altman, Janet Gurkin. *Epistolarity: Approaches to a Form.* Columbus: Ohio State University Press, 1982.

Anderson, Chas. E. et al. *After Fifty Years.* Idaho Falls: n.p., 1941.

Anderson, Philip J. "The Lively Exchange of Religious Ideals between the United States and Sweden during the Nineteenth Century." In *American Religious Influences in Sweden,* ed. Scott E. Erickson, 31–48. Special issue of *Tro & Tanke* 5 (1996).

Attebery, Jennifer Eastman. "Being Swedish-American in the Intermountain West: The Experiences of Immigrants to Idaho and Utah." *Swedish-American Historical Quarterly* 49 (1998): 234–44.

———. *Building with Logs: Western Log Construction in Context.* Moscow, Idaho: University of Idaho Press, 1998.

———. "Claiming Ethnicity: Implicit and Explicit Expressions of Ethnicity among Swedish Americans." In *Not English Only: Redefining "American" in American Studies,* ed. Orm Øverland, 12–28. Amsterdam: VU University Press, 2001.

———. "A Lonely Guy in Rocky Bar, Idaho: Imagining Swedish America from the Mines," *Swedish-American Historical Quarterly* 54 (2003): 164–84.

———. "Lonely Guys on the Fringe of Swedish America." *Swedish-American Historical Quarterly* 53 (2002): 163–78.

———. "Transplantations of Swedish America in Idaho: The Role of the Churches." *Swedish-American Historical Quarterly* 46 (1995): 122–40.

Baker, Ronald L. "Ritualized Violence and Local Journalism in the Development of a Lynching Legend." *Fabula* 29 (1988): 317–25.

Bakhtin, M. M. "The Problem of Speech Genres." In *Speech Genres and Other Late Essays,* ed. Caryl Emerson and Michael Holquist, 60–102. Trans. Vern W. McGee. Austin: University of Texas Press, 1986.

Barkan, Elliott Robert. "Turning Turner on His Head? The Significance of Immigration in Twentieth-century American Western History." *New Mexico Historical Review* 77, no. 1 (2002): 57–88.

Barton, David, and Nigel Hall. "Introduction." In *Letter Writing as a Social Practice,* ed. David Barton and Nigel Hall, 1–14. Amsterdam: John Benjamins, 2000.

Barton, H. Arnold. *A Folk Divided: Homeland Swedes and Swedish Americans, 1840–1940.* Carbondale: Southern Illinois University Press, 1994.

———. *Letters from the Promised Land: Swedes in America, 1840–1914.* Minneapolis: University of Minnesota Press, 1975.

———. "The Norrland Crop Failures of 1902 and the Swedish Americans." *Swedish-American Historical Quarterly* 50 (1999): 9–19.

Baughman, Ernest W. *Type and Motif Index of the Folktales of England and North America.* Indiana University Folklore Series 20. Bloomington: Folklore Institute, 1966.

Bauman, Richard. *Verbal Art as Performance.* Prospect Heights, Ill.: Waveland, 1977.

Beauchamp, Virginia Walcott. "The Persona and the Real Woman—A Case Study." In *Women's Personal Narratives: Essays in Criticism and Pedagogy,* ed. Leonore Hoffmann and Margo Culley, 40–47. New York: Modern Language Association, 1985.

Beijbom, Ulf. "The Historiography of Swedish America." *Swedish Pioneer Historical Quarterly* 31 (1980): 257–85.

———. "Swedish-American Organizational Life." In *Scandinavia Overseas: Patterns of Cultural Transformation in North America and Australia,* ed. Harald Runblom and Dag Blanck, 52–81. Uppsala Multiethnic Papers 7. Uppsala, Sweden: Uppsala University, 1986.

———. "Tegnér and America." In *Scandinavians in Old and New Lands,* ed. Philip J. Anderson, Dag Blanck, and Byron J. Nordstrom, 159–83. Chicago: Swedish-American Historical Society, 2004.

Berry, Mildred Freburg. "Memories of a Swedish Christmas." *Palimpsest* 59 (1978): 20–23.

Bjork, Kenneth O. "A Covenant Folk, with Scandinavian Colorings." *Norwegian-American Studies* 21 (1962): 212–51.

Björk, Ulf Jonas. "The Dangerous Prairies of Texas: The Western Dime Novel in Sweden, 1900–1908." *Swedish-American Historical Quarterly* 55 (2004): 165–78.

———. "'Folkets Röst,' the Pulse of the Public: *Svenska Amerikanska Posten* and Reader Letters, 1907–1911." *Swedish-American Historical Quarterly* 50 (1999): 4–17.

———. "Stories of America: The Rise of the 'Indian Book' in Sweden, 1862–1895." *Scandinavian Studies* 75 (2003): 509–26.

———. "A Swedish-American View of Sweden: The Journalism of Nils F. Brown, 1910–1953." *Swedish-American Historical Quarterly* 44 (1993): 21–38.

Björkborg, Gunnar. *Den Första Boken om Hovslätt.* Jönköping, Sweden: Hofslätts Hembygdsförening, 1979.

Blanck, Dag. *Becoming Swedish-American: The Construction of an Ethnic Identity in the Augustana Synod, 1860–1917.* Studia Historica Upsaliensia 182. Uppsala, Sweden: Uppsala University, 1997.

Blegen, Theodore. *Land of Their Choice: The Immigrants Write Home.* Minneapolis: University of Minnesota Press, 1955.

Bogart, Barbara Allen. *In Place: Stories of Landscape and Identity from the American West.* Glendo, Wyo.: High Plains Press, 1995.

Bringéus, Nils-Arvid. *Årets Festseder.* Stockholm: LTs Förlag, 1976.

Britsch, Ralph A. *Bierstadt and Ludlow: Painter and Writer in the West.* Provo, Utah: Brigham Young University, 1980.

Bruner, Jerome. "Self-Making and World-Making." In *Narrative and Identity: Studies in Autobiography, Self and Culture,* ed. Jens Brockmeier and Donal Carbaugh, 25–37. Amsterdam: John Benjamins, 2001.

Burke, Martin J. *The Conundrum of Class: Public Discourse on the Social Order in America.* Chicago: University of Chicago Press, 1995.

Cameron, Walter A. "Building the Northern Pacific in 1881." *Montana* 33, no. 3 (1983): 70–76.

Carlson, C. A. *Northmen Who Went West.* [Greeley: Colorado State College of Education], 1935.

Carter, Thomas. "Building Zion: Folk Architecture in the Mormon Settlements of Utah's Sanpete Valley, 1850–1890." PhD diss., Indiana University, 1984.

———. "North European Horizontal Log Construction in the Sanpete-Sevier Valleys." *Utah Historical Quarterly* 52 (1984): 50–71.

Cawelti, John G. *Adventure, Mystery, and Romance: Formula Stories as Art and Popular Culture.* Chicago: University of Chicago Press, 1976.

———. *The Six-Gun Mystique.* Bowling Green, Ohio: Bowling Green University Popular Press, [1971?].

Clute, John, and Peter Nicholls, ed. *The Encyclopedia of Science Fiction.* London: Orbit, 1993.

Conzen, Kathleen Neils. "A Saga of Families." In *The Oxford History of the American West,* ed. Clyde A. Milner II, Carol A. O'Connor, and Martha A. Sandweiss, 315–57. New York: Oxford University Press, 1994.

Cronon, William, George Miles, and Jay Gitlin. "Becoming West: Toward a New Meaning for Western History." In *Under an Open Sky: Rethinking America's Western Past,* ed. William Cronon, George Miles, and Jay Gitlin, 3–27. New York: Norton, 1992.

Culley, Margo. "Women's Vernacular Literature: Teaching the Mother Tongue." In *Women's Personal Narratives: Essays in Criticism and Pedagogy,* ed. Leonore Hoffmann and Margo Culley, 9–17. New York: Modern Language Association, 1985.

Danielson, Larry. "Religious Folklore." In *Folk Groups and Folklore Genres: An Introduction,* ed. Elliott Oring, 45–69. Logan: Utah State University Press, 1986.

Daun, Åke. *Swedish Mentality.* Trans. Jan Teeland. University Park: Pennsylvania State University Press, 1996. First published as *Svensk Mentalitet,* 1989.

Decker, William Merrill. *Epistolary Practices: Letter Writing in America before Telecommunications.* Chapel Hill: University of North Carolina Press, 1998.

Dégh, Linda. "Folk Narrative." In *Folklore and Folklife: An Introduction,* ed. Richard M. Dorson, 53–83. Chicago: University of Chicago Press, 1972.

―――. "Two Letters from Home." *Journal of American Folklore* 91 (1978): 808–22.

Del Giudice, Luisa. "Mountains of Cheese and Rivers of Wine: *Paesi di Cuccagna* and Other Gastronomic Utopias." In *Imagined States: Nationalism, Utopia, and Longing in Oral Cultures*, ed. Luisa Del Giudice and Gerald Porter, 11–63. Logan: Utah State University Press, 2001.

Djupedal, Knut. "Personal Letters as Research Sources." *Ethnologia Scandinavica* 19 (1989): 51–63.

Dolan, Jay P. "The Immigrants and Their Gods: A New Perspective in American Religious History." *Church History* 57 (1988): 61–72.

Dundes, Alan. "Folkloristics in the Twenty-first Century." *Journal of American Folklore* 118 (2005): 385–408.

―――. *The Study of Folklore*. Englewood Cliffs, N.J.: Prentice-Hall, 1965.

Edvinsson, Sören. "The Demographic Data Base at Umeå University: A Resource for Historical Studies." In *Handbook of International Historical Microdata for Population Research*, ed. Patricia Kelly Hall, Robert McCaa, and Gunnar Thorvaldsen, 231–49. IPUMS International, Minnesota Population Center, https://www.ipums.org/international/microdata_handbook-back.html (accessed 6 July 2005).

Erickson, Charlotte. *Invisible Immigrants: The Adaptation of English and Scottish Immigrants in Nineteenth-century America*. Ithaca, N.Y.: Cornell University Press, 1972.

Erling, Maria Elizabeth. "Crafting an Urban Piety: New England's Swedish Immigrants and Their Religious Culture from 1880 to 1915." PhD diss., Harvard University, 1995.

Esping, Mark, and Mardel Esping. "The Swedish-American Custom of Ljuskrona." *Mid-America Folklore* 18, no. 2 (1990): 108–15.

Fell, James E. *Ores to Metals: The Rocky Mountain Smelting Industry*. Lincoln: University of Nebraska Press, 1979.

Fitzpatrick, David. *Oceans of Consolation: Personal Accounts of Irish Migration to Australia*. Ithaca, N.Y.: Cornell University Press, 1994.

Foley, John Miles. *How to Read an Oral Poem*. Urbana: University of Illinois Press, 2002.

―――. *Immanent Art: From Structure to Meaning in Traditional Oral Epic*. Bloomington: Indiana University Press, 1991.

―――. "Word-Power, Performance, and Tradition." *Journal of American Folklore* 105 (1991): 275–301.

Franklin, H. Bruce. *Future Perfect: American Science Fiction of the Nineteenth Century*. New Brunswick, N.J.: Rutgers University Press, 1995.

Frykman, Jonas, and Orvar Löfgren. *Culture Builders: A Historical Anthropology of Middle-Class Life*. Trans. Alan Crozier. New Brunswick, N.J.: Rutgers University Press, 1987. First published as *Den Kultiverade Människan*, 1979.

Fur, Gunlög. "Romantic Relations: Swedish Attitudes towards Indians during the Twentieth Century." *Swedish-American Historical Quarterly* 55 (2004): 145–64.

Gerber, David A. *Authors of Their Lives: The Personal Correspondence of British Im-*

migrants to North America in the Nineteenth Century. New York: New York University Press, 2006.

———. "Epistolary Ethics: Personal Correspondence and the Culture of Emigration in the Nineteenth Century." *Journal of American Ethnic History* 19, no. 4 (2000): 3–23.

———. "Forming a Transnational Narrative: New Perspectives on European Migrations to the United States." *History Teacher* 35, no. 1 (2001). Available from http://www.historycooperative.org/journals/ht/35.1/gerber.html (accessed 4 February 2003).

Gernes, Todd S. "Recasting the Culture of Ephemera." In *Popular Literacy: Studies in Cultural Practices and Poetics,* ed. John Trimbur, 107–27. Pittsburgh: University of Pittsburgh Press, 2001.

Granquist, Mark Alan. "The Swedish Ethnic Denominations in the United States: Their Development and Relationships, 1880–1920." PhD diss., University of Chicago, 1992.

Grindal, Gracia. "The Swedish Tradition in Hymnals and Songbooks." *Lutheran Quarterly* 17 (2003): 435–68.

Hale, Frederick. *Danes in North America.* Seattle: University of Washington Press, 1984.

———. *Their Own Saga: Letters from the Norwegian Global Migration.* Minneapolis: University of Minnesota Press, 1986.

Hallberg, Carl V. "Nineteenth-century Colorado through Swedish Eyes." *Swedish-American Historical Quarterly* 36 (1985): 112–32.

———. *Swedish Heritage in Wyoming: A Reference Guide.* [Cheyenne: Wyoming State Archives, with funding from the Swedish Council of America], 2002.

Hansson, Stina. *Svensk Brevskrivning: Teori och Tillämpning.* Litteraturvetenskapliga Institutionen 18. Göteborg, Sweden: Göteborgs Universitet, 1988.

Harré, Rom. "Metaphysics and Narrative: Singularities and Multiplicities of Self." In *Narrative and Identity: Studies in Autobiography, Self, and Culture,* ed. Jens Brockmeier and Donal Carbaugh, 59–73. Amsterdam: John Benjamins, 2001.

Harvey, Anne-Charlotte. "Performing Ethnicity: The Role of Swedish Theatre in the Twin Cities." In *Swedes in the Twin Cities: Immigrant Life and Minnesota's Urban Frontier,* ed. Philip J. Anderson and Dag Blanck, 149–72. St. Paul: Minnesota Historical Society Press, 2001.

Hecker-Stampehl, Jan. "Nation-State Formation and Cultural Diversity in Sweden." Cultural Diversity in European Nation States Project, European Migration Network, http://www.emz_berlin.de/projekte_e/pj50_pdf/sweden.pdf (accessed 11 May 2005).

Hine, Robert V., and John Mack Faragher. *The American West: A New Interpretive History.* New Haven, Conn.: Yale University Press, 2000.

Historical Review of Vasa Order of America, 1896–1971. n.p., n.d. Copy available at SC.

Huhndorf, Shari M. *Going Native: Indians in the American Cultural Imagination.* Ithaca, N.Y.: Cornell University Press, 2001.

Isaacson, Carl. "They Did Not Forget Their Swedish: Class Markers in the Swedish American Community." In *Ethnolinguistic Chicago: Language and Literacy in the City's Neighborhoods*, ed. Marcia Farr, 223–49. Mahway, N.J.: Lawrence Erlbaum, 2004.

Jacobson, Matthew Frye. *Whiteness of a Different Color: European Immigrants and the Alchemy of Race*. Cambridge: Harvard University Press, 1998.

Jameson, Elizabeth. *All That Glitters: Class, Conflict, and Community in Cripple Creek*. Urbana: University of Illinois Press, 1998.

Jason, Heda. "Literature, Letters, Verbal Texts: What Is It That We Are Dealing With?" *Fabula* 33 (1992): 206–44.

Kalčik, Susan. ". . . like Ann's Gynecologist or the Time I Was Almost Raped: Personal Narratives in Women's Rap Groups." *Journal of American Folklore* 88 (1975): 3–11.

Klein, Barbro. "Folkets Röst: Svensk-Amerikanska Insändarbrev och Folklorens Betydelser." *Nord Nytt* 52 (1993): 85–97.

Klymasz, Robert B. "The Letter in Canadian Ukrainian Folklore." In *Folk Groups and Folklore Genres: A Reader*, ed. Elliott Oring, 53–62. Logan: Utah State University Press, 1989. First published in *Journal of the Folklore Institute* 6, no. 1 (1969): 39–49.

Kurunmäki, Jussi. "'National Representation' in Sweden in the Early Nineteenth Century: Erik Gustaf Geijer's Two Conceptions of 'National Representation.'" Paper for Workshop 2, "The History of Political Concepts," European Consortium for Political Research, Copenhagen, 14–19 April 2000.

Langlois, Janet L. "Belle Gunness, the Lady Bluebeard: Narrative Use of a Deviant Woman." In *Women's Folklore, Women's Culture*, ed. Rosan A. Jordan and Susan J. Kalčik, 109–24. Philadelphia: University of Pennsylvania Press, 1985.

Larn, Hubert. "'Fantastic Hilda'—Pioneer History Personified." *Swedish Pioneer Historical Quarterly* 15 2 (1964): 63–76.

Lawless, Elaine J. "Shouting for the Lord: The Power of Women's Speech in the Pentecostal Religious Service." *Journal of American Folklore* 96 (1983): 434–59.

Leonard, Stephen J. *Lynching in Colorado, 1859–1919*. Boulder: University Press of Colorado, 2002.

Limerick, Patricia Nelson. "Making the Most of Words: Verbal Activity and Western America." In *Under an Open Sky: Rethinking America's Western Past*, ed. William Cronon, George Miles, and Jay Gitlin, 167–84. New York: Norton, 1992.

———. *Something in the Soil: Legacies and Reckonings in the New West*. New York: Norton, 2000.

Lindgren, "The Swedes Come to Utah." In *American Swedish Historical Foundation Yearbook*, 13–27. Philadelphia: American Swedish Historical Foundation, 1949.

Lindquist, Emory. "Appraisals of Sweden and America by Swedish Emigrants: The Testimony of Letters in Emigrationsutredningen (1907)." *Swedish Pioneer Historical Quarterly* 15 (1964): 78–95.

———. "Swedish American Pseudonyms: One Aspect of the Swedish Immigrant Literary Tradition." *Swedish Pioneer Historical Quarterly* 18 (1967): 148–56.

Löfgren, Orvar. "The Great Christmas Quarrel and Other Swedish Traditions." In *Unwrapping Christmas*, ed. Daniel Miller, 217–34. Oxford: Oxford University Press, 2001.

Lord, Albert B. *The Singer of Tales*. 2nd ed. Ed. Stephen Mitchell and Gregory Nagy. Cambridge, Mass.: Harvard University Press, 2000.

Luebke, Frederick. C. "Introduction." In *European Immigrants in the American West*, ed. Frederick C. Luebke, vii–xix. Albuquerque: University of New Mexico Press, 1998.

Lund, Jennifer L. "Out of the Swan's Nest: The Ministry of Anthon H. Lund, Scandinavian Apostle." *Journal of Mormon History* 29, no. 2 (2003): 77–105.

MacMillan, Donald. *Smoke Wars: Anaconda Copper, Montana Air Pollution, and the Courts, 1890–1920*. Helena: Montana Historical Society Press, 2000.

Marshall, Linnea. "Swedish Immigrants to Latah County, Idaho." Master's thesis, University of Idaho, 2005.

Martin, Charles W. "John Ahmanson vs. Brigham Young: A Nebraska Legal Controversy, 1859–1861." *Nebraska History* 64, no. 1 (1983): 1–20.

Måwe, Carl-Erik. *Värmlänningar i Nordamerika: Sociologiska Studier i en Anpassningsprocess*. Säffle, Sweden: Säffle-Tidningens Tryckeri, 1971.

McDonald, Myrtle. *No Regrets: The Life of Carl A. Carlquist*. Encino, Calif.: n.p., n.d. Available at Brigham Young University.

Meinig, D. W. "The Mormon Culture Region: Strategies and Patterns in the Geography of the American West, 1847–1964." *Annals of the Association of American Geographers* 55 (1965): 191–220.

———. *The Shaping of America: A Geographical Perspective on 500 Years of History*. Vol. 3, *Transcontinental America 1850–1915*. New Haven, Conn.: Yale University Press, 1998.

Mieder, Wolfgang. "'Now I Sit Like a Rabbit in the Pepper': Proverbial Language in the Letters of Wolfgang Amadeus Mozart." *Journal of Folklore Research* 40 (2003): 33–70.

Mitman, Gregg. "Geographies of Hope: Mining the Frontiers of Health in Denver and Beyond, 1870–1965." *Osiris* 19 (2004): 93–111.

Mulder, William. *Homeward to Zion: The Mormon Migration from Scandinavia*. Minneapolis: University of Minnesota Press, 2000. First published 1957.

———. "Mormons from Scandinavia, 1850–1900: A Shepherded Migration." *Pacific Historical Review* 23 (1954): 227–46.

———. "Mother Tongue, 'Skandinavisme,' and 'The Swedish Insurrection' in Utah." *Swedish Pioneer Historical Quarterly* 7 (1956): 11–20.

———. "Utah's Ugly Ducklings: A Profile of the Scandinavian Immigrant." *Utah Historical Quarterly* 23 (1955): 233–59.

Murdoch, David Hamilton. *The American West: The Invention of a Myth*. Reno: University of Nevada Press, 2001.

Nelson, A. P. *Svenska Missionsvännernas Historia i Amerika*. Minneapolis: n.p., 1906.

Nelson, Helge. *The Swedes and the Swedish Settlements in North America*. New York:

Arno Press, 1979. First published by the Royal Society of Letters, Lund, Sweden, 1943.

Nilsson, Anders. "What Do Literacy Rates in the Nineteenth Century Really Signify?" *Paedagogica Historica* 35, no. 2 (1999): 275–96.

Olson, Adolf. *A Centenary History as Related to the Baptist General Conference of America.* Chicago: Baptist Conference Press, 1952.

Olson, Ernest L. "Otto Rydman, Satirist: An Immigrant Editor's Views of the Scandinavian Scene in Utah." Master's thesis, University of Utah, 1949.

Olsson, Karl A. *By One Spirit.* Chicago: Covenant Press, 1962.

Ong, Walter J. *Orality and Literacy: The Technologizing of the Word.* London: Routledge, 1982.

Oring, Elliott. "On the Concepts of Folklore." In *Folk Groups and Folklore Genres: An Introduction,* ed. Elliott Oring, 1–22. Logan: Utah State University Press, 1986.

Øverland, Orm. "Becoming White in 1881: An Immigrant Acquires an American Identity." *Journal of American Ethnic History* 23, no. 4 (2004): 132–41.

———. *Immigrant Minds, American Identities: Making the United States Home, 1870–1930.* Urbana: University of Illinois Press, 2000.

———. "Learning to Read Immigrant Letters: Reflections towards a Textual Theory." In *Norwegian-American Essays 1996,* ed. Øyvind T. Gulliksen, David C. Mauk, and Dina Tolfsby, 207–27. Oslo: NAHA-Norway and the Norwegian Emigrant Museum, 1996.

———. "Norwegian Texans Tell Their Story in Letters, 1843–1884." A lecture given at the Bosque Memorial Museum, Clifton, Texas, 16 March 2003.

———. "Religion and Church in Early Immigrant Letters: A Preliminary Investigation." In *Crossings: Norwegian-American Lutheranism as a Transatlantic Tradition,* ed. Todd W. Nichol, 31–56. Northfield, Minn.: Norwegian-American Historical Association, 2003.

Øverland, Orm, and Steinar Skærheim. *Fra Amerika til Norge.* 4 vols. Oslo: Solum, 1992–2002.

Palmenfelt, Ulf. "Bryt Ej Kedjan! Svenska Kedjebrev Förr och Nu." *Tradisjon: Tidsskrift för Folkeminnevitskap* 18 (1988): 41–54.

Peterson, Walter F. "Swedish Christmas in Iowa in 1879." *Swedish Pioneer Historical Quarterly* 11 (1960): 160–61.

Polson, D. Michol. "The Swedes in Grantsville, Utah, 1860–1900." *Utah Historical Quarterly* 56 (1988): 208–21.

Poulsen, Richard C. "Folk Material Culture of the Sanpete-Sevier Area: Today's Reflections of a Region Past." *Utah Historical Quarterly* 47 (1979): 130–47.

Quinn, D. Michael. "Religion in the American West." In *Under an Open Sky: Rethinking America's Western Past,* ed. William Cronon, George Miles, and Jay Gitlin, 145–66. New York: Norton, 1992.

Reed, Mary E. "Latah County's Scandinavians." *Latah Legacy* 19, no. 1 (1990): 13–28.

Rehnberg, Mats. *Swedish Holidays and Annual Festivals.* n.p.: Swedish Institute, 1973.

Rice, Cindy. "Spring City: A Look at a Nineteenth-century Mormon Village." *Utah Historical Quarterly* 43 (1975): 260–77.

Roediger, David R., and Philip S. Foner. *Our Own Time: A History of American Labor and the Working Day*. New York: Greenwood, 1989.

Rooney, John F., Wilbur Zelinsky, and Dean P. Louder. *This Remarkable Continent: An Atlas of United States and Canadian Society and Cultures*. College Station: Texas A&M University Press, 1982.

Sandahl, Charles Fredrick. *The Nebraska Conference of the Augustana Synod*. Rock Island, Ill.: Augustana Book Concern, 1931.

Sayers, William. "Joe Hill's *Pie in the Sky* and Swedish Reflexes of the Land of Cockaigne." *American Speech* 77 (2002): 331–36.

Schroubek, Georg R. "Das Kann Ich Nicht Vergessen." *Jahrbuch für Ostdeutsche Volkskunde* 17 (1974): 27–50.

Segerhammar, Carl W. *First Lutheran Church of the Rockies*. Longmont, Colo.: First Lutheran Church, 1946. Copy available at CHS.

Selander, Inger. *O Hur Saligt att Få Vandra: Motiv och Symboler i den Frikyrkliga Sången*. Stockholm: Gummessons Bokförlag, 1980.

Setterdahl, Lilly. *Swedish-American Newspapers*. Rock Island, Ill.: Augustana Library Publications 35, 1981.

Shipps, Jan. *Mormonism: The Story of a New Religious Tradition*. Urbana: University of Illinois Press, 1985.

Sinor, Jennifer. *The Extraordinary Work of Ordinary Writing: Annie Ray's Diary*. Iowa City: University of Iowa Press, 2002.

Skarstedt, Ernst. *Pennfäktare: Svensk-Amerikanska Författare och Tidningsmän*. Stockholm: Åhlén & Åkerlunds Förlag, 1930.

———. *Våra Penn-Fäktare*. San Francisco: Vestkustens Tryckeri, 1897.

Slotkin, Richard. *The Fatal Environment: The Myth of the Frontier in the Age of Industrialization, 1800–1890*. New York: Atheneum, 1985.

———. *Regeneration through Violence: The Mythology of the American Frontier, 1600–1860*. Middletown, Conn.: Wesleyan University Press, 1973.

Smith, Henry Nash. *Virgin Land: The American West as Symbol and Myth*. Cambridge, Mass.: Harvard University Press, 1978. First published 1950.

Snellman, Hanna. "Was It Actually So? A Foreign Exchange Student's Experiences as Portrayed in Diaries and Letters." *Ethnologia Scandinavica* 25 (1995): 43–49.

Sollors, Werner. *Beyond Ethnicity: Consent and Descent in American Culture*. New York: Oxford University Press, 1986.

Stahl, Sandra Dolby. *Literary Folkloristics and the Personal Narrative*. Bloomington: Indiana University Press, 1989.

Swedish-American Historical Quarterly 56, nos. 2–3 (2005). Special issue based on the conference "*Jag lever och har hälsan*: Letters and Diaries of Swedish Immigrants in North America," held at the Swenson Swedish Immigration Research Center, Augustana College, Rock Island, Ill., 15–16 October 2004.

Thomas, William I., and Florian Znaniecki. *The Polish Peasant in Europe and America*. Vol. 1. New York: Albert A. Knopf, 1927.

Toelken, Barre. *The Dynamics of Folklore*. Rev. and exp. ed. Logan: Utah State University Press, 1996.

———. "Ethnic Selection and Intensification in the Native American Powwow." In *Creative Ethnicity: Symbols and Strategies of Contemporary Ethnic Life*, ed. Stephen Stern and John Allan Cicala, 137–56. Logan: Utah State University Press, 1991.

———. *Morning Dew and Roses: Nuance, Metaphor, and Meaning in Folksongs*. Urbana: University of Illinois Press, 1995.

Tye, Diane. "The Traditional Craft of Christmas Form Letters." *Fabula* 42 (2001): 201–12.

Viola, Patrizia. "Letters." In *Discourse and Literature: New Approaches to the Analysis of Literary Genres*, ed. Teun A. Van Dijk, 149–67. Amsterdam: John Benjamins, 1985.

Wells, Merle W. *Gold Camps and Silver Cities: Nineteenth-century Mining in Central and Southern Idaho*. 2nd ed. Bulletin 22, Bureau of Mines and Geology, Idaho Department of Lands. Moscow, Idaho: Bureau of Mines and Geology and Idaho State Historical Society, 1983.

Wentz, Abdel Ross. *A Basic History of Lutheranism in America*. Philadelphia: Muhlenberg Press, 1955.

White, G. Edward. *The Eastern Establishment and the Western Experience: The West of Frederic Remington, Theodore Roosevelt, and Owen Wister*. New Haven, Conn.: Yale University Press, 1968.

Williamson, George, and Anne O. Williamson. *There Is an Old Swedish Saying*. n.p., n.d. Available at SC.

Wilson, William A. "Folklore of Utah's Little Scandinavia." *Utah Historical Quarterly* 47 (1979): 148–66.

Wolf-Knuts, Ulrika. "Contrasts as a Narrative Technique in Emigrant Accounts." *Folklore* 113 (2003): 91–105.

Woods, Fred E., and Nicholas J. Evans. "Latter-day Saint Scandinavian Migration through Hull, England, 1852–1894." *BYU Studies* 41 (2002): 75–102.

Wright, Robert L. *Swedish Emigrant Ballads*. Lincoln: University of Nebraska Press, 1965.

Zempel, Solveig. *In Their Own Words: Letters from Norwegian Immigrants*. Minneapolis: University of Minnesota Press, 1991.

Index

Abrahamsson, Anders (letter recipient), 161

African Americans, 45

agriculture, 47, 48, 57, 137

Alhambra (Montana), 108

Allen, Barbara. See Bogart, Barbara Allen

allusion, 11, 15, 16, 33, 34, 169, 170

Allwood, Jens, 24–25, 41

Altman, Janet Gurkin, 9

America fever, 72

American Indians, 45, 160; clubs, in Sweden, 113; image of, 111–15

Anaconda (Montana), 47, 63

Anderson, Anders August (missionary and writer), 137

Anderson, Charles E. (local history writer), 165

Anderson, Charles H. (letter writer), 72, 145, 177

Anderson, Jonas (letter writer), 140, 144, 177

Anderson, Karna (letter writer), 27, 146, 147–48, 149, 150–51, 168, 177, 254n2

Anderson, Otto (letter writer and journalist), 178, 254n2

Anderson, Peter (letter writer), 135, 136, 142, 143, 145, 146, 147–49, 171, 178

Andersson, Genny (letter writer), 27, 147–48, 149, 178–79, 254n2

anecdote, 33, 37, 38, 43, 128–32

Argo Smelting Works (Colorado), 50, 77, 78, 119

Aronson, Albert H. (newspaper publisher), 251n71

artifact (letter as), 22

Aspen (Colorado), 50, 55

audience, 36

Baker, Ronald L., 269n65

Bakhtin, M. M., 21

ballads, 15, 94, 100

Baptist church, 139, 140, 153

Barkan, Elliott Robert, 248n6

Barton, David, 9

Barton, H. Arnold, 2, 88, 104

Bay Horse (Idaho), 45, 65, 67, 74

Beauchamp, Virginia Walcott, 2

Bengtson, Charles E. (minister), 138

Bergs-Väktaren (Helena), 63, 64

Bible reading, 128, 137, 141, 154–55

Biblical scripture, 136, 145, 146, 148, 154–56

Bierstadt, Albert, 124

Bikuben (Salt Lake City), 59

Bingham (Utah), 139

Bjork, Kenneth, 58

Björk, Ulf Jonas, 112, 250n62, 258n60

Blackfoot (Idaho), 65, 139

Blanck, Dag, xv, 88, 104, 109

Blegen, Theodore, 2, 14, 39

Bloomberg, Charles M. (letter writer), 68, 118, 119, 140, 143, 144, 150, 179

Bogart, Barbara Allen, 31, 133

Boise (Idaho), 65

Boline, Carl (letter writer), 68, 108, 179

newspaper correspondents, 54–55, 60, 64; pen names of, 55, 60, 84

newspapers, xv, 14, 27, 36, 46, 52–55, 59–63, 64, 65, 66, 84, 127, 128, 161, 163; English, 127

New Sweden (Idaho), xv, 47, 65, 165–66

Newton, J. R. (newspaper publisher), 54, 251n71

Nilson, O. (letter writer), 211, 254n2

Nilsson, Christina (singer), 106

Nilsson, Leonard (letter writer), xv, 27, 28, 34–36, 43, 45, 65, 70, 73–74, 80, 82–83, 84, 87, 88, 89, 90, 93, 94, 95, 101, 109, 123–24, 128, 136–37, 145–46, 161, 167, 168, 212–15

Nora (Idaho), xv, 47

Norrbotten crop failure relief effort, 51

Norwegian Constitution Day (May 17), 63

occupation: and social status, 82–84; of Swedish Americans, 47–48, 57, 248n22

Ogden (Utah), 139

"Oleana," 98

Olson, Adolf, 139

Olson, Anna (letter writer), 72, 101, 143, 146, 216

Olson, Bengta (letter writer), 68, 216

Olson, Ernest, 61

Olson, Mounie (Swedish immigrant), xiii

Olson, Nils (letter writer), 216

Olson, Pit (letter writer), 217

Olsson, Karl A., 139

Olsson, Ole (letter writer), 217

Ong, Walter, 7, 15

oral formulaic composition, 6, 7, 15

orality in letters, 166–69

organization, of letters. *See* structure of letters

Orofino (Idaho), xv

Ouray (Colorado), 55

Øverland, Orm, 2, 8–9, 18, 88, 114, 159–60, 164

parataxis, 6, 36, 43

Park City (Utah), 139

Parry, Milman, 15

Payette (Idaho), xiii, 138

Pearson, Nels (letter writer), 24, 25, 26, 217–18

peasant letters, 7

Pedersen, Ole (letter writer), 84, 218

Pehrson, Elin (letter writer), 72, 99, 218–19

performance theory, 8

Person, Johan (writer), 92, 97, 99, 104, 105

personal experience narrative, 11, 16, 31, 33, 38, 43, 128–32, 159, 170–71

personal relationships, as a letter theme, 5, 20

Peterson, August (letter writer), 74, 76, 77–79, 118, 119, 219–20

Peterson, Effie (letter writer), 108, 220

Peterson, John (letter writer), 84, 157–58, 159, 169, 220–21

Peterson, Maria (letter writer), 221, 254n2

Peterson, Peter (letter writer), 36–37, 49, 57, 58, 59, 66, 84, 85, 96, 108, 119, 123, 128, 140, 154, 161–62, 164, 221–23

Petterson, Gust (letter writer), 223

photographs: as letter enclosures, 27, 77, 99, 130, 132

pilgrimage: as letter theme, 146–47, 151

plays, Swedish American, 51, 62, 250n47

poetry, 27, 60, 61, 65, 89–90, 94, 128, 256n35

political organizations, Swedish American, 51, 61

pollution, 74, 75–76

Porter, John Preston, Jr. (subject of crime anecdote), 127

pregnancy: as letter theme, 19

Jennifer Eastman Attebery is professor of English at Idaho State University, where she teaches folklore and American studies and directs the American Studies Program.